AN INTRODUCTION TO OPTICAL FIBERS

Allen H. Cherin

Bell Laboratories
Atlanta, Georgia

McGraw-Hill Publishing Company

New York   St. Louis   San Francisco   Auckland   Bogotá
Caracas   Hamburg   Lisbon   London   Madrid   Mexico   Milan
Montreal   New Delhi   Oklahoma City   Paris   San Juan
São Paulo   Singapore   Sydney   Tokyo   Toronto

This book was set in Times Roman.
The editor was T. Michael Slaughter;
the production supervisor was Diane Renda.

AN INTRODUCTION TO OPTICAL FIBERS

7 8 9 0   BRBBRB   90

ISBN 0-07-010703-3

Library of Congress Cataloging in Publication Data

Cherin, Allen H.
    An introduction to optical fibers.

    Includes index.
    1. Optical communications.   2. Fiber optics.
3. Optical fibers.   I. Title.
TK5103.59.C48   621.36′92   82-15316
ISBN 0-07-010703-3   AACR2

CONTENTS

Chapter 4   The Dielectric Slab Waveguide   62

Chapter 5   The Step-Index Fiber   85

Chapter 6   The Graded-Index Fiber   120

PREFACE

The field of fiber optic communications has been a rapidly changing one. Technological advances in the fabrication of optical fibers, interconnection devices, cables, sources, and detectors has propelled a field that was in its infancy in the early 1970s into a major industry of the 1980s. This book is addressed to people who wish to learn about fiber optic communications and emphasizes, in particular, the analysis and technology associated with optical fibers and related fiber optic components. My purpose in writing this book was to provide a textbook for senior level undergraduate and first year graduate engineering and physics students who wish to obtain both a theoretical and practical knowledge of the field of fiber optic communications. I also anticipate that this book will appeal to workers entering this field who want a tutorial introduction to the subject. The material and problems contained in this text have been classroom tested in senior and first year graduate fiber optics courses in the Electrical Engineering Department at the Georgia Institute of Technology.

This book begins with an introductory chapter that provides the reader with a general understanding of the characteristics of optical fibers and how they are used in a communication system. In Chaps. 2 and 3 basic electromagnetic theory is reviewed and the concepts and mathematical models needed to analyze a dielectric waveguide from a wave or ray optics point of view are derived. Chapter 4 deals with the analysis of the dielectric slab waveguide and is included for pedigogical reasons to illustrate how the mathematical models are used to analyze a simple dielectric waveguide. Concepts such as mode cutoff conditions and delay distortion are introduced in this chapter. Chapters 5 and 6 are the heart of the analysis portion of this text. In these chapters the step- and graded-index fibers are analyzed. Propagation conditions for single- and multi-mode fibers are derived and expressions for many important concepts such as numerical aperture, principal mode number, and delay distortion are developed. The last five chapters of this book consider many of the important applied experimental aspects of fiber optic technology. In Chap. 7 material considerations and fabrication techniques leading to the production of low-loss optical fibers are described. Chapter 8 discusses the techniques used to measure the transmission characteristics of optical fibers. In this chapter the measurement of a fiber's loss, bandwidth, and refractive-index profile are described. Chapter 9 deals with the packaging of optical fibers. The mechanical and optical characteristics of fibers that influence the design of an optical cable are discussed and examples of a variety of different cable designs are given. Chapter 10 is concerned with the coupling of energy from an optical source into a fiber and with the effect that interconnection devices (connectors and splices) have on an optical fiber link. In addition, examples of a number of different interconnection devices are given. Finally, in Chap. 11, general design considerations for fiber optic systems are discussed. Examples of intracity and undersea digital pulse code modulated (PCM) telecommunication systems are given as well as an example of a fiber optic system which transmits video signals using analog modulation of an optical carrier.

I would like to thank Laura Short for her invaluable contributions to the illustrative examples and problems used in this book. I would also like to acknowledge Raye Williams and J. C. Quakenbush for their work in preparing the manuscript of this text. Thanks are also in order to Dr. Terrance Lenahan for his constructive critique of the manuscript and to Professor Demetrius Paris of the Georgia Institute of Technology for his words of encouragement. Finally, I would like to express my appreciation to Bell Telephone Laboratories for supporting this project.

Allen H. Cherin

INTRODUCTION TO OPTICAL FIBERS

1-1 INTRODUCTION

Light wave communication systems, using optical fibers as the communications medium, will be an important configuration for transmission networks of the 1980s. Because of the low-loss and high-bandwidth transmission characteristics of optical fibers, they are ideally suited for carrying voice, data, and video signals in a high-information-capacity system. This introductory chapter is intended to give a reader beginning a study of optical fibers a general understanding of what an optical fiber is, how it is used in a communication system, and some of the attractive advantages that an optical communication system has that uses optical fibers as the transmission medium. In addition a very brief historical sketch of optical fiber communication will be given to provide the reader with a perspective from which he can view the current state of the art.

1-2 CLASSIFICATION OF OPTICAL FIBERS

Fibers that are used for optical communication are waveguides made of transparent dielectrics whose function is to guide visible and infrared light over long distances. An optical fiber consists of an inner cylinder of glass, called the core, surrounded by a cylindrical shell of glass or plastic of lower refractive index, called the cladding. Optical fibers (lightguides) may be classified in terms of the refractive index profile of the core and whether one mode (single-mode fiber) or many modes (multimode fiber) are propagating in the guide. If the core, which is typically made of a high-silica-content glass or multicomponent glass, has a

1

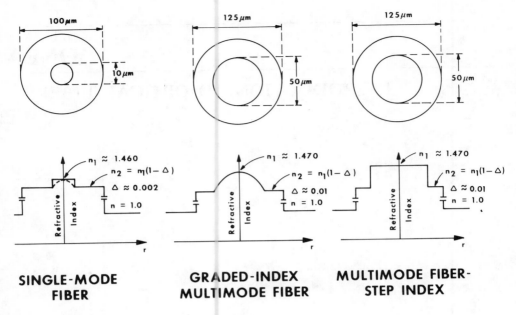

SINGLE-MODE FIBER

GRADED-INDEX MULTIMODE FIBER

MULTIMODE FIBER-STEP INDEX

Figure 1-1 Geometry of single- and multimode fibers.

uniform refractive index n_1 it is called a "step-index fiber." If the core has a nonuniform refractive index that gradually decreases from the center toward the core-cladding interface, the fiber is called, a "graded-index fiber." The cladding surrounding the core has a uniform refractive index $n_2 = n_1 (1 - \Delta)$ that is slightly lower than the refractive index of the core region. The cladding of the fiber is made of high-silica-content glass, multicomponent glass, or plastic. Figure 1-1 shows dimensions and refractive indices for commonly used telecommunication fibers. Figure 1-2 enumerates some of the advantages, contraints, and applications of the different types of fibers. In general, when the transmission medium must have a very high bandwidth, for example in an undersea cable system, a single-mode fiber is used. For intermediate system bandwidth requirements between 200 MHz and 2 GHz-km such as found in intracity trunks between telephone central offices, a graded-index multimode fiber would be the choice. For applications such as data links where lower bandwidth requirements are placed on the transmission medium, a step-index multimode fiber would be used.

1.3 FIBERS IN A SIMPLE COMMUNICATION SYSTEM

This book is primarily concerned with the analysis, fabrication, packaging, joining, and transmission characteristics of optical fibers. It is important, however, for the reader to understand how fibers are used in a communication system.

	SINGLE-MODE FIBER	GRADED-INDEX MULTIMODE FIBER	STEP-INDEX MULTIMODE FIBER
	Cladding, Core, Protective Plastic Coating		
SOURCE	REQUIRES LASER	LASER or LED	LASER or LED
BANDWIDTH	VERY VERY LARGE > 3 GHz-km	VERY LARGE 200 MHz to 3 GHz-km	LARGE < 200 MHz-km
SPLICING	VERY DIFFICULT DUE TO SMALL CORE	DIFFICULT BUT DOABLE	DIFFICULT BUT DOABLE
EXAMPLE OF APPLICATION	SUBMARINE CABLE SYSTEM	TELEPHONE TRUNK BETWEEN CENTRAL OFFICES	DATA LINKS
COST	LESS EXPENSIVE	MOST EXPENSIVE	LEAST EXPENSIVE

Figure 1-2 Applications and characteristics of fiber types.

3

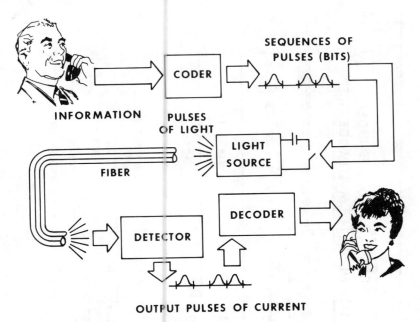

Figure 1-3 Optical system showing telephone call.

Figure 1-3 is a simple example of a telephone conversation being transmitted over an optical communication system. The system consists of a transmitter in the form of a semiconductor laser or light-emitting diode (LED) which is modulated by an information bearing signal. This light source usually radiates in the near-infrared portion of the electromagnetic spectrum (see Fig. 1-4) where the transmission characteristics of optical fibers are best utilized (see Fig. 1-5). The system receiver contains a PIN or avalanche photodiode (APD) that converts the optical signal into an information bearing electrical signal. This electrical signal is then demodulated to produce the audio signal heard in the telephone. The components in this simple system are present in most optical-fiber communication systems in existence today. Figure 1-6 illustrates the basic building blocks of a section of an optical communication system. Detailed examples of optical fiber communication systems will be given in Chap. 11 of this text.

1-4 A BRIEF HISTORICAL REVIEW

It is interesting to note that there is nothing new about using light as the carrier signal in a communication system. In 1880 Alexander Graham Bell invented the photophone.[1] He demonstrated, as shown in Fig. 1-7, that speech could be transmitted on a beam of light. A. G. Bell focused a narrow beam of sunlight onto a thin mirror. When the sound waves of human speech caused the mirror

ELECTROMAGNETIC SPECTRUM

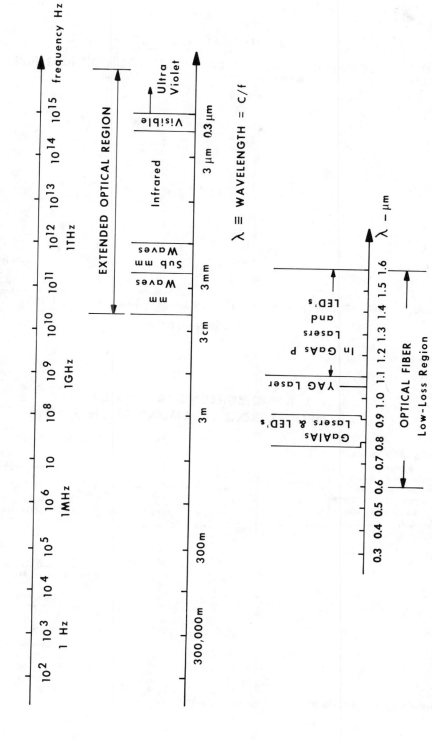

Figure 1-4 Electromagnetic spectrum.

5

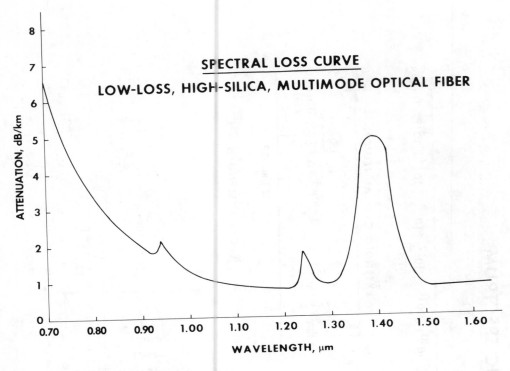

SPECTRAL LOSS CURVE

LOW-LOSS, HIGH-SILICA, MULTIMODE OPTICAL FIBER

Figure 1-5 Spectral loss curve of optical fiber.

**BASIC BUILDING BLOCKS OF
AN OPTICAL FIBER COMMUNICATION SYSTEM**

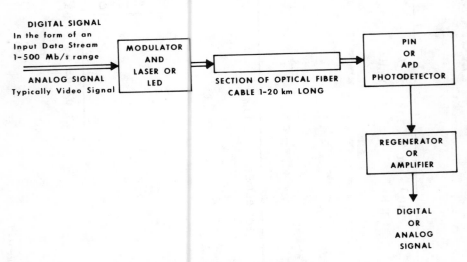

Figure 1-6 Basic building blocks of an optical communication system.

A.G. BELL'S PHOTOPHONE

Figure 1-7 Alexander Graham Bell's photophone.

to vibrate, the amount of energy transmitted to the light detector varied correspondingly. The light reaching the selenium detector caused its resistance, and therefore the intensity of the current in a telephone receiver, to vary, setting up speech waves at the receiver end. Bell managed to send voice signals 700 feet by using his ingenious invention.

What is new today, compared to the technology of earlier eras, are the techniques available for generating a light beam that can be modulated at extremely high rates and, equally important, transmitted through a low-loss optical fiber several miles long with acceptable loss of energy.

Modern light-wave communication had its birth in the 1960s. The first demonstration of the ruby laser in 1960[2] followed by a demonstration of laser operations in semiconductor devices in 1962[3,4] were the early stepping stones that led to the continuous operation of room temperature, long life-time, GaAlAs semiconductor lasers that are in common use today. The laser made available a coherent optical frequency carrier on the order of 3×10^{14} Hz. If a

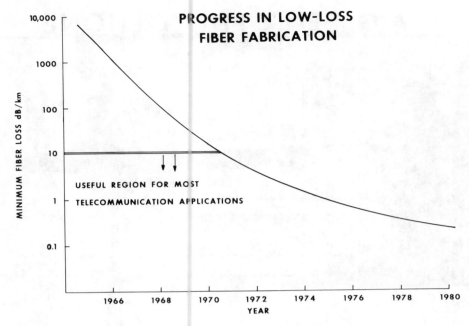

Figure 1-8 Progress in fiber fabrication.

communication system could be built that utilized only 0.01 percent of the carrier frequency its modulation bandwidth would be 30 GHz. The potential is there for enormous communication capacity.

In 1966 a parallel evolution of fiber technology was taking place. Although the best existing fibers at that time had loss greater than 1000 dB/km, researchers at Standard Telecommunications Laboratories in England[5] speculated that losses as low as 20 dB/km should be achievable and they further suggested that such fibers would be useful in telecommunication applications. And they were correct. In 1970 workers at Corning Glass Works[6] produced the first fiber with loss under 20 dB/km. Since that time fiber technology has advanced to the point of producing fibers with loss that is less than 0.5 dB/km at 1.55 μm.[7] These fibers are approaching the Rayleigh scattering limit of the glass being used to fabricate them. Figure 1-8 illustrates the trend of decreasing fiber loss from 1966 to 1980.

A window in history that brought together source and fiber technology and allowed communication engineers to produce practical high-capacity optical fiber communication systems occurred in the mid-1970s. Currently there are many examples of optical telecommunication systems.[8] A good example of one is the Bell Laboratories Lightguide system that was installed in Chicago in 1977.[9] This system connected two telephone-system central offices and provided voice, analog data, digital data, Picturephone®, and 4 MHz video service to customers in Chicago's Brunswick Building. The various services were put into a 44.7 Mb/s pulse code modulated format and transmitted over optical fibers. The 24-fiber optical cable used had the capacity of carrying 16,000 voice circuits in a cable whose cross section was less than 1 inch in diameter: a far cry from the days of Alexander Graham Bell's photophone.

1-5 ATTRACTIVE FEATURES OF OPTICAL FIBER TRANSMISSION

Because of their low-loss and wide-bandwidth capabilities, optical fibers have the potential for being used wherever twisted wire pairs or coaxial cables are used as the transmission medium in a communication system. If an engineer were interested in choosing a transmission medium for a given transmission objective, he would tabulate the required and desired features of alternate technologies that may be available for use in his application. With that process in mind, a summary of the attractive advantages of optical-fiber transmission will be given. Figure 1-9 itemizes some of these advantages.

To appreciate the low-loss and wide-bandwidth capabilities of optical fibers, consider the signal-attenuation-versus-frequency curve for three different transmission media shown in Fig. 1-10. Optical fibers have a "flat" transfer function well beyond 100 MHz. When compared with wire pairs or coaxial cables, optical fibers have far less loss for signal frequencies above a few megahertz. This is an important characteristic that strongly influences system economics since it allows the system designer to increase the distance between regenerators (amplifiers) in a communication system.

ATTRACTIVE FEATURES OF OPTICAL FIBERS

- ● LOW LOSS AND HIGH BANDWIDTH

- ● SMALL SIZE AND BENDING RADIUS

- ● NONCONDUCTIVE, NONRADIATIVE, AND NONINDUCTIVE

- ● LIGHT WEIGHT

- ● PROVIDES NATURAL GROWTH CAPABILITY

Figure 1-9 Attractive features of optical-fiber transmission.

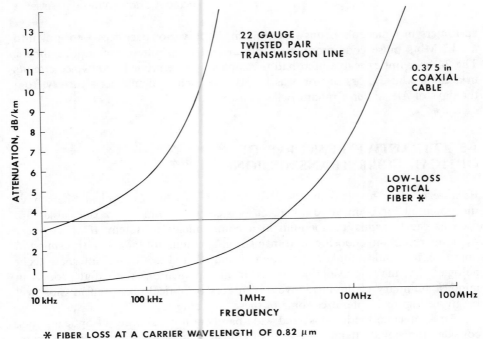

Figure 1-10 Attenuation versus frequency for three different transmission media.

GROWTH CAPABILITY
TRANSMISSION MEDIA COMPARISONS

Transmission Media	Loss in dB/km at Half Bit Rate Frequency (Digital Transmission Rates)		
	T1 (1.544 Mb/s)	T2 (6.312 Mb/s)	T3 (44.736 Mb/s)
26-GAUGE TWISTED WIRE PAIR	24	48	128
19-GAUGE TWISTED WIRE PAIR	10.8	21	56
0.375-in-DIAMETER COAXIAL CABLE	2.1	4.5	11
LOW-LOSS OPTICAL FIBER ✳	3.5	3.5	3.5

✳ FIBER LOSS AT A CARRIER WAVELENGTH OF 0.82 μm

Figure 1-11 Growth capability—transmission media comparisons.

The small size, small bending radius (a few centimeters), and light weight of optical fibers and cables are very important where space is at a premium, such as in aircraft, on ships, and in crowded ducts under city streets.

Because optical fibers are dielectric waveguides, they avoid many problems such as radiative interference, ground loops, and, when installed in a cable without metal, lightning-induced damage that exist in other transmission media.

Finally, the engineer using optical fibers has a great deal of flexibility. He can install an optical-fiber cable and use it initially in a low-capacity (low bit rate) system. As his system needs grow, he can take advantage of the broadband capabilities of optical fibers and convert to a high-capacity (high bit rate) system by simply changing the terminal electronics. A comparison of the growth capability of different transmission media is shown in Fig. 1-11. For the three digital-transmission rates considered (1.544, 6.312, and 44.7 Mb/s) the loss of the optical fiber is constant. The loss of the metallic transmission lines, however, increases with increasing transmission rates, thus limiting their use at the higher bit rates. The optical fiber system, on the other hand, could be used at all bit rates and can grow naturally to satisfy system needs.

REFERENCES

1. R. V. Bruce: *Alexander Graham Bell and the Conquest of Solitude*, Gollancz, London, 1973.
2. T. H. Maiman: "Stimulated Optical Radiation in Ruby," *Nature (London)*, **6**: 106 (1960).
3. R. N. Hall, G. E. Fenner, J. D. Kingsley, T. J. Soltys, and R. O. Carlson: "Coherent Light Emission from GaAs Junctions," *Phys. Rev. Lett.*, **9**: 366 (1962).
4. M. I. Nathan, W. P. Dumke, G. Burns, F. H. Dill, Jr., and G. Lasher: "Stimulated Emission of Radiation from GaAs *p-n* Junctions," *Appl. Phys. Lett.*, **1**: 62 (1962).
5. K. C. Kao and G. A. Hockham: "Dielectric-Fiber Surface Waveguides for Optical Frequencies," *Proc. IEE*, **133**: 1151 (1966).
6. F. P. Kapron, D. B. Keck, and R. D. Maurer: "Radiation Losses in Glass Optical Waveguides," *Appl. Phys. Lett.*, **17**: 423 (1970).
7. T. Miya, Y. Terunuma, T. Hosaka, and T. Miyashita: "Ultimate Low-Loss Single-Mode Fibre at 1.55 μm," *Electron. Lett.*, **15** (4) Feb. 15, 1979.
8. R. L. Gallawa, J. E. Midwinter, and S. Shimada: "A Survey of World-Wide Optical Waveguide Systems," Topical Meeting on Optical Fiber Communication, OSA-IEEE, March 1979, Washington, D.C.
9. M. I. Schwartz, W. A. Reenstra, J. H. Mullins, and J. S. Cook: "The Chicago Lightwave Communications Project," *BSTJ*, **57**: pp. 1881–1888, July/August 1978.

PROBLEMS

1-1 Describe three types of optical fibers. For each type of fiber give typical core and cladding diameters and a sketch of their refractive index profiles. Classify each fiber type by the number of modes propagating.

1-2 Draw a block diagram of an optical communication system with a bandwidth of 4 GHz · km (indicate a specific optical source type and fiber type).

1-3 List three advantages of using optical fibers as a transmission medium. Describe an application in which these advantages would be important.

1-4 Refer to Fig. 1-11. Which transmission medium is most attractive for a system initially installed to operate at the T1 rate but to be upgraded in the future to the T3 rate? Why?

REVIEW OF ELECTROMAGNETIC THEORY

2-1 INTRODUCTION

Our analysis of dielectric waveguides (step- and graded-index fibers and slab waveguides) is predicated upon an understanding of electromagnetic field theory in dielectric media. This chapter is written for the reader who has completed an undergraduate course in electromagnetic field theory but wishes to review some basic field theory concepts before undertaking the task of analyzing dielectric waveguides.

We will begin the study of field theory with Maxwell's equations and develop the wave equations needed to understand sinusoidal steady-state propagation of waves in a dielectric medium. Next, expressions for group and phase velocities of waves propagating in dispersive media will be developed along with the concept of group index and group delay. Fresnel's equations and Snell's law will then be derived by solving the simple problem of reflection and refraction of waves at a plane dielectric interface. Finally, total internal reflection and evanescent fields, both important concepts needed for understanding dielectric waveguides, will be investigated.

2-2 HEURISTIC DEFINITION OF A FIELD

Our object now is to analyze a physical device, namely a dielectric waveguide, with a model based upon basic physical laws and mathematics. To appreciate the physical laws, that find their embodiment in electromagnetic field theory, we must first understand the concepts of a field and a physical field theory.[1]

By a field we mean a set of values assumed by a physical quantity at various points in a region of space and at various instants of time. The region of space or the time interval may be either finite or infinite in extent. A physical field theory is comprised of physical laws which give the relationships between source fields and resultant fields.

2-3 MAXWELL'S EQUATIONS

The differential form of Maxwell's equations relate field vectors at arbitrary points in space and time. These differential equations constitute a physical field theory and govern the behavior of time-varying electromagnetic fields.

$$\nabla \times \bar{\mathscr{E}} = -\frac{\partial \bar{\mathscr{B}}}{\partial t} \tag{2-1}$$

$$\nabla \times \bar{\mathscr{H}} = \bar{\mathscr{J}} + \frac{\partial \bar{\mathscr{D}}}{\partial t} \tag{2-2}$$

$$\nabla \cdot \bar{\mathscr{B}} = 0 \tag{2-3}$$

$$\nabla \cdot \bar{\mathscr{D}} = \rho \tag{2-4}$$

$\bar{\mathscr{E}}$ = electric field intensity, V/m

$\bar{\mathscr{B}}$ = magnetic flux density, Wb/m^2

$\bar{\mathscr{D}}$ = electric flux density, C/m^2

$\bar{\mathscr{H}}$ = magnetic field intensity, A/m

$\bar{\mathscr{J}}$ = current density, A/m^2

ρ = charge density, C/m^3

The "script" notation used in this book denotes a general time-varying field. For example

$$\bar{\mathscr{E}}(x, y, z, t) = \mathscr{E}_x(x, y, z, t)\hat{a}_x + \mathscr{E}_y(x, y, z, t)\hat{a}_y + \mathscr{E}_z(x, y, z, t)\hat{a}_z \tag{2-5}$$

where $\hat{a}_x$, $\hat{a}_y$, and $\hat{a}_z$ are unit vectors along the coordinate axes of a rectangular coordinate system.

Within the region that Maxwell's equations are defined the following mathematical assumptions are made. The fields are:

(a) continuous functions of position and time with continuous derivatives
(b) single valued
(c) bounded

The field vectors have these properties except at points where there are abrupt changes in the distribution of current or charge. These changes usually occur at the interface between different media.

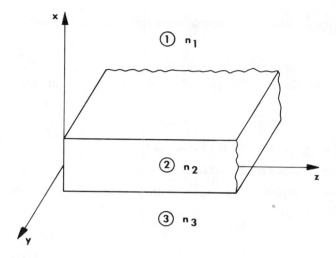

Figure 2-1 Slab waveguide viewed as a boundary-value problem.

The procedure followed in solving boundary value problems is to write down Maxwell's equations (or the derived wave equations) where the fields are continuous, and couple the solutions of these equations together by means of boundary conditions. For example, if we had a dielectric slab waveguide as shown in Fig. 2-1, we would write solutions to Maxwell's equations or the wave equation separately in regions (1), (2), and (3) and solve for the unknown coefficients associated with these solutions by applying the boundary conditions for the fields at the interfaces between mediums (1) and (2), (2) and (3), and at $x = \infty$.

Maxwell's equations form a macroscopic field theory. We are interested in fields which vary in space by a discernible amount over distances large compared with atomic dimensions. We will be concerned with an average field and not the field within the local vicinity of an atom.

2-4 CONSTITUTIVE RELATIONSHIPS—MEDIUM CHARACTERIZATION

Maxwell's equations are first-order linear coupled differential equations relating vector field quantities to each other. For a given medium, some of these field quantities can be written as a function of others. That is, the constitutive relationships for the medium under consideration are given by[2]

$$\bar{\mathscr{D}} = \mathscr{D}(\bar{\mathscr{E}}) \qquad \bar{\mathscr{B}} = \mathscr{B}(\bar{\mathscr{H}}) \qquad \bar{\mathscr{J}} = \mathscr{J}(\bar{\mathscr{E}}) \tag{2-6}$$

The specific functional form that the constitutive relationships take define the type of medium under consideration, for example for a linear, isotropic, homogeneous medium.

$$\bar{\mathscr{D}} = \varepsilon\bar{\mathscr{E}} \qquad \bar{\mathscr{B}} = \mu\bar{\mathscr{H}} \qquad \bar{\mathscr{J}} = \sigma\bar{\mathscr{E}} \tag{2-7}$$

with ε, μ, σ being scalar constants in this case. The units and names of these medium parameters are:

$$\varepsilon = \text{permittivity of medium, F/m}$$

$$\mu = \text{permeability of medium, H/m}$$

$$\sigma = \text{conductivity of medium, S/m}$$

We will be dealing with dielectrics and usually with lossless dielectrics with the following characteristics.

$$\sigma = 0$$

$$\mu_r = \frac{\mu}{\mu_0} = 1 \tag{2-8}$$

$$\varepsilon_r = \frac{\varepsilon}{\varepsilon_0}$$

where μ_r and ε_r are respectively the relative permeability and permittivity of the medium. ε_0 and μ_0 are the free space parameters equal to

$$\varepsilon_0 = \frac{1}{36\pi \times 10^9} = 8.854 \times 10^{-12} \text{ F/m} \tag{2-9}$$

$$\mu_0 = 4\pi \times 10^{-7} \text{ H/m}$$

When working in the optical part of the frequency spectrum and dealing with a dielectric medium one usually speaks in terms of the index of refraction of a medium rather than ε_r.

$$n = \sqrt{\varepsilon_r} \equiv \text{refractive index of the medium} \tag{2-10}$$

For the glass media that are used in dielectric waveguides, $n_{\text{glass}} \approx 1.5$.

In general the constitutive relationships can be complicated tensor relationships, i.e.,

$$\bar{\mathscr{D}} = \bar{\bar{\varepsilon}}\bar{\mathscr{E}} \tag{2-11}$$

where

$$\bar{\bar{\varepsilon}} = \begin{pmatrix} \varepsilon_{11} & \varepsilon_{12} & \varepsilon_{13} \\ \varepsilon_{21} & \varepsilon_{22} & \varepsilon_{23} \\ \varepsilon_{31} & \varepsilon_{32} & \varepsilon_{33} \end{pmatrix} \tag{2-12}$$

and

$$\mathscr{D}_x = \varepsilon_{11}\mathscr{E}_x + \varepsilon_{12}\mathscr{E}_y + \varepsilon_{13}\ \mathscr{E}_z$$

$$\mathscr{D}_y = \varepsilon_{21}\mathscr{E}_x + \varepsilon_{22}\mathscr{E}_y + \varepsilon_{23}\ \mathscr{E}_z \tag{2-13}$$

$$\mathscr{D}_z = \varepsilon_{31}\mathscr{E}_x + \varepsilon_{32}\mathscr{E}_y + \varepsilon_{33}\ \mathscr{E}_z$$

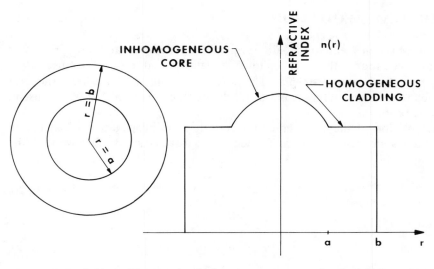

Figure 2-2 Graded-index fiber showing the inhomogeneous core refractive index.

For an anisotropic material such as crystalline quartz this type of tensor relationship applies. (Isotropic material exhibits the same properties in all directions.)

In addition, if the medium is inhomogeneous the permittivity is a function of position in the medium, that is $\varepsilon(x, y, z)$. An important example of an inhomogeneous medium, as shown in Fig. 2-2, is the core of a graded-index optical fiber.

Now let us specialize Maxwell's equations for the type of media we will be faced with when we analyze dielectric waveguides. For a charge-free, lossless, linear isotropic medium Maxwell's equations become

$$\nabla \times \bar{\mathscr{E}} = -\frac{\partial \bar{\mathscr{B}}}{\partial t} \tag{2-14}$$

$$\nabla \times \bar{\mathscr{H}} = \frac{\partial \bar{\mathscr{D}}}{\partial t} \tag{2-15}$$

$$\nabla \cdot \bar{\mathscr{D}} = 0 \tag{2-16}$$

$$\nabla \cdot \bar{\mathscr{B}} = 0 \tag{2-17}$$

the constitutive relationships for this type of dielectric medium are

$$\mu_r \approx 1$$
$$\bar{\mathscr{B}} = \mu_0 \bar{\mathscr{H}} \tag{2-18}$$

$$\bar{\mathscr{D}} = \varepsilon \bar{\mathscr{E}} \tag{2-19}$$

2-5 THE WAVE EQUATION

Although Maxwell's equations are simple in appearance and are first-order differential equations, they are coupled equations and difficult to use when solving boundary-value problems. The wave equation on the other hand is a decoupled (one vector only) second-order differential equation that is very useful for solving problems.

The solution of the wave equation describes the propagation of energy in the medium under consideration. To derive the wave equation first we take the curl of Eq. (2-14)

$$\nabla \times \nabla \times \bar{\mathscr{E}} = -\mu_0 \frac{\partial}{\partial t} (\nabla \times \bar{\mathscr{H}}) \tag{2-20}$$

Using Eq. (2-15) in (2-20)

$$\nabla \times \nabla \times \bar{\mathscr{E}} = -\mu_0 \frac{\partial^2 \bar{\mathscr{D}}}{\partial t^2} = -\mu_0 \varepsilon \frac{\partial^2 \bar{\mathscr{E}}}{\partial t^2} \tag{2-21}$$

Now consider the following vector identity

$$\nabla \times \nabla \times \bar{\mathscr{E}} = \nabla(\nabla \cdot \bar{\mathscr{E}}) - \nabla^2 \bar{\mathscr{E}} \tag{2-22}$$

Substituting Eq. (2-22) into (2-21) yields

$$\nabla^2 \bar{\mathscr{E}} - \mu_0 \varepsilon \frac{\partial^2 \bar{\mathscr{E}}}{\partial t^2} = \nabla(\nabla \cdot \bar{\mathscr{E}}) \tag{2-23}$$

Let us now investigate the right-hand side of Eq. (2-23) and specifically the term $\nabla \cdot \bar{\mathscr{E}}$.

Expanding Eq. (2-16)

$$\nabla \cdot \bar{\mathscr{D}} = \nabla \cdot (\varepsilon \bar{\mathscr{E}}) = 0$$

$$\nabla \cdot \bar{\mathscr{D}} = \varepsilon \nabla \cdot \bar{\mathscr{E}} + \bar{\mathscr{E}} \cdot \nabla \varepsilon = 0$$

Solving for $\nabla \cdot \bar{\mathscr{E}}$ yields

$$\nabla \cdot \bar{\mathscr{E}} = -\bar{\mathscr{E}} \cdot \frac{\nabla \varepsilon}{\varepsilon} \tag{2-24}$$

Returning to Eq. (2-23) and substituting (2-24) into it results in

$$\nabla^2 \bar{\mathscr{E}} - \mu_0 \varepsilon \frac{\partial^2 \bar{\mathscr{E}}}{\partial t^2} = -\nabla \left(\bar{\mathscr{E}} \cdot \frac{\nabla \varepsilon}{\varepsilon} \right) \tag{2-25}$$

If the medium we are considering is inhomogeneous ($\varepsilon(x, y, z)$), that is, the permittivity of the medium is a function of position in the medium, then the gradient of the permittivity is not equal to zero ($\nabla \varepsilon \neq 0$). If the medium is homogeneous, $\nabla \varepsilon = 0$, and the right-hand side of (2-25) will be equal to zero.

This will result in the familiar homogeneous wave equation

$$\nabla^2 \bar{\mathscr{E}} - \mu_0\,\varepsilon\,\frac{\partial^2 \bar{\mathscr{E}}}{\partial t^2} = 0 \qquad (2\text{-}26)$$

For the step-index waveguide the homogeneous wave equation can be solved in the core and cladding of the guide to obtain expressions for the fields. For the graded-index fiber, however, one must investigate under what conditions the homogeneous wave equation is a good approximation to Eq. (2-25), since this latter equation is far more difficult to handle and not very useful for actual calculations. Marcuse[3] analyzed the magnitudes of each of the terms in (2-25) and proved that the homogeneous wave equation (2-26) can be used even if ε is a function of position in the medium provided that its variation is slight over the distance of one optical wavelength. For the waveguides we will be analyzing, with the exception of interfaces between two different dielectric media, this condition is always satisfied. The propagation of light in slightly inhomogeneous media can be studied by solving the homogeneous wave equation. The difference between the homogeneous wave equation and the more accurate equation (2-25) is negligible in most cases of practical interest to us.

If we had started with Eq. (2-15) and derived the wave equation for the magnetic field intensity we would obtain

$$\nabla^2 \bar{\mathscr{H}} - \mu_0\,\varepsilon\,\frac{\partial^2 \bar{\mathscr{H}}}{\partial t^2} = 0 \qquad (2\text{-}27)$$

Equations (2-26) and (2-27) are vector equations that have three scalar components each. For example, Eq. (2-26) can be rewritten in rectangular coordinates as

$$\nabla^2 \mathscr{E}_x - \mu_0\,\varepsilon\,\frac{\partial^2 \mathscr{E}_x}{\partial t^2} = 0 \qquad (2\text{-}28a)$$

$$\nabla^2 \mathscr{E}_y - \mu_0\,\varepsilon\,\frac{\partial^2 \mathscr{E}_y}{\partial r^2} = 0 \quad \left.\begin{array}{l}\text{three-component} \\ \text{scalar} \\ \text{equation}\end{array}\right. \qquad (2\text{-}28b)$$

$$\nabla^2 \mathscr{E}_z - \mu_0\,\varepsilon\,\frac{\partial^2 \mathscr{E}_z}{\partial t^2} = 0 \qquad (2\text{-}28c)$$

where

$$\nabla^2 = \frac{\partial^2}{\partial x^2} + \frac{\partial^2}{\partial y^2} + \frac{\partial^2}{\partial z^2}$$

If we let

$$v = \frac{1}{\sqrt{\mu_0\,\varepsilon}} \quad \text{m/s} \qquad (2\text{-}29)$$

then

$$\frac{1}{v^2} = \mu_0\,\varepsilon$$

and each component of the wave equation has the following form and can be written symbolically as

$$\nabla^2 \psi - \frac{1}{v^2} \frac{\partial^2 \psi}{\partial t^2} = 0 \tag{2-30}$$

2-6 SOLUTIONS OF THE SCALAR WAVE EQUATION

The physical significance of the wave equation can be appreciated if we consider that every function of the form

$$\psi = f\left(t \mp \frac{1}{v} \hat{n} \cdot \bar{r} \right) \tag{2-31}$$

is a solution of Eq. (2-30) if the second derivative of f exists. Where $\bar{r}$ is a radius vector given by

$$\bar{r} = x\hat{a}_x + y\hat{a}_y + z\hat{a}_z \tag{2-32}$$

The components of $\bar{r}$ are the coordinates of the point at which the field is observed.

$$\hat{n} \equiv \text{a unit vector} = n_x \hat{a}_x + n_y \hat{a}_y + n_z \hat{a}_z \tag{2-33}$$

Equation (2-31) describes plane waves propagating in a dielectric medium. $\hat{n}$ is a unit vector perpendicular to surfaces of constant phase in the direction of propagation.

To appreciate that ψ is a plane wave consider a single-valued function $f(\beta)$. For a fixed value of $\beta = \beta_0$ the function has a corresponding fixed value $f(\beta_0)$. If we let

$$\beta = t - \frac{1}{v} \hat{n} \cdot \bar{r} \tag{2-34}$$

For a fixed time $t = t_1$, $\beta = \beta_0 = $ constant is realized on a plane given by the relation

$$\hat{n} \cdot \bar{r} = \text{const}$$
$$n_x x + n_y y + n_z z = \text{const} \tag{2-35}$$

To see how this plane propagates in space (see Fig. 2-3) let us look at the same fixed value of the function $f(\beta_0)$ at a perturbed value in time and space $t_1 + \Delta t$, $\bar{r} = \bar{r}_1 + \Delta \bar{r}$ such that

$$\beta_0 = t_1 + \Delta t - \frac{1}{v} \hat{n} \cdot (\bar{r}_1 + \Delta \bar{r}) = t_1 - \frac{1}{v} \hat{n} \cdot \bar{r}_1$$

or

$$v \, \Delta t = \hat{n} \cdot \Delta \bar{r}$$

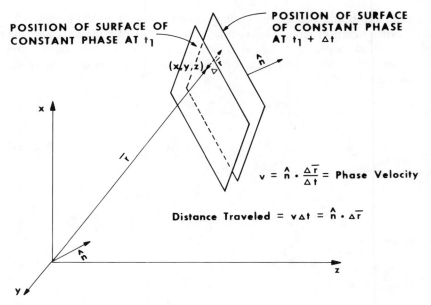

Figure 2-3 Geometry for propagating plane waves.

$\hat{n} \cdot \Delta \bar{r}$ is the distance traveled by the wave in time Δt, and

$$v = \hat{n} \cdot \frac{\Delta \bar{r}}{\Delta t} \tag{2-36}$$

v is the velocity of propagation of a surface of constant phase (that is, at $\beta = \beta_0$) of the wave in the dielectric medium.

Summarizing our results. Any arbitrary functions of the form $\psi = f[t \mp (1/v)\hat{n} \cdot \bar{r}]$ are solutions of the scalar wave equation. The solutions represent plane waves propagating with a velocity v in the $\pm \hat{n}$ direction.

2-7 SINUSOIDAL STEADY-STATE PROPAGATING WAVES

Let us assume that we have fields that vary consinusoidally in time. We can later expand the sinusoidal variation using Fourier analysis to represent general time functions. Let us look at the electric field and introduce the following notation

$$\bar{\mathscr{E}} = \mathscr{E}_x(x, y, z, t)\hat{a}_x + \mathscr{E}_y(x, y, z, t)\hat{a}_y + \mathscr{E}_z(x, y, z, t)\hat{a}_z \tag{2-37}$$

$$\mathscr{E}_x(x, y, z, t) = E_{x0}(x, y, z) \cos (\omega t + \phi_x) \tag{2-38}$$

$$\mathscr{E}_y(x, y, z, t) = E_{y0}(x, y, z) \cos (\omega t + \phi_y) \tag{2-39}$$

$$\mathscr{E}_z(x, y, z, t) = E_{z0}(x, y, z) \cos (\omega t + \phi_z) \tag{2-40}$$

where E_{x0}, E_{y0}, E_{z0} are real functions of position.

We are directing our efforts to obtain a complex vector notation that will allow us to write down in sinusoidal steady state Maxwell's equations and the Helmholtz equation (wave equation in steady state). We will then obtain the steady-state solution of the wave equation and define several wave parameters. Using the following relationship

$$e^{j(\omega t + \phi)} = \cos(\omega t + \phi) + j \sin(\omega t + \phi)$$

or

$$\text{Re}\left(e^{j(\omega t + \phi)}\right) = \cos(\omega t + \phi) \tag{2-41}$$

Let us write in complex vector notation $\mathscr{E}_x(x, y, z, t)$.

$$\mathscr{E}_x(x, y, z, t) = E_{x0}(x, y, z) \cos(\omega t + \phi_x)$$

$$= \text{Re}\left[E_{x0}(x, y, z)e^{j\phi_x}e^{j\omega t}\right] \tag{2-42}$$

Defining a complex function E_x

$$E_x = E_{x0}(x, y, z)e^{j\phi_x} \tag{2-43}$$

Then

$$\mathscr{E}_x = \text{Re}\left(E_x e^{j\omega t}\right) \tag{2-44}$$

Extending this notation to the y and z components of the electric field one obtains

$$\bar{\mathscr{E}} = \text{Re}\left[(E_{x0}e^{j\phi_x}\hat{a}_x + E_{y0}e^{j\phi_y}\hat{a}_y + E_{z0}e^{j\phi_z}\hat{a}_z)e^{j\omega t}\right]$$

$$= \text{Re}\left[(E_x \hat{a}_x + E_y \hat{a}_y + E_z \hat{a}_z)e^{j\omega t}\right] \tag{2-45}$$

We now define a complex vector $\bar{E}$ that is a function of space coordinates only

$$\bar{E} = E_x \hat{a}_x + E_y \hat{a}_y + E_z \hat{a}_z \tag{2-46}$$

$$\therefore \bar{\mathscr{E}} = \text{Re}\left(\bar{E}e^{j\omega t}\right) \tag{2-47}$$

We are now in a position to work directly with the vectors

$$\bar{E}, \bar{H}, \bar{D}, \bar{B}$$

and obtain equations in sinusoidal steady state, solve them, and then obtain the physical fields by substituting in Eq. (2-47).

Using the vector notation for the fields and taking the explicit derivatives with respect to time in Eqs. (2-14) through (2-17) yields Maxwell's equations in sinusoidal steady state.

$$\nabla \times \bar{E} = -j\omega\mu\bar{H} \tag{2-48}$$

$$\nabla \times \bar{H} = j\omega\varepsilon\bar{E} \tag{2-49}$$

$$\nabla \cdot \bar{H} = 0 \tag{2-50}$$

$$\nabla \cdot \bar{D} = 0 \tag{2-51}$$

Now following the same procedure that was used to derive the homogeneous wave equation (2-26) we can derive directly the wave equations in sinusoidal steady state known as Helmholtz equations.

$$\nabla^2 \bar{E} + k^2 \bar{E} = 0 \tag{2-52}$$

$$\nabla^2 \bar{H} + k^2 \bar{H} = 0 \tag{2-53}$$

where

$$k = \omega \sqrt{\mu \varepsilon} = \frac{\omega}{v} \tag{2-54}$$

Defining a propagation vector $\bar{\mathbf{k}}$

$$\bar{\mathbf{k}} = k\hat{n} = \frac{\omega}{v} \hat{n} \tag{2-55}$$

A solution for each component of the Helmholtz equation is a propagating wave. For example, the x component of the electric field is of the form

$$E_x = E_x^+ e^{-j\bar{k} \cdot \bar{r}} + E_x^- e^{+j\bar{k} \cdot \bar{r}} \tag{2-56}$$

The actual physical field for each component of the electric and magnetic fields is of the form:

$$\psi = A^+ \cos(\omega t - k\hat{n} \cdot \bar{r}) + A^- \cos(\omega t + k\hat{n} \cdot \bar{r}) \tag{2-57}$$

Equation (2-57) is physically two plane waves propagating in the $\pm \hat{n}$ directions, respectively. This solution is analogous to the one we obtained for the wave equation but now a cosinusoidal variation in time is explicitly stated.

Example 2-1 Sinusoidal steady-state wave propagation This example illustrates how a sinusoidal steady state wave propagates. Let us assume the wave is propagating in the z direction.

Each component of the field is of the form given by Eq. (2-57)

$$\psi = A^+ \cos(\omega t - k\hat{n} \cdot \bar{r}) + A^- \cos(\omega t + k\hat{n} \cdot \bar{r})$$

For this example $\hat{n} = \hat{a}_z$ and the equation becomes

$$\psi = A^+ \cos(\omega t - kz) + A^- \cos(\omega t + kz)$$

This is the sum of a plane wave traveling in the $+z$ direction and a plane wave traveling in the $-z$ direction. Sketches of each plane wave at fixed instants of time will show how it is propagating along the z axis. We will look at times $t = 0$, $t = \pi/2\omega$, and $t = \pi/\omega$.

At $t = 0$

$$\cos(\omega t - kz) = \cos(\omega t + kz) = \cos kz$$

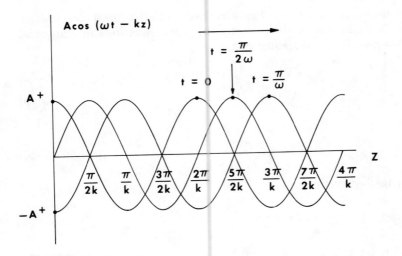

Figure 2-4 Sinusoidal steady state wave propagating in $+z$ directions.

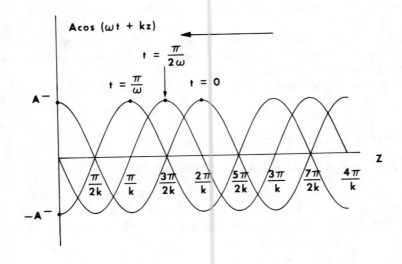

Figure 2-5 Sinusoidal steady state wave propagating in $-z$ direction.

At $t = \pi/2\omega$

$$\cos(\omega t - kz) = \cos\left(\frac{\pi}{2} - kz\right) = \sin kz$$

$$\cos(\omega t + kz) = \cos\left(\frac{\pi}{2} + kz\right) = -\sin kz$$

At $t = \pi/\omega$

$$\cos(\omega t - lz) = \cos(\pi - kz) = -\cos kz$$

$$\cos(\omega t + kz) = \cos(\pi + kz) = -\cos kz$$

Let us first consider the wave $A^+ \cos(\omega t - kz)$ shown in Fig. 2-4. If we examine the peak marked in Fig. 2-4, we see that as time increases, the peak moves in the $+z$ direction. Now consider the other wave described by $A^- \cos(\omega t + kz)$ as shown in Fig. 2-5. As time increases the marked peak moves in the $-z$ direction.

Note that the two plane waves start in the same place for $t = 0$ but move in opposite directions. The sinusoidal steady-state wave will be the sum of these two distributions.

2-8 WAVE PARAMETERS

Consider a plane wave propagating in the $+\hat{n}$ direction

$$\psi = A \cos(\omega t - \bar{k} \cdot \bar{r}) \tag{2-58}$$

Following a surface of constant phase, let us advance the wave a spatial wavelength λ requiring that ψ changes through a full cycle as $\bar{r}$ changes to $\bar{r} + \Delta\bar{r} = \bar{r} + \lambda\hat{n}$. That is

$$\Delta\bar{r} = \lambda\hat{n}$$

and

$$\omega t - \bar{k} \cdot \bar{r} = \omega t + 2\pi - \bar{k} \cdot (\bar{r} + \lambda\hat{n}) = \text{const}$$

solving for k in terms of λ

$$k\lambda = 2\pi$$

or

$$k = \frac{2\pi}{\lambda} = \frac{\omega}{v} \tag{2-59}$$

where $\lambda \equiv$ spatial wavelength of wave in medium of parameters ε, μ_0
  k is sometimes called the wave number
  $v \equiv$ phase velocity of the wave in medium of parameters ε, μ_0

Writing the wave parameters v, λ, and k in terms of free space parameters ε_0, μ_0, and the speed of light in free space c

$$v = \frac{1}{\sqrt{\mu_0 \varepsilon}} = \frac{c}{\sqrt{\varepsilon_r}} = \frac{c}{n} \tag{2-60}$$

$$\lambda = \frac{2\pi v}{\omega} = \frac{2\pi}{\omega}\left(\frac{c}{n}\right) = \frac{c}{f}\left(\frac{1}{n}\right) = \frac{\lambda_0}{n} \tag{2-61}$$

where λ_0 is the spatial wavelength of the wave in free space and n is the refractive index of medium whose permittivity is ε.

Finally

$$k = \frac{2\pi}{\lambda} = \left(\frac{2\pi}{\lambda_0}\right)n = nk_0 \tag{2-62}$$

where k_0 is the wave number in free space.

2-9 DISPERSIVE MEDIA; GROUP VELOCITY

In our study of dielectric waveguides we will be dealing with dispersive dielectric media, i.e., media whose refractive indices are a function of wavelength (frequency). When propagating energy from a quasi or nonmonochromatic source, such as a laser or light-emitting diode, through a dispersive dielectric medium, one is concerned with the group velocity or group delay of the energy being transmitted. In this section the concept of group velocity will be developed by means of a simplified example designed to give the reader a physical understanding of how nonmonochromatic waves propagate through a dispersive medium.

First consider one component of a monochromatic electric field, say the y component, propagating in the z direction in a dielectric medium. By letting $\hat{n} = \hat{a}_z$ in Eq. (2-58) one obtains

$$E_y = A \cos(\omega t - kz) \tag{2-63}$$

The phase velocity of this wave can be obtained by setting the phase of this wave equal to a constant and finding dz/dt. That is

$$\omega t - kz = \text{const}$$

$$v = \frac{dz}{dt} = \frac{\omega}{k} \tag{2-64}$$

Now consider that the wave has two frequencies of equal amplitude expressed by (nonmonochromatic wave)

$$\omega + \Delta\omega$$

and

$$\omega - \Delta\omega$$

It follows that the wave numbers corresponding to these two frequencies are

$$k + \Delta k$$

and

$$k - \Delta k$$

For frequency 1

$$E_y^1 = A \cos [(\omega + \Delta\omega)t - (k + \Delta k)z] \tag{2-65}$$

For frequency 2

$$E_y^2 = A \cos [(\omega - \Delta\omega)t - (k - \Delta k)z] \tag{2-66}$$

Adding equations (2-65) and (2-66) gives the total field

$$E_y = E_y^1 + E_y^2 \tag{2-67}$$

$$E_y = A\{\cos [(\omega + \Delta\omega)t - (k + \Delta k)z] + \cos [(\omega - \Delta\omega)t - (k - \Delta k)z]\} \tag{2-68}$$

Letting

$$x = \omega t - kz$$

$$y = \Delta\omega t - \Delta kz$$

and using the trigonometric identity

$$2 \cos x \cos y = \cos (x + y) + \cos (x - y)$$

one obtains

$$E_y = 2A \cos (\omega t - kz) \cos (\Delta\omega t - \Delta kz) \tag{2-69}$$

The two cosine functions indicate the presence of beats, that is, a slow variation superimposed upon a more rapid one. For those readers who have studied modulation theory equation (2-69) is of the same form as a suppressed carrier AM wave. If we consider $\omega \gg \Delta\omega$ the first cosine term in (2-69) varies very rapidly and the second cosine term has the effect of slowly varying the amplitude of the first term. To obtain the phase velocity of this wave for a constant phase point

$$\omega t - kz = \text{const}$$

and

$$v = \frac{dz}{dt} = \frac{\omega}{k} \equiv \text{phase velocity} \tag{2-70}$$

Setting the argument of the second cosine term equal to a constant

$$\Delta\omega t - \Delta k z = \text{const}$$

Defining group velocity v_g as

$$v_g = \frac{dz}{dt} = \frac{\Delta\omega}{\Delta k} \equiv \text{group velocity} \tag{2-71}$$

In the limit as $\Delta\omega \to 0$, v_g becomes

$$v_g = \lim_{\Delta\omega \to 0} \frac{\Delta\omega}{\Delta k} = \frac{d\omega}{dk} \tag{2-72}$$

The group velocity is actually the phase velocity of the wave envelope and the velocity that information modulated on a wave will propagate at. Let us now define the concept of group delay τ_g

$$\tau_g = \frac{1}{v_g} = \frac{dk}{d\omega} \equiv \text{group delay} \tag{2-73}$$

For an infinite dispersive dielectric medium whose refractive index n is a function of ω we will now derive expressions for v, τ_g, and v_g.

Recalling that

$$k = nk_0 = n\left(\frac{\omega}{c}\right)$$

then

$$v = \frac{\omega}{k} = \frac{c}{n} \tag{2-74}$$

This expression for phase velocity was previously developed in (2-60). For a dispersive medium the refractive index is evaluated at the center wavelength of a nonmonochromatic source to calculate the phase velocity.

Calculating group delay τ_g

$$\tau_g = \frac{dk}{d\omega} = \frac{1}{c}\frac{d}{d\omega}(n\omega)$$

$$\tau_g = \frac{1}{c}\left(n + \omega\frac{dn}{d\omega}\right) \tag{2-75}$$

Now for the sake of notational simplicity let us define a group index N_g

$$N_g = n + \omega\frac{dn}{d\omega} \equiv \text{group index} \tag{2-76}$$

then

$$\tau_g = \frac{N_g}{c} \tag{2-77}$$

Table 2-1 Wave parameters

Free space	Nondispersive dielectric medium	Dispersive dielectric medium
$\lambda_0 = \dfrac{c}{f}$	$\lambda = \dfrac{\lambda_0}{n}$	$\lambda = \dfrac{\lambda_0}{n(\lambda_0)}$
$k_0 = \dfrac{2\pi}{\lambda_0}$	$k = \dfrac{2\pi}{\lambda} = nk_0$	$k = \dfrac{2\pi}{\lambda} = n(\lambda_0)k_0$
$v = c$	$v = \dfrac{c}{n}$	$v = \dfrac{c}{n(\lambda_0)}$
$N_g = n_0 = 1$	$N_g = n$	$N_g = n(\lambda_0) - \lambda\,\dfrac{dn}{d\lambda_0}$
$v_g = v = c$	$v_g = v$	$v_g = \dfrac{c}{N_g}$

and the group velocity is

$$v_g = \frac{c}{N_g} \tag{2-78}$$

Since in the optical portion of the electromagnetic spectrum one normally thinks in terms of wavelength λ_0 rather than frequency ω let us transform the group index to show the variation of the refractive index with λ_0.

$$N_g = n + \omega\,\frac{dn}{d\omega} = n + \omega\,\frac{dn}{d\lambda_0}\left(\frac{d\lambda_0}{d\omega}\right)$$

with

$$\lambda_0 = \frac{c}{f} = \frac{2\pi c}{\omega}$$

$$\frac{d\lambda_0}{d\omega} = -\frac{\lambda_0}{\omega}$$

Therefore

$$N_g = n - \lambda_0\,\frac{dn}{d\lambda_0} \tag{2-79}$$

Notice that for a nondispersive medium where the refractive index is a constant, independent of λ_0, $N_g = n$ and $v = v_g$. Table 2-1 shows the relationships for the various wave parameters in free space, in a nondispersive dielectric medium, and in a dispersive dielectric medium.

Example 2.2 Group and phase velocities in a dispersive medium In general, the group and phase velocities of a wave in a dispersive medium will be different. Fused silica is a dispersive medium whose refractive index is a function of wavelength as shown in Fig. 5-5. To illustrate propagation in a dispersive medium we will calculate the group and phase velocities of a wave propagating in fused silica with a source wavelength $\lambda_0 = 1$ μm.

For a 1 μm source wavelength the refractive index $n(\lambda_0)$ is 1.4505 from Fig. 5-5. The phase velocity v_p is given by

$$v_p = \frac{c}{n(\lambda_0)}$$

$$= \frac{3 \times 10^8 \text{ m/s}}{1.4505}$$

$$= 2.068 \times 10^8 \text{ m/s}$$

To obtain the group velocity we must first calculate the group index N_g. We will calculate $dn/d\lambda_0$ by approximating the slope of the curve in Fig. 5-5

$$\text{at } \lambda_0 = 1 \text{ } \mu\text{m, } n(\lambda_0) = 1.4505$$

$$\text{at } \lambda_0 = 1.05 \text{ } \mu\text{m, } n(\lambda_0) = 1.4500$$

$$\frac{dn}{d\lambda_0} = -0.01/\mu\text{m} = \frac{1.4505 - 1.4500}{(1 - 1.05) \text{ } \mu\text{m}}$$

The group index

$$N_g = n(\lambda_0) - \lambda_0 \frac{dn}{d\lambda_0}$$

$$= 1.4505 + 1(0.01)$$

$$= 1.4605$$

$$v_g = \frac{c}{N_g}$$

$$= \frac{3 \times 10^8 \text{ m/s}}{1.4605}$$

$$= 2.054 \times 10^8 \text{ m/s}$$

The group velocity, at which information will propagate, is slower than the phase velocity.

2-10 TRANSVERSE ELECTROMAGNETIC (TEM) WAVES; POYNTING VECTOR

Generalizing the concepts we have developed for uniform propagating plane waves in dielectric media, one can obtain the relationships between the $\bar{E}$ and $\bar{H}$ vectors and the direction of propagation of a wave defined by the unit vector $\hat{n}$.

Writing $\bar{E}$ and $\bar{H}$ as

$$\bar{E} = \bar{E}_1 e^{-j\bar{k}\cdot\bar{r}} + \bar{E}_2 e^{+j\bar{k}\cdot\bar{r}} \tag{2-80}$$

and

$$\bar{H} = \bar{H}_1 e^{-j\bar{k}\cdot\bar{r}} + \bar{H}_2 e^{+j\bar{k}\cdot\bar{r}}$$

where $\bar{E}_1$, $\bar{E}_2$, $\bar{H}_1$, and $\bar{H}_2$ are vectors contained in planes normal to $\hat{n}$.

We can by direct substitution of Eq. (2-80) into Maxwell's equations show that

$$\hat{n} \cdot \bar{E} = 0 \tag{2-81}$$

$$\bar{H}_1 = \frac{1}{\eta}\,\hat{n} \times \bar{E}_1 \tag{2-82}$$

$$\bar{H}_2 = \frac{-1}{\eta}\,\hat{n} \times \bar{E}_2 \tag{2-83}$$

and

$$\eta = \sqrt{\frac{\mu_0}{\varepsilon}} \equiv \text{the characteristic impedance of the medium} \tag{2-84}$$

The characteristics of a wave defined by Eqs. (2-81) to (2-83) are those of a uniform TEM plane wave propagating in a direction fixed by the unit vector $\hat{n}$. Notice that the $\bar{E}$ and $\bar{H}$ vectors are perpendicular to each other and that they are both perpendicular to the direction of propagation of the plane waves defined by $\hat{n}$.

Another important parameter that is a measure of the time average power flow in an electromagnetic field is the complex Poynting vector $\bar{S}$

$$\bar{S} = \tfrac{1}{2}(\bar{E} \times \bar{H}^*) \tag{2-85}$$

The time average power flow is given by

$$\bar{P}_{\text{av}} = \text{Re }\bar{S} = \tfrac{1}{2}\,\text{Re }(\bar{E} \times \bar{H}^*) \tag{2-86}$$

Using the notation developed in Eqs. (2-80) to (2-83) the general expression for $\bar{S}$ can be obtained

$$\bar{S} = \bar{S}_1 + \bar{S}_2 \tag{2-87}$$

$$\bar{S}_1 = \tfrac{1}{2}\bar{E}_1 \times \bar{H}_1^* = \tfrac{1}{2}\bar{E}_1 \times \left(\frac{1}{\eta}\,\hat{n} \times \bar{E}_1^*\right)$$

$$\bar{S}_1 = \frac{1}{2\eta}\left[(\bar{E}_1 \cdot \bar{E}_1^*)\hat{n} - (\bar{E}_1 \cdot \hat{n})\bar{E}_1^*\right] \tag{2-88}$$

$$\bar{S}_1 = \frac{1}{2\eta}\,|E_1|^2\hat{n} \tag{2-89}$$

and

$$\bar{S}_2 = \tfrac{1}{2}\bar{E}_2 \times \bar{H}_2^* = \tfrac{1}{2}\bar{E}_2 \times \left(\frac{-1}{\eta}\,\hat{n} \times \bar{E}_2^*\right)$$

$$\bar{S}_2 = \frac{1}{2\eta}\,|E_2|^2(-\hat{n}) \tag{2-90}$$

Notice that $\bar{S}_1$ and $\bar{S}_2$, the Poynting vectors, are in the propagating directions $(\pm\hat{n})$ of their respective waves.

2-11 BOUNDARY CONDITIONS IN DIELECTRIC MEDIA

To solve for the fields in a dielectric waveguide the procedure followed is to write down Maxwell's equations (or the derived wave equations) where the fields are continuous, and couple the solutions of these equations together by means of boundary conditions. When the dielectric waveguide has an inhomogeneous core with no discontinuous regions of the dielectric constant the only boundary condition is the requirement that the field vanish at infinity and be finite everywhere else. The most common type of boundary condition occurs when there are discontinuities in the dielectric constant. Such a discontinuity exists, for example at the core-cladding interface of a step-index fiber. The desired boundary conditions for time varying fields at the interface between dielectric media can be obtained from Maxwell's equations in integral form.

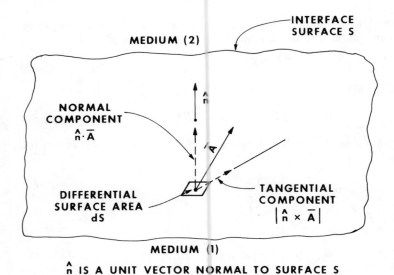

Figure 2-6 Orientation of normal and tangential components of vector at interface of dielectric media.

Figure 2-6 illustrates the orientation of the normal and tangential components of a field vector with respect to a unit vector $\hat{n}$ normal to a surface that forms the interface between two dielectric media. For the dielectric media we are considering the general boundary conditions for the fields are[5]

$$\hat{n} \times (\bar{E}_2 - \bar{E}_1) = 0 \tag{2-91}$$

(Tangential components of E field are continuous.)

$$\hat{n} \times (\bar{H}_2 - \bar{H}_1) = 0 \tag{2-92}$$

(Tangential components of H field are continuous.)

$$\hat{n} \cdot (\bar{B}_2 - \bar{B}_1) = 0 \tag{2-93}$$

(Normal components of B field are continuous.)

$$\hat{n} \cdot (\bar{D}_2 - \bar{D}_1) = 0 \tag{2-94}$$

(Normal components of D field are continuous.)

2-12 REFLECTION AND REFRACTION AT A PLANE DIELECTRIC INTERFACE

Let us now utilize the background material we have developed in this chapter to solve a simple but important problem of wave propagation in dielectric media. Consider a plane TEM wave incident upon an interface (boundary surface) between two dielectric media as shown in Figure 2-7. It is our purpose to study the phenomena of reflection and refraction of the wave as it crosses the

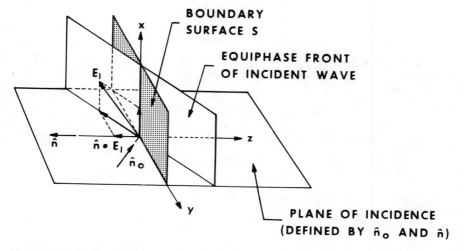

Figure 2-7 Geometry of plane wave incident at dielectric interface, arbitrary polarization.

interface. In general the incident electric field vector can be decomposed into two components. Each component or polarization of the electric field will ultimately yield a different answer for the amplitude of the reflected and transmitted waves. For pedagogical reasons we will analyze the problem for the case of perpendicular polarization, that is, for the component of the electric field perpendicular to the plane of incidence. (Referring to Fig. 2-7, the plane of incidence is formed by $\hat{n}_0$, a unit vector in the direction of the incident wave, and $\hat{n}$ a unit vector normal to the boundary surface.) We will then state the answer to the problem for the case of parallel polarization when the component of the electric field is in the plane of incidence.

Consider a perpendicularly polarized plane wave incident upon a dielectric boundary at some angle θ_1, relative to the normal to the boundary. (See Fig. 2-8.) Using the vector notation we have developed, we can write the incident electric field as

$$\bar{E}_I = \bar{E}e^{-j\bar{k}_0 \cdot \bar{r}} \tag{2-95}$$

where

$$\bar{E} = E_i \hat{a}_x \tag{2-96}$$

Our objective is to obtain expressions for reflected and transmitted fields in terms of the known parameters E_i, θ_1, ε_1, and ε_2.

We can write general expressions for the reflected and transmitted fields as

$$\bar{E}_R = E_r e^{-j\bar{k}_1 \cdot \bar{r}} \hat{a}_x \tag{2-97}$$

$$\bar{E}_T = E_t e^{-j\bar{k}_2 \cdot \bar{r}} \hat{a}_x \tag{2-98}$$

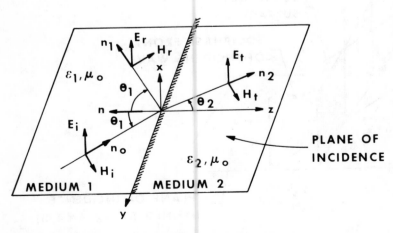

Figure 2-8 Field configuration of perpendicularly polarized waves.

where the propagation and unit vectors associated with incident, reflected, and transmitted fields are:

$$\bar{k}_0 = k_1 \hat{n}_0$$
$$\hat{n}_0 = \cos\theta_1 \hat{a}_z - \sin\theta_1 \hat{a}_y \qquad (2\text{-}99)$$
$$k_1 = \omega\sqrt{\varepsilon_1 \mu_0}$$

$$\bar{k}_1 = k_1 \hat{n}_1$$
$$\hat{n}_1 = -\cos\theta_1 \hat{a}_z - \sin\theta_1 \hat{a}_y \qquad (2\text{-}100)$$

and

$$\bar{k}_2 = k_2 \hat{n}_2$$
$$\hat{n}_2 = \cos\theta_2 \hat{a}_z - \sin\theta_2 \hat{a}_y \qquad (2\text{-}101)$$
$$k_2 = \omega\sqrt{\varepsilon_2 \mu_0}$$

The stategy for obtaining E_r, E_t, and θ_2 in terms of the given parameters E_i, θ_1, ε_1, and ε_2 is to first take advantage of the properties of a TEM wave and write expressions for the electric and magnetic fields in media 1 and 2. We will then apply the boundary conditions at the interface between the media (at $z = 0$) to obtain the amplitudes and directions of the reflected and transmitted waves.

Using Eqs. (2-99) to (2-101) we can expand the exponents in Eqs. (2-95), (2-97), and (2-98) to obtain the following expressions for the electric fields:

$$\bar{E}_I = E_i e^{-jk_1(\cos\theta_1 z - \sin\theta_1 y)} \hat{a}_x \qquad (2\text{-}102)$$

$$\bar{E}_R = E_r e^{-jk_1(-\cos\theta_1 z - \sin\theta_1 y)} \hat{a}_x \qquad (2\text{-}103)$$

$$\bar{E}_T = E_t e^{-jk_2(\cos\theta_2 z - \sin\theta_2 y)} \hat{a}_x \qquad (2\text{-}104)$$

For a TEM wave we know that the $\bar{E}$ and $\bar{H}$ fields are perpendicular to each other and perpendicular to the direction of propagation. Utilizing Eq. (2-82) the expressions for the magnetic fields become

$$\bar{H}_I = \frac{\hat{n}_0 \times \bar{E}_I}{\eta_1} \qquad (2\text{-}105)$$

$$\bar{H}_R = \frac{\hat{n}_1 \times \bar{E}_R}{\eta_1} \qquad (2\text{-}106)$$

$$\bar{H}_T = \frac{\hat{n}_2 \times \bar{E}_T}{\eta_2} \qquad (2\text{-}107)$$

and

$$\eta_1 = \sqrt{\frac{\mu_0}{\varepsilon_1}} \qquad \eta_2 = \sqrt{\frac{\mu_0}{\varepsilon_2}} \qquad (2\text{-}108)$$

Since $\bar{E}_I$, $\bar{E}_R$, and $\bar{E}_T$ are in the $\hat{a}_x$ direction, we are interested in the terms, $\hat{n}_0 \times \hat{a}_x$, $\hat{n}_1 \times \hat{a}_x$ and $\hat{n}_2 \times \hat{a}_x$. For example

$$\hat{n}_0 \times \hat{a}_x = (\cos \theta_1 \hat{a}_z - \sin \theta_1 \hat{a}_y) \times \hat{a}_x$$

$$\hat{n}_0 \times \hat{a}_x = \cos \theta_1 \hat{a}_y + \sin \theta_1 \hat{a}_z$$

and similarly

$$\hat{n}_1 \times \hat{a}_x = -\cos \theta_1 \hat{a}_y + \sin \theta_1 \hat{a}_z$$

$$\hat{n}_2 \times \hat{a}_x = \cos \theta_2 \hat{a}_y + \sin \theta_2 \hat{a}_z$$

Substituting these cross products into Eqs. (2-105) to (2-107) results in the following expressions for the magnetic fields:

$$\bar{H}_I = \left(\frac{E_i}{\eta_1} \cos \theta_1 \hat{a}_y + \frac{E_i}{\eta_1} \sin \theta_1 a_z \right) e^{jk_1 y \sin \theta_1 - jk_1 z \cos \theta_1} \tag{2-109}$$

$$\bar{H}_R = \left(-\frac{E_r}{\eta_1} \cos \theta_1 \hat{a}_y + \frac{E_r}{\eta_1} \sin \theta_1 \hat{a}_z \right) e^{jk_1 y \sin \theta_1 + jk_1 z \cos \theta_1} \tag{2-110}$$

$$\bar{H}_T = \left(\frac{E_t}{\eta_2} \cos \theta_2 \hat{a}_y + \frac{E_t}{\eta_2} \sin \theta_2 \hat{a}_z \right) e^{jk_2 y \sin \theta_2 - jk_2 z \cos \theta_2} \tag{2-111}$$

To solve for the unknown parameters E_r, E_t, and θ_2 we will apply the boundary conditions for the tangential components of the $\bar{E}$ and $\bar{H}$ fields and $z = 0$. That is

$$\hat{n} \times (\bar{E}_I + \bar{E}_R) = \hat{n} \times \bar{E}_T \tag{2-112}$$

$$\hat{n} \times (\bar{H}_I + \bar{H}_R) = \hat{n} \times \bar{H}_T \tag{2-113}$$

where

$$\hat{n} = -\hat{a}_z$$

Substituting Eqs. (2-102) to (2-104) into (2-112) at $z = 0$ yields

$$-\hat{a}_z \times (E_i e^{jk_1 y \sin \theta_1} \hat{a}_x + E_r e^{jk_1 y \sin \theta_1} \hat{a}_z) = -\hat{a}_z \times (E_t e^{jk_2 y \sin \theta_2} \hat{a}_z)$$

or

$$(E_i + E_r)e^{jk_1 y \sin \theta_1} \hat{a}_y = E_t e^{jk_2 y \sin \theta_2} \hat{a}_y \tag{2-114}$$

The continuity of magnitudes in Eq. (2-114) requires that

$$E_i + E_r = E_t \tag{2-115}$$

The continuity of phase requires

$$k_1 \sin \theta_1 = k_2 \sin \theta_2$$

or

$$\frac{\sin \theta_1}{\sin \theta_2} = \frac{k_2}{k_1} \equiv \text{Snell's law} \tag{2-116}$$

Following an identical procedure of substituting Eqs. (2-109) to (2-111) into (2-113) results in the boundary condition equation at $z = 0$ for the magnetic field

$$\frac{E_i}{\eta_1} \cos \theta_1 - \frac{E_r}{\eta_1} \cos \theta_1 = \frac{E_t}{\eta_2} \cos \theta_2 \qquad (2\text{-}117)$$

We will use Eqs. (2-115) and (2-117) to develop the reflection and transmission coefficients (Fresnel's equations) for perpendicular polarization. Substituting Eq. (2-115) into (2-117) to eliminate E_t we obtain:

$$E_i\left(\frac{\cos \theta_1}{\eta_1} - \frac{\cos \theta_2}{\eta_2}\right) = E_r\left(\frac{\cos \theta_1}{\eta_1} + \frac{\cos \theta_2}{\eta_2}\right)$$

or simplifying

$$E_i(\eta_2 \cos \theta_1 - \eta_1 \cos \theta_2) = E_r(\eta_2 \cos \theta_1 y_1 \cos \theta_2)$$

We can now define a reflection coefficient

$$\Gamma_\perp = \frac{E_r}{E_i} = \frac{\eta_2 \cos \theta_1 - \eta_1 \cos \theta_2}{\eta_2 \cos \theta_1 + \eta_1 \cos \theta_2} \qquad (2\text{-}118)$$

We now have an expression for E_r in terms of E_i, that is,

$$E_r = \Gamma_\perp E_i \qquad (2\text{-}119)$$

Substituting Eq. (2-119) into (2-115), thus eliminating E_r, allows us to define a transmission coefficient

$$\tau_\perp = \frac{E_t}{E_i} = \frac{2\eta_2 \cos \theta_1}{\eta_2 \cos \theta_1 + \eta_1 \cos \theta_2} \qquad (2\text{-}120)$$

and

$$E_t = \tau_\perp E_i \qquad (2\text{-}121)$$

$\Gamma_\perp$ and $\tau_\perp$ are two of Fresnel's equations for perpendicular polarization. If we choose to solve the problem for the case of parallel polarization where the incident electric field vector is in the plane of incidence, we would obtain the following results:

$$\Gamma_\parallel = \frac{\eta_1 \cos \theta_1 - \eta_2 \cos \theta_2}{\eta_1 \cos \theta_1 + \eta_2 \cos \theta_2} \qquad (2\text{-}122)$$

$$\tau_\parallel = \frac{2\eta_2 \cos \theta_1}{\eta_1 \cos \theta_1 + \eta_2 \cos \theta_2} \qquad (2\text{-}123)$$

$\Gamma_\perp, \tau_\perp, \Gamma_\parallel, \tau_\parallel$ form the complete set of Fresnel's equations. Using Fresnel's equations and Snell's law, we can determine the relationships between the incident and the reflected and transmitted fields at a dielectric interface for the two polarizations of the electric field.

An interesting example of the use of Fresnel's equations occur when one calculates the amount of power reflected and transmitted at an air-glass boundary. To determine the power reflection and transmission coefficients we will write the expressions for the incident, reflected, and transmitted powers in the z direction in terms of Γ, τ, and E_i. Using Eq. (2-97)

$$P_{Iz} = \frac{1}{2\eta_1} |E_i|^2 \hat{n}_0 \cdot \hat{a}_z = \frac{1}{2\eta_1} |E_1|^2 \cos \theta_1$$

$$P_{Rz} = \frac{1}{2\eta_1} |\Gamma E_i|^2 \hat{n}_1 \cdot \hat{a}_z = \frac{1}{2\eta_1} |\Gamma|^2 |E_i|^2 \cos \theta_1$$

$$P_{Tz} = \frac{1}{2\eta_2} |\tau E_i|^2 \hat{n}_2 \cdot \hat{a}_z = \frac{1}{2\eta_2} |\tau|^2 |E_i|^2 \cos \theta_2$$

Now defining the power reflection and transmission coefficients as

$$R = \frac{P_{Rz}}{P_{Iz}} = |\Gamma|^2 \tag{2-124}$$

and

$$T = \frac{P_{Tz}}{P_{Iz}} = \frac{\eta_1}{\eta_2} |\tau|^2 \frac{\cos \theta_2}{\cos \theta_1} = \frac{n_2}{n_1} |\tau|^2 \frac{\cos \theta_2}{\cos \theta_1} \tag{2-125}$$

One can write R and T for perpendicular and parallel polarization in terms of the input angle θ_1 only by using Snell's law (2-116) to write θ_2 in terms of θ_1. Following this procedure $\Gamma_\perp$, $\Gamma_\parallel$, $\tau_\perp$, and $\tau_\parallel$ can be substituted into Eqs. (2-124) and (2-125) to obtain $R_\perp$, $R_\parallel$, $T_\perp$, and $T_\parallel$. After some tedious algebra,

$$R_\perp = \frac{[n_1 \cos \theta_1 - \sqrt{n_2^2 - n_1^2 \sin^2 \theta_1}]^2}{[n_1 \cos \theta_1 + \sqrt{n_2^2 - n_1^2 \sin^2 \theta_1}]^2} \tag{2-126}$$

$$R_\parallel = \frac{[n_2 \cos \theta_1 - n_1/n_2\sqrt{n_2^2 - n_1^2 \sin^2 \theta_1}]^2}{[n_2 \cos \theta_1 + n_1/n_2\sqrt{n_2^2 - n_1^2 \sin^2 \theta_1}]^2} \tag{2-127}$$

$$T_\perp = \frac{4n_1 \cos \theta_1\sqrt{n_2^2 - n_1^2 \sin^2 \theta_1}}{[n_1 \cos \theta_1 + \sqrt{n_2^2 - n_1^2 \sin^2 \theta_1}]^2} \tag{2-128}$$

$$T_\parallel = \frac{4n_1 \cos \theta_1\sqrt{n_2^2 - n_1^2 \sin^2 \theta_1}}{[n_2 \cos \theta_1 + n_1/n_2\sqrt{n_2^2 - n_1^2 \sin^2 \theta_1}]^2} \tag{2-129}$$

Figure 2-9 is a plot of $R_\perp$ and $T_\perp$ as a function of θ_1 for an air-glass interface. Notice that for small angles, less than twenty degrees, the reflection coefficient is 0.04 (4 percent). That is 4 percent of the power is reflection and 96 percent transmitted at an air-glass boundary such as a dry junction of an optical fiber splice. Figure 2-10 shows how $R_\parallel$ and $T_\parallel$ vary as a function of θ_1. Notice there is an input angle $\theta_1 = \theta_B$ at which the reflection coefficient $R_\parallel = 0$.

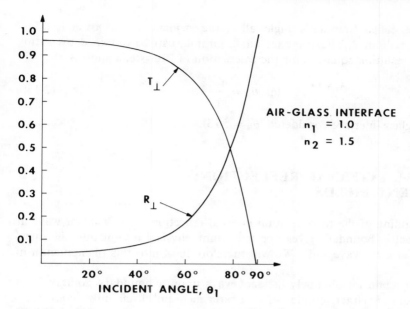

Figure 2-9 Power reflection and transmission coefficients—perpendicular polarization.

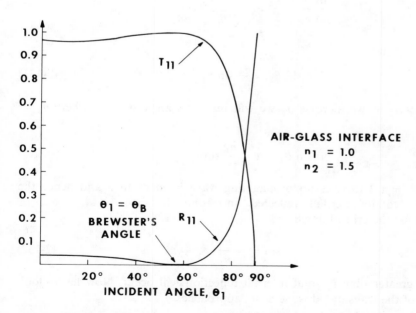

Figure 2-10 Power reflection and transmission coefficients—parallel polarization.

At this angle, called Brewster's angle, all of the incident waves power is transmitted into medium 2. The Brewster angle formula can be obtained by setting $\Gamma_{\parallel} = 0$. The resulting equation for the calculation of Brewster's angle is

$$\tan \theta_B = \frac{n_2}{n_1} \tag{2-130}$$

For the air-glass interface considered, $\theta_B = 56.3°$.

2-13 TOTAL INTERNAL REFLECTION; EVANESCENT FIELDS

An understanding of the topic of total internal reflection of an incident wave at a plane dielectric boundary gives one important physical insight into the operation of a dielectric waveguide. We will therefore look into this phenomenon in depth.

Consider again an obliquely incident wave upon a boundary going from a denser medium of refractive index n_1 to a rarer medium of refractive index n_2.

Total reflection of the incident wave will occur for certain angles of incidence equal to or greater than an angle known as the "critical" angle.

The directional relationship between the incident wave and transmitted wave is given by Snell's law

$$\frac{\sin \theta_1}{\sin \theta_2} = \frac{k_2}{k_1} = \frac{\omega \sqrt{\mu_0 \varepsilon_2}}{\omega \sqrt{\mu_0 \varepsilon_1}} = \frac{n_2}{n_1}$$

or

$$\sin \theta_2 = \frac{n_1}{n_2} \sin \theta_1 \tag{2-131}$$

For $n_1 > n_2$ as we increase θ_1 we will reach an angle $\theta_1 = \theta_c$ where $\theta_2 = \pi/2$, that is

$$\sin \theta_2 = 1 = \frac{n_1}{n_2} \sin \theta_c$$

When $\theta_2 = \pi/2$ there is no propagating wave in medium 2 and hence the wave will be "totally internally reflected" in medium 1.

Solving for the critical angle

$$\sin \theta_c = \frac{n_2}{n_1} \tag{2-132}$$

For angles greater than θ_c total internal reflection will occur. Now let us look at the field of the transmitted wave as θ_1 approaches θ_c.

$$\bar{E}_T = \bar{E}_2 \, e^{-jk_2(\cos \theta_2 z - \sin \theta_2 y)} \tag{2-133}$$

where $\bar{E}_2$ is dependent upon the state of polarization. For example, for perpendicular polarization,

$$\bar{E}_2 = E_t \hat{a}_x$$

Using Eq. (2-131) and noting that

$$\cos \theta_2 = \sqrt{1 - \frac{n_1^2}{n_2^2} \sin^2 \theta_1} \qquad (2\text{-}134)$$

We can rewrite (2-133) in terms of θ_1

$$\bar{E}_T = \bar{E}_2 \exp\left[jk_2 \left(\frac{n_1}{n_2} \sin \theta_1 y - \sqrt{1 - \frac{n_1^2}{n_2^2} \sin^2 \theta_1} \, z \right) \right] \qquad (2\text{-}135)$$

As θ_1 is increased from 0 to θ_c we have a component of the propagation vector of $\bar{E}_t$ propagating in the $-y$ direction and a component propagating in the $+z$ direction.

When

$$\theta_1 = \theta_c$$

$$\sin^2 \theta_c = \left(\frac{n_2}{n_1} \right)^2$$

and

$$\sqrt{1 - \frac{n_1^2}{n_2^2} \sin^2 \theta_c} = \sqrt{1 - \frac{n_1^2}{n_2^2} \left(\frac{n_2^2}{n_1^2} \right)} = 0$$

Therefore

$$\bar{E}_T = \bar{E}_2 \, e^{jk_2 y} \qquad (2\text{-}136)$$

The field is propagating in the $-y$ direction only. Let us now look at the flow of power for the critical angle case. The complex Poynting vector for the transmitted wave is

$$\bar{S}_T = \frac{1}{2} \frac{|E_2|^2}{\eta_2} \hat{n}_2 \qquad (2\text{-}137)$$

where

$$\hat{n}_2 = \cos \theta_2 \, \hat{a}_z - \sin \theta_2 \, \hat{a}_y$$

when

$$\theta_1 = \theta_c \qquad \theta_2 = \frac{\pi}{2}$$

and

$$\cos \theta_2 = 0 \qquad \sin \theta_2 = 1$$

Therefore

$$\hat{n}_2 = -\hat{a}_y$$

and

$$\bar{S}_T = -\frac{1}{2}\frac{|E_2|^2}{\eta_2}\,\hat{a}_y \qquad (2\text{-}138)$$

Equation (2-138) illustrates the fact that the time average power flow in the $+z$ direction into medium 2 is zero. The time average power flows only in the $-y$ direction at the critical angle.

What happens to the fields and power flow when $\theta_1 > \theta_c$?

Observe that

$$\sin^2\theta_1 > \frac{n_2^2}{n_1^2} \qquad \text{and} \qquad \sqrt{1 - \frac{n_1^2}{n_2^2}\sin^2\theta_1}$$

becomes imaginary. Therefore we can write

$$\sqrt{1 - \frac{n_1^2}{n_2^2}\sin^2\theta_1} = -j\sqrt{\frac{n_1^2}{n_2^2}\sin^2\theta_1 - 1} \qquad (2\text{-}139)$$

(the choice of $-j$ in the above expression was dictated by energy considerations at $z \to \infty$).

Substituting Eq. (2-139) into (2-135) yields an expression for the electric field in medium 2 for $\theta_1 > \theta_c$

$$\bar{E}_T = \bar{E}_2\left(e^{-k_2\sqrt{\frac{n_1^2}{n_2^2}\sin^2\theta_1 - 1}\,z}\right)\left(e^{jk_2\frac{n_1}{n_2}\sin\theta_1 y}\right) \qquad (2\text{-}140)$$

To physically understand Eq. (2-140) let us make the following definitions. Let

$$\alpha = k_2\sqrt{\frac{n_1^2}{n_2^2}\sin^2\theta_1 - 1} = \omega\sqrt{\mu_0\varepsilon_2}\sqrt{\frac{n_1^2}{n_2^2}\sin^2\theta_1 - 1} \qquad (2\text{-}141)$$

$$\beta = k_2\left(\frac{n_1}{n_2}\right)\sin\theta_1 = \omega\sqrt{\mu_0\varepsilon_2}\left(\frac{n_1}{n_2}\right)\sin\theta_1 \qquad (2\text{-}142)$$

Substituting α and β into Eq. (2-140) gives a simple expression for the electric field in medium 2 for $\theta_1 > \theta_c$

$$\bar{E}_T = \bar{E}_2\,e^{-\alpha z}e^{j\beta y} \qquad (2\text{-}143)$$

$\bar{E}_T$ is the electric field portion of a nonuniform plane wave that is propagating in the $-y$ direction. Notice that this is an attenuated or "evanescent" wave in the $+z$ direction that is propagating in the $-y$ direction. α is an attenuation constant that determines the spatial rate of decay of the field in medium 2. β is a phase propagation constant. This wave is guided along the reflecting surface with no average transport of power into medium 2. To illustrate this fact let us calculate the average power transmitted in the z direction in medium 2.

$$\hat{a}_z \cdot \bar{S}_T = \frac{1}{2} \frac{|E_2|^2}{\eta_2} \hat{a}_z \cdot \hat{n}_2 = \frac{1}{2} \frac{|E_2|^2}{\eta_2} \cos \theta_2 \qquad (2\text{-}144)$$

But for $\theta_1 > \theta_c$ from Eq. (2-134) $\cos \theta_2$ is an imaginary number. Therefore the power transmitted in the z direction is imaginary (reactive). There is no average transport of energy into medium 2 even though an evanescent field exists. The concept of total internal reflection and an evanescent field will be very useful to us when we analyze the fields in the cladding of dielectric waveguides.

REFERENCES

1. J. L. Synge: *Talking about Relativity*, Elsevier, New York, 1970.
2. D. T. Paris and K. F. Hurd: *Basic Electromagnetic Theory*, McGraw-Hill Book Co., New York, 1969.
3. D. Marcuse: *Light Transmission Optics*, Van Nostrand Reinhold Co., New York, 1972.
4. J. D. Kraus: *Electro-Magnetics*, McGraw-Hill Book Co., New York, 1953.
5. R. B. Adler, L. J. Chu, and R. M. Fano: *Electromagnetic Energy Transmission and Radiation*, John Wiley & Sons, Inc., 1960.

PROBLEMS

2-1 Derive the wave equation for the magnetic field intensity (Eq. (2-27)) from Maxwell's equations for a charge-free, lossless, linear isotropic medium (assume the medium is also homogeneous).

2-2 Derive the Helmholtz equation (2-52) for the electric field from Maxwell's equations in sinusoidal steady state (assume a homogeneous medium).

2-3 Calculate the wave parameters v, λ, and k of a wave propagating in a medium of refractive index $n = 1.530$ whose free space wavelength $\lambda_0 = 1$ μm. Calculate the characteristic impedance of the medium. Compare these values with the values of the parameters in free space.

2-4 Given

1. A perpendicularly polarized TEM wave incident on a plane dielectric boundary as shown in Fig. 2-11

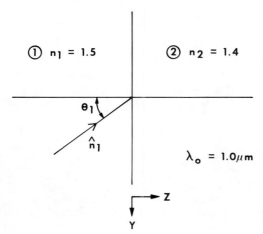

Figure 2-11 Geometry of TEM wave incident on a plane dielectric boundary. (Prob. 2-4)

2. The incident field $\bar{E}_1 = 5e^{-j\beta_1\hat{n}_1 \cdot \bar{r}}\hat{a}_x$
3. $\theta_1 = 30°$
   I. Find
      a. The magnitude of the field in medium 2 at $z = 10 \ \mu m$
      b. The z component of the Poynting vector in medium 2
   II. What is the smallest value of θ_1 at which total internal reflection will occur?

2-5 Refer again to Fig. 2-11. What happens to the wave in medium 2 if $\theta_1 = 75°$? Assume for this case that the wave in medium 2 is given by

$$\bar{E}_T = \bar{E}_2 \, e^{-jk_2\hat{n}_2 \cdot \bar{r}}$$

Find the magnitude of the wave in medium 2 at $z = 10 \ \mu m$ and the z component of the Poynting vector.

2-6 Calculate the group and phase velocities of a wave of free-space wavelength $\lambda_0 = 1.2 \ \mu m$
   (a) in free space,
   (b) in a nondispersive medium of refractive index 1.4482, and
   (c) in fused silica (refer to Fig. 5-5 for the $n(\lambda_0)$ curve of fused silica).

THREE

BASIC WAVEGUIDE EQUATIONS, WAVE AND RAY OPTICS

3-1 INTRODUCTION

This chapter is concerned with the development of the basic equations needed for the analysis of dielectric waveguides. Both wave and ray optics models will be developed to analyze the slab waveguide and the round optical fiber.

Since our intent is to design a guiding structure, we will choose the z axis as the longitudinal axis of our waveguide and assume that energy in the guide is propagating in the z direction. Our wave optics analysis will use the field theory notation of Chap. 2 to derive a wave equation in terms of the longitudinal components of the fields in the guide. Simple transformation equations will also be derived allowing one to calculate the transverse components of the fields in terms of the longitudinal components.

An alternate ray optics model for analyzing dielectric waveguides will also be developed. The Eikonal equation, which forms the basis of geometric optics, will be derived from the general wave equation. Ray optics equations for inhomogeneous dielectric media will then be transformed in cylindrical coordinates for future use in the analysis of the round optical fiber.

3-2 BASIC WAVEGUIDE EQUATIONS; WAVE OPTICS

Consider the general waveguide structure shown in Fig. 3-1. Our purpose in this section is to develop the mathematical model that will enable us to analyze and design a structure. We will ultimately apply this general model to obtain

45

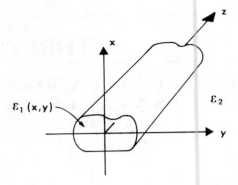

Figure 3-1 General dielectric waveguide structure used to propagate energy in the z direction.

the "modes" in a dielectric slab waveguide and in a round optical fiber. A mode is an allowable field configuration, for a given waveguide geometry, that satisfies Maxwell's equations (or the derived wave equations) and all of the boundary conditions of the problem. Our wave optics model will yield a complete description of the fields, that is, expressions for the amplitude and components of the propagation vector of the fields associated with a mode will be obtained.

We will assume that our design objective is to create a dielectric waveguide that propagates energy in a given direction. We define the longitudinal axis of our waveguide as the z axis and design it such that energy is propagating in the guide in the z direction with a longitudinal propagation constant β. (β is the longitudinal component of the propagation vector $\bar{\mathbf{k}}$.) We will assume that the permittivity $\varepsilon(x, y)$ does not depend on z but can vary with x and y. This special case of an inhomogeneous medium in which ε is independent of one space coordinate is an excellent representation of an optical fiber.

Using the notation developed in Chap. 2 and the assumptions cited above, we can write the fields in a waveguide as follows:

$$\bar{E} = \bar{E}_0(x, y)e^{-j\beta z} \tag{3-1}$$

$$\bar{H} = \bar{H}_0(x, y)e^{-j\beta z} \tag{3-2}$$

where the propagation constant β is to be determined.

If we substitute the fields into Maxwell's equations (2-49) and (2-48) we obtain in expanded component form

$$\left(\frac{\partial H_z}{\partial y} - \frac{\partial H_y}{\partial z}\right)\hat{a}_x + \left(\frac{\partial H_x}{\partial z} - \frac{\partial H_z}{\partial x}\right)\hat{a}_y + \left(\frac{\partial H_y}{\partial x} - \frac{\partial H_x}{\partial y}\right)\hat{a}_z$$

$$= \varepsilon\frac{\partial E_x}{\partial t}\hat{a}_x + \varepsilon\frac{\partial E_y}{\partial t}\hat{a}_y + \varepsilon\frac{\partial E_z}{\partial t}\hat{a}_z \tag{3-3}$$

and

$$\left(\frac{\partial E_z}{\partial y} - \frac{\partial E_y}{\partial z}\right)\hat{a}_x + \left(\frac{\partial E_x}{\partial z} - \frac{\partial E_z}{\partial x}\right)\hat{a}_y + \left(\frac{\partial E_y}{\partial x} - \frac{\partial E_x}{\partial y}\right)\hat{a}_z$$

$$= -\mu\frac{\partial H_x}{\partial t}\hat{a}_x - \mu\frac{\partial H_y}{\partial t}\hat{a}_y - \mu\frac{\partial H_z}{\partial t}\hat{a}_z \quad (3\text{-}4)$$

Since we are assuming that the fields are varying with respect to time as $e^{j\omega t}$, we can use Eqs. (3-1) and (3-2) to write the derivatives with respect to t and z explicitly as

$$\frac{\partial E_x}{\partial t} = j\omega E_x \qquad \frac{\partial E_y}{\partial t} = j\omega E_y \qquad \frac{\partial E_z}{\partial t} = j\omega E_z \qquad (3\text{-}5a)$$

$$\frac{\partial H_x}{\partial t} = j\omega H_x \qquad \frac{\partial H_y}{\partial t} = j\omega H_y \qquad \frac{\partial H_z}{\partial t} = j\omega H_z \qquad (3\text{-}5b)$$

$$\frac{\partial E_y}{\partial z} = -j\beta E_y \qquad \frac{\partial E_x}{\partial z} = -j\beta E_x \qquad (3\text{-}5c)$$

$$\frac{\partial H_y}{\partial z} = -j\beta H_y \qquad \frac{\partial H_x}{\partial z} = -j\beta H_x \qquad (3\text{-}5d)$$

Substituting (3-5) into (3-3) and (3-4) and writing in component form we obtain

$$\frac{\partial H_z}{\partial y} + j\beta H_y = j\omega\varepsilon E_x \qquad (3\text{-}6a)$$

$$-j\beta H_x - \frac{\partial H_z}{\partial x} = j\omega\varepsilon E_y \qquad (3\text{-}6b)$$

$$\frac{\partial H_y}{\partial x} - \frac{\partial H_x}{\partial y} = j\omega\varepsilon E_z \qquad (3\text{-}6c)$$

$$\frac{\partial E_z}{\partial y} + j\beta E_y = -j\omega\mu H_x \qquad (3\text{-}7a)$$

$$-j\beta E_x - \frac{\partial E_z}{\partial x} = -j\omega\mu H_y \qquad (3\text{-}7b)$$

$$\frac{\partial E_y}{\partial x} - \frac{\partial E_x}{\partial y} = -j\omega\mu H_z \qquad (3\text{-}7c)$$

We would like to manipulate Eqs. (3-6) and (3-7) to express E_x, E_y, H_x, H_y in terms of E_z and H_z (the transverse components in terms of the longitudinal components).

Once we accomplish that task our ultimate goal is to derive equations in terms of the longitudinal field components only (E_z and H_z). We will then use these equations to analyze dielectric waveguides.

Working with Eqs. (3-6a) and (3-7b), for example, we can obtain E_x in terms of H_z and E_z. Substituting (3-7b) into (3-6a)

$$j\omega\varepsilon E_x = \frac{\partial H_z}{\partial y} + \frac{j\beta}{-j\omega\mu}\left(-j\beta E_x - \frac{\partial E_z}{\partial x}\right)$$

or

$$\left(j\omega\varepsilon + \frac{-j\beta^2}{\omega\mu}\right)E_x = \frac{\partial H_z}{\partial y} + \frac{\beta}{\omega\mu}\frac{\partial E_z}{\partial x}$$

Multiplying both sides of the above equation by $-j\omega\mu$

$$(\omega^2\mu\varepsilon - \beta^2)E_x = -j\left(\omega\mu\frac{\partial H_z}{\partial y} + \beta\frac{\partial E_z}{\partial x}\right)$$

Let

$$\kappa^2 = k^2 - \beta^2 \qquad k^2 = \omega^2\mu\varepsilon \tag{3-8}$$

We obtain

$$E_x = \frac{-j}{\kappa^2}\left(\omega\mu\frac{\partial H_z}{\partial y} + \beta\frac{\partial E_z}{\partial x}\right) \tag{3-9}$$

Starting with (3-6b) and (3-7a) in a similar fashion we can obtain

$$E_y = \frac{-j}{\kappa^2}\left(\beta\frac{\partial E_z}{\partial y} - \omega\mu\frac{\partial H_z}{\partial x}\right) \tag{3-10}$$

Using Eqs. (3-7a) and (3-6b) we obtain

$$H_x = \frac{-j}{\kappa^2}\left(\beta\frac{\partial H_z}{\partial x} - \omega\varepsilon\frac{\partial E_z}{\partial y}\right) \tag{3-11}$$

and using (3-7b) and (3-6a) we obtain

$$H_y = \frac{-j}{\kappa^2}\left(\beta\frac{\partial H_z}{\partial y} + \omega\varepsilon\frac{\partial E_z}{\partial x}\right) \tag{3-12}$$

If we could solve for the longitudinal components of the fields we can, using Eqs. (3-9) to (3-12), obtain the transverse components.

We are now interested in deriving equations in terms of the longitudinal field components only (E_z and H_z).

If in Eq. (3-6c) we substitute (3-11) and (3-12) we obtain

$$\frac{-j}{\kappa^2}\beta\frac{\partial^2 H_z}{\partial x\,\partial y} - \frac{j}{\kappa^2}\omega\varepsilon\frac{\partial^2 E_z}{\partial x^2} + \frac{j}{\kappa^2}\beta\frac{\partial^2 H_z}{\partial x\,\partial y} - \frac{j}{\kappa^2}\omega\varepsilon\frac{\partial^2 E_z}{\partial y^2} = j\omega\varepsilon E_z$$

multiplying by $j\kappa^2/\omega\varepsilon$ we obtain

$$\frac{\partial^2 E_z}{\partial x^2} + \frac{\partial^2 E_z}{\partial y^2} + \kappa^2 E_z = 0 \tag{3-13}$$

This is a partial differential equation in E_z only. In a similar manner, starting with Eq. (3-7c) and substituting Eqs. (3-9) and (3-10) we can derive

$$\frac{\partial^2 H_z}{\partial x^2} + \frac{\partial^2 H_z}{\partial y^2} + \kappa^2 H_z = 0 \tag{3-14}$$

Equations (3-13) and (3-14) are modified forms of a wave equation and can be rewritten as follows:

$$\nabla_T^2 E_z + \kappa^2 E_z = 0 \tag{3-15}$$

$$\nabla_T^2 H_z + \kappa^2 H_z = 0 \tag{3-16}$$

where

$$\nabla_T^2 \equiv \frac{\partial^2}{\partial x^2} + \frac{\partial^2}{\partial y^2} \tag{3-17}$$

∇_T^2 is the transverse laplacian operator.

We will use Eqs. (3-15) and (3-16) transformed into cylindrical coordinates to derive the fields in a round optical fiber. In general when ε depends on x and y, (3-15) and (3-16) are no longer exact, since derivatives with respect to x and y of ε were not taken. (ε was assumed to be a constant.) However, they are still good approximations if the variation in ε is small over the region of one wavelength. For the graded index optical fiber this approximation is a very good one.

It is interesting to note that Eqs. (3-15) and (3-16) are uncoupled equations in the longitudinal component of the fields only. In general coupling of the two longitudinal fields occurs when satisfying the boundary conditions of a problem. This is the case for the round optical fiber. If the boundary conditions do not

Table 3-1 Listing of the various types of modes

Nomenclature	Longitudinal components	Transverse components
TEM (transverse electromagnetic)	$E_z = 0$ $H_z = 0$	E_T, H_T
TE (transverse electric)	$E_z = 0$ $H_z \neq 0$	E_T, H_T
TM (transverse magnetic)	$H_z = 0$ $E_z \neq 0$	E_T, H_T
HE or EH (hybrid)	$H_z \neq 0$ $E_z \neq 0$	E_T, H_T

achieve coupling of the longitudinal components, it is possible to obtain mode solutions with either $E_z = 0$ (transverse electric (TE) mode) or $H_z = 0$ (transverse magnetic (TM) mode). A list of the different types of modal solutions that can exist in an infinite dielectric medium or in a dielectric waveguide are given in Table 3-1.

> **Example 3-1 Transverse components of a TM mode** Using Eqs. (3-9) to (3-12) we can illustrate how to calculate the transverse field components of a TM mode in a waveguide in terms of the longitudinal field components.
>
> For a TM mode, $H_z = 0$. The transverse field components are given by Eqs. (3-9) to (3-12) with $H_z = 0$.

$$E_x = \frac{-j}{\kappa^2} \beta \frac{\partial E_z}{\partial x}$$

$$E_y = \frac{-j}{\kappa^2} \beta \frac{\partial E_z}{\partial y}$$

$$H_x = \frac{j}{\kappa^2} \omega\varepsilon \frac{\partial E_z}{\partial y}$$

$$H_y = \frac{-j}{\kappa^2} \omega\varepsilon \frac{\partial E_z}{\partial x}$$

3-3 WAVEGUIDE EQUATIONS IN CYLINDRICAL COORDINATES

In Sec. 3-2 we developed a mathematical model for analyzing dielectric waveguides with their fields propagating in the z direction. This model consisted of a set of equations ((3-9) to (3-12)) relating the transverse components to the longitudinal components of the fields, and two modified wave equations (3-15) and (3-16) written in terms of the longitudinal components of the fields of the waveguide only. Now we will convert the above equations from cartesian coordinates to cylindrical coordinates so that we may apply them in Chap. 5 to the geometry of the round optical fiber. The geometry considered in converting from cartesian coordinates to cylindrical coordinates is shown in Fig. 3-2. The z coordinate, which is the optical axis of our system, is common to both coordinate systems. As an example of the coordinate conversion process consider expressing E_r in cylindrical coordinates

$$E_r = E_x \cos \phi + E_y \sin \phi \qquad (3-18)$$

where in cartesian coordinates E_x and E_y are given by Eqs. (3-9) and (3-10).

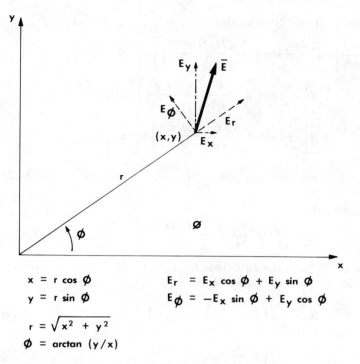

$$x = r \cos \phi \qquad E_r = E_x \cos \phi + E_y \sin \phi$$

$$y = r \sin \phi \qquad E_\phi = -E_x \sin \phi + E_y \cos \phi$$

$$r = \sqrt{x^2 + y^2}$$

$$\phi = \arctan (y/x)$$

Figure 3-2 Geometry for conversion from cartesian to cylindrical coordinates.

Substituting these equations into (3-18)

$$E_r = \frac{-j}{\kappa^2} \left(\omega\mu \frac{\partial H_z}{\partial y} \cos \phi + \beta \frac{\partial E_z}{\partial x} \cos \phi + \beta \frac{\partial E_z}{\partial y} \sin \phi - \omega\mu \frac{\partial H_z}{\partial x} \sin \phi \right) \quad (3\text{-}19)$$

Using the chain rule to obtain the required partial derivatives in cylindrical coordinates

$$\frac{\partial f}{\partial x} = \frac{\partial f}{\partial r} \frac{\partial r}{\partial x} + \frac{\partial f}{\partial \Phi} \frac{\partial \Phi}{\partial x}$$

$$\frac{\partial f}{\partial y} = \frac{\partial f}{\partial r} \frac{\partial r}{\partial y} + \frac{\partial f}{\partial \phi} \frac{\partial \phi}{\partial y} \qquad (3\text{-}20)$$

where

$$\frac{dr}{dx} = \frac{x}{r} = \cos \phi \qquad \frac{d\phi}{dx} = \frac{-y}{r^2} = \frac{-\sin \phi}{r}$$

$$\frac{dr}{dy} = \frac{y}{r} = \sin \phi \qquad \frac{d\phi}{dy} = \frac{x}{r^2} = \frac{\cos \phi}{r} \qquad (3\text{-}21)$$

Using Eqs. (3-20) and (3-21) in (3-19) yields

$$
E_r = \frac{-j}{\kappa^2} \left\{ \omega\mu \left[\frac{\partial H_z}{\partial r} \sin\phi + \frac{\partial H_z}{\partial \phi}\left(\frac{\cos\phi}{r}\right) \right] \cos\phi \right.
$$

$$
+ \beta \left[\frac{\partial E_z}{\partial r} \cos\phi + \frac{\partial E_z}{\partial \phi}\left(\frac{-\sin\phi}{r}\right) \right] \cos\phi
$$

$$
+ \beta \left[\frac{\partial E_z}{\partial r} \sin\phi + \frac{\partial E_z}{\partial \phi}\left(\frac{\cos\phi}{r}\right) \right] \sin\phi
$$

$$
\left. - \omega\mu \left[\frac{\partial H_z}{\partial r} \cos\phi + \frac{\partial H_z}{\partial \phi}\left(\frac{-\sin\phi}{r}\right) \right] \sin\phi \right\}
\tag{3-22}
$$

Simplifying Eq. (3-22) yields

$$
E_r = \frac{-j}{\kappa^2}\left(\beta \frac{\partial E_z}{\partial r} + \omega\mu \frac{1}{r}\frac{\partial H_z}{\partial \phi} \right)
\tag{3-23}
$$

Following the same procedures the equations for E_ϕ, H_r, H_ϕ can be written in cylindrical coordinates in terms of E_z and H_z as

$$
E_\phi = \frac{-j}{\kappa^2}\left(\beta \frac{1}{r}\frac{\partial E_z}{\partial \phi} - \omega\mu \frac{\partial H_z}{\partial r} \right)
\tag{3-24}
$$

$$
H_r = \frac{-j}{\kappa^2}\left(\beta \frac{\partial H_z}{\partial r} - \omega\varepsilon \frac{1}{r}\frac{\partial E_z}{\partial \phi} \right)
\tag{3-25}
$$

$$
H_\phi = \frac{-j}{\kappa^2}\left(\beta \frac{1}{r}\frac{\partial H_z}{\partial \phi} + \omega\varepsilon \frac{\partial E_z}{\partial r} \right)
\tag{3-26}
$$

In addition the modified wave equations (3-15) and (3-16) in cylindrical coordinates become

$$
\frac{\partial^2 E_z}{\partial r^2} + \frac{1}{r}\frac{\partial E_z}{\partial r} + \frac{1}{r^2}\frac{\partial^2 E_z}{\partial \phi^2} + \kappa^2 E_z = 0
\tag{3-27}
$$

and

$$
\frac{\partial^2 H_z}{\partial r^2} + \frac{1}{r}\frac{\partial H_z}{\partial r} + \frac{1}{r^2}\frac{\partial^2 H_z}{\partial \phi^2} + \kappa^2 H_z = 0
\tag{3-28}
$$

Equations (3-27) and (3-28) will be solved in Chap. 5 to obtain expressions for E_z and H_z in a round optical fiber. These expressions will then be substituted into (3-23) to (3-26) to obtain a complete description of the fields in a fiber.

3-4 RAY OPTICS; THE EIKONAL AND RAY EQUATIONS

An alternate method of analyzing optical waveguides is through the use of a geometric or ray optics model. Ray optics allows us to treat light propagation in a way that is far simpler than would be possible by solving Maxwell's equations or the wave equation. Ray optics can be applied to all phenomena that are described by the wave equation and that satisfy the additional requirement that the wavelength of light is short compared to the dimensions of the guide through which it passes. For example, ray optics can be used in a large-core multimode optical fiber. Ray optics is also useful because it allows one to visualize propagation of light rays in a simple way. One can think of ray optics as being very similar to the classical mechanics of a point particle.[2] In fact the relation between wave and ray optics is analogous to the relation between wave mechanics and ordinary mechanics of a point particle.

In this section the relationship between wave and ray optics will be shown by deriving the equations of ray optics from the wave equation developed in Chap. 2. If you will recall the Helmholtz equation (2-52)

$$\nabla^2 \bar{E} + k^2 \bar{E} = 0 \tag{3-29}$$

and if ψ is any rectangular component of $\bar{E}$

$$\nabla^2 \psi + k^2 \psi = 0 \tag{3-30}$$

where

$$k = nk_0 = n\left(\frac{2\pi}{\lambda_0}\right) \tag{3-31}$$

We will seek a solution to Eq. (3-30) of the form

$$\psi = \psi_0(x, y, z)e^{-jk_0 S(x, y, z)} \tag{3-32}$$

Where $\psi_0(x, y, z)$ and $S(x, y, z)$ are real functions of position. $S(x, y, z)$ is a phase function associated with the medium and is called an "eikonal."

Substituting Eq. (3-32) into (3-30), we obtain

$$\nabla^2(\psi_0 e^{-jk_0 S}) + k^2 \psi_0 e^{-jk_0 S} = 0 \tag{3-33}$$

Note that the laplacian of the product of the two scalar functions in the first term of Eq. (3-33) is

$$\nabla^2(\psi_0 e^{-jk_0 S}) = \psi_0 \nabla^2 e^{-jk_0 S} + e^{-jk_0 S}\nabla^2 \psi_0 + 2\nabla\psi_0 \cdot \nabla e^{-jk_0 S}$$

and

$$\nabla^2 e^{-jk_0 S} = \nabla \cdot \nabla e^{-jk_0 S} = \nabla \cdot [-jk_0(\nabla S)e^{-jk_0 S}]$$
$$= [-k_0^2(\nabla S)^2 - jk_0 \nabla^2 S]e^{-jk_0 S}$$

where

$$(\nabla S)^2 = \nabla S \cdot \nabla S = \left(\frac{\partial S}{\partial x}\right)^2 + \left(\frac{\partial S}{\partial y}\right)^2 + \left(\frac{\partial S}{\partial z}\right)^2$$

Therefore

$$\nabla^2(\psi_0 e^{-jk_0 S}) = \psi_0[-k_0^2(\nabla S)^2 - jk_0 \nabla^2 S]e^{-jk_0 S}$$
$$+ e^{-jk_0 S}\nabla^2 \psi_0 - j2k_0 e^{-jk_0 S}\nabla S \cdot \nabla\psi_0 \tag{3-34}$$

Substituting Eq. (3-34) into (3-33) and dividing out the common $e^{-jk_0 S}$ term results in

$$\psi_0[-k_0^2(\nabla S)^2 - jk_0 \nabla^2 S] + \nabla^2 \psi_0 - j2k_0 \nabla S \cdot \nabla \psi_0 + k^2 \psi_0 = 0 \qquad (3\text{-}35)$$

Finally equating the real and imaginary parts of Eq. (3-35) we obtain real part

$$-\psi_0 k_0^2(\nabla S)^2 + \nabla^2 \psi_0 + k^2 \psi_0 = 0 \qquad (3\text{-}36a)$$

and imaginary part

$$\psi_0 \nabla^2 S + 2\nabla S \cdot \nabla \psi_0 = 0 \qquad (3\text{-}36b)$$

Equations (3-36a) and (3-36b) represent an exact solution to the original wave equation (3-30). To obtain the simplifying geometric optics approximation to Eq. (3-36a) we will rewrite it in convenient form and show that one of the terms may be neglected as λ_0 becomes very small.

Rearranging Eq. (3-36a)

$$(\nabla S)^2 - \frac{\nabla^2 \psi_0}{k_0^2 \psi_0} = n^2 \qquad (3\text{-}37)$$

notice that $k_0 = 2\pi/\lambda_0$ and

$$\frac{\nabla^2 \psi_0}{k_0^2 \psi_0} = \frac{\lambda_0^2(\nabla^2 \psi_0)}{(2\pi)^2 \psi_0} \qquad (3\text{-}38)$$

As λ_0 becomes very small, that is, as λ_0 approaches zero, Eq. (3-38) approaches zero and Eq. (3-37) becomes

$$(\nabla S)^2 = n^2 \qquad (3\text{-}39)$$

Equation (3-39) is known as the "eikonal" equation. It determines the function S, which allows us to define the surfaces of constant phase by the equation

$$S(x, y, z) = \text{const} \qquad (3\text{-}40)$$

These surfaces of constant phase define the shape of the fields. The eikonal equation determines, within the geometrical optics approximation, the wave propagation in a guide.

We know from Chap. 2 that the surfaces of constant phase are perpendicular to the direction of light propagation of a plane wave. We will now define light rays as the locus of points that form the orthogonal trajectories to the constant phase fronts of a light wave. If we know the surfaces of constant phase, we can construct the light rays by drawing lines perpendicular to the phase fronts. As the phase fronts curve in an inhomogeneous medium, so do the light rays.

It is often desirable to calculate the trajectories of the light rays directly without having to construct the phase fronts from the eikonal equation. In order to develop the equations for the trajectories of light rays consider the

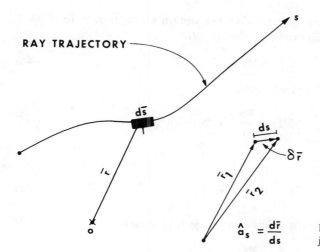

RAY TRAJECTORY

$$\hat{a}_s = \frac{d\bar{r}}{ds}$$

Figure 3-3 Geometry for ray trajectory equations.

geometry of a ray path shown in Fig. 3-3. A radius vector $\bar{r}$ is drawn from a fixed origin O to an arbitrary point on a ray path. If this vector $\bar{r}$ were known for all points along the ray, we would have a mathematical description of the light ray. Our strategy will be to develop an equation in terms of the radius vector $\bar{r}$, the distance measured along the ray s, and the refractive index of the medium n.

From the eikonal equation we have information about a vector ∇S that is perpendicular to the phase fronts in the direction of a ray. That is

$$\nabla S = n\hat{a}_s \tag{3-41}$$

where $\hat{a}_s$ is a unit vector tangent to the light ray. From Fig. 3-3 it is evident that

$$\hat{a}_s = \frac{d\bar{r}}{ds} \tag{3-42}$$

therefore

$$\nabla S = n\frac{d\bar{r}}{ds} \tag{3-43}$$

We wish now to incorporate the information in Eq. (3-43) into the eikonal equation so that we can eliminate S and obtain an equation in terms of $\bar{r}$, s, and n. To accomplish this first observe that

$$\frac{d}{ds} = \frac{d\bar{r}}{ds} \cdot \nabla = \frac{d}{ds}(x\hat{a}_x + y\hat{a}_y + z\hat{a}_z) \cdot \left(\frac{\partial}{\partial x}\hat{a}_x + \frac{\partial}{\partial y}\hat{a}_y + \frac{\partial}{\partial z}\hat{a}_z\right) \tag{3-44}$$

Using (3-44)

$$\frac{d}{ds}(\nabla S) = \hat{a}_s \cdot \nabla(\nabla S) = \hat{a}_s \cdot (\nabla\nabla S) \tag{3-45}$$

where $\nabla\nabla$ is the dyadic tensor operator. We can obtain an expression for $\nabla\nabla S$ if we take the gradient of the eikonal equation (3-39)

$$\nabla S \cdot \nabla\nabla S = n\nabla n \tag{3-46}$$

Now from Eqs. (3-41) and (3-46) we obtain

$$\hat{a}_s \cdot (\nabla\nabla S) = \frac{\nabla S}{n} \cdot \nabla\nabla S = \nabla n \tag{3-47}$$

Using Eq. (3-45) yields

$$\frac{d}{ds}(\nabla S) = \nabla n \tag{3-48}$$

or using Eq. (3-43) we obtain the desired ray trajectory equation

$$\frac{d}{ds}\left(n\frac{d\bar{r}}{ds}\right) = \nabla n \tag{3-49}$$

All of ray optics can be derived from the ray equation (3-49). The ray equation describes the trajectory of a light beam by the position vector $\bar{r} = \bar{r}(s)$, which is a function of the length of the ray measured from some arbitrary starting point. The ray equation contains the refractive index, $n(x, y, z)$, as well as the gradient of the refractive index $\nabla n(x, y, z)$. As shown in Example 3-2 when the medium is homogeneous the rays will be straight lines. When the medium is inhomogeneous ($\nabla n \neq 0$) the ray trajectories will be curved paths.

The ray equation is expressed in vector form in Eq. (3-49) and is independent of the choice of the coordinate system it is expressed in. In cartesian coordinates, the component equations of the ray equation are

$$\frac{d}{ds}\left(n\frac{dx}{ds}\right) = \frac{\partial n}{\partial x} \tag{3-50}$$

$$\frac{d}{ds}\left(n\frac{dy}{ds}\right) = \frac{\partial n}{\partial y} \tag{3-51}$$

$$\frac{d}{ds}\left(n\frac{dz}{ds}\right) = \frac{\partial n}{\partial z} \tag{3-52}$$

One of the most important theorems of ray optics (Snell's law) can be derived from Eq. (3-52). If we consider three dielectric media as shown in Fig. 3-4 and assume that the refractive indices of these media are a function of x only, then Eq. (3-52) becomes

$$\frac{d}{ds}\left(n\frac{dz}{ds}\right) = 0 \tag{3-53}$$

since $\partial n/\partial z = 0$.

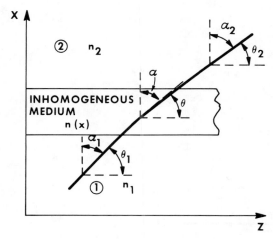

Figure 3-4 Geometry for light-ray development of Snell's law.

Integrating Eq. (3-53) we obtain

$$n \frac{dz}{ds} = \text{const} \tag{3-54}$$

From the geometry shown in Fig. 3-4, dz/ds can be written as follows:

$$\frac{dz}{ds} = \sin \alpha = \cos \theta \tag{3-55}$$

Using Eq. (3-55), Eq. (3-54) becomes

$$n \frac{dz}{ds} = n \cos \theta = n \sin \alpha = \text{const} \tag{3-56}$$

Equation (3-56) is Snell's law derived from a ray optics point of view. Snell's law illustrates the fact that $n \cos \theta$ is constant along a ray trajectory provided that the refractive index of the media does not depend upon z. The form of Snell's law that was derived in Chap. 2 (Eq. (2-116)) can be obtained from Eq. (3-56) if we consider media 1 and 2 in Fig. 3-4. Equation (3-56) applied in the regions of constant refractive index n_1 and n_2 becomes

$$n_1 \cos \theta_1 = n_2 \cos \theta_2 \tag{3-57}$$

or, by using the complement of the angles,

$$n_1 \sin \alpha_1 = n_2 \sin \alpha_2 \tag{3-58}$$

Equations (3-57) and (3-58) hold regardless of the shape of the index profile in the transition region and contain only n_1 and n_2, the refractive indices in the two homogeneous half-space regions.

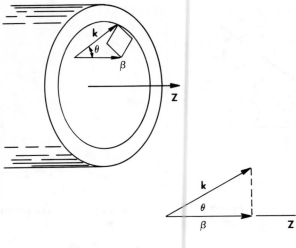

$$\cos \theta = \frac{\beta}{k}$$

Figure 3-5 Components of propagation vector; ray optics.

For a waveguide of the type shown in Fig. 3-1, Eq. (3-53) can be written in terms of β and k, that is,

$$n \frac{dz}{ds} = n \cos \theta = \text{const} = n \frac{\beta}{k} \qquad (3\text{-}59)$$

where k is the magnitude and β the z component of the propagation vector of the plane wave defining the ray. As shown in Fig. 3-5, θ is now the ray angle relative to the z axis. This physical interpretation of Snell's law will be useful to us when we analyze the round optical fiber in Chaps. 5 and 6.

Example 3-2 Ray propagation in homogeneous media Using the ray equation (3-49) it is easy to show that in homogeneous media light rays are straight lines.

For a homogeneous medium, the refractive index is a constant and $\nabla n = 0$. Therefore the solution of the ray equation (3-49) is immediately obtained as

$$\frac{d\bar{r}}{ds} = \bar{a} = \text{const}$$

Integrating we obtain

$$\bar{r} = \bar{a}s + \bar{b}$$

The above equation for $\bar{r}$ is the equation of a straight line.

3.5 RAY EQUATION IN CYLINDRICAL COORDINATES

For applications involving optical fibers, we need to know the ray equation in cylindrical coordinates. We will assume once again that the refractive index is independent of z (longitudinal coordinate) but can be a function of the transverse coordinates r and ϕ. That is, $n = n(r, \phi)$. The transformation from cartesian to cylindrical coordinates of Eqs. (3-50) and (3-51) require the following sets of equations:

$$x = r \cos \phi \tag{3-60a}$$

$$y = r \sin \phi \tag{3-60b}$$

$$r = (x^2 + y^2)^{1/2} \tag{3-61a}$$

$$\phi = \arctan (y/x) \tag{3-61b}$$

The partial derivatives of n with respect to x and y may be expressed as

$$\frac{\partial n}{\partial x} = \frac{\partial n}{\partial r}\frac{\partial r}{\partial x} + \frac{\partial n}{\partial \phi}\frac{\partial \phi}{\partial x} = \frac{\partial n}{\partial r} \cos \phi - \frac{\partial n}{\partial \phi}\frac{\sin \phi}{r} \tag{3-62}$$

$$\frac{\partial n}{\partial y} = \frac{\partial n}{\partial r}\frac{\partial r}{\partial y} + \frac{\partial n}{\partial \phi}\frac{\partial \phi}{\partial y} = \frac{\partial n}{\partial r} \sin \phi + \frac{\partial n}{\partial \phi}\frac{\cos \phi}{r} \tag{3-63}$$

and the derivatives of x and y with respect to s become

$$\frac{dx}{ds} = \frac{\partial r}{\partial s} \cos \phi - r \frac{\partial \phi}{\partial s} \sin \phi \tag{3-64}$$

$$\frac{dy}{ds} = \frac{\partial r}{\partial s} \sin \phi + r \frac{\partial \phi}{\partial s} \cos \phi \tag{3-65}$$

Using Eqs. (3-61) to (3-65) the ray equation can be derived in cylindrical coordinates.[4] Example 3-3 illustrates the derivation of the r component of the ray equation. Listed below are the components r, ϕ, and z in cylindrical coordinates of the ray equation.

$$\frac{d}{ds}\left(n\frac{dr}{ds}\right) - nr\left(\frac{d\phi}{ds}\right)^2 = \frac{\partial n}{\partial r} \qquad (r \text{ component}) \tag{3-66}$$

$$\frac{d}{ds}\left(nr^2\frac{d\phi}{ds}\right) = \frac{\partial n}{\partial \phi} \qquad (\phi \text{ component}) \tag{3-67}$$

$$\frac{d}{ds}\left(n\frac{dz}{ds}\right) = \frac{\partial n}{\partial z} \qquad (z \text{ component}) \tag{3-68}$$

Equations (3-66) to (3-68) are valid even if $n(r, \phi, z)$. If n is independent of z, Eq. (3-68) becomes Eq. (3-59). If, as is often the case for optical fibers, n is independent of ϕ, then Eq. (3-67) becomes

$$nr^2 \frac{d\phi}{ds} = \text{const} \tag{3-69}$$

In addition, it is often convenient to approximate the ray equation by replacing ds with dz. This approximation is valid if the angle of the ray relative to the z axis remains small. This approximate form of the ray equation is called the paraxial ray equation since all the rays are nearly parallel to the z axis. The paraxial approximation also requires that $n(x, y)$ or $n(r, \phi)$ varies only a small amount. This allows us to replace $n(x, y)$ with an average value $n(x, y) = n_a$. We will, however, retain the derivative term of n, since these terms will provide the information about the refracting properties of rays in a medium with a graded index.

The paraxial form of the ray equation (3-49) is

$$\frac{d^2 \bar{r}}{dz^2} = \frac{1}{n_a} \nabla n \tag{3-70}$$

and finally the paraxial ray equations in cylindrical coordinates are

$$\frac{d^2 r}{dz^2} - r \left(\frac{d\phi}{dz} \right)^2 = \frac{1}{n_a} \frac{\partial n}{\partial r} \tag{3-71}$$

$$\frac{d}{dz} \left(r^2 \frac{d\phi}{dz} \right) = \frac{1}{n_a} \frac{\partial n}{\partial \phi} \tag{3-72}$$

Equations (3-71) and (3-72) will be used in Chap. 6 to analyze the ray trajectories of a graded-index fiber with a parabolic-shaped refractive index profile.

Example 3-3 Derivation of the radial component of the ray equation To derive the radial component of the ray equation, we will start with Eqs. (3-50) and (3-51). If we multiply Eq. (3-50) by x and Eq. (3-51) by y and add the resulting equations we obtain

$$x \frac{d}{ds} \left(n \frac{dx}{ds} \right) + y \frac{d}{ds} \left(n \frac{dy}{ds} \right) = x \frac{\partial n}{\partial x} + y \frac{\partial n}{\partial y}$$

If we then use Eqs. (3-62) and (3-63) along with Eqs. (3-60a,b) in the above equation we obtain

$$\cos \phi \, \frac{d}{ds} \left(n \frac{dx}{ds} \right) + \sin \phi \, \frac{d}{ds} \left(n \frac{dy}{ds} \right) = \frac{\partial n}{\partial r}$$

Substituting Eqs. (3-64) and (3-65) into the above equation, rearranging terms, and differentiating the resulting equation, yields the desired radial component of the ray equation

$$\frac{d}{ds}\left(n\frac{dr}{ds}\right) - nr\left(\frac{d\phi}{ds}\right)^2 = \frac{\partial n}{\partial r}$$

REFERENCES

1. D. Marcuse: *Light Transmission Optics*, Van Nostrand Reinhold Co., New York, 1972.
2. J. A. Arnaud: *Beam and Fiber Optics*, Academic Press, New York, 1976.
3. M. Born, and E. Wolf: *Principles of Optics*, Pergamon Press, London, 1970.
4. D. Marcuse: *Principles of Optical Fiber Measurement*, Academic Press, New York, 1981.

PROBLEMS

3-1 Starting with Eq. (3-7c), derive the modified wave equation in terms of H_z (Eq. (3-14)).

3-2 For a dielectric waveguide, define the transverse field components of a TE mode in terms of H_z (longitudinal field component). Which of these field components exist if the field is uniform in the y direction (i.e., $\partial/\partial y = 0$)?

3-3 Starting with Eq. (3-15), derive the modified wave equation for E_z in cylindrical coordinates (Eq. (3-27)).

$$\left(\text{In cylindrical coordinates } \nabla_T^2 = \frac{1}{r}\frac{\partial}{\partial r} + r\frac{\partial}{\partial r} + \frac{1}{r^2}\frac{\partial^2}{\partial\theta^2}\right)$$

FOUR

THE DIELECTRIC SLAB WAVEGUIDE

4-1 INTRODUCTION

The analysis of the dielectric slab waveguide results in solutions that are mathematically simple and physically easy to understand. As such the slab waveguide provides a good pedagogical example for illustrating how the analytical techniques developed in Chaps. 2 and 3 are used to analyze a dielectric waveguide. Once the reader is familiar with the general approach of solving a dielectric waveguide problem he will be better prepared to analyze the mathematically complicated round optical fiber in Chaps. 5 and 6.

In this chapter the slab waveguide will be treated as a boundary value problem.[1-4] The wave equation will be solved subject to boundary conditions to obtain expressions for the fields of the propagating modes. The propagating modes will be divided into even and odd TE and TM modes. The characteristic or eigenvalue equations obtained for the guide will yield expressions for the propagation constants associated with the modes. A mode will then be decomposed into two plane waves and the cutoff condition for the mode shown to be equivalent to a plane wave striking the core-cladding interface at the critical angle. Finally, to complete our study of the dielectric slab guide, the concept of multimode group delay will be developed along with an alternate ray optics analysis of the guide.[5]

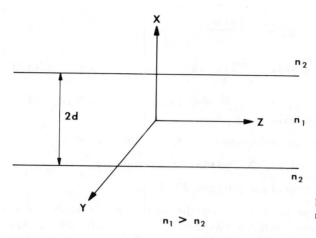

Figure 4-1 Geometry of symmetric dielectric slab waveguide.

4-2 PROPAGATING MODES OF THE SYMMETRIC SLAB WAVEGUIDE

In Chap. 3 we developed a set of equations relating the transverse components to the longitudinal components of the fields in a guide with cylindrical symmetry, that is, a guide with identical transverse cross sections and fields propagating in the z direction. Now, using the set of equations previously developed, we would like to analyze the dielectric slab waveguide shown in Fig. 4-1 and obtain expressions for the guided modes.

The waves in the slab waveguide will be traveling in the z direction. The guide is infinitely extended in the y direction. There is no variation in the waveguide geometry in the z direction and by symmetry no variation in the field distributions in the y direction. Mathematically the limitation imposed by guide symmetry can be expressed as

$$\frac{\partial}{\partial y} = 0 \tag{4-1}$$

A functional expression for the electric field in the guide can be symbolically written as

$$\bar{E} = \bar{E}_0(x)e^{-j\beta z}e^{j\omega t} \tag{4-2}$$

The symmetry restriction $\partial/\partial y = 0$ allows us to decompose the fields of the guide into TE and TM modes. To appreciate this fact we will rewrite Eqs. (3-9) through (3-12) with $\partial/\partial y = 0$.

$$E_x = \frac{-j\beta}{\kappa^2}\left(\frac{\partial E_z}{\partial x}\right) \tag{4-3}$$

$$E_y = \frac{j\omega\mu}{\kappa^2}\left(\frac{\partial H_z}{\partial x}\right) \tag{4-4}$$

$$H_x = \frac{-j\beta}{\kappa^2}\left(\frac{\partial H_z}{\partial x}\right) \tag{4-5}$$

$$H_y = \frac{-j\omega\varepsilon}{\kappa^2}\left(\frac{\partial E_z}{\partial x}\right) \tag{4-6}$$

If we first consider the TE modes, $E_z = 0$, $H_z \neq 0$. From Eqs. (4-3) through (4-5) the following field components exist.

TE mode field components: E_y, H_x, and H_z

For the TM modes, $H_z = 0$ and $E_z \neq 0$. The filed components are

TM mode field components: E_x, E_z, H_y

The strategy we will follow in analyzing the dielectric slab waveguide is first to consider the TE modes and then the TM modes.[1-3] For each case we will investigate subcases of even and odd modes separately. This approach is taken to simplify our physical understanding of the mode structures and characteristic equations. In our analysis we will start with the Helmholtz equation derived in Chap. 2.

$$\nabla^2 \bar{E} + k^2 \bar{E} = 0 \tag{4-7}$$

with

$$k^2 = \omega^2 \mu_0 \varepsilon \tag{4-8}$$

For the TE mode case E_y is the only component of the electric field. Rewriting (4-7) using (4-1) yields

$$\frac{\partial^2 E_y}{\partial x^2} + \frac{\partial^2 E_y}{\partial z^2} + k^2 E_y = 0 \tag{4-9}$$

From Eq. (4-2) the functional form of E_y is

$$E_y(x, z) = E_y(x)e^{-j\beta z} \tag{4-10}$$

Substituting Eq. (4-10) into (4-9) yields

$$\frac{d^2 E_y}{dx^2} + \kappa^2 E_y = 0 \tag{4-11}$$

where

$$\kappa^2 = k^2 - \beta^2 \tag{4-12}$$

The solutions for Eq. (4-11) will be different inside the slab and in the surrounding medium (cladding). Once we have solved for E_y we can obtain H_x and H_z from Maxwell's equations. From Eqs. (3-7a) and (3-7c),

$$H_x = \frac{-\beta}{\omega\mu_0} E_y \tag{4-13}$$

$$H_z = \frac{j}{\omega\mu_0} \frac{\partial E_y}{\partial x} \tag{4-14}$$

The general solution of Eq. (4-11) for E_y inside the slab can be written as

$$E_{y1} = A \cos \kappa x + B \sin \kappa x \qquad (4\text{-}15)$$

for

$$|x| \leq d$$

where

$$\kappa^2 = n_1^2 k_0^2 - \beta^2 \qquad (4\text{-}16)$$

Equation (4-15) can be decomposed into even and odd modes where

$$A \cos \kappa x \text{ represents the } even \text{ TE modes}$$

and

$$B \sin \kappa x \text{ represents the } odd \text{ TE modes}$$

Because the field in the cladding will be an evanescent field that approaches zero as x approaches infinity, the solution of Eq. (4-11) in the cladding is of the form

$$E_{y2} = Ce^{-\gamma(|x|-d)} \qquad (4\text{-}17)$$

for

$$|x| \geq d$$

where γ is the decay constant of the evanescent field.

If we chose to solve this problem directly using the fields described by Eqs. (4-15) and (4-17), we would apply the boundary conditions associated with the tangential components of the E and H fields at $x = \pm d$. This procedure would yield a characteristic or eigenvalue equation for the guide that would allow us to determine the values of κ and γ for the propagating TE modes. This general procedure was followed by Marcuse,[1] and the resulting characteristic equation obtained was (see Prob. 4-3)

$$\tan(2dk) = \frac{2\gamma\kappa}{\kappa^2 - \gamma^2} \qquad (4\text{-}18)$$

We will refer to this result in Sec. 4-8 when we analyze the guide from a ray optics point of view.

In order to obtain a simple physical model and characteristic equations for the slab guide, it is instructive to separate the even and odd mode solutions in the core and obtain characteristic equations for each case. Superposition can then be used to obtain expressions for the total fields.

4-3 EVEN TE MODES IN A DIELECTRIC SLAB WAVEGUIDE

Inside the slab waveguide for $|x| \leq d$ the even TE mode solution for the electric field is of the form

$$E_{y_1} = A_e \cos \kappa x \qquad (4\text{-}19)$$

Using Eqs. (4-13) and (4-14) the magnetic field components are of the form

$$H_{x_1} = \frac{-\beta}{\omega\mu_0} A_e \cos \kappa x \tag{4-20}$$

and

$$H_{z_1} = \frac{-j\kappa_1}{\omega\mu_0} A_e \sin \kappa x \tag{4-21}$$

In the cladding of the guide we require an evanescent field that approaches zero as $|x|$ approaches infinity. Therefore

$$E_{y_2} = B_e e^{-\gamma(|x|-d)} \qquad |x| \geq d \tag{4-22}$$

substituting Eq. (4-22) into (4-9) and remembering that the z variation of the field is $e^{-j\beta z}$ we obtain

$$\gamma^2 = \beta^2 - n_2^2 k_0^2 \tag{4-23}$$

The magnetic fields in the cladding are

$$H_{x2} = \frac{-\beta}{\omega\mu_0} B_e e^{-\gamma(|x|-d)} \tag{4-24}$$

and

$$H_{z2} = \frac{j\gamma}{\omega\mu_0} \left(\frac{-x}{|x|}\right) B_e e^{-\gamma(|x|-d)} \tag{4-25}$$

Our task now is to obtain the characteristic equation for the even TE mode case by applying boundary conditions at the core-cladding interface. The boundary conditions for the tangential components of the fields require that E_y and H_z are continuous at $|x| = d$. For example at $x = d$

$$E_{y1} = E_{y2} \tag{4-26}$$

$$A_e \cos \kappa d = B_e \tag{4-27}$$

Using Eq. (4-27) in (4-25) and applying the boundary condition for the magnetic fields at $x = d$

$$H_{z1} = H_{z2} \tag{4-28}$$

$$\frac{-j\kappa}{\omega\mu_0} A_e \sin \kappa d = A_e \cos \kappa d \left(\frac{-d}{|d|}\right)\left(\frac{j\gamma}{\omega\mu_0}\right) \tag{4-29}$$

Simplifying Eq. (4-29) results in the characteristic equation for the even TE modes of the guide

$$\frac{\sin \kappa d}{\cos \kappa d} = \tan \kappa d = \frac{\gamma}{\kappa} \tag{4-30}$$

Before we discuss the characteristic equation (4-30) in detail, let us derive a similar equation for the odd TE modes. We will then discuss the solutions of the two characteristic equations together in Sec. 4-5.

4-4 ODD TE MODES IN A DIELECTRIC SLAB WAVEGUIDE

For the odd TE modes the fields in the core of the guide can be written, for $|x| \leq d$, as

$$E_{y1} = A_0 \sin \kappa x \tag{4-31}$$

$$H_{x1} = \frac{-\beta}{\omega\mu_0} E_{y1} = \frac{-\beta A_0}{\omega\mu_0} \sin \kappa x \tag{4-32}$$

$$H_{z1} = \frac{j}{\omega\mu_0} \frac{\partial E_{y1}}{\partial x} = \frac{j\kappa}{\omega\mu_0} A_0 \cos \kappa x \tag{4-33}$$

In the cladding of the guide for $|x| \geq d$ the fields are

$$E_{y2} = B_0 e^{-\gamma(|x|-d)} \tag{4-34}$$

$$H_{x2} = \frac{-\beta}{\omega\mu_0} B_0 e^{-\gamma(|x|-d)} \tag{4-35}$$

and

$$H_{z2} = \frac{j\gamma}{\omega\mu_0} \left(\frac{-x}{|x|}\right) B_0 e^{-\gamma(|x|-d)} \tag{4-36}$$

Following the same procedure as before, we will apply the boundary condition for the tangential components of the fields at $x = \pm d$.

Applying the boundary conditions at $x = +d$

$$E_{y1} = E_{y2}$$

$$A_0 \sin \kappa d = B_0 \tag{4-37}$$

at $x = -d$

$$-A_0 \sin \kappa d = B_0 \tag{4-38}$$

Combining Eqs. (4-37) and (4-38) we can obtain a general equation for B_0

$$B_0 = \frac{x}{|x|} A_0 \sin \kappa d \tag{4-39}$$

for $x = \pm d$

Substituting (4-39) into (4-36) and applying the boundary conditions for $H_{z1} = H_{z2}$ at $x = d$ we obtain

$$\frac{j\kappa_1}{\omega\mu_0} A_0 \cos \kappa d = \frac{-j\gamma}{\omega\mu_0} A_0 \sin \kappa d \tag{4.40}$$

Simplifying Eq. (4-40) yields the characteristic equation for the odd TE modes of the dielectric slab waveguide

$$\frac{\sin \kappa d}{\cos \kappa d} = \tan \kappa d = \frac{-\kappa}{\gamma} \qquad (4\text{-}41)$$

The analysis of Eqs. (4-30) and (4-41) will give us the information we need to obtain the propagation constants for the TE modes in the waveguide.

4-5 CHARACTERISTIC EQUATIONS; TE MODES

In this section we will analyze the characteristic equations of the guided TE modes of a dielectric slab waveguide. We will obtain values for the propagation constants for each of the modes in terms of the physical parameters of the guide n_1, n_2, d, and the source-propagating wavelength λ_0. For ease of reference in our analysis let us rewrite Eqs. (4-16), (4-23), (4-30), and (4-41).

$$\kappa^2 = n_1^2 k_0^2 - \beta^2 \qquad (4\text{-}42)$$

$$\gamma^2 = \beta^2 - n_2^2 k_0^2 \qquad (4\text{-}43)$$

$$\tan \kappa d = \frac{\gamma}{\kappa} \qquad (4\text{-}44)$$

(characteristic equation TE even modes)

$$\tan \kappa d = \frac{-\kappa}{\gamma} \qquad (4\text{-}45)$$

(characteristic equation TE odd modes).

We will rearrange Eqs. (4-42) to (4-45) with the goal of finding a solution for them in simply graphical form. Let us start this process by adding Eqs. (4-42) and (4-43) and multiplying the sum by d^2. The resulting equation is

$$\gamma^2 d^2 + \kappa^2 d^2 = (n_1^2 - n_2^2)k_0^2 d^2 \qquad (4\text{-}46)$$

If we let

$$X = \kappa d$$

$$Y = \gamma d$$

$$R = \sqrt{n_1^2 - n_2^2}\, k_0\, d$$

Eq. (4-46) can be plotted graphically in the form of a circle whose equation is given by

$$X^2 + Y^2 = R^2 \qquad (4\text{-}47)$$

Let us now rewrite the characteristic equations for the even and odd TE modes for similar presentation in graphical form. For the even TE modes if we multiply Eq. (4-44) by d and rearrange we obtain

$$\gamma d = \kappa d \tan (\kappa d) \qquad (4.48)$$

For the odd TE modes, multiplying Eq. (4-45) by d and rearranging yields

$$\gamma d = -\kappa d \cot (\kappa d) \qquad (4.49)$$

Rewriting in terms of X and Y, Eqs. (4-48) and (4-49) become

$$Y = X \tan X \qquad (4-50)$$

and

$$Y = -X \cot X \qquad (4-51)$$

Equations (4-47), (4-50), and (4-51) can now be plotted on an X-Y diagram to obtain the propagation constants of the guided TE modes of the waveguide. Figure 4-2 is a plot of these equations. The intersections of the circle, Eq. (4-47), with Eqs. (4-50) and (4-51), define the propagation conditions for the modes in the guide. For example for the first even mode, the TE_0 mode, the values of κ_{10} and γ_0 can be obtained, for a given slab half-width d, directly from the coordinates of the first intersection in Fig. 4-2. β_0 can then be calculated from Eq. (4-42). The propagation constants for the other TE_M modes can be obtained successively in the same manner.

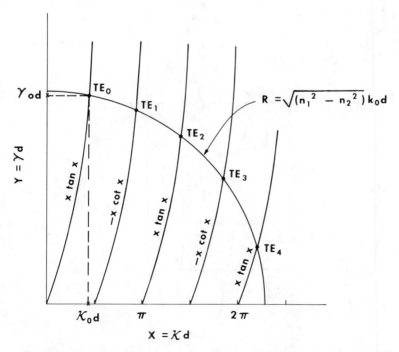

Figure 4-2 Characteristic equation diagram TE modes of dielectric slab waveguide.

Table 4-1

Increasing physical parameter	Number of propagating modes
Core refractive index, n_1	Increases
Cladding refractive index, n_2	Decreases
Slab half-width, d	Increases
Source wavelength, $\lambda_0 = 2\pi/k_0$	Decreases

Notice that the number of propagating modes in the guide is proportional to R. For

$$R = \sqrt{n_1^2 - n_2^2}\, k_0 d < \frac{\pi}{2} \tag{4-52}$$

The only propagating mode is the TE_0 mode since the circle in Fig. 4-2 will intersect only the first branch of the $X \tan X$ curve. One can obtain an understanding of how the physical parameters n_1, n_2, d, and λ_0 effect the number of propagating modes in a guide simply by observing their effect on R. Table 4-1

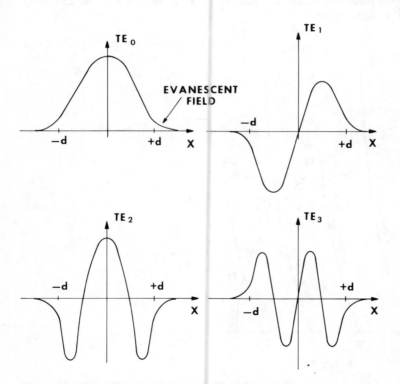

Figure 4-3 TE modes in a dielectric slab waveguide as a function of x.

shows how increasing the parameters influences the number of propagating modes.

The guide will have many propagating modes when

$$R = \sqrt{n_1^2 - n_2^2}\left(\frac{2\pi}{\lambda_0}\right)d \gg 2\pi \tag{4-53}$$

To design a highly multimoded guide the slab half-width d should be chosen such that

$$d \gg \frac{\lambda_0}{\sqrt{n_1^2 - n_2^2}} = \frac{\lambda_0}{\text{NA}} \tag{4-54}$$

where NA is the numerical aperture of the guide.

$$NA = \sqrt{n_1^2 - n_2^2} \tag{4-55}$$

Figure 4-3 illustrates in graphical form the fields corresponding to the first few TE_M modes. Notice the different structure of the fields in the core for the even and odd modes and the presence of the evanescent field in the cladding.

4-6 MODE CUTOFF CONDITIONS (PLANE WAVE REPRESENTATION)

In the last section we developed the relationships for determining the number of propagating modes in a slab waveguide. We will now determine the cutoff condition for a given propagating mode. A propagating mode is considered cut off when its field in the cladding ceases to be evanescent and is detached from the guide. When this condition occurs the mode is no longer guided by the structure and becomes a radiation mode. To determine the cutoff condition recall that the field in the cladding is of the form $e^{-\gamma(|x|-d)}$, when

$$\gamma = \gamma_c = 0 \tag{4-56}$$

The field is detached from the guide and the mode is cut off. At cutoff κ_c and β_c of the mode can be obtained from Eqs. (4-46) and (4-43). That is for $\gamma_c = 0$

$$\kappa_c^2 d^2 = (n_1^2 - n_2^2)k_0^2 d^2$$

and solving for κ_c

$$\kappa_c = \sqrt{n_1^2 - n_2^2}\, k_0 \tag{4-57}$$

and, from Eq. (4-43),

$$\beta_c = n_2 k_0 \tag{4-58}$$

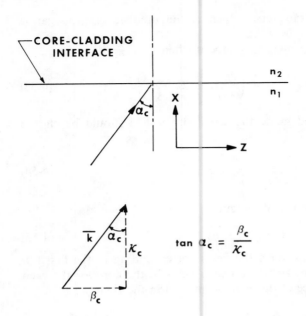

Figure 4-4 Components of propagation vector at mode cutoff condition.

κ and β are respectively the transverse and longitudinal components of the propagation vector $\bar{k}$. Figure 4-4 shows the propagation vector and the angle it makes with the core-cladding interface at cutoff. Using Eqs. (4-57) and (4-58)

$$\tan \alpha_c = \frac{\beta_c}{\kappa_c} = \frac{n_2}{\sqrt{n_1^2 - n_2^2}} \tag{4-59}$$

It is instructive to relate α_c to a plane wave incident upon the core-cladding interface at the critical angle. To illustrate the relationship between a mode and propagating plane waves let us rewrite the expression for the electric field of an even TE mode in the core of the slab guide.

$$E_y = A \cos \kappa x e^{-j\beta z} \tag{4-60}$$

Notice that

$$\cos \kappa x = \frac{e^{j\kappa x} + e^{-j\kappa x}}{2} \tag{4-61}$$

and therefore

$$E_y = \frac{A}{2}(e^{j(\kappa x - \beta z)} + e^{-j(\kappa x + \beta z)}) \tag{4-62}$$

Physically $e^{j(\kappa x - \beta z)}$ and $e^{-j(\kappa x + \beta z)}$ represent two plane waves propagating respectively in the $-x$, $+z$ direction and $+x$, $+z$ direction. The direction of propagation of the two plane waves in the slab is given by

$$\tan \alpha = \pm \frac{\beta}{\kappa} \tag{4-63}$$

where the angle α is formed by the direction of propagation of the plane wave and the normal to the interface between the slab core and cladding. Our study of total internal reflection in Chap. 2 suggests that the plane waves cannot leave the core of the guide if their angle of incidence with respect to the interface is larger than the critical angle. Recall that the critical angle relationships are given by

$$\sin \alpha_c = \frac{n_2}{n_1} \tag{4-64}$$

and

$$\cos \alpha_c = (1 - \sin^2 \alpha_c)^{1/2} = \frac{\sqrt{n_1^2 - n_2^2}}{n_1} \tag{4-65}$$

Dividing Eq. (4-64) by (4-65) yields

$$\tan \alpha_c = \frac{n_2}{\sqrt{n_1^2 - n_2^2}} \tag{4-66}$$

Since Eqs. (4-66) and (4-59) are identical we have proved that the cutoff condition for a mode can be identified with a plane wave traveling inside the dielectric slab at the limiting critical angle α_c for total internal reflection.

A physical explanation for the existence of a guided mode can now be given as follows. Inside the dielectric slab, two plane waves travel at an angle to the interface formed by the core and cladding. The plane waves are totally internally reflected at the boundary and bounce back and forth between the two dielectric interfaces of the guide. The evanescent field that exists outside the core of the slab is associated with a wave in the core that is totally reflected at the dielectric interface. The angle at which the plane waves propagate inside the slab is obtained by solving the characteristic equation for the guide and is calculated from the components of the propagation vector β and κ.

Example 4-1 Symmetric slab waveguide In this example we will illustrate how to calculate the numerical aperture (NA), R number, and the cutoff angle α_c for the TE modes of a symmetric dielectric slab waveguide. For the guide shown in Fig. 4-1 the following parameters are chosen:

$$d = 1 \ \mu\text{m}, \quad n_1 = 2.234, \quad n_2 = 2.214, \quad \text{and} \quad \lambda_0 = 0.6328 \ \mu\text{m}$$

$$NA = \sqrt{n_1^2 - n_2^2}$$

$$= \sqrt{(2.234)^2 - (2.214)^2}$$

$$= 0.298$$

$$R = \sqrt{n_1^2 - n_2^2} \, k_0 \, d$$

$$= 2.96$$

$$\tan \alpha_c = \frac{n_2}{\sqrt{n_1^2 - n_2^2}}$$

$$= 7.42$$

$$\alpha_c = 82.33°$$

At cutoff the propagation vector makes an angle of 82.33° with the normal to the core-cladding interface.

4-7 TM MODES IN A DIELECTRIC SLAB WAVEGUIDE

To complete our modal analysis of the slab waveguide from a field theory point of view, we will now outline the procedures to be followed for obtaining expressions for the fields and characteristic equations for the TM modes. Recall from Sec. 4-2 for the TM modes that the following fields exist within the guide: H_y, E_x, and E_z. Since H_y is the only component of the magnetic field it can be written in the form

$$H_y = H_y(x)e^{-j\beta z} \tag{4-67}$$

Substituting into the Helmholtz equation for the magnetic field, derived in Chap. 2, the following equation in terms of H_y is obtained:

$$\frac{d^2 H_y}{dx^2} + (n^2 k_0^2 - \beta^2)H_y = 0 \tag{4-68}$$

Solving for H_y in the core and cladding of the guide, for the even and odd TM modes, will yield expressions of the same form as previously obtained for E_y for the TE mode case. In terms of H_y, E_x and E_z can be expressed using Eqs. (3-6a) and (3-6c) as

$$E_x = \frac{\beta}{\omega \varepsilon} H_y \tag{4-69}$$

and

$$E_z = \frac{-j}{\omega \varepsilon} \frac{\partial H_y}{\partial x} \tag{4-70}$$

Since the remaining procedures for solving for the TM modes are identical to those followed for the TE modes, we will leave the details of the solution as an exercise for the reader and summarize the results below.

For the TM even modes In the core, $|x| \leq d$

$$H_y = B_e \cos \kappa x \tag{4-71}$$

$$E_x = \frac{\beta}{\omega \varepsilon_1} B_e \cos \kappa x \tag{4-72}$$

$$E_z = \frac{j\kappa_1}{\omega \varepsilon_1} B_e \sin \kappa x \tag{4-73}$$

$$\kappa^2 = n_1^2 k_0^2 - \beta^2 \tag{4-74}$$

In the cladding, $|x| \geq d$

$$H_y = B_e \cos \kappa d e^{-\gamma(|x|-d)} \tag{4-75}$$

$$E_x = \frac{\beta}{\omega \varepsilon_2} (B_e \cos \kappa d) e^{-\gamma(|x|-d)} \tag{4-76}$$

$$E_z = \frac{x}{|x|} \left(\frac{j\gamma}{\omega \varepsilon_2} \right) (B_e \cos \kappa d) e^{-\gamma(|x|-d)} \tag{4-77}$$

$$\gamma^2 = \beta^2 - n_2^2 k_0^2 \tag{4-78}$$

and the characteristic equation for the TM even modes is

$$\tan \kappa d = \frac{n_1^2}{n_2^2} \left(\frac{\gamma}{\kappa} \right) \tag{4-79}$$

For the TM odd modes In the core, $|x| \leq d$

$$H_y = B_0 \sin \kappa x \tag{4-80}$$

$$E_x = \frac{\beta}{\omega \varepsilon_1} B_0 \sin \kappa x \tag{4-81}$$

$$E_z = \frac{-j\kappa}{\omega \varepsilon_1} B_0 \cos \kappa x \tag{4-82}$$

In the cladding, $|x| \geq d$

$$H_y = \frac{x}{|x|} B_0 \sin \kappa d e^{-\gamma(|x|-d)} \tag{4-83}$$

$$E_x = \frac{x}{|x|} \left(\frac{\beta}{\omega \varepsilon_2} \right) (B_0 \sin \kappa d) e^{-\gamma(|x|-d)} \tag{4-84}$$

and

$$E_z = \frac{j\gamma}{\omega\varepsilon_2}(B_0 \sin \kappa d)e^{-\gamma(|x|-d)} \tag{4-85}$$

Finally the characteristic equation for the TM odd modes is

$$\tan \kappa d = \frac{-n_2^2}{n_1^2}\left(\frac{\kappa}{\gamma}\right) \tag{4-86}$$

The TE and TM modes form the set of guided modes in the waveguide. The complete set of modes in a dielectric slab waveguide includes a finite number of guided modes and an infinite number of radiation modes.

The interested reader should refer to Marcuse[2] for an excellent discussion of the radiation modes.

4-8 RAY OPTICS EXPLANATION OF MODES IN A DIELECTRIC SLAB WAVEGUIDE

To illustrate how ray optics can be used to analyze a waveguide let us now derive the general characteristic equation (4-18) for the TE modes from a ray optics point of view. Ray optics describes the propagation of light fields by defining rays as the lines that cross the surfaces of constant phase of the light field at right angles. Snell's law, the critical angle, and Fresnel's equations carry directly over from field theory and apply as laws in ray optics. Let us consider a dielectric slab guide with a plane wave propagating in it that traces out a ray trajectory as shown in Fig. 4-5a. All rays that travel in the same direction ψ are associated with the same plane wave. (Surfaces of constant phase of the reflected wave in Fig. 4-5a have been omitted for the sake of clarity.) Consider points A and B. The surfaces of constant phase that go through these two points (CF and BD) belong to the same plane wave. The ray going from A to B (ray AB) has not been reflected from the slab boundary. The longer ray going from C to D (ray CD) is associated with the reflected wave and experiences two total internal reflections at the boundaries as it travels from the surface of constant phase at A to the surface of constant phase at B. Since all points on a surface of constant phase of a plane wave must be in phase, we require that the phase change experienced by the ray AB differ from that of the ray CD by a multiple of 2π. This coherent reinforcement of the rays is the physical criterion that is equivalent to the existence of a mode in the guide. That is, we will prove that the rays traveling at an angle ψ that satisfy the phase requirement will yield the same characteristic equation as obtained from the modal solution. The angle can then be related to the direction of the propagation vector associated with the mode.

If a ray of physical length s traveled in a medium whose refractive index is

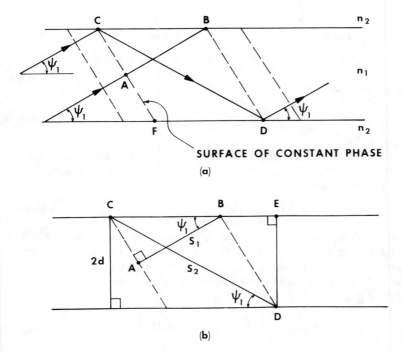

Figure 4-5 (*a*) Light rays in a dielectric slab waveguide. (*b*) Detailed geometry for ray paths.

n, its optical path length is defined as ns. Its phase change relative to a starting point $s = 0$ is defined as

$$\phi = -nsk_0 \tag{4-87}$$

If we look at the geometry shown in Fig. 4-5*b* we can obtain the distance $AB(s_1)$ and $CD(s_2)$ in terms of d and ψ_1. Notice that ray CD experiences two internal reflections that result in phase changes equal to $2\phi_R$. The coherent phase change relationship between AB and CD can be expressed as

$$n_1(s_2 - s_1)k_0 + 2\phi_R = 2N\pi \tag{4-88}$$

where N is an integer.

We can now develop the characteristic equation for the guide by solving for s_1, s_2, and ϕ_R in Eq. (4-88) in terms of d and ψ_1. From Fig. 4-5*b*, s_1 and s_2 can be written as

$$s_2 = \frac{2d}{\sin \psi_1} \tag{4-89}$$

$$s_1 = CB \cos \psi_1$$

where

$$CB = 2d\left(\frac{1}{\tan \psi_1} - \tan \psi_1\right)$$

Therefore

$$s_1 = 2d\left(\frac{\cos \psi_1}{\tan \psi_1} - \cos \psi_1 \tan \psi_1\right)$$

and simplifying s_1 becomes

$$s_1 = \frac{2d}{\sin \psi_1}(\cos^2 \psi_1 - \sin^2 \psi_1) \tag{4-90}$$

The expression for ϕ_R is obtained by realizing that for incident angles greater than the critical angle, the reflection coefficient associated with the reflected wave is complex, that is,

$$\Gamma = |\Gamma| \underline{/\phi_R} \tag{4-91}$$

ϕ_R will be dependent upon the polarization of the incident wave. For TE waves the electric vector E_y is parallel to the core-cladding boundary. In the language of Chap. 2, the incident plane wave is perpendicularly polarized. Using Eqs. (2-118) and (2-134) the phase of the reflected wave, in terms of the angle ψ shown in Fig. 4-5, is given by

$$\phi_R = -2 \tan^{-1}\left[\frac{\sqrt{\cos^2 \psi_1 - (n_2/n_1)^2}}{\sin \psi_1}\right] \tag{4-92}$$

Using the notation developed earlier in this chapter we can write γ and the components of the propagation vector β and κ in terms of ψ_1, that is,

$$\beta = n_1 k_0 \cos \psi_1 \tag{4-93}$$

$$\kappa = n_1 k_0 \sin \psi_1 \tag{4-94}$$

$$\gamma = \sqrt{\beta^2 - n_2^2 k_0^2} \tag{4-95}$$

Rewriting ϕ_R in terms of β, κ, and γ we obtain

$$\phi_R = -2 \tan^{-1}\left(\frac{\sqrt{\beta^2 - n_2^2 k_0^2}}{\kappa}\right) = -2 \tan^{-1}\left(\frac{\gamma}{\kappa}\right) \tag{4-96}$$

Developing the term $n_1(s_2 - s_1)$ in Eq. (4-88) we obtain from Eqs. (4-89) and (4-90)

$$n_1(s_2 - s_1)k_0 = \frac{n_1 2d}{\sin \psi}(1 - \cos^2 \psi_1 + \sin^2 \psi_1)k_0$$

which reduces to

$$n_1(s_2 - s_1)k_0 = 4n_1 d \sin \psi_1 k_0 \tag{4-97}$$

substituting Eq. (4-94) into (4-97) yields

$$n_1(s_2 - s_1)k_0 = 4d\kappa \tag{4-98}$$

If we now substitute Eqs. (4-96) and (4-98) into the coherent phase equation (4-88) we obtain

$$4d\kappa - 4\tan^{-1}\left(\frac{\gamma}{\kappa}\right) = 2N\pi \tag{4-99}$$

or

$$2\tan^{-1}\left(\frac{\gamma}{\kappa}\right) + N\pi = 2d\kappa \tag{4-100}$$

If we take the tangent of both sides of Eq. (4-100)

$$\tan\left\{\left[2\tan^{-1}\left(\frac{\gamma}{\kappa}\right)\right] + N\pi\right\} = \tan(2d\kappa) \tag{4-101}$$

and use the following trigonometric identities

$$\tan(a+b) = \frac{\tan a + \tan b}{1 - \tan a \tan b} \tag{4-102}$$

$$\tan 2a = \frac{2\tan a}{1 - \tan^2 a} \tag{4-103}$$

we obtain

$$\tan(2d\kappa) = \frac{2\gamma\kappa}{\kappa^2 - \gamma^2} \tag{4-104}$$

Equation (4-104) is identical to the characteristic equation for the TE modes obtained from analyzing the guide from a field theory point of view and using the modal approach (see Eq. (4-18)). We have therefore shown that the ray and modal analysis of the dielectric slab guide are equivalent.

We have illustrated, using the ray approach, that only rays satisfying the coherent phase relationship and propagating at discrete angles associated with the guided modes can exist in the guide.

4-9 MULTIMODE GROUP DELAY IN A DIELECTRIC SLAB WAVEGUIDE

A optical waveguide is used as a transmission medium for communicating information. Typically a pulse code modulated signal in the form of a stream of pulses will be sent at a defined bit rate between two points in a transmission system. It is important to understand how the shapes of the pulses being transmitted are changed as they propagate down the length of the guide. One form of distortion that can cause pulse broadening in a multimode dielectric waveguide is known as modal delay distortion. We will illustrate how a pulse is broadened in a dielectric slab waveguide by calculating the difference in transit times between information in the lowest- and highest-order modes as it propagates down the length of the guide, from the guide's input to its output. An estimate of the maximum difference in group delay in a guide can be obtained by calculating the differential group delay between the highest- and lowest-order modes

$$\Delta\tau_g = \tau_{g_L} - \tau_{g_H} \tag{4-105}$$

where τ_{g_L} and τ_{g_H} are respectively the group delay of the lowest- and highest-order propagating modes in the guide. Utilizing Fig. 4-2, the characteristic equation diagram for the slab guide, we can obtain the range of values for group delays of the propagating modes. Notice the range of values of X and, in turn, κ for the propagating modes is

$$0 < \kappa < \sqrt{n_1^2 - n_2^2}\, k_0 \tag{4-106}$$

If we recall that

$$\beta = \sqrt{n_1^2 k_0^2 - \kappa^2} \tag{4-107}$$

we can substitute the extreme values of κ in Eq. (4-106) into (4-107) to obtain the range of values of β, that is, for $\kappa = 0$ (κ associated with lowest-order modes),

$$\beta = n_1 k_0$$

For $\kappa = \sqrt{n_1^2 - n_2^2}\, k_0$ (κ associated with highest-order modes)

$$\beta = n_2 k_0$$

Therefore the range of values for β for the propagating modes is

$$\underbrace{n_2 k_0}_{\substack{\text{higher-order} \\ \text{modes}}} < \beta < \underbrace{n_1 k_0}_{\substack{\text{lower-order} \\ \text{modes}}} \tag{4-108}$$

To obtain the range of group delays, recall from Sec. 2-9 that

$$\tau_g = \frac{d\beta}{d\omega} \tag{4-109}$$

Differentiating Eq. (4-108) with respect to ω and remembering that $k_0 = \omega/c$ we obtain

$$\frac{d}{d\omega}\left(n_2\frac{\omega}{c}\right) < \frac{d\beta}{d\omega} < \frac{d}{d\omega}\left(n_1\frac{\omega}{c}\right) \tag{4-110}$$

Introducing the concept of group index from Eqs. (2-75) and (2-76) we can rewrite Eq. (4-110) as

$$\frac{N_{g2}}{c} < \tau_g < \frac{N_{g1}}{c} \tag{4-111}$$

where

$$N_{g1} = n_1 + \omega \, \frac{dn_1}{d\omega} \tag{4-112}$$

$$N_{g2} = n_2 + \omega \, \frac{dn_2}{d\omega} \tag{4-113}$$

An estimate of the differential group delay between the highest- and lowest-ordered modes for a guide of length L is

$$\Delta\tau_g = \frac{L}{c} \, (N_{g1} - N_{g2}) \tag{4-114}$$

where

$$N_{g1} - N_{g2} = (n_1 - n_2) + \omega \left(\frac{dn_1}{d\omega} - \frac{dn_2}{d\omega} \right) \tag{4-115}$$

For a waveguide in which the dispersive properties of the core and cladding glasses are similar

$$\frac{dn_1}{d\omega} - \frac{dn_2}{d\omega} \approx 0 \tag{4-116}$$

and Eq. (4-114) becomes

$$\Delta\tau_g = \frac{L}{c} \, (n_1 - n_2) \tag{4-117}$$

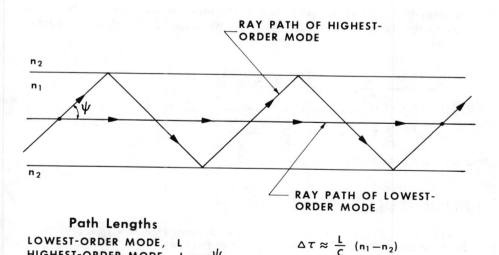

RAY PATH OF HIGHEST-ORDER MODE

n_2

n_1

ψ

n_2

RAY PATH OF LOWEST-ORDER MODE

Path Lengths

LOWEST-ORDER MODE, L

HIGHEST-ORDER MODE, L sec ψ

$$\Delta\tau \approx \frac{L}{c} \, (n_1 - n_2)$$

Figure 4-6 Multimode group delay. Ray paths in a multimode dielectric slab waveguide.

Equation (4-117) allows us to estimate the difference in arrival times of information propagating in the highest- and lowest-order modes of a dielectric slab waveguide of length L (see Fig. 4-6). The information to be transmitted in a waveguide is often in the form of a train of very narrow pulses (impulses) whose energy is distributed among the modes of the guide at its input. The delay difference $\Delta\tau_g$ will be a conservative estimate of the width of the pulses at the output of the waveguide. Thus, $\Delta\tau_g$ is an indication of the pulse broadening caused by modal delay distortion.

Example 4-2 Multimode group delay in a dispersionless guide Different plane waves propagating in a multimode slab waveguide will trace out ray paths of different lengths. The time for energy to propagate from the input to the output of the guide will be different along each path.

For example, if the guide in Fig. 4-7 is 1 km long, ray path 1 will be 1 km long. Energy will propagate through the guide along path 1 in time

$$t = \frac{L_1}{n_{\text{core}} c} = \frac{1000}{1.53(3 \times 10^8)}$$

$$= 5.1 \ \mu s$$

In the same guide, ray path 2 is 1 km (sec 15°) = 1035 m long. Energy will propagate through the guide along this path in time

$$t = \frac{L_2}{n_{\text{core}} c} = \frac{1035}{1.53(3 \times 10^8)}$$

$$= 5.28 \ \mu s$$

Energy launched at the same time at the input of the guide will propagate along the different paths and arrive at the output of the guide at different times.

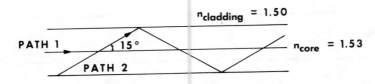

Figure 4-7 Ray paths, Example 4-2.

REFERENCES

1. D. Marcuse: *Theory of Dielectric Optical Waveguides*, Academic Press, New York, 1974.
2. D. Marcuse: *Light Transmission Optics*, Van Nostrand Reinhold Co., New York, 1972.
3. M. K. Barnoski: *Introduction to Integrated Optics*, Plenum Press, New York, 1973.
4. N. S. Kapany and J. J. Burke: *Optical Waveguides*, Academic Press, New York, 1972.
5. T. Tamir: *Integrated Optics*, Springer-Verlag, New York, 1975.

PROBLEMS

4-1(*a*) Calculate the numerical aperture, $R\#$ and cutoff conditions for the TE modes of the slab waveguide shown in Fig. 4-8 if $n_1 = 1.60$, $n_2 = 1.46$, $d = 0.6$ μm, and $\lambda_0 = 1$ μm.

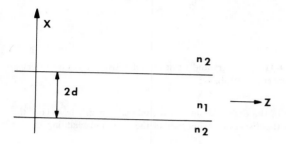

Figure 4-8 Geometry of symmetric slab waveguide, Probs. 4-1, 3.

(*b*) What happens to the number of propagating modes if d is increased to 3 μm?

(*c*) What happens to the number of propagating modes if λ_0 is increased to 1.3 μm?

4-2 For the asymmetric slab waveguide shown in Fig. 4-9, derive the characteristic equations for the TE and TM modes. Show that the TE mode equation reduces to that for the symmetric case (Eq. (4-18)).

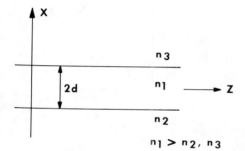

Figure 4-9 Geometry of asymmetric slab waveguide, Prob. 4-2.

4-3 Derive the characteristic equation for propagating TE modes in a symmetric slab waveguide (Eq. (4-18)) without separating the solutions into even and odd modes. Refer to Fig. 4-8 for the geometry of the guide.

4-4 Design a symmetric slab waveguide with an NA = 0.45, an R number between 2.0 and 2.25,

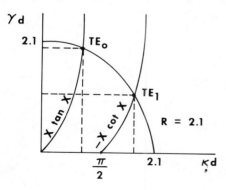

Figure 4-10

and a source wavelength of 0.82 μm. Specify n_1, n_2, and d for the guide. Use a diagram similar to Fig. 4-2 to find κ and γ for the TE modes in the guide.

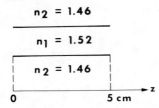

Figure 4-11 Geometry and values of refractive indices of dielectric slab waveguide, Prob. 4-5.

4-5 Estimate the multimode group delay of the dielectric slab waveguide shown in Fig. 4-11 if the length of the guide is 5 cm. Assume that the dispersive properties of the core and cladding glasses are similar.

THE STEP-INDEX FIBER

5-1 INTRODUCTION

In this chapter the step-index optical fiber is treated as a boundary-value problem and expressions for the modes in the fiber are obtained. Mode cutoff conditions are then analyzed and a design equation for a single-mode fiber is developed. Next, linearly polarized (LP) modes are introduced along with the concept of a principle mode number to simplify our understanding and analysis of a fiber. Using this simplified notation, expressions that describe the power and delay distortion characteristics in a multimode step-index fiber are derived. Finally a discussion of delay distortion in both single- and multimode fibers is included in this chapter to provide the reader with an understanding of the mechanisms that limit the bandwidth of a step-index fiber.

5-2 BASIC EQUATIONS AND PHYSICAL CONSTRAINTS; THE STEP-INDEX FIBER

In the last chapter we developed the concept of propagating modes in a dielectric waveguide by using electromagnetic field theory to rigorously solve the boundary-value problem of the homogeneous slab waveguide. Solutions to a wave equation were found in the core and cladding of the guide and these solutions were matched via the boundary conditions at the core-cladding interface to yield the "characteristic" equations of the guide. Solution of the characteristic equations produced a finite set of propagation constants and their

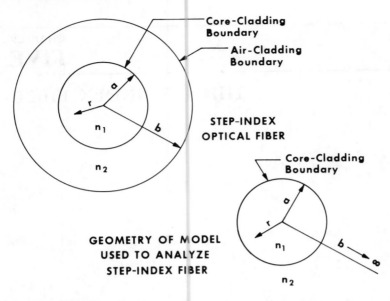

Figure 5-1 Geometry of the step-index fiber and model used for analysis.

associated modes that exist in the guide. To analyze the round optical fiber with a homogeneous core (the step-index fiber) the same general approach that was used for the dielectric slab waveguide will be followed.

First we will assume that b, the radius of the fiber cladding, is large enough to ensure that the cladding field decays exponentially and approaches zero at the cladding-air interface. This will allow us, as shown in Fig. 5-1, to analyze the fiber as a two-media boundary-value problem. This assumption agrees well with the condition that exists within a properly designed optical fiber. The steps we will follow to solve the boundary-value problem of the step-index fiber are outlined in Table 5-1.

In Sec. 3-3 a set of equations were developed in cylindrical coordinates relating the transverse components to the longitudinal components of the fields for an optical system with cylindrical symmetry. That is a system with fields

Table 5-1 Analysis of step-index fiber—Procedures followed

1. Mathematically model the step-index fiber using the wave equations in cylindrical coordinates.
2. Use the technique of separation of variables to partition the wave equations.
3. Define the physical requirements that influence the solutions of the fields in the core and cladding.
4. Select the proper functional form of the solution of the modified wave equation (Bessel's equation) in the core and cladding.
5. Apply the boundary conditions at the core-cladding interface.
6. Obtain the "characteristic" equation and its resulting modal solutions.
7. Analyze the resulting modes and their cutoff conditions.

propagating in the z direction. To obtain the modes in a step-index optical fiber, one must solve the modified wave equations (5-1) and (5-2) shown below for E_z and H_z in both the core and cladding regions of the fiber. Having obtained expressions for E_z and H_z we can directly obtain expressions for the transverse components of the fields E_r, E_ϕ, H_r, and H_ϕ from Eqs. (3-23) to (3-26).

$$\frac{\partial^2 E_z}{\partial r^2} + \frac{1}{r}\frac{\partial E_z}{\partial r} + \frac{1}{r^2}\frac{\partial^2 E_z}{\partial \phi^2} + \kappa^2 E_z = 0 \tag{5-1}$$

$$\frac{\partial^2 H_z}{\partial r^2} + \frac{1}{r}\frac{\partial H_z}{\partial r} + \frac{1}{r^2}\frac{\partial^2 H_z}{\partial \phi^2} + \kappa^2 H_z = 0 \tag{5-2}$$

Since Eqs. (5-1) and (5-2) have the same mathematical form we will solve (5-1) understanding that solutions obtained for it will be valid for Eq. (5-2). To obtain Eq. (5-1) we have already assumed an optical system with cylindrical symmetry. The longitudinal direction of propagation is the z axis and the z and time dependence of the fields is of the form $e^{j(\omega t - \beta z)}$.

The technique of separation of variables will now be applied to obtain a solution of Eq. (5-1). We will assume that we can obtain independent solutions for E_z in ϕ and r, that is,

$$E_z(\phi, r) = A\Phi(\phi)F(r) \tag{5-3}$$

Since the fiber has circular symmetry we will choose a circular function as a trial solution for $\Phi(\phi)$.

$$\Phi(\phi) = e^{jv\phi} \tag{5-4}$$

where v is a positive or negative integer, and

$$E_z = AF(r)e^{jv\phi} \tag{5-5}$$

Taking the derivatives with respect to r and ϕ for substitution into Eq. (5-1) we obtain

$$\frac{\partial E_z}{\partial r} = Ae^{jv\phi}\frac{dF(r)}{dr} \tag{5-6}$$

$$\frac{\partial^2 E_z}{\partial r^2} = Ae^{jv\phi}\frac{d^2 F(r)}{dr^2} \tag{5-7}$$

and

$$\frac{\partial^2 E_z}{\partial \phi^2} = -Av^2 e^{jv\phi}F(r) \tag{5-8}$$

substituting Eqs. (5-6) to (5-8) into (5-1) and multiplying the resulting equation by $1/Ae^{jv\phi}$ one obtains

$$\frac{d^2 F(r)}{dr^2} + \frac{1}{r}\frac{dF(r)}{dr} + \left(\kappa^2 - \frac{v^2}{r^2}\right)F(r) = 0 \tag{5-9}$$

Equation (5-9) is a form of Bessel's equation. This well-known second-order differential equation has two independent solutions. Numerous cylinder functions, as illustrated in App. 1, satisfy Bessel's equation. Energy considerations will dictate the choice of the functions selected as solutions of Eq. (5-9), that is,

1. The field must be finite in the core of the fiber. Specifically the cylinder function chosen in the core of the fiber must be finite at $r = 0$.
2. The field in the cladding of the fiber must have an exponentially decaying behavior at large distances from the center of the fiber.

5-3 THE FIELDS IN THE CORE AND CLADDING OF THE STEP-INDEX FIBER

To obtain the proper field configurations in the round optical fiber, one must select the appropriate cylinder function solutions of Bessel's equation—(5.9)—in the core, and the cladding that satisfy the physical requirements listed in Sec. 5-2.

Since the fields must be finite at the center of the fiber core, we will choose $J_v(\kappa r)$ (see App. 1) as the form of the solution for $r < a$. Therefore, for $r < a$

$$E_z = AJ_v(\kappa r)e^{jv\phi} \tag{5-10}$$

$$H_z = BJ_v(\kappa r)e^{jv\phi} \tag{5-11}$$

We require that the field in the cladding of the fiber decay in the r direction and be of the form $e^{-\gamma r}$.

If we define $\kappa = j\gamma$ we can choose a modified Hankel function of the first kind as shown in App. 1, to describe the decaying behavior of the field in the cladding for large r.

That is, for $r > a$

$$E_z = CH_v^{(1)}(j\gamma r)e^{jv\phi} \tag{5-12}$$

$$H_z = DH_v^{(1)}(j\gamma r)e^{jv\phi} \tag{5-13}$$

where A, B, C, D are unknown constants.

To obtain the transverse fields in the core and cladding of the guide, one must use Eqs. (3-23) to (3-26).

For example, to obtain E_r one must differentiate the longitudinal fields with respect to r and ϕ.

$$E_r = \frac{-j}{\kappa^2}\left(\beta\,\frac{\partial E_z}{\partial r} + \omega\mu\,\frac{1}{r}\,\frac{\partial H_z}{\partial \phi}\right) \tag{5-14}$$

In the core for $r < a$

$$\frac{\partial E_z}{\partial r} = A\kappa J_v'(\kappa r)e^{jv\phi} \tag{5-15}$$

where

$$J'_\nu(\kappa r) = \frac{\partial J_\nu(\kappa r)}{\partial(\kappa r)} \tag{5-16}$$

$$\frac{\partial H_z}{\partial \phi} = B(j\nu)J_\nu(\kappa r)e^{j\nu\phi} \tag{5-17}$$

Substituting Eqs. (5-15) and (5-17) into Eq. (5-14) results in

$$E_r = \frac{-j}{\kappa^2}\left[A\beta\kappa J'_\nu(\kappa r)e^{j\nu\phi} + B(j\nu)(\omega\mu)\frac{1}{r}J_\nu(\kappa r)e^{j\nu\phi} \right] \tag{5-18}$$

In a similar way using Eqs. (3-24) to (3-26) one can obtain

$$E_\phi = \frac{-j}{\kappa^2}\left[j\beta\frac{\nu}{r}AJ_\nu(\kappa r) - \kappa\omega\mu BJ'_\nu(\kappa r) \right]e^{j\nu\phi} \tag{5-19}$$

$$H_r = \frac{-j}{\kappa^2}\left[-j\omega\varepsilon_1\frac{\nu}{r}AJ_\nu(\kappa r) + \kappa\beta BJ'_\nu(\kappa r) \right]e^{j\nu\phi} \tag{5-20}$$

and

$$H_\phi = \frac{-j}{\kappa^2}\left[\kappa\omega\varepsilon_1 AJ'_\nu(\kappa r) + j\beta\frac{\nu}{r}BJ_\nu(\kappa r) \right]e^{j\nu\phi} \tag{5-21}$$

where

$$\kappa^2 = k_1^2 - \beta^2 \tag{5-22}$$

$$k_1^2 = \omega^2\mu_0\varepsilon_1 \tag{5-23}$$

The transverse fields in the cladding of the fiber can be obtained in the same fashion by differentiating Eqs. (5-12) and (5-13) with respect to r and ϕ and substituting into Eqs. (3-23) to (3-26). If one goes through this exercise one obtains for $r > a$

$$E_r = \frac{-1}{\gamma^2}\left[\beta\gamma CH_\nu^{(1)\prime}(j\gamma r) + \omega\mu_0\frac{\nu}{r}DH_\nu^{(1)}(j\gamma r) \right]e^{j\nu\phi} \tag{5-24}$$

$$E_\phi = \frac{-1}{\gamma^2}\left[\beta\frac{\nu}{r}CH_\nu^{(1)}(j\gamma r) - \gamma\omega\mu_0 DH_\nu^{(1)\prime}(j\gamma r) \right]e^{j\nu\phi} \tag{5-25}$$

$$H_r = \frac{-1}{\gamma^2}\left[-\omega\varepsilon_2\frac{\nu}{r}CH_\nu^{(1)}(j\gamma r) + \gamma\beta DH_\nu^{(1)\prime}(j\gamma r) \right]e^{j\nu\phi} \tag{5-26}$$

$$H_\phi = \frac{-1}{\gamma^2}\left[\gamma\omega\varepsilon_2 CH_\nu^{(1)\prime}(j\gamma r) + \beta\frac{\nu}{r}DH_\nu^{(1)}(j\gamma r) \right]e^{j\nu\phi} \tag{5-27}$$

where

$$\frac{\partial H_\nu^{(1)}(j\gamma r)}{\partial(j\gamma r)} = H_\nu^{(1)\prime}(j\gamma r) \tag{5-28}$$

and

$$\gamma^2 = \beta^2 - k_2^2 \qquad (5\text{-}29)$$

$$k_2^2 = \omega^2 \mu_0 \varepsilon_2 \qquad (5\text{-}30)$$

The total field configurations in the round optical fiber are described by Eqs. (5-18) to (5-21) and (5-24) to (5-27). The constants A, B, C, D, and β will be determined by applying the boundary conditions for the two tangential components of the electric and magnetic fields at the core-cladding interface ($r = a$).

5-4 BOUNDARY CONDITIONS AND CHARACTERISTIC EQUATION FOR STEP-INDEX FIBER

The boundary conditions for the fields at the core-cladding interface ($r = a$) can be written as

$$\left.\begin{aligned} Ez_1 &= Ez_2 \\ E\phi_1 &= E\phi_2 \\ Hz_1 &= Hz_2 \\ H\phi_1 &= H\phi_2 \end{aligned}\right\} r = a$$

where the subscripts 1 and 2 refer to the fields in the core and cladding respectively. Applying these conditions yields four simultaneous equations for the unknowns A, B, C, and D.

Using Eqs. (5-10) and (5-12) the boundary condition equation for E_z is,

$$J_\nu(\kappa a)A - H_\nu^{(1)}(j\gamma a)C = 0 \qquad (5\text{-}31)$$

Substituting $r = a$ into Eqs. (5-19) and (5-25) yields the equation for E_ϕ

$$\left(\frac{\beta}{\kappa^2}\frac{\nu}{a}\right)J_\nu(\kappa a)A + j\frac{\omega\mu_0}{\kappa}J_\nu'(\kappa a)B$$

$$+ \left(\frac{\beta}{\gamma^2}\frac{\nu}{a}\right)H_\nu^{(1)}(j\nu a)C - \frac{\omega\mu_0}{\gamma}H_\nu^{(1)\prime}(j\gamma a)D = 0 \quad (5\text{-}32)$$

From Eqs. (5-11) and (5-13) the boundary-condition equation for H_z is

$$J_\nu(\kappa a)B - H_\nu^{(1)}(j\gamma a)D = 0 \qquad (5\text{-}33)$$

Finally using Eqs. (5-21) and (5-27) the resulting boundary condition equation for H_ϕ is

$$\left(\frac{-j\omega\varepsilon_1}{\kappa}\right)J_\nu'(\kappa a)A + \left(\frac{\beta}{\kappa^2}\frac{\nu}{a}\right)J_\nu(\kappa a)B$$

$$+ \left(\frac{\omega\varepsilon_2}{\gamma}\right)H_\nu^{(1)\prime}(j\gamma a)C + \left(\frac{\beta}{\gamma^2}\frac{\nu}{a}\right)H_\nu^{(1)}(j\gamma a)D = 0 \quad (5\text{-}34)$$

Equations (5-31) to (5-34) form a set of simultaneous equations that have a nontrivial solution provided that the system determinant for the four equations vanishes, that is,

$$
\begin{vmatrix}
J_v(\kappa a) & 0 & -H_v^{(1)}(j\gamma a) & 0 \\
\dfrac{v}{a}\dfrac{\beta}{\kappa^2} J_v(\kappa a) & \dfrac{j\omega\mu_0}{\kappa} J_v'(\kappa a) & \dfrac{v}{a}\dfrac{\beta}{\gamma^2} H_v^{(1)}(j\gamma a) & \dfrac{-\omega\mu_0}{\gamma} H_v^{(1)\prime}(j\gamma a) \\
0 & J_v'(\kappa a) & 0 & -H_v^{(1)\prime}(j\gamma a) \\
\dfrac{-j\omega\varepsilon_1}{\kappa} J_v'(\kappa a) & \dfrac{v}{a}\dfrac{\beta}{\kappa^2} J_v(\kappa a) & \dfrac{\omega\varepsilon_2}{\gamma} H_v^{(1)\prime}(j\gamma a) & \dfrac{v\beta}{a\gamma^2} H_v^{(1)}(j\gamma a)
\end{vmatrix} = 0 \quad (5\text{-}35)
$$

Expansion of this determinant results in what is known as the "eigenvalue" or characteristic equation of the waveguide. This equation defines the modes in the guide and yields the permissible values of β, κ, and γ associated with each mode. In App. 2 the system determinant (5-35) is expanded and the resulting characteristic equation for the step-index fiber is

$$
\left[\frac{\varepsilon_1}{\varepsilon_2} \frac{a\gamma^2}{\kappa} \frac{J_v'(\kappa a)}{J_v(\kappa a)} + j\gamma a \frac{H_v^{(1)\prime}(j\gamma a)}{H_v^{(1)}(j\gamma a)} \right]\left[\frac{a\gamma^2 J_v'(\kappa a)}{\kappa J_v(\kappa a)} + j\gamma a \frac{H_v^{(1)\prime}(j\gamma a)}{H_v^{(1)}(j\gamma a)} \right]
$$
$$
= \left[v\left(\frac{\varepsilon_1}{\varepsilon_2} - 1 \right) \frac{\beta k_2}{\kappa^2} \right]^2 \quad (5\text{-}36)
$$

Although mathematically more complicated, Eq. (5-36) is conceptually similar to the characteristic equations derived in Chap. 4 for the dielectric slab waveguide. In the next section the characteristic equation (5-36) will be analyzed to determine the types of modes that exist in an optical fiber.

The coefficients in Eqs. (5-31) to (5-34) can be rewritten so that A is the only unknown coefficient. For example Eqs. (5-31) and (5-33) relate respectively A and C and B and D to each other.

$$
C = \frac{J_v(\kappa a)}{H_v^{(1)}(j\gamma a)} A \quad (5\text{-}37)
$$

$$
D = \frac{J_v(\kappa a)}{H_v^{(1)}(j\gamma a)} B \quad (5\text{-}38)
$$

The coefficients A and B are related to each other via Eqs. (5-32) or (5-34) using Eqs. (5-37), (5-38), and (5-34). Solving for B in terms of A yields[1]

$$
B = \frac{j}{v} \frac{a\kappa\gamma[\varepsilon_1\gamma J_v'(\kappa a)H_v^{(1)}(j\gamma a) + j\varepsilon_2 \kappa J_v(\kappa a)H_v^{(1)\prime}(j\gamma a)]}{\omega(\varepsilon_1 - \varepsilon_2)\mu_0 \beta J_v(\kappa a)H_v^{(1)}(j\gamma a)} A \quad (5\text{-}39)
$$

If Eq. (5-32) were used instead of (5-34) the resulting relationship between B and A would be

$$
B = jv \frac{\omega(\varepsilon_1 - \varepsilon_2)\beta J_v(\kappa a)H_v^{(1)}(j\gamma a)}{\kappa\gamma a[\gamma J_v'(\kappa a)H_v^{(1)}(j\gamma a) + j\kappa J_v(\kappa a)H_v^{(1)\prime}(j\gamma a)]} A \quad (5\text{-}40)
$$

Equations (5-39) and (5-40) will be used in Sec. 5-5 when we determine the types of modes that can propagate in a step-index fiber.

5-5 CHARACTERIZATION OF MODES IN A STEP-INDEX OPTICAL FIBER

In general the permissible field configurations or modes that exist in a step-index fiber have six field components. For the round fiber hybrid modes exist as well as the TE and TM modes that we observed in the dielectric slab wave-guide. The hybrid modes will be denoted as HE and EH modes and have both longitudinal electric and magnetic field components present. In terms of a ray analogy for the step-index fiber, the hybrid modes correspond to propagating skew rays and the TE and TM modes to meridional rays. For the special case $v = 0$, only meridional rays propagate in the guide. For this case the right-hand side of the characteristic equation (5-36) is equal to zero and one obtains two characteristic equations that define the TE and TM modes. These equations are written below.

$$\left[\frac{a\gamma^2}{\kappa} \frac{J_0'(\kappa a)}{J_0(\kappa a)} + j\gamma a \frac{H_0^{(1)\prime}(j\gamma a)}{H_0^{(1)}(j\gamma a)} \right] = 0 \tag{5-41}$$

$$\left[\frac{\varepsilon_1}{\varepsilon_2} \frac{a\gamma^2}{\kappa} \frac{J_0'(\kappa a)}{J_0(\kappa a)} + \frac{j\gamma a H_0^{(1)\prime}(j\gamma a)}{H_0^{(1)}(j\gamma a)} \right] = 0 \tag{5-42}$$

To understand that Eq. (5-41) is the defining equation for the TE modes and Eq. (5-42) the defining equation for the TM modes let us recall that for TE modes $E_z = 0$ and for TM modes $H_z = 0$. Since

$$E_z = AJ_v(\kappa r)e^{jv\phi} \tag{5-43}$$

and

$$H_z = BJ_v(kr)e^{jv\phi} \tag{5-44}$$

E_z is equal to zero when $A = 0$, and $H_z = 0$ when $B = 0$. Referring to Eq. (5-39) when $v \to 0$, $B \to \infty$ unless $A = 0$. Equation (5-41) is the characteristic equation for the guide when $v \to 0$ and $A = 0$. That is, Eq. (5-41) is the defining equation for the TE modes. Using Eq. (5-40) when $v = 0$, $B = 0$, Eq. (5-42) is the characteristic equation for the guide for the TM modes when $v = 0$ and $B = 0$.

Equations (5-41) and (5-42) can be rewritten in a simpler way if we recall from Eq. (A1-19) that for any cylinder function

$$Z_0' = -Z_1 \tag{5-45}$$

Then Eqs. (5-41) and (5-42) become,

Defining equation for TE modes, $\dfrac{\gamma}{\kappa} \dfrac{J_1(\kappa a)}{J_0(\kappa a)} + j \dfrac{H_1^{(1)}(j\gamma a)}{H_0^{(1)}(j\gamma a)} = 0 \tag{5-46}$

and,

Defining equation for TM modes, $\quad \dfrac{\varepsilon_1}{\varepsilon_2}\dfrac{\gamma}{\kappa}\dfrac{J_1(\kappa a)}{J_0(\kappa a)} + j\,\dfrac{H_1^{(1)}(j\gamma a)}{H_0^{(1)}(j\gamma a)} = 0 \qquad$ (5-47)

In summary the characteristic equation (5-36) defines the propagating modes in a step-index optical fiber. The solutions to this equation are, to say the least, extremely complicated and normally obtained numerically on a computer. The general solution for $v \neq 0$ has six field components and defines the propagation conditions for the (HE, EH) hybrid modes. For the special case of $v = 0$ we can derive two separate characteristic equations, (5-46) and (5-47), that describe the conditions for propagation of the TE and TM modes.

5-6 MODE CUTOFF CONDITIONS

An important parameter for each propagating mode is its cutoff frequency. As we have already discussed in Chap. 4, a mode is cut off when its field in the cladding ceases to be evanescent and is detached from the guide, that is, the field in the cladding does not decay. The rate of decay of the field in the cladding is determined by the value of the constant γ. In App. 1 we developed the expression for the asymptotic approximation of the modified Hankel function for large values of its argument[5]

$$H_v^{(1)}(j\gamma r) = \sqrt{\frac{2}{\pi j \gamma r}}\,(e^{-j(\pi v/2 + \pi/4)})e^{-\gamma r} \qquad (5\text{-}48)$$

For large values of γ, the field is tightly concentrated inside and close to the core. With decreasing values of γ, the field reaches farther out into the cladding. Finally, for $\gamma = 0$, the field detaches itself from the guide. The frequency at which this happens is called the cutoff frequency. At cutoff

$$\gamma = 0 = \sqrt{\beta_c^2 - k_{2c}^2} \qquad (5\text{-}49)$$

or

$$\beta_c^2 = k_{2c}^2 \qquad (5\text{-}50)$$

where

$$k_{2c}^2 = \omega_c^2 \mu_0 \varepsilon_2 \qquad (5\text{-}51)$$

In the core of the guide at cutoff we have

$$\kappa_c^2 = k_{1c}^2 - \beta_c^2 \qquad (5\text{-}52)$$

$$k_{1c}^2 = \omega_c^2 \mu_0 \varepsilon_1 \qquad (5\text{-}53)$$

We can obtain an expression for the cutoff frequency of a mode by substituting Eq. (5-50) into (5-52)

$$\kappa_c^2 = k_{1c}^2 - k_{2c}^2 = \omega_c^2 \mu_0(\varepsilon_1 - \varepsilon_2) \qquad (5\text{-}54)$$

Solving for ω_c from Eq. (5-54)

$$\omega_c = \frac{\kappa_c}{\sqrt{\mu_0(\varepsilon_1 - \varepsilon_2)}} \tag{5-55}$$

The cutoff frequency of a mode can be zero if $\kappa_c = 0$. One, and only one, mode can exist in an optical fiber with $\omega_c = 0$. This mode is the hybrid HE_{11} mode which exists for all frequencies. It is therefore possible to design and operate a single-mode optical fiber. The single-mode fiber has a very small core diameter and small refractive index difference between the core and cladding. These parameters must be chosen to ensure that all other guided modes are below their cutoff frequency. Before we can develop the design equation for a single-mode fiber, we must develop the equations for the cutoff conditions (and solve for the κ_c's) for the different types of modes that can exist in a step-index optical fiber.

In App. 3 the characteristic equation (5-36) has been reworked for convenient solution at mode cutoff. By allowing γ to approach zero, and using an approximation for the modified Hankel function for small arguments, we obtain the following mode cutoff conditions.

TE and TM modes $v = 0$

The cutoff conditions for the $TE_{0\mu}$ and $TM_{0\mu}$ modes are obtained from the μth roots of Eq. (5-56) shown below

$$J_0(\kappa a) = 0 \tag{5-56}$$

That is, the value of $\kappa_c a$ is obtained from the roots of Eq. (5-56), as shown in Fig. 5-2. The corresponding cutoff frequency for a mode is calculated using this value of κ_c in Eq. (5-55).

Hybrid Modes

$HE_{1\mu}$ modes

The cutoff condition of the $HE_{1\mu}$ modes is described by Eq. (5-57)

$$\kappa_c a = x_{v\mu} \qquad \text{for} \qquad v = 1, 2, 3, \ldots \tag{5-57}$$

where the parameter $x_{v\mu}$ is the μth root of the equation

$$J_v(x_{v\mu}) = 0 \tag{5-58}$$

As previously discussed the fundamental or HE_{11} mode exists for all frequencies. It will propagate when all other modes are cut off. The equation that describes its cutoff condition is:

HE_{11} mode

$$\kappa_c a = 0 \tag{5-59}$$

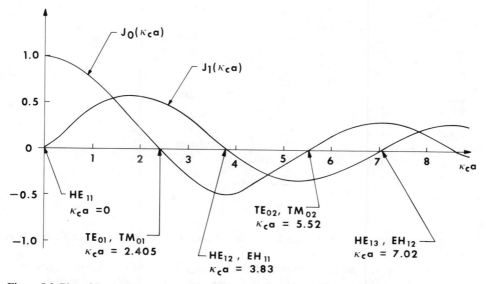

Figure 5-2 Plot of Bessel functions used for calculating cutoff conditions of modes.

$EH_{\nu\mu}$ modes

The cutoff condition equation for the $EH_{\nu\mu}$ modes is also Eq. (5-58) but with the added constraint $x_{\nu\mu} \neq 0$.

Figure 5-2 shows a graphical example of how to calculate the cutoff condition for the $HE_{1\mu}$ and $EH_{1\mu}$ modes. Finally, the remaining $HE_{\nu\mu}$ modes have the following cutoff condition equation that must be solved.

$HE_{\nu\mu}$ modes   for $\nu = 2, 3, 4, \ldots$

$$\left(\frac{\varepsilon_1}{\varepsilon_2} + 1\right) J_{\nu-1}(\kappa_c a) = \frac{a\kappa_c}{\nu - 1} J_\nu(\kappa_c a) \tag{5-60}$$

For the hybrid modes there are two types of modes for each integral value of $\nu > 1$. The modes whose cutoff frequency is determined by Eq. (5-58) are designated $EH_{\nu\mu}$ modes. Equation (5-60) determines the cutoff frequencies of the $HE_{\nu\mu}$ modes. Both the $EH_{1\mu}$ and $HE_{1(\mu+1)}$ modes have the same cutoff frequency. However, they are not degenerate modes since at frequencies other than cutoff, they have different propagation constants. For $\nu = 0$ we have the nondegenerate TE and TM modes, whose identical cutoff condition is given by Eq. (5-56). One can calculate the cutoff parameter $\kappa_c a$ for the different types of modes that exist in a step-index fiber from Eqs. (5-56) to (5-60). Table 5-2 lists the first few low-order modes and their respective cutoff parameter values. To calculate the cutoff parameter for the $HE_{\nu\mu}$ modes (Eq. (5-60)) a knowledge of the ratio of the refractive indices of the core and cladding of the fiber is required. The cutoff parameters for all the other modes are obtained directly, for a given order ν and

Table 5-2

Mode	Cutoff parameter, $\kappa_c a$	Mode	Cutoff parameter, $\kappa_c a$
HE_{11}	0.0	EH_{31}	6.38
TE_{01}, TM_{01}	2.405	E_{51}	6.41
HE_{21}	2.42	HE_{13}, EH_{12}	7.02
HE_{12}, EH_{11}	3.83	HE_{32}	7.02
HE_{31}	3.86	EH_{41}	7.59
EH_{21}	5.14	HE_{61}	7.61
HE_{41}	5.16	EH_{22}	8.42
TE_{02}, TM_{02}	5.52	HE_{52}	8.43
HE_{22}	5.53		

corresponding root μ, from the Bessel functions. It is assumed in Table 5-2 that $n_1/n_2 = 1.02$. ($\varepsilon_1/\varepsilon_2 = 1.0404$.)

To appreciate the significance of the cutoff parameter $\kappa_c a$ let us define it in terms of the physical parameters of the fiber. From Eq. (5-54)

$$\kappa_c a = \omega_c \sqrt{\mu_0 \varepsilon_0}(\sqrt{n_1^2 - n_2^2})a \qquad (5\text{-}61)$$

noting that

$$\omega_c \sqrt{\mu_0 \varepsilon_0} = \frac{2\pi}{\lambda_0} \qquad (5\text{-}62)$$

we obtain

$$V \equiv \kappa_c a = \frac{2\pi a}{\lambda_0} \sqrt{n_1^2 - n_2^2} \qquad (5\text{-}63)$$

The cutoff parameter $\kappa_c a$ is usually called the "V" number of the fiber. Notice that the V number for the fiber is analogous to the parameter R for the dielectric slab waveguide. The number of propagating modes in the step-index fiber is proportional to its V number. Table 5-3 illustrates how increasing a, n_1, n_2, or λ_0 influences the number of propagating modes in the fiber.

Table 5-3

Increasing physical parameter	Number of propagating modes
Core radius a	Increases
Core refractive index, n_1	Increases
Cladding refractive index, n_2	Decreases
Source wavelength, λ_0	Decreases

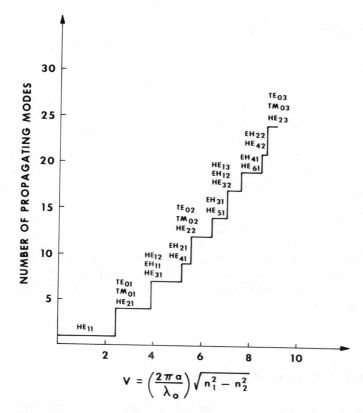

Figure 5-3 Plot of number of propagating modes vs. fiber V number.

Using Table 5-2, a plot of the number of propagating modes in a step-index fiber as a function of its V number can be made (see Fig. 5-3). Notice that for $V < 2.405$ it is possible to design a single-mode fiber that supports only the HE_{11} mode.

Example 5.1 Multimode step-index fiber We wish to design a multimode step-index fiber with a V number, $V = 100$ and a numerical aperture, $NA = 0.30$. This fiber will be used in a data link with a 0.82 μm light-emitting diode (LED) source. We will determine the fiber parameters a, n_1, and n_2 as follows:

$$V = \frac{2\pi a}{\lambda_0} \sqrt{n_1^2 - n_2^2}$$

$$NA = \sqrt{n_1^2 - n_2^2}$$

Choose a fused silica core $n_1 = 1.458$.

$$n_2 = \sqrt{n_1^2 - NA^2}$$

$$= 1.427$$

$$a = \frac{\lambda_0 V}{2\pi(NA)}$$

$$= 43.5 \ \mu m$$

The fiber design is

$$a = 43.5 \ \mu m$$

$$n_1 = 1.458$$

$$n_2 = 1.427$$

To fully design the fiber we would also need to specify a value for the cladding radius b which would ensure that the evanescent fields in the cladding approach zero before the cladding-air interface. A typical cladding radius that satisfies this requirement is:

$$b = 62.5 \ \mu m$$

5-7 SINGLE-MODE OPTICAL FIBER

In this section we will develop an equation and use it to design a single-mode step-index fiber. Recall from Fig.5-3 that the number of propagating modes in a step-index fiber is a function of its V number. For $V < 2.405$ the only mode that propagates in a fiber is the fundamental HE_{11} mode. To develop the design equation for a single-mode fiber let us rewrite Eq. (5-63) in terms of Δ, the fractional refractive index difference between the core and cladding

$$V = \frac{2\pi a}{\lambda_0} \sqrt{n_1^2 - n_2^2} = \frac{2\pi a}{\lambda_0} n_1 \sqrt{2\Delta - \Delta^2} \tag{5-64}$$

where

$$n_2 = n_1(1 - \Delta) \tag{5-65}$$

and

$$\Delta = \frac{n_1 - n_2}{n_1} \tag{5-66}$$

for small Δ, $\Delta^2 \ll 2\Delta$ and Eq. (5-64) becomes

$$V \approx \frac{2\pi a}{\lambda_0} \sqrt{2} \, n_1 \sqrt{\Delta} = 8.886 \frac{a n_1}{\lambda_0} \sqrt{\Delta} \tag{5-67}$$

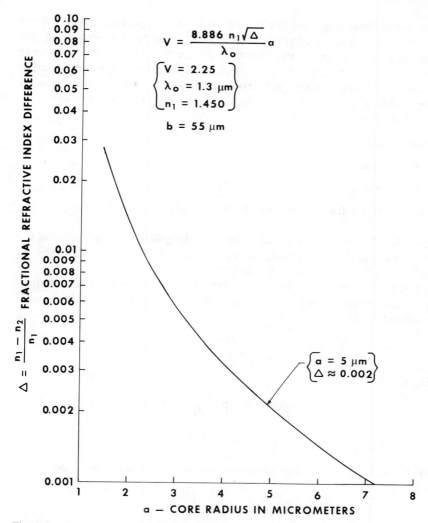

Figure 5-4 Design curve for single-mode fiber.

Using Eq. (5-67) we can design a single mode if $V < 2.405$. Let us assume the following values for our design:

$$V = 2.25$$

$$\lambda_0 = 1.3 \ \mu m$$

$$n_1 = 1.450$$

Substituting these values into Eq. (5-67) we can obtain a design curve (Fig. 5-4) showing the relationship between Δ and the core radius a for a single-mode fiber. Referring to Fig. 5-4, we wish to choose the radius a large enough to make the splicing of single-mode fibers a viable task. We must also choose Δ large enough to make the fiber manufacturable. We are free to choose a value for the cladding radius b. Our choice will be made to ensure that the power in the evanescent cladding field approaches zero at the outside diameter of the fiber. With these considerations in mind, the following parameters for a single-mode fiber were chosen:

$$a = 5 \ \mu m$$

$$b = 55 \ \mu m$$

$$\Delta = 0.002$$

$$n_1 = 1.450 \text{ (refractive index of high-silica glass at } \lambda = 1.3 \ \mu m)$$

Example 5-2 Cutoff wavelength of a single-mode guide Let us determine the cutoff wavelength, for single-mode operation, of the guide designed in Sec. 5.7 ($a = 5 \ \mu m$, $n_1 = 1.450$, $\Delta = 0.002$).

If the V number of the fiber is greater than 2.405, the fiber will support more than one mode. We will calculate the cutoff wavelength for single-mode operation as follows:

$$V = 2.405 = \frac{2\pi a}{\lambda_0} \sqrt{n_1^2 - n_2^2}$$

Solving for λ_0

$$2.405 = \frac{2\pi(5 \ \mu m)}{\lambda_0} \sqrt{(1.450)^2 - (1.447)^2}$$

$$\lambda_0 = 1.218 \ \mu m$$

If λ_0 is less than 1.218 μm the guide will support more than one mode.

5-8 DELAY DISTORTION IN A SINGLE-MODE FIBER

When a very high-capacity optical communication system is designed, such as a transatlantic undersea link, the transmission medium used must have a bandwidth in excess of 10 GHz-km. Single-mode fibers would be the transmission medium of choice for this type of application because their bandwidths are very large and limited only by intramodal delay distortion (chromatic and waveguide dispersion). Single-mode fibers with measured bandwidths of 30 GHz-$\sqrt{km}$ have been reported in the literature.[6]

An optical fiber can be described in terms of its baseband frequency characteristic (bandwidth) or equivalently in terms of its impulse response (rms pulse width) in the time domain (see Chap. 8). Since most applications of fibers in communication systems use some form of digital envelope modulation of an optical signal, the fiber performance is usually characterized in the time domain in terms of the degradation of an optical pulse propagating through the fiber (impulse response). In this section we will follow this practice by describing the mechanisms that cause the degradation of the shape of an optical pulse (group delay distortion) as it propagates through a single-mode fiber. The two mechanisms that contribute to delay distortion are: (1) chromatic (material) dispersion and (2) waveguide dispersion. Chromatic dispersion is the dominant effect and is a result of the fact that the group delay of an optical wave propagating in a glass medium is wavelength-dependent. Let us now develop the expression for group delay due to chromatic dispersion in a single-mode optical fiber.

If you recall from Chap. 2, the group delay of a mode is given by

$$\tau_g = \frac{1}{v_g} = \frac{N_g}{c} \tag{5-68}$$

where N_g is the group index of the medium

$$N_g = n - \lambda_0 \frac{dn}{d\lambda_0} \tag{5-69}$$

Since the glass that is used in optical fibers is a dispersive medium, the refractive index of the core of a single-mode fiber is dependent upon the communication system source wavelength λ_0. Suppose that the system source has a relative spectral bandwidth $\Delta\lambda/\lambda$

$$\text{Relative spectral bandwidth of source} \equiv \frac{\Delta\lambda}{\lambda_0} \tag{5-70}$$

where $\Delta\lambda = \lambda_2 - \lambda_1$ is a spread of wavelengths about a center wavelength λ_0.

Now consider that energy is propagating in a range of wavelengths $\Delta\lambda$ in a single-mode fiber. If the energy propagates a distance L in the fiber, the spread in the arrival times of energy propagating at the different wavelengths λ_1 and λ_2 is

$$\Delta\tau_c = \frac{L}{c} N_g(\lambda_1) - \frac{L}{c} N_g(\lambda_2)$$

$$= -\frac{L}{c} \frac{dN_g}{d\lambda} \Delta\lambda \tag{5-71}$$

Using Eq. (5-69)

$$\frac{dN_g}{d\lambda} = \frac{dn_1}{d\lambda} - \lambda \frac{d^2 n_1}{d\lambda^2} - \frac{dn_1}{d\lambda}$$

$$= -\lambda \frac{d^2 n_1}{d\lambda^2} \tag{5-72}$$

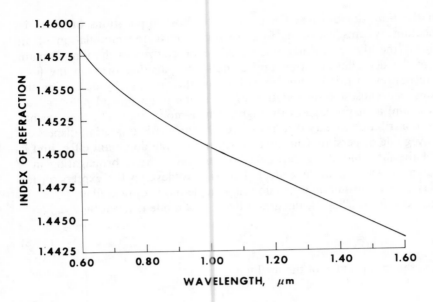

Figure 5-5 Refractive index of fused silica vs. wavelength.

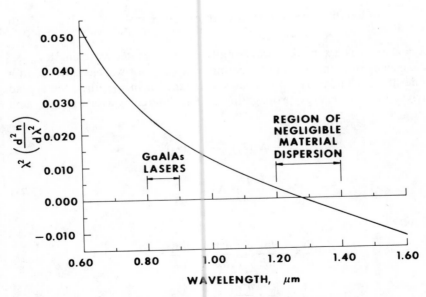

Figure 5-6 $\lambda^2(d^2n/d\lambda^2)$ vs. wavelength showing zero material dispersion region.

and

$$\Delta\tau_c = \frac{L}{c}\,\lambda\,\frac{d^2 n_1}{d\lambda^2}\,\Delta\lambda \tag{5-73}$$

Writing Eq. (5-73) in terms of the relative bandwidth of the source

$$\Delta\tau_c = \frac{L}{c}\left(\frac{\Delta\lambda}{\lambda_0}\right)\lambda_0^2\,\frac{d^2 n_1}{d\lambda^2} \tag{5-74}$$

Equation (5-74) can be used to approximate the chromatic dispersion component of delay distortion in a single-mode fiber. Figures 5-5 and 5-6 show respectively n_1[7] and $\lambda^2(d^2 n_1/d\lambda^2)$ versus λ for fused silica.

To obtain an estimate of pulse broadening due to chromatic dispersion let us consider a GaAs laser operating at $\lambda_0 = 0.82\ \mu$m with a linewidth $\Delta\lambda = 1$ nm. The source relative bandwidth is $\Delta\lambda/\lambda = 0.12$ percent.

Using Fig. 5-6 and Eq. (5-74) the pulse broadening due to chromatic dispersion for a kilometer of fiber would be approximately 100 ps. This effect can be substantially reduced if sources are operated at longer wavelengths. Referring to Fig. 5-6, in the region $\lambda = 1.2\ \mu$m to 1.4 μm,

$$\lambda^2\,\frac{d^2 n}{d\lambda^2} \approx 0 \tag{5-75}$$

This indicates that it is theoretically possible to find a source-wavelength region where pulse-spreading due to chromatic dispersion approaches zero. Experimental evidence[8,9] suggests that for germanium- or phosphorus-doped silica fibers the zero material dispersion region would occur at a longer wavelength than Fig. 5-6 suggests.

Let us now consider waveguide dispersion, the second mechanism that can cause some pulse broadening in a single-mode fiber. Waveguide dispersion is a result of the fact that the propagating characteristics of the mode are a function of the ratio between the core radius and the wavelength. An expression for waveguide dispersion has been developed in the literature.[3,10] It is presented here to give the reader an understanding of the size of the contributions to the total pulse-broadening due to this mechanism

$$\Delta\tau_w = \frac{L}{c}\left(\frac{\Delta\lambda}{\lambda}\right)(n_2 - n_1)D_w\,V \tag{5-76}$$

$D_w(V)$ is a dimensionless dispersion coefficient that is a function of the V number of the fiber. A plot of $D_w(V)$ versus V is shown in Fig. 5-7. For the fiber parameters of the single-mode fiber designed in Sec. 5-7, and assuming a source linewidth $\Delta\lambda = 1$ nm, the pulse-broadening due to waveguide dispersion is approximately two picoseconds for a kilometer of fiber, a very small part of the total pulse-broadening due to intramodal delay distortion in an optical fiber.

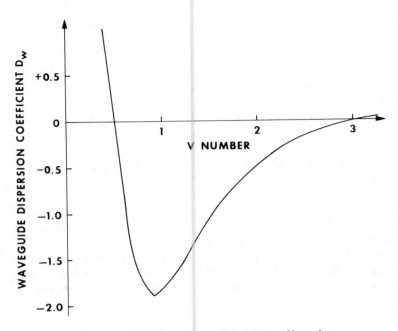

Figure 5-7 Plot of waveguide dispersion coefficient, D_w vs. V number.

5-9 WEAKLY GUIDING FIBERS; SIMPLIFIED CHARACTERISTIC EQUATION

In Secs. 5-4 and 5-5 we obtained a rigorous solution for the fields in a step-index fiber. Unfortunately the characteristic equation and the description of the six component hybrid fields obtained from this analysis was mathematically very complicated. To proceed farther with our analysis of a fiber with many modes would be an extremely difficult task unless some simplifying assumptions can be made. The simplification in the descriptions of the modes in a fiber is made possible by realizing that most fibers used for practical telecommunication applications have core materials whose refractive index is only slightly higher than that of the surrounding cladding, that is, we will assume that $\Delta \ll 1$ and typically Δ is less than 0.05. By making this assumption, considerable analytical simplifications result. In this section we will make use of the assumption $\Delta \ll 1$ to derive the simplified characteristic equation for a weakly guiding fiber.

Starting with the exact characteristic equation (A3-8) for the step-index fiber

$$\left(\frac{\varepsilon_1}{\varepsilon_2} J^- - H^-\right)(J^+ - H^+) + \left(\frac{\varepsilon_1}{\varepsilon_2} J^+ - H^+\right)(J^- - H^-) = 0 \qquad (5\text{-}77)$$

where J^+, J^-, H^+, and H^- are defined by Eqs. (A3-2) to (A3-5). We can obtain the simplified characteristic equation by setting $n_1 = n_2$ $(\varepsilon_1 = \varepsilon_2)$. Equation (5-77) becomes

$$(J^- - H^-)(J^+ - H^+) = 0 \qquad (5\text{-}78)$$

Using Eqs. (A3-2) to (A3-5) we immediately obtain the two characteristic equations

$$\frac{J_{v-1}(\kappa a)}{\kappa a J_v(\kappa a)} = \frac{H^{(1)}_{v-1}(j\gamma a)}{j\gamma a H^{(1)}_v{}'(j\gamma a)} \qquad \text{for HE modes} \qquad (5\text{-}79)$$

$$\frac{J_{v+1}(\kappa a)}{\kappa a J_v(\kappa a)} = \frac{H^{(1)}_{v+1}(j\gamma a)}{j\gamma a H^{(1)}_v{}'(j\gamma a)} \qquad \text{for EH modes} \qquad (5\text{-}80)$$

The approximate characteristic equations (5-79) and (5-80) are much more convenient for obtaining solutions for the propagation constants than the exact characteristic equation (5-36). Marcuse[1] has shown that approximate expressions for the fields far from cutoff can be written in cartesian coordinates. The interested reader should refer to Marcuse's excellent book for the details of the derivation of these approximate fields. A further simplification of the approximate fields can be made if we realize that the HE modes of order $v = v' + 1$ are almost degenerate with the EH modes of order $v = v' - 1$. Linear superposition of an HE and a EH mode results in a linearly polarized (LP) mode[1,11,13] that has only four field components. These new modes are much simpler in structure than the original HE and EH modes that have six field components. It is important to keep in mind that LP modes are not exact modes of the step-index fiber. Since the parent HE and EH modes have slightly different propagation constants as a function of z (degeneracy between the modes is not exact), the superposition of these modes changes with z. Therefore LP modes are not true modes but are useful and allow us to visualize the field structures of a step-index fiber in a simpler way.

5-10 LINEARLY POLARIZED (LP) MODES

We begin our analysis of the LP modes by drawing an analogy with the slab waveguide studied in Chap. 4. If you recall, we reduced the slab waveguide to a two-dimensional problem with the symmetry restriction $\partial/\partial y = 0$. This resulted in a separation of the solution into TE modes (E_y, H_x, and H_z field components) and TM modes (E_x, E_z, and H_y field components). By analogy the three-dimensional fiber solution can be simplified by assuming $\Delta \ll 1$. The waves in the structure propagate at small angles to the axis and we can construct modes whose transverse fields are essentially polarized in one direction (E_y, H_x, E_z, and H_z field components or the orthogonal polarization where the field components are E_x, H_y, E_z, and H_z).

Let us postulate transverse field components in a weakly guiding fiber as follows: in the core $r < a$

$$E_y = \frac{\eta_0}{n_1} H_x = \frac{A J_l(\kappa r)}{J_l(U)} \cos l\phi \qquad (5\text{-}81)$$

and in the cladding $r > a$

$$E_y = \frac{\eta_0}{n_2} H_x = \frac{A H_l^{(1)}(j\gamma r)}{H_l^{(1)}(jW)} \cos l\phi \qquad (5\text{-}82)$$

where $l = 0, 1, 2, 3, \ldots$

A is the electric field strength at the core-cladding interface

$\eta_0 = \sqrt{\mu_0/\varepsilon_0}$ is the characteristic impedance of free space, and

$$U = ka \qquad (5\text{-}83)$$

$$W = \gamma a \qquad (5\text{-}84)$$

$$V^2 = U^2 + W^2 \qquad (5\text{-}85)$$

The longitudinal components E_z and H_z can be obtained from H_x and E_y using Eqs. (3-6c) and (3-7c). Rewriting these equations in terms of η_0 we obtain

$$E_z = \frac{j\eta_0}{k_0 n_1^2} \frac{\partial H_x}{\partial y} \qquad \text{in core of fiber} \qquad (5\text{-}86)$$

$$E_z = \frac{j\eta_0}{k_0 n_2^2} \frac{\partial H_x}{\partial y} \qquad \text{in cladding of fiber} \qquad (5\text{-}87)$$

and

$$H_z = \frac{j}{k_0 \eta_0} \left(\frac{\partial E_y}{\partial x} \right) \qquad \text{in the core and cladding of the fiber} \qquad (5\text{-}88)$$

For the interested reader expressions for E_z, H_z, E_ϕ and H_ϕ are obtained in App. 4. In addition the characteristic equation for the LP modes is derived by assuming $n_1 = n_2$ and matching the tangential components of the fields at the core-cladding interface. The resultant characteristic equation is

$$U \left[\frac{J_{l-1}(U)}{J_l(U)} \right] = jW \left[\frac{H_{l-1}^{(1)}(jW)}{H_l^{(1)}(jW)} \right] \qquad (5\text{-}89)$$

This characteristic equation is much simpler than the exact characteristic equation (5-36) developed in Sec. 5-4. It has been shown[11] to be accurate to within one and ten percent for $\Delta \leq 0.1$ and $\Delta \leq 0.25$ respectively.

The approximate characteristic equations (5-79) and (5-80) can be shown to be equal to (5-89). To do this for example for the HE modes, we invert (5-79) and let $v = v' + 1$. After using the recursion relation (A1-20) and simplifying, Eq. (5-89) is obtained. For the EH modes we follow the same procedure but let $v = v' - 1$.

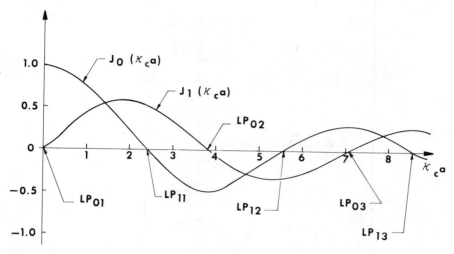

Figure 5-8 Plot of Bessel functions used for calculating cutoff conditions of LP_{0m} and LP_{1m} modes.

To obtain the cutoff condition for the LP modes, we require $\gamma = 0$. For the cutoff condition $W = \gamma a = 0$ and the characteristic equation (5-89) becomes

$$J_{l-1}(\kappa_c a) = 0 \tag{5-90}$$

The lowest-order mode, characterized by $l = 0$, has a cutoff equation given by

$$J_1(\kappa_c a) = -J_{-1}(\kappa_c a) = 0 \tag{5-91}$$

This mode is labeled the LP_{01} mode having a field pattern described by $l = 0$ and a cutoff characteristic of the first zero of the Bessel function. Referring to Fig. 5-8 the first zero occurs at $\kappa_c a = 0$, that is the lowest-order mode cuts off only when $a = 0$. The LP_{01} mode corresponds to the fundamental HE_{11} mode obtained from the exact analysis of the fiber. The next mode of the $l = 0$ type cuts off when $J_1(\kappa_c a)$ next equals zero, that is when $\kappa_c a = 3.83$. This mode is called the LP_{02} mode. Similarly the modes characterized by $l = 1$ have cutoffs when $J_0(\kappa_c a) = 0$. Thus the LP_{11} mode cuts off when $k_c a = 2.405$. The notation for labelling the LP modes obviously is no longer the same as used for the exact solution since the integer l now refers to a superposition of exact modes with labels $v + 1$ and $v - 1$. A comparison of the simplified-mode solutions with the exact modes shows that the LP_{lm} modes are actually a superposition of $HE_{v+1,\mu}$ and $EH_{v-1,\mu}$ modes.[11,13]

One of the attractive features of the LP mode theory is the ease with which we can visualize a mode. A complete set of modes exist in which only one electric and one magnetic field component are significant. The E vector can be chosen to lie along an arbitrary radius with the H vector along a perpendicular radius. Having made this choice there will always be a second independent polarization with the E and H vectors orthogonal to the first pair. Since each of

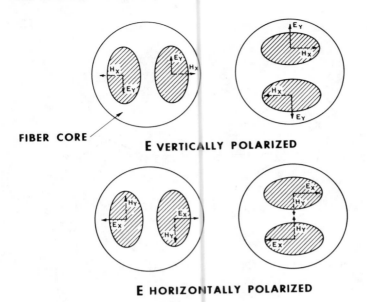

FIBER CORE

E VERTICALLY POLARIZED

E HORIZONTALLY POLARIZED

Figure 5-9 Four possible field distributions of LP_{11} mode.

the two possible polarization directions can be coupled with either a cos $l\phi$ or a sin $l\phi$ azimuthal dependence, four discrete mode patterns can be obtained from a single LP_{lm} label. Figure 5-9 illustrates four possible field distributions for the LP_{11} mode. We have previously noted that the LP_{lm} mode is formed from a linear combination of the $HE_{v+1,\mu}$ mode and the $EH_{v-1,\mu}$ mode, each of which has the possibility of a cos $l\phi$ or sin $l\phi$ dependence. Thus the new labeling system substitutes four LP mode patterns for four discrete HE and EH mode patterns, and each system forms a complete set.

5-11 TOTAL NUMBER OF MODES; PRINCIPAL MODE NUMBERS

It is often useful to be able to quickly estimate the total number of modes in a step-index fiber with a large V number. To develop this estimate we will approximate the characteristic equation (5-89) for tightly bound LP modes far from cutoff. Far from cutoff, $W = \gamma a$ becomes large, and the asymptotic approximation for the modified Hankel functions (Eq. (5-48)) for large values of their arguments can be used in the characteristic equation (5-89), that is, for large γ

$$\frac{H_{l-1}^{(1)}(jW)}{H_l^{(1)}(jW)} = \frac{\sqrt{2/j\pi W}\, e^{-\{j[(l-1)(\pi/2)+\pi/4]\}}e^{-W}}{\sqrt{2/j\pi W}\, e^{-\{j[l(\pi/2)+\pi/4]\}}e^{-W}} = j \qquad (5\text{-}92)$$

and the characteristic equation becomes

$$U \frac{J_{l-1}(U)}{J_l(U)} = -W \tag{5-93}$$

The limiting value $U = U_\infty$, which is reached when $W \to \infty$, is given as the root of the equation

$$J_l(U_\infty) = 0 \tag{5-94}$$

For very large values of V we obtain an approximate value for the total number of modes by estimating the number of roots of the equation

$$J_l(U_m) = 0 \tag{5-95}$$

where

$$U_m \le V$$

For large values of m an approximate formula for the roots of Eq. (5-95) is:[14]

$$U_m = (l + 2m - \tfrac{1}{2}) \frac{\pi}{2} \tag{5-96}$$

or approximately

$$U_m = (l + 2m) \frac{\pi}{2} \tag{5-97}$$

Referring to the mode-space diagram, Fig. 5-10, each point with integer coordinate values l and m represents one solution of Eq. (5-95) and is associated with one mode of a given polarization and ϕ dependence. Each point can be thought of as representing a square of unit area in the mode-space diagram (l-m plane). The area in this space thus represents the number of modes. For constant values of U_m, the integer values of l and m satisfy Eq. (5-97) and lie along lines parallel to the dashed line shown in Fig. 5-11. Since the largest value of U_m is V the boundary for the modes in the mode-space diagram can be obtained by

$$V = (l + 2m) \frac{\pi}{2} \tag{5-98}$$

From Fig. 5-11 we see that all of the values of l and m that are allowed by Eq. (5-98) lie inside the triangle formed by the two coordinate axes and the slanted solid line passing through the points $m_{max} = V/\pi$ and $l_{max} = 2V/\pi$.

The total number of modes in a fiber is four times the area of the triangle shown in Fig. 5-11 since each mode can appear in two mutually orthogonal polarizations and can have a cosine or sine ϕ dependence. The area of the triangle is $(V/\pi)^2$. The approximate total number of modes that can exist in a step-index fiber, for a given value of V, is therefore

$$N = \frac{4V^2}{\pi^2} \tag{5-99}$$

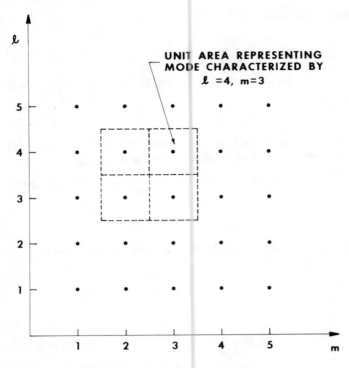

Figure 5-10 Mode-space diagram, each point represents a mode in the *l, m* plane.

Equation (5-97) suggests that it is possible to associate a single-mode number, called the principal mode number, with all the modes characterized by the integer

$$M = l + 2m \qquad (5\text{-}100)$$

The group of modes characterized by Eq. (5-100) form a degenerative mode group with the characteristic

$$\beta_M = \beta_{lm} \qquad (5\text{-}101)$$

and have common cutoff values in the region of

$$U = \frac{M\pi}{2} \qquad (5\text{-}102)$$

We can write an expression for the total number of modes in terms of the maximum principal mode number $M_{\max}$.

$$M_{\max} = l_{\max} + 2m_{\max}$$

$$M_{\max} = \frac{2V}{\pi} + \frac{2V}{\pi} = \frac{4V}{\pi} \qquad (5\text{-}103)$$

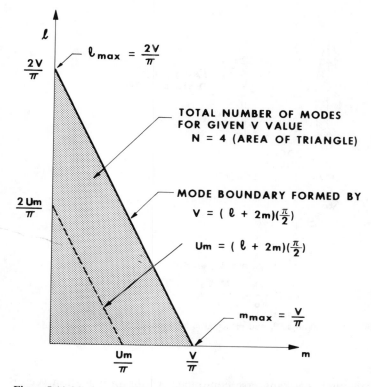

Figure 5-11 Mode-space diagram showing maximum boundary formed by $V = (l + 2m)\pi/2$.

Substituting Eq. (5-103) into (5-99) yields

$$N = \frac{M_{max}^2}{4} \tag{5-104}$$

In addition to being a convenient notational tool, the principal mode number M, can be related directly to the far-field angle of the radiation leaving a step-index fiber. The components of the propagation vector $\bar{k}$ which defines the propagation direction of a mode (i.e., its representative plane wave) can be written in terms of M as follows:

$$\kappa = \frac{U}{a} = \frac{M\pi}{2a} \tag{5-105}$$

$$\beta = \sqrt{k^2 - \kappa^2} = \sqrt{k^2 - \frac{M^2\pi^2}{4a^2}} \tag{5-106}$$

where

$$k^2 = n_1^2 k_0^2 = \kappa^2 + \beta^2 \tag{5-107}$$

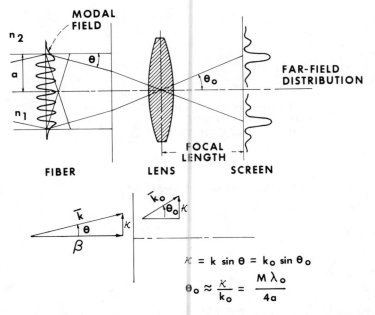

Figure 5-12 Relationship of far-field angle θ_0 and principal mode number, M.

Figure 5-12 illustrates that the transverse component of the propagation vector κ is conserved (by Snell's law) when the wave enters free space at the end of the waveguide, that is,

$$\kappa = k \sin \theta_1 = k_0 \sin \theta_0 \tag{5-108}$$

For weakly guiding fibers where the waves in the structure propagate at small angles to the axis, $\sin \theta \approx \theta$. Therefore in the far field (or the focal plane of the lens shown in Fig. 5-12) the wave will radiate into a cone of semiangle

$$\theta_0 = \frac{\kappa}{k_0} = \frac{(M\pi/2a)}{(2\pi/\lambda_0)} = \frac{M\lambda_0}{4a} \tag{5-109}$$

In the far field the angular concentration of the two far-field spots is about the directions $+\theta_0$ and $-\theta_0$. The propagation directions of neighboring mode groups (for example mode groups M and $M - 1$) differ by

$$\Delta\theta_0 = \frac{\lambda_0}{4a} \tag{5-110}$$

The mode groups thus form a partly overlapping sequence of spots in the far field, ordered according to principal mode number. Consequently the far-field distribution represents a direct image of the modal power distribution in a step-index fiber.[15]

5-12 POWER DISTRIBUTION IN A STEP-INDEX FIBER

In this section we will derive the distribution of the power that is carried by the guided modes in the core and in the cladding of a step-index fiber. By integrating the Poynting vector the amount of power contained in the core of the fiber is given by

$$P_{core} = \frac{1}{2} \int_0^{2\pi} \int_0^a r(E_x H_y^* - E_y H_x^*) \, dr \, d\phi \tag{5-111}$$

and the power in the cladding is given by

$$P_{clad} = \frac{1}{2} \int_0^{2\pi} \int_a^\infty r(E_x H_y^* - E_y H_x^*) \, dr \, d\phi \tag{5-112}$$

Using Eq. (5-81) to obtain E_y and H_x in the core and substituting into Eq. (5-111) yields

$$P_{core} = \frac{1}{2} \frac{A^2 n_1}{\eta_0 [J_l(U)]^2} \int_0^{2\pi} \int_0^a \cos^2 l\phi [J_l(\kappa r)]^2 \, dr \, d\phi \tag{5-113}$$

Integrating with respect to ϕ

$$P_{core} = \frac{\pi A^2 n_1}{2\eta_0 [J_l(U)]^2} \int_0^a [J_l(\kappa r)]^2 \, dr \tag{5-114}$$

and integrating with respect to r

$$P_{core} = \frac{\pi n_1 A^2 a^2}{4\eta_0 [J_l(U)]^2} \{[J_l(U)]^2 - J_{l-1}(U) J_{l+1}(U)\} \tag{5-115}$$

To obtain the power in the cladding, Eq. (5-82) is substituted into Eq. (5-112). Upon integration with respect to r and ϕ, P_{clad} becomes

$$P_{clad} = \frac{\pi n_2 A^2}{4\eta_0 [H_l^{(1)}(jW)]^2} \{H_{l+1}^{(1)}(jW) H_{l-1}^{(1)}(jW) - [H_l^{(1)}(jW)]^2\} \tag{5-116}$$

To simplify our notation, let

$$\alpha = \frac{[H_l^{(1)}(jW)]^2}{H_{l+1}^{(1)}(jW) H_{l-1}^{(1)}(jW)} \tag{5-117}$$

$$B = \frac{\pi n_2 A^2}{4\eta_0} \tag{5-118}$$

then

$$P_{clad} = B\left(\frac{1}{\alpha} - 1\right) \tag{5-119}$$

Using the characteristic equations (A4-24) and (A4-25) we can rewrite P_{core} as

$$P_{core} = B\left[1 + \left(\frac{W}{U}\right)^2 \frac{1}{\alpha}\right] \qquad (5\text{-}120)$$

The total power in the fiber is

$$P_{tot} = P_{core} + P_{clad} = \frac{B}{\alpha}\left[1 + \left(\frac{W}{U}\right)^2\right] \qquad (5\text{-}121)$$

and since $V^2 = U^2 + W^2$

$$P_{tot} = \frac{B}{\alpha}\left(\frac{V^2}{U^2}\right) \qquad (5\text{-}122)$$

To determine the fraction of the power in the core and cladding the following ratios are of interest

$$\frac{P_{core}}{P_{tot}} = \frac{B[1 + (W/U)^2 1/\alpha]}{B/\alpha[1 + (W/U)^2]} \qquad (5\text{-}123)$$

Using $W^2 = V^2 - U^2$ and simplifying yields

$$\frac{P_{core}}{P_{tot}} = 1 - \frac{U^2}{V^2}(1 - \alpha) \qquad (5\text{-}124)$$

and

$$\frac{P_{clad}}{P_{tot}} = \frac{U^2}{V^2}(1 - \alpha) \qquad (5\text{-}125)$$

An approximate expression for α can be written as[12]

$$\alpha \approx 1 - (W^2 + l^2 + 1)^{-1/2} \qquad (5\text{-}126)$$

For a mode close to cutoff, $W \ll 1$ and $U \approx V$

$$\alpha \approx 1 - \frac{1}{\sqrt{l^2 + 1}} \qquad (5\text{-}127)$$

$$\frac{P_{core}}{P_{tot}} \approx 1 - \frac{1}{\sqrt{l^2 + 1}} \qquad (5\text{-}128)$$

and

$$\frac{P_{clad}}{P_{tot}} \approx \frac{1}{\sqrt{l^2 + 1}} \qquad (5\text{-}129)$$

We see that for $l = 0$ (a meridional mode) the mode's power moves into the cladding at cutoff. For highly skew modes ($l \gg 0$), the power remains primarily concentrated in the core, even at cutoff. Figure 5-13 shows the ratio P_{clad}/P_{tot} for several modes as a function of the fiber V number.[12]

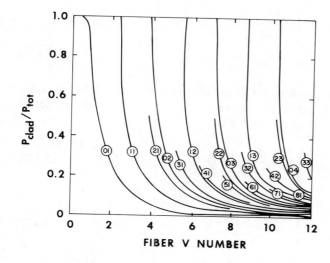

Figure 5-13 Plot of the ratio P_{clad}/P_{tot} vs. fiber V number.

5-13 DELAY DISTORTION IN A STEP-INDEX MULTIMODE FIBER

Pulse delay distortion in step-index multimode fibers is caused predominantly by the different group delays of the modes (modal delay distortion). This is the mechanism that limits the bandwidth of a step-index fiber and in turn the types of applications it can be used for in a communication system. We will now develop an expression for group delay τ_g in a step-index fiber. Group delay determines the transit time of a pulse traveling through the fiber of length L. Using Eq. (4-109)

$$\tau_g = L \frac{d\beta}{d\omega} = \frac{L}{c} \frac{d\beta}{dk_0} = \frac{L}{c} \left(\frac{V}{k_0}\right) \frac{d\beta}{dV} \qquad (5\text{-}130)$$

The equivalent forms of Eq. (5-130) are obtained from a knowledge of

$$k_0 = \frac{\omega}{c} \qquad (5\text{-}131)$$

$$\frac{d\beta}{d\omega} = \frac{d\beta}{dk_0} \frac{dk_0}{d\omega} \qquad (5\text{-}132)$$

$$\frac{dk_0}{d\omega} = \frac{1}{c} \qquad (5\text{-}133)$$

$$V^2 = (n_1^2 - n_2^2)a^2 k_0^2 \qquad (5\text{-}134)$$

$$\frac{d\beta}{dk_0} = \frac{d\beta}{dV} \frac{dV}{dk_0} \qquad (5\text{-}135)$$

and

$$\frac{dV}{dk_0} = \frac{V}{k_0} \tag{5-136}$$

We must now obtain an expression for β to substitute into the defining equation (5-130) for group delay. To be able to write β in a simple form let us define a normalized propagation constant b such that

$$b = \frac{W^2}{V^2} = \frac{(\gamma a)^2}{V^2} \tag{5-137}$$

or

$$\gamma = \frac{V\sqrt{b}}{a} \tag{5-138}$$

for weakly guiding fibers $\Delta = (n_1 - n_2)/n_2 \ll 1$, Eq. (5-134) can be written as

$$V = \sqrt{2}\,n_2\,k_0\,a\sqrt{\Delta} \tag{5-139}$$

and

$$\gamma = n_2\,k_0\,\sqrt{2b\Delta} \tag{5-140}$$

We can now write β in a simplified form

$$\beta^2 = n_2^2\,k_0^2 + \gamma^2 = n_2^2\,k_0^2(1 + 2\Delta b) \tag{5-141}$$

and

$$\beta \approx n_2\,k_0\,\sqrt{1 + 2\Delta b} \tag{5-142}$$

Using the expansion:

$$\sqrt{1 + x} \approx 1 + \frac{x}{2} \qquad \text{for} \qquad x \ll 1 \tag{5-143}$$

we obtain

$$\beta \approx n_2\,k_0(1 + \Delta b) \tag{5-144}$$

Substituting (5-144) into (5-130), the group delay becomes

$$\tau_g = \frac{L}{c}\frac{d(n_2\,k_0)}{dk_0} + \frac{L}{c}\frac{V}{k_0}\frac{d}{dV}(n_2\,k_0\,\Delta b) \tag{5-145}$$

We can separate the group delay given by Eq. (5-145) as follows:

$$\tau_g = \tau_c + \tau_m \tag{5-146}$$

where

$$\tau_c = \frac{L}{c} \frac{d(n_2 k_0)}{dk_0} \equiv \begin{array}{l} \text{modal delay characteristic} \\ \text{of material (chromatic dispersion)} \end{array} \tag{5-147}$$

$$\tau_m = \frac{L}{c} \frac{V}{k_0} \frac{d}{dV} (n_2 k_0 \Delta b) \equiv \text{modal waveguide delay} \tag{5-148}$$

τ_c is the group delay which is characteristic of the material of the fiber and is independent of a particular mode. Chromatic (material) dispersion is the mechanism that limits the bandwidth of single-mode fibers and is discussed in Sec. 5-8.

τ_m, the modal waveguide delay, is different for every mode. Consider a light pulse injected into and shared by many guided modes in the fiber. The light pulse will be split up into many pulses arriving at the end of the fiber at different times due to differences in the delays of the modes (modal delay distortion). We have encountered this phenomena before for the slab waveguide (Sec. 4-9). In order to obtain τ_m we must use the characteristic equation (5-89), and can ultimately obtain the derivative with respect to V required in Eq. (5-148). For the interested reader, this procedure is followed in App. 5, and the arrival time difference between the mode with the largest waveguide group delay and the least delay is calculated. The resulting expression from App. 5 is

$$\Delta \tau_m = \frac{L}{c} n_1 - n_2 \left(1 - \frac{\pi}{V}\right) \tag{5-149}$$

The difference $\Delta \tau_m$ in the arrival times of the leading and trailing edge of the resultant output pulse of the fiber is given by Eq. (5-149). For a typical step-index fiber with the following parameters

$$a = 25 \ \mu m$$

$$\Delta = 0.01$$

$$L = 1 \ km$$

$$\lambda_0 = 0.85 \ \mu m$$

$$V \approx 38$$

the modal pulse delay distortion $\Delta \tau_m \approx 45$ ns.

Pulse distortion in step-index multimode fibers is caused predominantly by different group delays of the modes. Modal delay distortion is the primary mechanism that limits the use of step-index fibers to relatively low-bandwidth systems (less than 100 MHz-km). The contribution to the total delay distortion due to chromatic dispersion ($\Delta \tau_c$) is much less than that due to modal delay distortion ($\Delta \tau_m$). If the system source were a GaAs light-emitting diode with a relative bandwidth of four percent the delay distortion due to chromatic dispersion would be less than 5 ns.

Example 5-3 Modal waveguide delay Let us calculate the modal waveguide delay for 1 km of the multimode step-index fiber in Example 5-1.

$$\Delta\tau_m = \frac{L}{c}\,(n_1 - n_2)\left(1 - \frac{\pi}{V}\right)$$

$$= \frac{1\ \text{km}}{3 \times 10^8\ \text{m/s}}\,(1.458 - 1.427)\left(1 - \frac{\pi}{100}\right)$$

$$= 100\ \text{ns}$$

REFERENCES

1. D. Marcuse: *Light Transmission Optics*, Van Nostrand Reinhold Co., New York, 1972.
2. J. E. Midwinter: *Optical Fibers for Transmission*, John Wiley and Sons, New York, 1979.
3. S. E. Miller and A. G. Chynoweth: *Optical Fiber Telecommunications*, Academic Press, New York, 1979.
4. E. Snitzer: "Cylindrical Dielectric Waveguide Modes," *JOSA*, **51**(5) May 1961.
5. E. Jahnke and P. Emde: *Table of Functions with Formulas and Curves*, Dover Publications, New York, 1945.
6. T. Kimura, M. Saruwatari, J. Yamada, S. Uehura, and T. Miyashita: "Optical Fiber (800 Mbit/sec) Transmission Experiment at 1.05 μm," *Appl. Opt.*, **17**: 2420, Aug. 1, 1978.
7. D. E. Gray: *American Institute of Physics Handbook*, McGraw-Hill Book Co., New York, 1972.
8. D. N. Payne and W. A. Gambling: "Zero Material Dispersion Optical Fibers," *Electron. Lett.*, **11**: 176–178 (1975).
9. A. Kawana, M. Kawachi, and T. Miyashuta: "Pulse Broadening in Long-Span Single Mode Fibers Around a Material-Dispersion Free Wavelength," *Opt. Lett.*, **2**(4), April 1978.
10. D. Gloge: "Dispersion in Weakly Guiding Fibers," *Appl. Opt.*, **10**(11), November 1971.
11. A. W. Snyder: "Asymptotic Expressions for Eigenfunctions and Eigenvalues of a Dielectric Optical Waveguide," *IEEE Trans. Microwave Theory Tech.*, **MTT-17**: 1130–1138, December 1969.
12. D. Gloge: "Weakly Guiding Fibers," *Appl. Opt.*, **10**: 2252–2258, October 1971.
13. D. Marcuse: *Theory of Dielectric Optical Waveguides*, Academic Press, New York, 1974.
14. M. Abnomovitz and I. A. Stegun: "Handbook of Mathematical Functions with Formulas, Graphs and Mathematical Tables," *Natl. Bur. Stand. U.S. Appl. Math. Ser.*, **55** (1965).
15. D. Gloge: "Optical Power Flow in Multimode Fibers," *BSTJ*, **51**(8), October 1972.

PROBLEMS

5-1 Starting with Eq. (3-25) for H_r in cylindrical coordinates, derive Eqs. (5-20) and (5-26) for H_r in the core and cladding of a step-index fiber.

5-2 Calculate the pulse-delay distortion for a 1-km single-mode fused-silica step-index guide if $\lambda_0 = 1.0\ \mu\text{m}$, $\Delta\lambda/\lambda = 0.12\%$, $V = 1.5$, $n_1 = 1.453$, $n_2 = 1.450$. Compare the pulse-delay distortion of the single-mode guide to the modal waveguide delay of a 1-km step-index multimode guide, $V = 38$, $n_1 = 1.453$, $n_2 = 1.438$.

5-3 Design a single-mode guide for operation at $\lambda = 1.3\ \mu\text{m}$ with a fused silica core ($n_1 = 1.458$). Specify n_2 and a for the guide. Will the guide still be single-mode if $\lambda = 0.82\ \mu\text{m}$? If not, how many modes will exist?

5-4 Calculate the V number and numerical aperture of a multimode guide if $n_1 = 1.450$, $\Delta = 1.3\%$, $\lambda_0 = 0.82$ μm and $a = 25$ μm. What happens to the number of modes in the guide if n_1 increases? If n_1 decreases? If λ_0 increases? If λ_0 decreases?

5-5 Obtain the characteristic equation for the step-index fiber equation (5-36) by expanding the determinant (5-35).

5-6 Starting with Eq. (5-36) derive the cutoff conditions for the $HE_{1\mu}$ and $EH_{1\mu}$ modes.

5-7 Identify which modes exist and specify the cutoff parameter ($\kappa_c a$) for each mode in a step-index fiber with $V = 5.5$.

5-8 Calculate the material dispersion component of delay distortion for $\lambda_0 = 0.8$, 0.9, 1.3, and 1.5 μm for a fused silica single-mode fiber. Assume in each case the source linewidth $\Delta\lambda = 3$ nm and the guide length $L = 1$ km.

5-9 Starting with Eqs. (5-81) and (5-82), derive Eq. (5-89), the characteristic equation for the LP modes. State the assumptions used in this analysis.

5-10 For a step-index fiber with $V = 20$, $\lambda = 0.82$ μm and $a = 25$ μm, calculate the principal mode number M, the number of propagating modes, the semiangle of radiation θ_0, and the difference in propagation direction of two neighboring mode groups $\Delta\theta_0$.

5-11 Calculate the percentage of power in the core and in the cladding for an LP_{11} mode with $\kappa_c a = 2.400$.

SIX

THE GRADED-INDEX FIBER

6-1 INTRODUCTION

The graded-index fiber, because of its relatively large bandwidth and core diameter, is the type of fiber that is used in a large majority of the fiber optic telecommunication systems in existence today. The step-index fiber bandwidth is severely limited (less than 100 MHz-km) due to modal delay distortion. The grading of the refractive index profile of a fiber core has the effect of increasing the bandwidth of a fiber (typically 300 MHz-km to 3 GHz-km) by equalizing the group delays of the various propagating mode groups. In this chapter the graded-index fiber is analyzed using the Wentzel, Kramers, Brillouin, and Jefferies (WKBJ) approximation technique. Wave number diagrams are used to illustrate the general propagation characteristics of the fiber. In addition a simple ray optics picture of the graded-index fiber will be given and expressions describing pulse-delay distortion will be obtained.

6-2 BASIC ASSUMPTIONS AND ANALYSIS PROCEDURES; THE GRADED-INDEX FIBER

Let us consider a multimode fiber with an inhomogeneous core as shown in Fig. 6-1. We will analyze this fiber by following the same general approach that was used for the step-index fiber in Chap. 5. We are interested in obtaining the modes and, specifically, information related to the propagation constants associated with these modes in the guide. From our study of the slab waveguide and

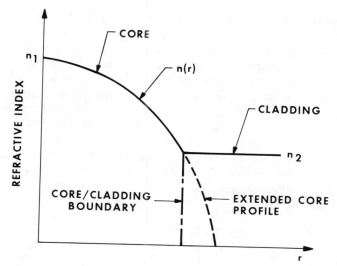

Figure 6-1 Refractive-index profile of graded-index fiber.

step-index fiber, we know that the propagation constant β of a bound mode must fall within the range

$$n_1 k_0 \geq \beta \geq n_2 k_0 \tag{6-1}$$

To find β, we must solve the wave equation for a cylindrical structure having the refractive index profile $n(r)$. The wave equation (5-9) is rewritten below showing the variation of the refractive index with r

$$\frac{d^2 F(r)}{dr^2} + \frac{1}{r}\frac{dF(r)}{dr} + \left[k^2(r) - \beta^2 - \frac{v^2}{r^2} \right] F(r) = 0 \tag{6-2}$$

where

$$k(r) = \frac{2\pi}{\lambda_0} n(r) = k_0 n(r) \tag{6-3}$$

and

$$\kappa^2 = k^2(r) - \beta^2 \tag{6-4}$$

The solution of the wave equation leads to a "characteristic equation" for the guide which relates β to k. If $n(r)$ is constructed of two different functions in the core and cladding of the guide, the field-matching boundary conditions at $r = a$ will result in an extremely complicated characteristic equation. To simplify our analysis we could assume that the refractive index continues to decrease in the cladding following the core profile shown by the dashed curve in Fig. 6-1. If we computed the propagation constants of the modes on this basis we would use Eq. (6-1) to determine which of these modes are bound when the profile has a minimum index n_2. This approach misrepresents a certain fraction of the modes in the guide that have substantial power in the region beyond $r = a$. For a waveguide with a parabolic refractive index profile, the approach leads to mode solutions in the guide in terms of Laguerre–Gauss functions.[1] For other profiles, we must resort to a ray optics method of analysis or equivalently follow the procedure developed in this text of obtaining an approximate mode solution of the wave equation (6-2) using the WKBJ method. The WKBJ approach, named after Wentzel, Kramers, Brillouin, and Jefferies,[2] is a geometrical optics approximation that works whenenever the refractive index of the fiber varies only slightly over distances on the order of the optical wavelength. Specifically the following simplifying assumptions will be made about the multimode fibers we will analyze:

1. The refractive index profile is circularly symmetric.
2. The fiber is a multimode fiber with a large core diameter measuring 50 wavelengths or more.
3. The total index change within the guiding core region is small ($\Delta \ll 1$), so that modes can be considered transverse electromagnetic (equivalent to the LP mode assumption made in Chap. 5).
4. Index variations are very small over distances of a wavelength so that the conditions of geometric optics (or the zeroth order of the WKBJ method) apply.

6-3 WKBJ ANALYSIS OF THE GRADED-INDEX FIBER

Using the technique of separation of variables we have shown in Chap. 5 that the z component of the electric field can be expressed as follows:

$$E = AF(r)\begin{pmatrix} \cos v\phi \\ \sin v\phi \end{pmatrix} e^{-j\beta z} \tag{6-5}$$

where $F(r)$ is the radial variation of the field that satisfies Eq. (6-2). The general approach of the WKBJ method is to recognize that if the refractive index of the core is a constant or is slowly varying with r (the assumption made for the graded index fibers we are analyzing), the general solution $F(r)$ can be written as the superposition of nonuniform plane waves of the form

$$F(r) = e^{jk_0 S(r)} \tag{6-6}$$

We will now substitute Eq. (6-6) into Bessel's equation (6-2), observing that

$$\frac{dF(r)}{dr} = jk_0 e^{jk_0 S(r)} \frac{dS(r)}{dr} \tag{6-7}$$

$$\frac{d^2 F(r)}{dr^2} = jk_0 \frac{d^2 S(r)}{dr^2} e^{jk_0 S(r)} - k_0^2 \left[\frac{dS(r)}{dr}\right]^2 e^{jk_0 S(r)} \tag{6-8}$$

Substituting Eqs. (6-6) to (6-8) into (6-2) yields

$$jk_0 \frac{d^2 S(r)}{dr^2} - k_0^2 \left[\frac{dS(r)}{dr} \right]^2 + \frac{jk_0}{r} \frac{dS(r)}{dr} + \left[k^2(r) - \beta^2 - \frac{v^2}{r^2} \right] = 0 \qquad (6\text{-}9)$$

If the index variation with r is gradual so that $S(r)$ is nearly constant over a distance of one wavelength, $S(r)$ can be expanded in a power series in terms of k_0^{-1}, where k_0^{-1} is proportional to the free space wavelength $\lambda_0 (\lambda_0 = 2\pi/k_0)$. Let

$$S(r) = S_0(r) + \frac{1}{k_0} S_1(r) + \frac{1}{k_0^2} S_2(r) + \cdots \qquad (6\text{-}10)$$

Using the first two terms of this series and collecting the derivatives needed for substitution back into Eq. (6-9) results in the following terms:

$$\frac{dS(r)}{dr} = \frac{dS_0}{dr} + \frac{1}{k_0} \frac{dS_1}{dr} \qquad (6\text{-}11)$$

$$\left[\frac{dS(r)}{dr} \right]^2 = \left(\frac{dS_0}{dr} \right)^2 + \frac{1}{k_0^2} \left(\frac{dS_1}{dr} \right)^2 + \frac{2}{k_0} \frac{dS_0}{dr} \frac{dS_1}{dr} \qquad (6\text{-}12)$$

and

$$\frac{d^2 S(r)}{dr^2} = \frac{d^2 S_0}{dr^2} + \frac{1}{k_0} \frac{d^2 S_1}{dr^2} \qquad (6\text{-}13)$$

Using Eqs. (6-11) to (6-13) in Eq. (6-9) yields

$$jk_0 \frac{d^2 S_0}{dr^2} + j \frac{d^2 S_1}{dr^2} - k_0^2 \left(\frac{dS_0}{dr} \right)^2 - \left(\frac{dS_1}{dr} \right)^2 - 2k_0 \frac{dS_0}{dr} \frac{dS_1}{dr}$$

$$+ j \frac{k_0}{r} \frac{dS_0}{dr} + \frac{j}{r} \frac{dS_1}{dr} + \left[k^2(r) - \beta^2 - \frac{v^2}{r^2} \right] = 0 \quad (6\text{-}14)$$

If we equate equal powers of k_0 in Eq. (6-14) we obtain the following two equations:

$$-\left(\frac{dS_0}{dr} \right)^2 k_0^2 + \left[k^2(r) - \beta^2 - \frac{v^2}{r^2} \right] = 0 \qquad (6\text{-}15)$$

and

$$jk_0 \frac{d^2 S_0}{dr^2} - 2k_0 \frac{dS_0}{dr} \frac{dS_1}{dr} + j \frac{k_0}{r} \frac{dS_0}{dr} = 0 \qquad (6\text{-}16)$$

To obtain a physical understanding of how waves (rays) propagate in a graded-index guide, we are primarily concerned with understanding the behavior of the propagation constants of the modes. Solving Eq. (6-15) for $S_0(r)$ (zero-order WKBJ approximation) will provide the required information about the propagation constants. If we were interested in obtaining a complete field description of the modes in the guide, the solution of Eq. (6-16) to obtain $S_1(r)$ would also be required.

6-4 PROPAGATION CONSTANTS
IN A GRADED-INDEX FIBER

To obtain information about the modes in a graded-index fiber let us now solve
Eq. (6-15) for $S_0(r)$. Taking the square root of Eq. (6-15) we obtain

$$\frac{dS_0}{dr} = \pm \frac{1}{k_0} \left[k^2(r) - \beta^2 - \frac{v^2}{r^2} \right]^{1/2} \qquad (6\text{-}17)$$

Now integrating with respect to r yields

$$S_0(r) = \pm \frac{1}{k_0} \int \left[k^2(r) - \beta^2 - \frac{v^2}{r^2} \right]^{1/2} dr \qquad (6\text{-}18)$$

A knowledge of $S_0(r)$ will yield, as a zero-order WKBJ approximation, that
$F(r)$ from Eq. (6-6) is

$$F(r) = e^{jk_0 S_0(r)} \qquad (6\text{-}19)$$

From Eq. (6-19), for a propagating mode to exist, $S_0(r)$ must be real. This
requires that the integrand in Eq. (6-18) is real or that

$$k^2(r) - \beta^2 - \frac{v^2}{r^2} > 0 \qquad \text{(positive quantity)} \qquad (6\text{-}20)$$

To obtain a physical interpretation of bound modes, Eq. (6-20) will be
analyzed graphically. Figure 6-2a illustrates $k^2(r)$ and v^2/r^2 as a function of the
radius r. The solid curve in Fig. 6-2b shows $k^2(r) - v^2/r^2$ as a function of r. For
a fixed value of β there exists two values of r (r_1 and r_2) at which

$$k^2(r) - \frac{v^2}{r^2} - \beta^2 = 0 \qquad (6\text{-}21)$$

It is between these two radii that the ray associated with the assumed plane
wave solution is constrained to move. Outside of these two values of r, called
the turning points (or caustics), $S_0(r)$ becomes imaginary leading to decaying
fields.

For a fixed value of β, as v increases, the region between the two turning
points becomes narrower. As v is further increased a point will be reached
where the turning points merge. Beyond this point the wave is no longer bound.
The propagation conditions of a wave depend upon the values of both β and v.
For a fixed value of v, modes far from cutoff have large β values and correspondingly more closely spaced turning points. In general, a bound hybrid
mode in a graded-indexed optical fiber can be pictorially represented by a skew
ray spiraling down the fiber between the two turning points or caustics as
shown in Fig. 6-3. Both inside ($r < r_1$) and outside ($r > r_2$) the turning points,
the field corresponding to the hybrid mode decays.

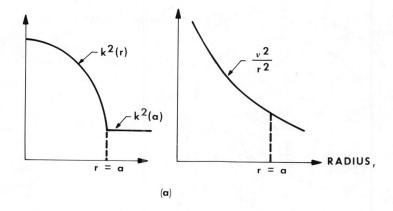

(a)

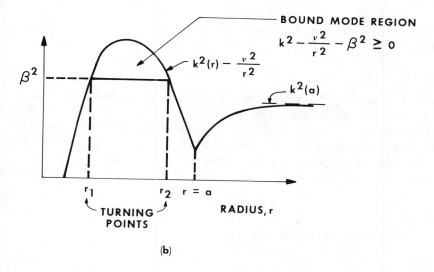

(b)

Figure 6-2 Wave-number diagram for graded-index fiber (hybrid modes).

A special class of modes, that are analogous to the TE and TM modes in the step-index fiber, exist for $v = 0$. These modes correspond to meridional rays (rays that go through the center of the fiber). Figure 6-4 illustrates the wave number diagram for meridional rays in a graded-index fiber. Meridional rays have only one turning point at $r = r_1$.

To complete our wave number diagram picture of rays propagating in a fiber let us consider the step-index fiber as a special case of the graded-index fiber. Figure 6-5a shows k^2 amd v^2/r^2 as a function of r for a step-index fiber.

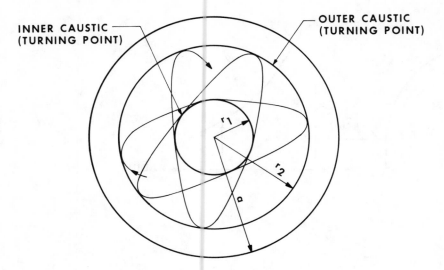

Figure 6-3 Ray projection showing caustics in graded-index fiber.

Figure 6-5*b* is the wave number diagram for the hybrid modes ($v \neq 0$) in a step-index fiber. Notice the rays follow straight-line trajectories in the core between $r = r_1$ and $r = a$, the core-cladding boundary. For meridional rays in a step-index fiber as shown in Fig. 6-5*c* the ray paths pass through the center of the fiber and extend to the core-cladding interface at $r = a$.

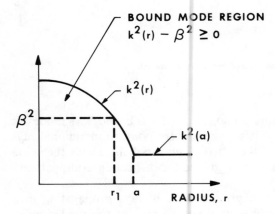

Figure 6-4 Wave-number diagram for graded-index fiber (meridional modes).

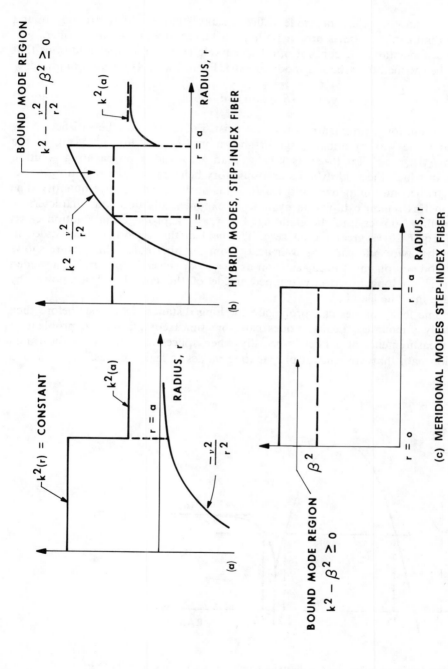

Figure 6-5 Wave-number diagrams for step-index fiber.

127

6-5 LEAKY MODES IN A GRADED-INDEX FIBER

There is another class of mode called "leaky" modes[3] that are not bound modes but can sometimes propagate long distances in a graded-index fiber.

To understand the concept of a leaky mode let us recall the conditions that must be satisfied for a bound mode to exist. From Eq. (6-1) for a bound mode

$$\beta \geq k(a) = n_2 k_0 \tag{6-22}$$

In addition, for a propagating mode to exist, Eq. (6-20) must be satisfied. Now consider the wave number diagram shown in Fig. 6-6. For $\beta_l < k(a)$, in the region $r_1 < r < r_2$ Eq. (6-20) is greater than zero and a propagating solution exists in which the field exhibits an oscillatory behavior. In the region $r_2 < r < r_3$, $S_0(r)$ becomes imaginary and Eq. (6-20) is no longer a positive quantity. The field in this region exhibits an evanescent exponentially decaying characteristic "tunneling" power into the cladding. For $r > r_3$ a propagating solution exists since Eq. (6-20) is greater than zero. The field in this region resumes its oscillatory behavior and carries power away from the fiber core. This picture shows that mode cutoff must occur as soon as $\beta = n_2 k_0$ since, for $\beta < n_2 k_0$, a guided mode is no longer perfectly trapped inside of the core but loses power by leakage into the cladding.

Some leaky modes can propagate for long distances in a fiber before they are fully attenuated. Leaky modes can sometimes complicate the problem of loss measurements of a fiber, especially when splices are present in the transmission path that can convert propagating modes to leaky modes.

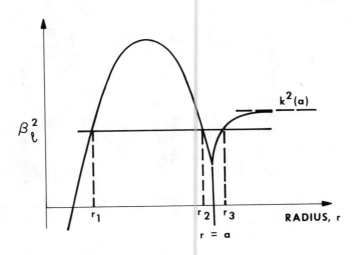

Figure 6-6 Wave-number diagram illustrating leaky modes in a graded-index fiber.

6-6 TOTAL NUMBER OF MODES IN A GRADED-INDEX FIBER

We have pictured a bound hybrid mode in a graded-index fiber by a ray optics equivalent of a skew ray spiraling down a fiber between two turning points at r_1 and r_2. Both inside $(r < r_1)$ and outside $(r > r_1)$ the turning points, the field corresponding to the hybrid mode decays. In Sec. 4-8, for the slab waveguide, we developed the concept of coherent phase reinforcement of rays as the physical criterion that is equivalent to the existence of a mode in the guide. If we use an analogous argument for the graded-index fiber we require that for the bound mode solutions the phase $k_0 S_0(r)$ evaluated between the turning points must be a multiple of π, that is,

$$\mu\pi = \int_{r_1}^{r_2} \left[k^2(r) - \beta^2 - \frac{v^2}{r^2} \right]^{1/2} dr \qquad (6\text{-}23)$$

where $\mu = 0, 1, 2, \ldots$ is the radial mode number which counts the number of half periods between the turning points. The guided modes can therefore be labeled by v and μ, the azimuthal and radial mode numbers. Each pair of integers μ and v characterizes a discrete mode pattern; and just as with the LP modes of the step-index guide, each mode can appear in two mutually orthogonal polarizations and can have a sine or cosine ϕ dependence. Following the procedure developed in Sec. 5-11, a mode space diagram (v-μ plane) shown in Fig. 6-7 can be drawn where the area in this space represents the number of

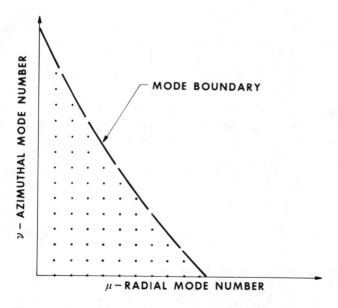

Figure 6-7 Mode-space diagram for graded-index fiber.

modes in the guide. The mode boundary defined by the function $\mu = F(v)$ separates the guided modes from the leaky and radiation modes. We can express the total number of guided modes by the formula[4]

$$N = 4 \int_0^{v_{max}} F(v) \, dv \tag{6-24}$$

because each representation point (representing a group of four degenerate modes) occupies an element of unit area in the v, μ space. For the purpose of calculating the number of modes, let us consider the limits of μ, v, and β. From Eq. (6-22) for a bound mode the minimum value of β which defines mode cutoff is

$$\beta_c = n_2 k_0 \tag{6-25}$$

The largest value of v occurs for $\beta = \beta_c$ and $\mu = 0$. Alternately, μ is largest for $\beta = \beta_c$ and $v = 0$. From Eq. (6-23), μ can be written as a function of v as

$$\mu = F(v) = \frac{1}{\pi} \int_{r_1(v)}^{r_2(v)} \left[k^2(r) - \beta_c^2 - \frac{v^2}{r^2} \right]^{1/2} dr \tag{6-26}$$

Substituting Eq. (6-26) into (6-24) yields the total number of modes

$$N = \frac{4}{\pi} \int_0^{v_{max}} \int_{r_1(v)}^{r_2(v)} \left[k^2(r) - \beta_c^2 - \frac{v^2}{r^2} \right] dr \, dv \tag{6-27}$$

Since v_{max} occurs when $\mu = 0$, from Eq. (6-26)

$$v_{max} = r[k^2(r) - \beta_c^2]^{1/2} \tag{6-28}$$

Equation (6-27) becomes, after changing the order of integration,

$$N = \frac{4}{\pi} \int_0^a \int_0^{r(k^2 - \beta_c^2)^{1/2}} \left[k^2(r) - \beta_c^2 - \frac{v^2}{r^2} \right]^{1/2} dv \, dr \tag{6-29}$$

When the turning points range from $r = 0$ ($v = 0$ corresponds to meridional ray) to $r = a$ where the refractive index $n(r)$ reaches the cladding value n_2. Integrating Eq. (6-29) with respect to v by using the integral of the form[5]

$$\int \sqrt{a^2 - x^2} \, dx = \frac{1}{2} \left(x \sqrt{a^2 - x^2} + a^2 \sin^{-1} \frac{x}{a} \right) \tag{6-30}$$

yields

$$N = \int_0^a [k^2(r) - \beta_c^2] r \, dr \tag{6-31}$$

Since $k(r) = n(r) k_0$ and $\beta_c = n_2 k_0$, Eq. (6-31) can be written as

$$N = k_0^2 \int_0^a [n^2(r) - n_2^2] r \, dr \tag{6-32}$$

For a known core refractive index profile $n(r)$, the total number of possible bound propagating modes that the guide can support is calculated by Eq. (6-32). Let us now write Eq. (6-31) in a different form so that we can later develop a concept analogous to the principle mode number (see Sec. 5-11) for the WKBJ solution.

$$m(\beta) = \int_0^{r_2} [k^2(r) - \beta^2] r \, dr \qquad (6\text{-}33)$$

where $m(\beta)$ is the number of bound modes having a propagation constant greater than β. The radius r_2, at which $k(r) = \beta$, defines the upper limit of the integration in Eq. (6-33).

6-7 POWER LAW PROFILES

To proceed farther in our analysis of the graded-index fiber we will consider the general class of refractive index profile classified by the two-parameter system defined by[6]

$$n(r) = \begin{cases} n_1 \left[1 - 2\Delta \left(\dfrac{r}{a} \right)^\alpha \right]^{1/2} & \text{for} \quad r < a \\ n_1 (1 - 2\Delta)^{1/2} & \text{for} \quad r > a \end{cases} \qquad (6\text{-}34)$$

and

$$\Delta = \frac{n_1^2 - n_2^2}{2n_1^2} = \frac{(n_1 - n_2)(n_1 + n_2)}{2n_1^2} \qquad (6\text{-}35)$$

where α is a parameter that describes the shape of the profile

Δ is a measure of the index difference between the peak refractive index n_1 at the center of the core and n_2, the cladding refractive index.

For the weakly guiding fibers that we are considering $\Delta \ll 1$ and $n_1 \approx n_2$. Equation (6-35) can be simplified and written as

$$\Delta \approx \frac{n_1 - n_2}{n_1} \qquad (6\text{-}36)$$

Figure 6-8 is a plot of Eq. (6-34) for α values ranging from 1 to ∞.

N, the total number of modes in the fiber and $m(\beta)$, the number of bound modes having a propagation constant greater than β, can be calculated using the power-law profile described by Eq. (6-34). These parameters have been derived in App. 6 and the following results obtained:

$$N = a^2 \Delta k_0^2 n_1^2 \left(\frac{\alpha}{\alpha + 2} \right) \qquad (6\text{-}37)$$

$$m(\beta) = N \left(\frac{n_1^2 k_0^2 - \beta^2}{2\Delta n_1^2 k_0^2} \right)^{(\alpha + 2)/\alpha} \qquad (6\text{-}38)$$

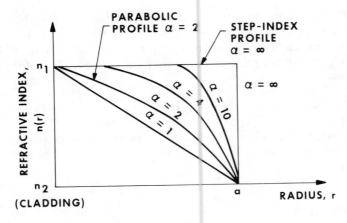

Figure 6-8 Power-law refractive-index profile.

Using Eq. (6-37) we can show that the total number of modes in a graded-index wave guide with a parabolic profile ($\alpha = 2$) is half the number that exist in a step-index ($\alpha = \infty$) wave guide, that is,

$$N_{\text{parabolic}} = \frac{N_{\text{step}}}{2} \qquad (6\text{-}39)$$

If we use the definition for the V number of the guide developed in Chap. 5, we can write the total number of modes in a graded-index fiber from Eq. (5-64) as follows:

$$V = k_0\, a\, \sqrt{n_1^2 - n_2^2} \approx k_0\, an_1\sqrt{2\Delta} \qquad (6\text{-}40)$$

Substituting Eq. (6-40) into (6-37) we obtain

$$N = \frac{V^2}{2}\left(\frac{\alpha}{\alpha + 2}\right) \qquad (6\text{-}41)$$

Example 6-1 Number of modes in a graded-index and step-index fiber Given the following fiber parameters

$$a = 25 \ \mu m$$

$$\Delta = 0.013$$

$$\lambda_0 = 0.82 \ \mu m$$

$$n_1 = 1.453$$

let us calculate the total number of modes in the fiber if

1. The fiber has a parabolic-index profile ($\alpha = 2$)
2. The fiber has a step-index profile

The total number of modes in the fiber is given by Eq. (6-37).

$$N = a^2 \Delta k_0^2 n_1^2 \left(\frac{\alpha}{\alpha + 2} \right)$$

For $\alpha = 2$

$$N = 504 \text{ modes}$$

For a step-index profile $N_{\text{parabolic}} = N_{\text{step}}/2$

$$N_{\text{step}} = 1008 \text{ modes}$$

6-8 NEAR- AND FAR-FIELD POWER DISTRIBUTIONS IN A GRADED-INDEX FIBER

In this section we will obtain expressions for the near- and far-field power distributions at the output end face of a graded-index fiber excited at its input end by a lambertian (diffuse) source. For this type of source the incident power per unit solid angle at any point in the core cross section is constant (all modes are excited uniformly). To compute the power accepted by the fiber we have to know the solid angle of acceptance at any point on the core. To calculate this angle consider the wave vector diagram shown in Fig. 6-9

$$\cos \theta(r) = \frac{\beta}{k(r)} \tag{6-42}$$

The maximum angle θ_c results when $\beta = \beta_c = n_2 k_0$. Therefore

$$\cos \theta_c(r) = \frac{\beta_c}{k(r)} = \frac{n_2 k_0}{n(r) k_0} = \frac{n_2}{n(r)} \tag{6-43}$$

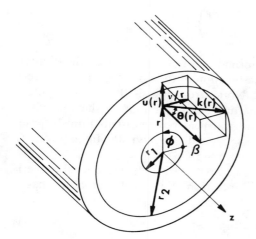

Figure 6-9 Wave-vector diagram in the propagating region of a graded-index multimode fiber.

if we define the local numerical aperture on a point on the fiber front face as

$$NA(r) = n(r) \sin \theta_c(r) = n(r)(1 - \cos^2 \theta_c)^{1/2} \qquad (6\text{-}44)$$

From Eq. (6-43) the local numerical aperture becomes

$$NA(r) = [n^2(r) - n_2^2]^{1/2} \qquad (6\text{-}45)$$

The normalized power accepted at r relative to the power accepted at $r = 0$ can be written as[6-8]

$$\frac{p(r)}{p(0)} = \frac{[NA(r)]^2}{[NA(0)]^2} \qquad (6\text{-}46)$$

If we assume an ideal fiber without loss, mode mixing, or leaky mode excitation, the same power distribution described by Eq. (6-46) should hold at the fiber output end face. Using the power-law profiles the local numerical aperture in the core of the fiber can be obtained by substituting Eq. (6-34) into (6-45)

$$NA(r) = \left\{ n_1^2 \left[1 - 2\Delta \left(\frac{r}{a} \right)^\alpha \right] - n_2^2 \right\}^{1/2} \qquad (6\text{-}47)$$

From Eq. (6-35)

$$n_1^2 - n_2^2 = 2n_1^2 \Delta \qquad (6\text{-}48)$$

Substituting Eq. (6-48) into (6-47) yields

$$NA(r) = n_1 \sqrt{2\Delta} \left[1 - \left(\frac{r}{a} \right)^\alpha \right]^{1/2} \qquad (6\text{-}49)$$

and the near-field power $p(r)$ becomes

$$p(r) = p(0) \left[1 - \left(\frac{r}{a} \right)^\alpha \right] \qquad (6\text{-}50)$$

Using Eq. (6-50) a plot of the normalized near-field power distribution $p(r)/p(0)$ (see Fig. 6-10) can be made as a function of the fiber radius for different values of the profile shape parameter α. Notice from Fig. 6-10 that α can potentially be measured by launching a lambertian distribution into a short length of wave guide and measuring the emergent near-field power distribution. In practice a leaky mode-correction term must be added to Eq. (6-50) to properly obtain α from the measured near-field distribution.[7,9]

To calculate the far-field pattern, let us first consider how the local numerical aperture $NA(r)$ varies with radius. Note from Eq. (6-45) that $NA(r)$ has a maximum value at $r = 0$

$$NA(0) = \sqrt{n_1^2 - n_2^2} \qquad (6\text{-}51)$$

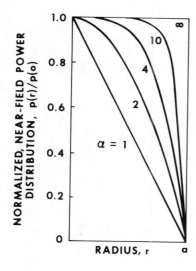

Figure 6-10 Normalized near-field power distribution in the core of a multimode graded-index fiber.

The local numerical aperture decreases with r to zero at $r = a$

$$NA(a) = 0 \tag{6-52}$$

For the lambertian source we have assumed every incremental area of the core cross section at the fiber end uniformly illuminates its cone of acceptance. For this reason, all areas that have a numerical aperture $NA(r) \geq \sin \theta$ contribute equally to the far-field power at θ and, as shown in Fig. 6-11,

$$\frac{P(\theta_1)}{P(\theta_2)} = \frac{\pi r_1^2}{\pi r_2^2} = \frac{r_1^2}{r_2^2} \tag{6-53}$$

The areas contributing to $P(\theta)$ are within a circle whose radius is obtained by solving Eq. (6-47) for r with $NA(r) = \sin \theta$.

$$r = a\left(1 - \frac{\sin^2 \theta}{2\Delta n_1^2}\right)^{1/\alpha} \tag{6-54}$$

Normalizing the power with respect to $\theta = 0$ at $r = a$, Eq. (6-53) becomes

$$\frac{P(\theta)}{P(0)} = \frac{a^2[1 - (\sin^2 \theta/2\Delta n_1^2)]^{2/\alpha}}{a^2}$$

or

$$\frac{P(\theta)}{P(0)} = \left(1 - \frac{\sin^2 \theta}{2\Delta n_1^2}\right)^{2/\alpha} \tag{6-55}$$

Figure 6-12 is a plot of Eq. (6-55) showing the normalized far-field power distribution as a function of $\sin \theta/\sqrt{2\Delta}\,n_1$. Once α is determined from the near-field pattern the far-field pattern can be used to obtain $\sin \theta_{max} = 2\Delta n_1^2$. Where θ_{max} is the maximum angle the propagation vector $\bar{k}$ can make with respect to the z axis and still be accepted by the waveguide.

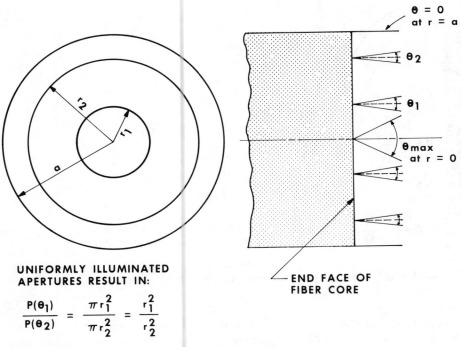

UNIFORMLY ILLUMINATED
APERTURES RESULT IN:

$$\frac{P(\theta_1)}{P(\theta_2)} = \frac{\pi r_1^2}{\pi r_2^2} = \frac{r_1^2}{r_2^2}$$

Figure 6-11 Geometry for calculating far-field power distribution.

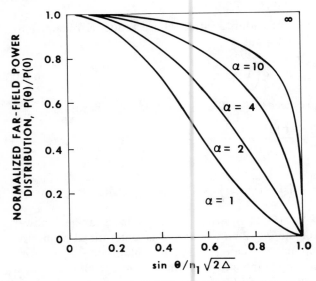

Figure 6-12 Normalized far-field power distribution of a multimode graded-index fiber.

As shown in Sec. 5-11, for the step-index guide ($\alpha = \infty$) there is a perfect correspondence between the mode angle and mode number. The far-field pattern from a step-index waveguide therefore corresponds exactly to the mode spectrum of the guide. For any other value of α, however, the mode angle and mode number are not linearly related. That is, in a graded-index guide no single angle uniquely characterizes a mode.

6-9 DELAY DISTORTION IN A MULTIMODE GRADED-INDEX FIBER

We have observed in our analysis of the step-index fiber (Sec. 5-13) that the transit times of the modes in a multimode optical fiber are different. Differential modal delay is the primary cause of pulse distortion in a highly multimoded step-index fiber and severely limits its bandwidth. The modal transit times of a fiber can be equalized to a good approximation by grading its core-refractive index profile with a near-parabolic profile. To understand the causes of delay distortion in a graded-index fiber let us first analyze the group delay for a given mode of a fiber whose refractive index is described by the power-law profile given by Eq. (6-34). To obtain the group delay of a given mode we will calculate

$$\tau_g = \frac{L}{c} \frac{d\beta}{dk_0} \tag{6-56}$$

From Eq. (6-38) we can obtain a simple expression for β for the mth mode group as follows:

$$\frac{n_1^2 k_0^2 - \beta^2}{2\Delta n_1^2 k_0^2} = \left(\frac{m}{N}\right)^{\alpha/(\alpha+2)} \tag{6-57}$$

Solving for β

$$\beta = n_1 k_0 \left[1 - \left(\frac{m}{N}\right)^{\alpha/(\alpha+2)} (2\Delta)\right]^{1/2} \tag{6-58}$$

where N is the total number of modes in the fiber (Eq. (6-37)). m counts the number of modes with propagation constant β in the range

$$n_1 k_0 \geq \beta \geq \beta_m \tag{6-59}$$

To obtain the group delay of a mode we must differentiate Eq. (6-58) with respect to k_0 and substitute the results into Eq. (6-56). Obtaining $d\beta/dk_0$ is a tedious process since Δ, n_1, and N are all functions of k_0. After much algebra the delay time τ_g of a mode is[10]

$$\tau_{g_m} = \frac{L N_{g1}}{c} \left[1 + \Delta\left(\frac{\alpha - 2 - \varepsilon}{\alpha + 2}\right)\left(\frac{m}{N}\right)^{\alpha/(\alpha+2)}\right.$$

$$\left. + \frac{\Delta^2}{2} \frac{(3\alpha - 2 - 2\varepsilon)}{\alpha + 2} \left(\frac{m}{N}\right)^{2\alpha/(\alpha+2)}\right] + 0(\Delta^3) \tag{6-60}$$

where

$$\varepsilon = \frac{-2n_1}{N_{g_1}} \left(\frac{\lambda_0}{\Delta}\right)\left(\frac{d\Delta}{d\lambda_0}\right) \tag{6-61}$$

and

$$N_{g_1} = n_1 - \lambda_0 \frac{dn_1}{d\lambda_0} \tag{6-62}$$

N_{g_1} is the group index associated with the peak refractive index at the center of the core n_1. Notice in Eq. (6-60) that the delay differences among the modes would vanish, at least to first order in Δ, when

$$\alpha = \alpha_0 = 2 - \frac{2n_1}{N_{g_1}} \left(\frac{\lambda_0}{\Delta}\right)\left(\frac{d\Delta}{d\lambda_0}\right) \tag{6-63}$$

This optimal profile shape parameter α_0 is a function of the variation of Δ with λ_0. This material effect is often referred to as profile dispersion.[11] Figure 6-13 shows how α_0 varies for two different core glass dopant materials as a function of λ_0.[12] For binary compound materials such as GeO_2-SiO_2 or P_2O_5-SiO_2 where α_0 is a strong function of wavelength, a fiber designed for high bandwidth at one wavelength may not be optimum for operation at a second wavelength. Thus, a fiber designed to operate at 0.85 μm wavelength with a GaAs laser will not in general be optimum for operation at 1.3 μm with an InGaAsP LED or

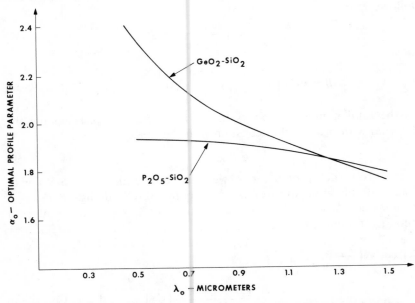

Figure 6-13 Optimal profile parameter α_0 for two binary compound dopant materials.

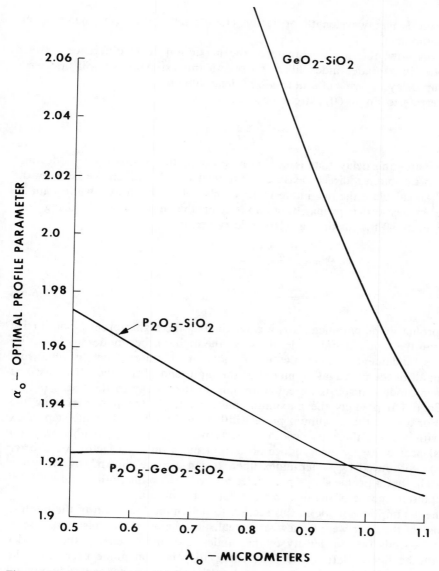

Figure 6-14 α_0 vs. λ_0 for binary and ternary compound materials.

laser. To increase the spectral range of the optimal profile, ternary compound materials such as $P_2O_5\text{-}GeO_2\text{-}SiO_2$ could be used. As shown in Fig. 6-14, these materials decrease the dependence of $\alpha_0(\lambda)$ on wavelength.[13] An optimal α profile over a wide range of wavelengths would allow the installation of wide-band graded-index fiber networks that could be operated simultaneously at multiple wavelengths or operated initially at a shorter wavelength (0.85 μm) and later refitted for longer wavelength operation (1.3–1.5 μm) by simply changing terminal equipment.

Let us now obtain an estimate of the maximum delay difference between the modes in a graded-index fiber. To obtain this estimate, we will first write the group delay in terms of a normalized delay time $\Delta\tau$.

Referring to Eq. (6-60), $\Delta\tau$ can be written as

$$\Delta\tau = \frac{c\tau_{gm}}{LN_{g_1}} - 1 \tag{6-64}$$

$\Delta\tau$ eliminates the delay that is common to all of the propagating modes and allows us to obtain a direct measure of the relative delay difference between the modes. To calculate the maximum relative delay of the modes we will obtain $\Delta\tau$ for the highest-order propagating mode. For this mode $m = N$. Using Eqs. (6-60) and (6-64) the maximum relative delay becomes

$$\Delta\tau_{max} \approx \Delta\frac{\alpha - \alpha_0}{\alpha + 2} \qquad \text{for } \alpha \neq \alpha_0$$

$$= \frac{\Delta^2}{2} \qquad \text{for } \alpha = \alpha_0 \tag{6-65}$$

If the profile shape parameter α is greater than α_0 the higher-order modes arrive later than the fundamental mode. If $\alpha < \alpha_0$ the higher-order modes arrive earlier than the fundamental mode. Let us consider an impulse of energy uniformly exciting all of the propagating modes at the input end of the fiber. If we assume that each mode transports an equal amount of the energy to the fiber's output end, Eq. (6-65) predicts the maximum pulse width of the power exciting the fiber. For $\alpha = \alpha_0$ the maximum pulse width would be $\Delta^2/2$. For the step-index fiber with $\alpha = \infty$, the pulse width is Δ. Hence a graded-index fiber with an optimal profile $\alpha = \alpha_0$ can produce an output pulse that is a factor $\Delta/2$ shorter than that produced by a step-index fiber. It can also be shown,[6] by analyzing Eq. (6-60), that a profile shape parameter $\alpha = \alpha_0 - 2\Delta$ reduces the total width of the impulse response of the fiber by another factor of four.

The assumptions made in this section to determine the width of the impulse response of the fiber were somewhat unrealistic. The actual impulse response of a fiber depends on the density of the modes and on the energy these modes carry at the fiber's output end. The energy depends on mode excitation, the variation of loss with mode number, and on the energy exchange (mode-mixing) among the modes. Since these factors are difficult to evaluate, the assumption of uniform energy distribution in all of the propagating modes was made as a first-order approximation to analytically predict the modal delay distortion characteristics of the fiber. In any case the basic point to be understood is that the limitations to the bandwidth of a graded-index multimode fiber are caused by both intermodal and intramodal delay distortion mechanisms. A choice of the source wavelength near the zero material dispersion region of the fiber core and the proper grading of the fiber's refractive index profile can produce a broadband transmission medium with a bandwidth of a few gigahertz-kilometers.

Example 6-2 Delay distortion; bandwidth The theory developed in Sec. 6-9 can be used to calculate and compare the maximum relative delay $\Delta\tau_{max}$ for a group of fibers of different composition.

Let us consider three fibers with the following characteristics:

(a) a P_2O_5-GeO_2-SiO_2 fiber with $\alpha = 1.922$, $\Delta = 0.013$
(b) a P_2O_5-SiO_2 fiber with $\alpha = 1.940$, $\Delta = 0.013$
(c) a P_2O_5-SiO_2 fiber with $\alpha = 1.98$, $\Delta = 0.013$.

Using Fig. 6-14 and Eq. (6-65) we can calculate $\Delta\tau_{max}$ for a given wavelength. For example, for $\lambda = 0.8$ μm

(a) From Fig. 6-14, $\alpha = \alpha_0 = 1.922$
From Eq. (6-55), $\Delta\tau_{max} = \Delta^2/2 = 8.45 \times 10^{-5}$
(b) $\alpha = \alpha_0 = 1.940$, $\Delta\tau = \Delta^2/2 = 8.45 \times 10^{-5}$
(c) $\alpha \neq \alpha_0$,

$$\Delta\tau = \Delta\left[\frac{(\alpha - \alpha_0)}{(\alpha + 2)}\right] = 0.013\left[\frac{(1.98 - 1.94)}{3.96}\right] = 1.313 \times 10^{-4}$$

If we assume that each mode in a fiber carries an equal amount of the input pulse's energy to the fiber's end, $\Delta\tau_{max}$ becomes an estimate of the output pulse width of a fiber. If, in addition, we recall that the bandwidth of a fiber is inversely proportional to pulse width we can compare the relative bandwidths of the above fibers at different wavelengths.

At $\lambda = 0.8$ μm, fibers a and b have optimal profile parameters and will have equal bandwidths that are higher than fiber c ($\alpha \neq \alpha_0$).

At $\lambda = 1.1$ μm, using Fig. 6-14 we observe that the two P_2O_5-SiO_2 fibers (fibers b and c) will be far from their optimum profile parameter ($\alpha \neq \alpha_0$). However, the optimal profile parameter curve for the P_2O_5-GeO_2-SiO_2 fiber (fiber a) is almost independent of wavelength. Therefore, for this fiber $\alpha \approx \alpha_0$. Hence, fiber a will have the highest bandwidth of the three fibers at $\lambda = 1.1$ μm.

6-10 RAY OPTICS ANALYSIS OF THE GRADED-INDEX FIBER

In this chapter we have analyzed the graded-index fiber using the WKBJ method. The solution of the ray equations developed in Chap. 3 is an alternative method of analysis that will describe the trajectory of a ray in a graded-index fiber. To illustrate this ray optics method, we will now solve the paraxial ray equations (3-71) and (3-72) (rewritten below for the reader's convenience) for a fiber with a parabolic-shaped refractive-index profile (exact solutions for the case of the arbitrarily shaped refractive-index profile cannot be obtained).[14]

$$\frac{d}{dz}\left(r^2\frac{d\phi}{dz}\right) = \frac{1}{n_a}\frac{\partial n}{\partial \phi} \tag{6-66}$$

$$\frac{d^2r}{dz^2} - r\left(\frac{d\phi}{dz}\right)^2 = \frac{1}{n_a}\frac{\partial n}{\partial r} \tag{6-67}$$

$$n(r) = n_1\left[1 - \left(\frac{r}{a}\right)^2\Delta\right] \tag{6-68}$$

To start our analysis we recognize that the refractive index profile described by Eq. (6-68) is independent of ϕ. Hence the ϕ derivative of the refractive index in Eq. (6-66) is equal to zero and this equation can be integrated to yield

$$r^2\frac{d\phi}{dz} = k_1 \tag{6-69}$$

where k_1 is a constant.

To obtain a differential equation for the radial function $r(z)$ of the ray we must obtain the terms $\partial n/\partial r$ and $d\phi/dz$ from Eqs. (6-68) and (6-69) for substitution into Eq. (6-67), that is,

$$\frac{\partial n}{\partial r} = -2n_1\left(\frac{\Delta}{a^2}\right)r \tag{6-70}$$

and

$$\frac{d\phi}{dz} = \frac{k_1}{r^2} \tag{6-71}$$

Substituting Eqs. (6-70) and (6-71) into Eq. (6-67) and recognizing that $n_1 \approx n_a$ we obtain

$$\frac{d^2r}{dz^2} + 2\frac{\Delta}{a^2}r - \frac{k_2}{r^3} = 0 \tag{6-72}$$

where k_2 is a constant equal to k_1^2. The solutions of Eqs. (6-72) and (6-69) will yield $r(z)$ and $\phi(z)$, the radial and azimuthal ray trajectory functions.

To obtain $r(z)$ we first note that if we multiply Eq. (6-72) by dr/dz we obtain the expression for the derivative

$$\frac{d}{dz}\left[\frac{1}{2}\left(\frac{dr}{dz}\right)^2 + \Delta\frac{r^2}{a^2} + \frac{k_2}{2r^2}\right] = 0 \tag{6-73}$$

whose integral is

$$\frac{1}{2}\left(\frac{dr}{dz}\right)^2 + \Delta\frac{r^2}{a^2} + \frac{k_2}{2r^2} = k_3 \tag{6-74}$$

where k_3 is a constant of integration. Rewriting Eq. (6-74) with the intent of solving for dz we obtain

$$\left(\frac{dr}{dz}\right)^2 = \frac{2k_3 r^2 - 2\Delta(r^4/a^2) - k_2}{r^2} \tag{6-75}$$

Solving Eq. (6-75) for dz and integrating yields

$$z - z_0 = \int \frac{r \, dr}{[2k_3 r^2 - 2\Delta(r^4/a^2) - k_2]^{1/2}} \tag{6-76}$$

where z_0 is again an integration constant. Using a standard table of integrals,[15] Eq. (6-76) can be directly integrated to yield

$$z - z_0 = \frac{a}{2\sqrt{2\Delta}} \arcsin\left\{\frac{(4\Delta/a^2)r^2 - 2k_3}{[4k_3^2 - (8\Delta/a^2)k_2]^{1/2}}\right\} \tag{6-77}$$

Remembering that we are trying to solve for $r(z)$ we can invert the arcsine function in Eq. (6-77) to obtain

$$\frac{(4\Delta/a^2)r^2 - 2k_3}{[4k_3^2 - (8\Delta/a^2)k_2]^{1/2}} = \sin\left[2\frac{\sqrt{2\Delta}}{a}(z - z_0)\right] \tag{6-78}$$

if we make the following definitions:[14]

$$\Omega = \frac{\sqrt{2\Delta}}{a} \tag{6-79}$$

$$b^2 = k_2\left(\frac{\Omega}{k^3}\right)^2 \tag{6-80}$$

$$A = \frac{\sqrt{k_3}}{\Omega} \tag{6-81}$$

We can directly solve for $r(z)$ from Eq. (6-78) and obtain

$$r(z) = A\{1 + \sqrt{1 - b^2} \sin[2\Omega(z - z_0)]\}^{1/2} \tag{6-82}$$

By substituting Eq. (6-82) into (6-69) and integrating (Prob. 6-14) we obtain a solution for $\phi(z)$

$$\phi = \phi_0 + \arctan\frac{1}{b}\{\sqrt{1 - b^2} + \tan[\Omega(z - z_0)]\} \tag{6-83}$$

where ϕ_0 is an integration constant.

After a lot of work we have finally obtained the results we were after, namely $r(z)$ and $\phi(z)$. Equations (6-82) and (6-83) provide us with a description of the ray trajectory in the form $r = r(z)$, $\phi = \phi(z)$ for a graded-index fiber with a parabolic-shaped refractive index profile.

It is of interest now to interpret the equations for $r(z)$ and $\phi(z)$ and see how this interpretation compares with the description obtained using the WKBJ method. From Eq. (6-82) we can immediately observe the ray is trapped inside the fiber core between two turning points given by

$$r_{max} = A(1 + \sqrt{1 - b^2})^{1/2} \tag{6-84}$$

and

$$r_{min} = A(1 - \sqrt{1 - b^2})^{1/2} \tag{6-85}$$

Hence the ray spirals down the fiber between r_{max} and r_{min}. Two simple trajectories corresponding to meridional and helical rays can be derived easily from Eqs. (6-82) and (6-83). An expression for the meridional rays can be obtained by setting $k_2 = 0$. For this case from Eq. (6-80), we see that b is also equal to zero. Therefore Eq. (6-82) becomes

$$r(z) = A\{1 + \sin [2\Omega(z - z_0)]\}^{1/2} \tag{6-86}$$

which can be written as

$$r(z) = A[\cos^2 \Omega(z - z_0) + \sin^2 \Omega(z - z_0) + 2 \sin \Omega(z - z_0) \cos \Omega(z - z_0)]^{1/2} \tag{6-87}$$

The expression under the square root in Eq. (6-87) is a perfect square, hence $r(z)$ can be written as

$$r(z) = A[\cos \Omega(z - z_0) + \sin \Omega(z - z_0)]$$
$$= \sqrt{2} A \sin \left[\Omega(z - z_0) + \frac{\pi}{4} \right] \tag{6-88}$$

In addition with $b = 0$ Eq. (6-83) is simplified and becomes

$$\phi(z) = \phi_0 + \frac{\pi}{2} \tag{6-89}$$

From Eq. (6-89) the azimuthal angle ϕ is a constant for this case. This means that the ray moves, as described by Eq. (6-88), on a sinusoidal trajectory in the meridional plane crossing the axis $r = 0$ (meridional ray) as it propagates down the z axis. The spatial radian frequency of this sinusoidal meridional ray path is Ω.

The second special case that is easy to interpret from the ray equations occurs when $b = 1$. In this case r is independent of z and Eqs. (6-82) and (6-83) become

$$r(z) = A \tag{6-90}$$

and

$$\phi(z) = \phi_0 + (z - z_0)\Omega \tag{6-91}$$

Since the ray travels at a fixed distance from the axis ($r = A$) on a helical path described by Eq. (6-91), it is called a helical ray. Meridional and helical rays are limiting cases of the general ray which travels along a spiraling trajectory whose distance from the fiber axis varies periodically between the turning points.

We have shown in this section that the analysis of the ray equation provides an alternate geometric description of propagation in a multimode guide that is consistent with the results we obtained from the WKBJ method of analysis.

REFERENCES

1. P. K. Tien, J. P. Gordon, and J. R. Whinnery: "Focusing of a Light Beam of Gaussian Field Distribution in Continuous and Parabolic Lens-Like Media," *Proc. IEEE*, **53**: 129–136 (1965).
2. P. M. Morse and H. Feshbach: *Methods of Theoretical Physics*, Part II, McGraw-Hill Book Company, New York, 1953.
3. A. W. Snyder and D. J. Mitchell: "Leaky Rays on Circular Fibers," *JOSA*, **64**: 599–607 (1974).
4. S. E. Miller and A. G. Chynoweth: *Optical Fiber Telecommunications*, Academic Press, New York, 1979.
5. W. H. Beyer: *CRC Standard Mathematical Tables*, 25th ed. CRC Press, Boca Raton, Florida, 1979.
6. D. Gloge and E. A. J. Marcatili: "Multimode Theory of Graded-Core Fibers," *BSTJ*, **52**(9): 1563–1578, November 1973.
7. J. E. Midwinter: *Optical Fibers for Transmission*, John Wiley and Sons, New York, 1979.
8. M. K. Barnoski: *Fundamentals of Optical Fiber Communications*, Academic Press, Inc., New York, 1976.
9. M. J. Adams, D. N. Payne, and F. M. E. Sladen: "Leaky Rays on Optical Fibers of Arbitrary (Circularly Symmetric) Index Profiles," *Electron. Lett.*, **11**: 238 (1975).
10. R. Olshansky and D. B. Keck: "Pulse Broadening in Graded-Index Optical Fibers," *Appl. Opt.* **15**(2): 483–491, February 1976.
11. D. Gloge: "Propagation Effects in Optical Fibers," *IEEE Trans. Microwave Theory Tech.*, **MII-23**: 106–120, January 1975.
12. I. P. Kaminow and H. W. Presby: "Profile Synthesis in Multicomponent Glass Optical Fiber," *Appl. Opt.*, **16**: 108–112 (1977).
13. I. P. Kaminow, H. M. Presby, J. B. MacChesney, and P. B. O'Connor: "Ternary Fiber Glass Composition for Minimum Modal Dispersion Over a Range of Wavelengths," Technical Digest Optical Fiber Transmission II, *Opt. Soc. Am.* PD5-1, February 1977.
14. D. Marcuse: *Principles of Optical Fiber Measurements*, Academic Press, New York, 1981.
15. I. S. Gradshteyn and I. M. Ryzhik: *Table of Integrals, Series, and Products*, Academic Press, Inc., New York, 1980.

PROBLEMS

6-1 Starting with the wave equation in cylindrical coordinates (Eq. (6-2)) derive Eq. (6-15). What assumptions are made in using the WKBJ approach?

6-2 Use the wave number diagrams in Figs. 6-2b and 6-4 to describe the propagation of hybrid and meriodional modes in a graded-index fiber.

6-3 For a fixed value of β how do the conditions for propagation of hybrid modes change as v increases?

6-4 What are the regions of propagation for meriodional and hybrid modes in a step-index fiber?

6-5 What are the conditions for propagation of leaky modes in a graded-index fiber? (Refer to Fig. 6-6).

6-6 Use Eq. (6-32) to derive Eq. (6-37), the total number of modes in a graded-index fiber with refractive-index profile $n(r) = n_1[1 - 2\Delta(r/a)^\alpha]^{1/2}$ for $r < a$.

6-7 Calculate the number of bound modes having a propagation constant β, greater than $1.11 \times 10^7/\mu m$ for a graded-index fiber with the power-law profile given by Eq. (6-34) and

$$\Delta = 0.013$$

$$\lambda_0 = 0.82 \ \mu m$$

$$n_1 = 1.453$$

$$\alpha = 2$$

$$a = 25 \ \mu m$$

6-8 Use Eq. (6-32) to derive the number of modes in a step-index guide. Show Eq. (6-39) is valid by comparing your answer to the total number of modes in a graded-index guide with a parabolic ($\alpha = 2$) power-law profile.

6-9 Calculate the numerical aperture of a graded-index fiber at the fiber center ($r = 0$) and at the core-cladding boundary ($r = a$) if the fiber has a parabolic power-law profile.

6-10 How does the shape of the normalized near-field power distribution in Fig. 6-10 for $\alpha = 2$ and $\alpha = \infty$ compare with the shape of the refractive-index profile $n(r)$ for the same α parameter? What assumptions are made in using the normalized near-field power distribution to measure the profile shape parameter α?

6-11 What happens to the delay differences among modes in a fiber with the optimal profile shape parameter α_0? How does this affect the bandwidth of the fiber?

6-12 What value of the profile-shape parameter α will maximize the bandwidth of a P_2O_5-SiO_2 fiber to be operated with a source $\lambda = 0.82 \ \mu m$? $\lambda = 1.3 \ \mu m$?

6-13 Calculate the maximum relative delay difference between modes for a P_2O_5-SiO_2 composition fiber which is to be operated with a source $\lambda = 1.3 \ \mu m$ with $\Delta = 0.015$ for (1) $\alpha = \alpha_0$; (2) $\alpha = 2.0$.

Do the higher-order modes arrive before or after the fundamental mode when $\alpha = 2 \neq \alpha_0$?

6-14 Derive Eq. (6-83) the solution for $\phi(z)$. Start your derivation with Eq. (6-69) and use Eq. (6-82) to obtain Eq. (6-83).

SEVEN

FABRICATION OF OPTICAL FIBERS

7-1 INTRODUCTION

Starting with this chapter and continuing in the succeeding chapters of this text we will consider many of the important applied experimental aspects of fiber optic technology. In this chapter the material considerations and fabrication techniques leading to the production of fibers with low loss and high bandwidth are described.

Emphasis will be placed on the two-step process of producing high-silica fibers. This process consists of first making a preform (a rod of glass containing both the core and cladding materials) by a deposition process, and then drawing the preform into a fiber on a fiber-drawing machine. The production of low-temperature compound silicate glass fibers formed by the double crucible method will also be described.

7-2 MATERIAL CONSIDERATIONS

Fibers used for communication purposes are made from material systems that satisfy the following basic requirements:

1. The dielectric material used in the core must have a higher refractive index than the cladding material to ensure that the fiber is a guiding structure.
2. The dielectric materials used must have low loss (< 10 dB/km) in the infrared region of the optical spectrum. This is the region (0.8 to 0.9 μm and 1.3 to 1.6 μm) where economical semiconductor light sources exist.

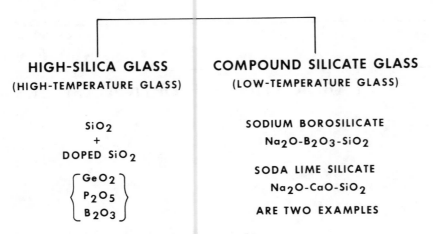

Figure 7-1 Glass systems used to fabricate optical fibers.

3. To obtain a high-bandwidth fiber, the materials and fabrication processes used must be capable of producing a graded refractive-index profile in the fiber's core.
4. The dielectric materials used must be capable of being drawn into a fiber, that is, the core and cladding materials must have compatible thermal and mechanical properties.

These requirements limit the field of dielectric material systems to glasses and plastics. Many plastics are excluded from further consideration because the presence of hydrogen in their structures gives rise to very high losses and because their molecular size leads to large scattering losses. For these reasons we will concern ourselves with fibers whose core and cladding are both glass.

There are two general types of glass systems that are in use today as shown in Fig. 7-1. The first type of glass system consists of glasses produced by a deposition process.[1,2] The vapor phase reaction of oxygen with mixtures of compounds such as $SiCl_4$, $GeCl_4$, BCl_3, and $POCl_3$ produces an ultrapure glass rod called a preform. The preform has a doped silica core and generally a pure silica (SiO_2) cladding. To obtain the desired variation of the refractive index of the core, the concentration of the dopants (GeO_2, P_2O_5, and B_2O_3) is varied radially. The preforms are pulled into fibers at high temperatures (typically 2000°C). The resultant fibers made by this technique are referred to as "high-silica" fibers. This type of fiber is used in the vast majority of optical telecommunication systems in existence today.[3]

The second type of glass system is made by starting with very pure powdered raw materials that are processed using classical glass-making techniques to produce compound silicate glasses. With this technique, two glasses (core and cladding) of different chemical compositions are melted separately (at relatively low temperatures, 850 to 1100°C) and fed into two concentric crucibles (double crucible method) with a hole at the bottom through which a fiber is pulled. The fibers made by this process are referred to as "multicomponent glass" fibers.[4]

7-3 LOSS AND BANDWIDTH LIMITING MECHANISMS

Let us now consider the mechanisms that are inherent in the glass materials and in the fiber fabrication process that cause loss and limit the bandwidth of an optical fiber. Figure 7-2 itemizes these mechanisms. The loss of a fiber, which is a function of wavelength, is due to a number of material absorption and scattering mechanisms which we shall describe below.

7-3-1 Intrinsic Material Absorption Loss

High-silica glass fibers are used in a "window" between ultraviolet and infrared absorption regions. The absorption tails, which are low-level appendages of the absorption peaks on a plot of absorption versus wavelength, are shown in Fig. 7-3.[5] Absorption in the ultraviolet region of the spectrum results when light photons contain enough energy to excite electrons of the glass materials from a valence band to a conduction band. For pure fused silica the oxygen ions have very tightly bound electrons and the energy gap between the valence and conduction bands is approximately 8.9 eV. To excite these electrons requires ultraviolet photons of wavelength $\lambda \approx 0.14$ μm. Thus the UV absorption peak for fused silica occurs at approximately 0.14 μm and its absorption tail becomes almost negligible in the infrared portion of the spectrum. The infrared absorption tail is caused by molecular vibrations. If only the fundamental vibrations of the fused silica molecules were important, the infrared absorption peak would be at 8 μm. However, combination and overtone bands exist at 3.2 μm, 3.8 μm, and 4.4 μm which influence the infrared absorption tail and cause loss of less than 0.5 dB/km at 1.5 μm.[1]

LOSS MECHANISMS

I . INTRINSIC MATERIAL ABSORPTION LOSS
   (a) ULTRAVIOLET ABSORPTION TAIL
   (b) INFRARED ABSORPTION TAIL

II . ABSORPTION LOSS DUE TO IMPURITY IONS

III . RAYLEIGH SCATTERING LOSS

IV . WAVEGUIDE SCATTERING LOSS

V . MICROBENDING LOSS

BANDWIDTH LIMITING MECHANISMS

I . INDEX PROFILE ERRORS DUE TO PREFORM FABRICATION

Figure 7-2 Transmission loss and bandwidth limiting mechanisms.

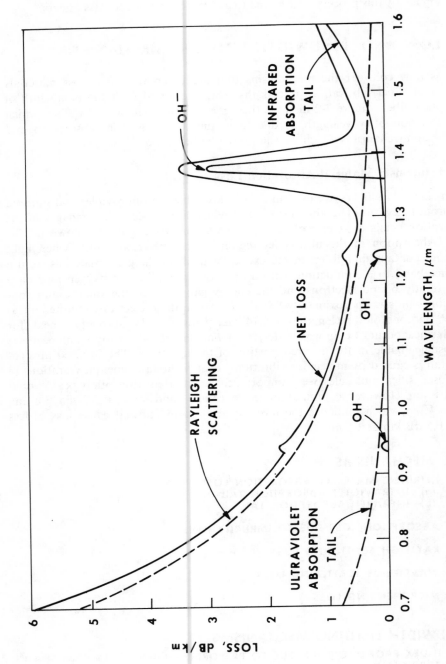

Figure 7-3 Spectral loss curve of fiber showing components of absorption and scattering loss.

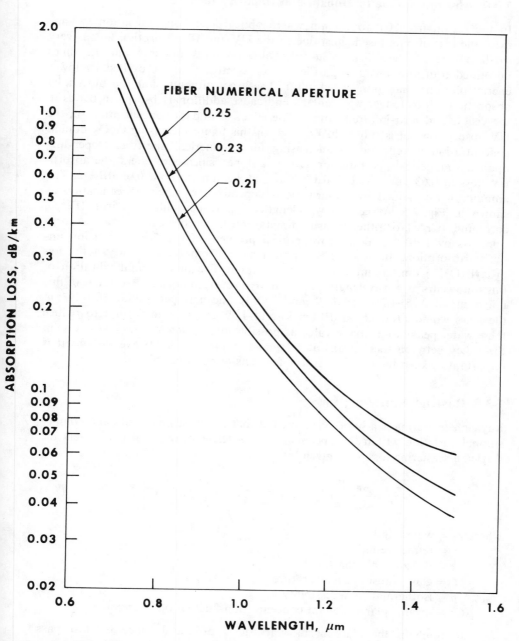

Figure 7-4 Absorption loss due to GeO_2 dopant as a function of wavelength.

7-3-2 Absorption Due to Dopant and Impurity Ions

In the region from 0.8 to 1.5 μm where optical-fiber communication systems exist, the loss of pure fused silica due to the UV and IR absorption tails is very small. However, the silica in a fiber also contains dopants and at times unwanted transition-metal impurities whose electrons can be excited by lower energy photons than pure fused silica. These constituents shift the ultraviolet absorption tail to longer wavelengths and cause additional absorption bands in the visible and near-infrared ranges. The effect of dopant concentration on the UV absorption tail is shown in Fig. 7-4. In this figure increasing GeO_2 dopant concentration is reflected by increasing fiber numerical aperture. Depending upon the numerical aperture, for germania-doped silica-core fibers, the absorption loss at 0.63 μm is 1 to 2 dB/km and at 1.3 μm is about 0.05 dB/km. The amount of loss added by impurity ions depends upon their concentration as shown in Fig. 7-5. At certain wavelengths 1 part per billion of iron (Fe^{2+}), chromium (Cr^{+3}), or other transition-metal ion impurities can increase absorption loss by 1 dB/km. Besides the critical problem of transition-metal ion impurity absorption, an additional problem arises from the presence of the hydroxyl (OH^-) ion, commonly known as water. The fundamental vibration of this ion occurs at a wavelength of 2.7 μm. However, important overtones of this ion occur at 0.95, 1.25, and 1.39 μm.[1,5] Only one part per million of OH^- in the glass would produce 30 dB/km loss at 1.39 μm. It is important to reduce these water peaks to as low a value as possible and to achieve the lowest loss in the valley between these peaks at 1.3 μm. For low-loss lightwave systems it is important to keep the OH^- level to a few tens of parts per billion.

7-3-3 Rayleigh Scattering Loss

Rayleigh scattering is a basic phenomenon that results from density and compositional variation within the fiber material. In terms of material parameters the Rayleigh scattering loss α_R is given by[6,7,8]

$$\alpha_R = \frac{8\pi^3}{3\lambda_0^4} \left[(n^2 - 1)kT\beta + 2n\left(\frac{\partial n}{\partial C}\right)^2 \overline{\Delta C^2}\, \delta V \right] \tag{7-1}$$

where λ_0 = wavelength
n = refractive index
k = Boltzmann's constant
T = glass transition temperature
β = isothermal compressibility
$\overline{\Delta C^2}$ = mean-squared dopant concentration fluctuation over volume δV

Variations in the glass occur when it is produced, since it must pass through the glass transition point in becoming an amorphous solid. There is a level of thermal agitation occurring at the transition point causing thermal and compositional fluctuations which are "frozen" into the lattice at the softening

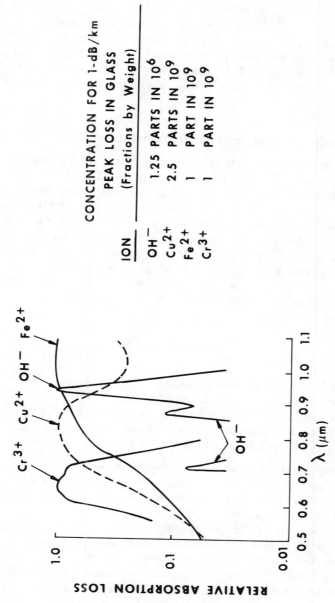

Figure 7-5 Relative absorption loss vs. wavelength of transition metal and OH ion impurities in glass.

point and are dependent upon material composition. In high-silica glasses, dopants are added in the core to increase its refractive index. Dopants having large index variation with concentration tend to increase the Rayleigh scattering coefficient $(\partial n/\partial c)^2$. The scale of the frozen-in thermal and compositional fluctuations is smaller than the wavelength of light. They are fundamental to glass materials and cannot be eliminated. It is important to note that Rayleigh scattering loss α_R is strongly dependent upon wavelength and in fact is proportional to $1/\lambda^4$. As shown in Fig. 7-3 the intersection of the Rayleigh scattering loss curve with the infrared absorption tail usually determines the lower limit of a fiber's loss.

7-3-4 Waveguide Scattering and Microbending Loss

An important goal of waveguide fabrication is to reduce the impurity absorption loss to zero so that only intrinsic absorption and Rayleigh scattering loss are left. However, other forms of scattering loss may occur during the waveguide fabrication processes that add additional loss. This additional scattering loss is due to waveguide imperfections such as variations in the size of the fiber core and microbubbles in the core or at the core-cladding interface. These imperfections can cause light to radiate out of the fiber or cause energy conversion from one guided mode to another. Mode conversion can cause a loss of energy if the coupling is to a leaky or higher-loss mode. The loss due to waveguide imperfections can be determined by plotting the overall loss versus λ^{-4} according to the equation[8]

$$\alpha = \frac{A}{\lambda^4} + B + C(\lambda) + \sum \alpha_i \tag{7-2}$$

where $A \equiv$ the Rayleigh scattering coefficient

$B \equiv$ the loss due to waveguide imperfections

$C(\lambda) \equiv$ the loss in a narrow band due to impurities such as OH^-

$\alpha_i \equiv$ the intrinsic absorption loss of fused silica (S_iO_2) and intentional dopants (α_i is less than 1 dB/km for 1 μm $< \lambda < 1.6$ μm)

The Rayleigh scattering loss A/λ^4 approaches zero as λ^4 approaches infinity. Therefore the ordinate intercept of the curve of loss versus λ^{-4} is a good measure of the value of B. Since B is the loss due to waveguide imperfections, for good fibers B is close to zero.

Figure 7-6 is a plot of the loss of a high-silica fiber doped with germanium and phosphorus (germania-phosphosilicate fiber) as a function of λ^{-4}. In this figure the dashed curve shows the fiber with a coating that induced "microbending" loss.[5] A rough stiff coating can cause the fiber axis to deflect by a few microns in a period along the fiber's length of a few millimeters.[9] These microbends in the fiber can cause scattering losses. It is important that the fiber coating buffer the fiber from microbending forces due to subsequent cabling and installation operations.

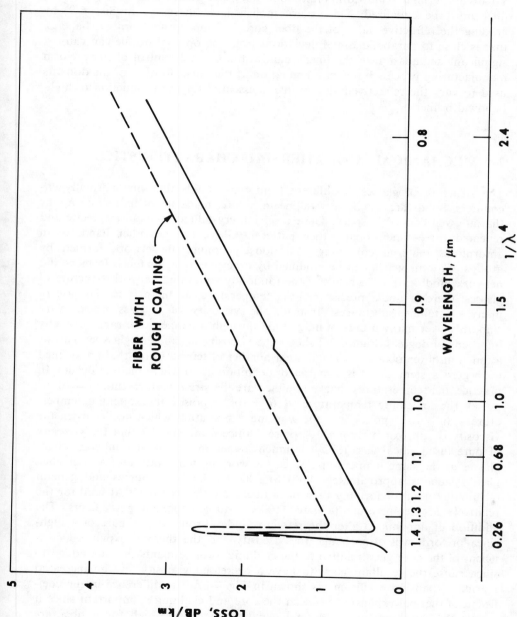

Figure 7-6 Loss vs. λ^{-4} for a germania-phosphosilicate fiber.

7-3-5 Bandwidth Limiting Mechanisms

To obtain a high bandwidth multimode fiber the modal transit times of the fiber must be equalized. This is accomplished, as discussed in Sec. 6-9, by grading the refractive index of the fiber core with an optimal profile shape α_0 that is close to parabolic. Small deviations from the optimal profile can cause a significant degradation in the fiber's bandwidth. Careful control of the preform manufacturing process by precise regulation of the concentration of the dopants used to vary the refractive-index profile is essential for the production of high-bandwidth fibers.

7-4 MECHANICAL AND THERMAL CHARACTERISTICS

The structure of glasses is different from most solids that one normally encounters. Solids are usually crystalline in nature, made up of individual atoms that are well defined in space. These atoms in crystalline solids form precise and repeated three-dimensional lattice patterns. Glass, on the other hand, is an amorphous material consisting of a loosely connected network formed by groups of atoms which can be modified by other components (glass formers and network modifiers). As a result of the randomly connected network structure of glasses, there is not a precise melting temperature, as there is in the case of many crystalline substances. Instead, the viscosity of a glass η can vary smoothly over many orders of magnitude through a temperature range of many hundreds of degrees. Figure 7-7 shows the viscosity of different glass systems as a function of temperature.[1] There are a number of temperatures that are defined for a glass system and it is a matter of definition as to where melting occurs. In practice, the temperatures that are defined are the strain temperature ($\eta = 10^{14.5}$ poise), the annealing temperature T_g ($\eta = 10^{13.5}$ poise), the softening temperature T_s ($\eta = 10^{7.5}$ poise), and the working temperature which occurs when the viscosity is approximately $\eta \approx 10^4$ poise. Notice from Fig. 7-7 that the viscosity of pure fused silica glass (SiO_2) is much higher than that of multicomponent glasses at the same temperature. Since the working temperature of a high-silica glass system is approximately 1700 to 2000°C, the heat sources and general technology used for forming high-silica fibers is different from that used for the relatively low-temperature (850 to 1100°C) multicomponent glass fibers. The addition of dopants to alter the refractive-index profile of the core of a high-silica preform will also change the viscosity and the thermal expansion coefficient of the core glass relative to the cladding. Most dopants that are added to silica cause the resultant glass to have a decreased viscosity and an increased thermal expansion coefficient as shown in Fig. 7-8.[1] The difference in the coefficient of thermal expansion between the core and cladding is important since it causes the development of thermal expansion stresses which for a fiber are tangential, radial, and axial. These stresses can be harmful or can be utilized in a beneficial way to influence the strength of the fiber. It is desirable to have the

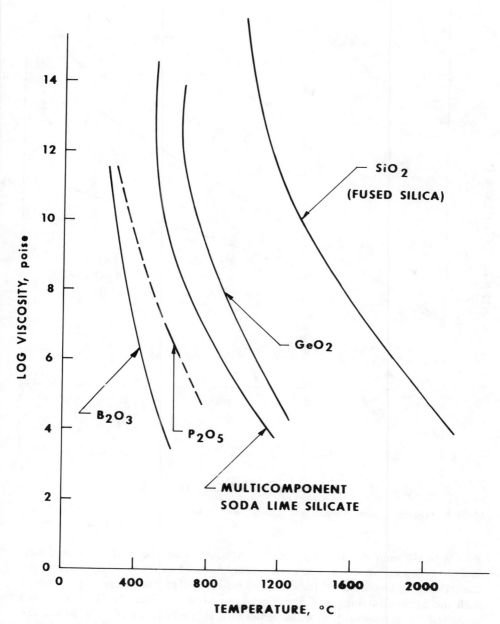

Figure 7-7 Viscosity vs. temperature for a number of glass systems and dopants.

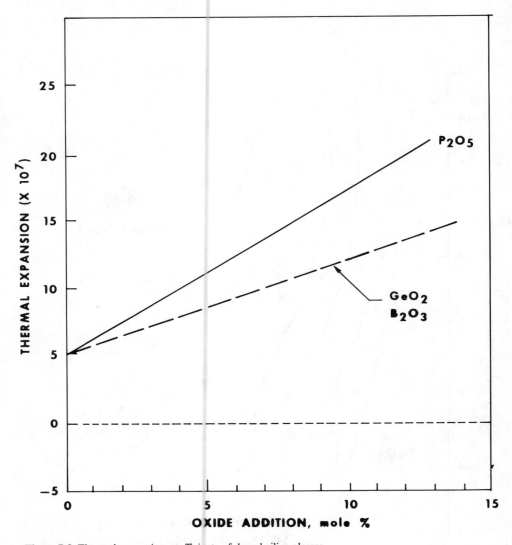

Figure 7-8 Thermal expansion coefficients of doped silica glasses.

glass with the smaller expansion coefficient as the cladding glass. This will lead to axial compressive stresses in the cladding and aid in the strengthening of the fiber. Differing viscosities of the core and cladding glass may cause a problem in both the preform-making and fiber-drawing processes. Since the viscosity of the more viscous glass will dictate the temperature at which the fiber is drawn, the softer glass may have to be drawn in a very fluid condition. While this may tend to distort both a preform and its index profile it has been shown that if the temperature gradient across the preform and fiber are small, plane flow will be maintained and the index profile will not be affected.[1] In conclusion, the most important general point to understand is that the thermal expansion coefficients and viscosities of the core and cladding glasses must be closely matched to ensure that a preform can be made and that a fiber can be drawn from it.

7-5 PREFORM FABRICATION TECHNIQUES

High-silica glass preforms consisting of a rod of glass containing a cladding surrounding a higher-index core material have been made by a number of different techniques that are based on vapor phase processes. These techniques use pure silica (SiO_2) as a base material and then add to it small amounts of dopants to change its refractive index sufficiently to allow a waveguide to be formed. In a typical vapor phase reaction, chloride precursors such as $SiCl_4$, $GeCl_4$, $POCl_3$ and BCl_3 undergo a high-temperature oxidation or hydrolysis to form oxides of silicon and the dopant elements. For oxidation, the completed chemical reactions are as follows:[8]

$$SiCl_4 + O_2 \rightarrow SiO_2 + 2Cl_2 \qquad (7\text{-}3)$$

$$GeCl_4 + O_2 \rightarrow GeO_2 + 2Cl_2 \qquad (7\text{-}4)$$

$$2POCl_3 + \tfrac{3}{2}O_2 \rightarrow P_2O_5 + 3Cl_2 \qquad (7\text{-}5)$$

$$2BCl_3 + \tfrac{3}{2}O_2 \rightarrow B_2O_3 + 3Cl_2 \qquad (7\text{-}6)$$

(For hydrolysis, combustion in a hydrogen-containing flame introduces water of hydration, which is subsequently removed.) The dopant materials GeO_2 and P_2O_5 increase the refractive index of silica, whereas B_2O_3 reduces it as shown in Fig. 7-9. Phosporus and boron dopants are used as fining agents, lowering the fusion temperature and the viscosity of the deposited glass thus making it more homogeneous.

The different processes that are used to fabricate preforms are shown in Fig. 7-10. They are classified into two categories: the inside deposition processes, and the outside deposition processes,[10] where inside and outside refer to the general environment in which the glass materials are deposited. For an inside process, deposition occurs on the inside surface of a fused silica tube. For an outside process the materials are deposited directly onto an external target surface called a bait rod. We shall now describe these preform fabrication processes in some detail.

7-5-1 Inside Process

The most commonly used inside process, the MCVD[11] (modified chemical vapor deposition) process, was developed at Bell Laboratories and is shown schematically in Fig. 7-11. The idea of this process is to form glassy layers of doped silica on the inside surface of a silica tube. One then heats the tube to a

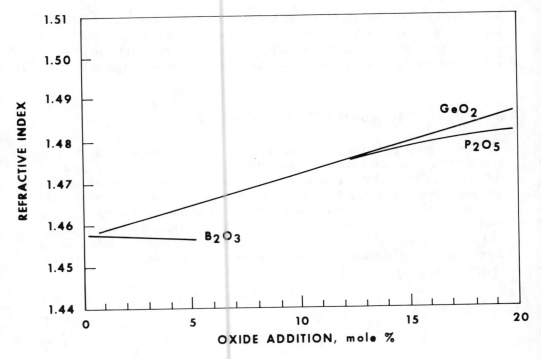

Figure 7-9 Refractive index of doped silica glasses.

high temperature (approximately 1900°C) so that surface tension and/or external pressure cause it to shrink radially until the center hole is eliminated. The
solid rod that is obtained is the "preform" that is ultimately drawn into a fiber.
For a multimode waveguide, the silica tube becomes the fiber's cladding and the
deposited layers of higher-refractive index glass ultimately form the fiber's core.

The MCVD process involves externally heating a rotating fused-silica tube
mounted between synchronous chucks of a glass-working lathe (see Fig. 7-12) to
thermally trigger (1300 to over 1600°C) oxidation of chloride precursors that are
flowing inside the tube.[8] In the hot zone both homogeneous (gas-phase) and

1. INSIDE PROCESSES (e.g. MCVD process)

2. OUTSIDE PROCESSES
    (a) LATERAL DEPOSITION
    (b) VAPOR PHASE AXIAL DEPOSITION (VAD)

Figure 7-10 High-silica glass preform preparation techniques.

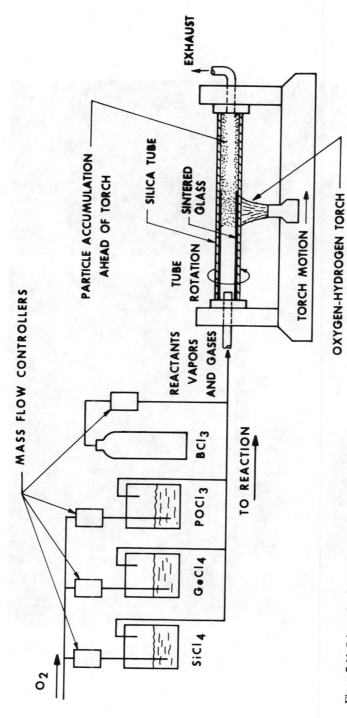

Figure 7-11 Schematic of MCVD process.

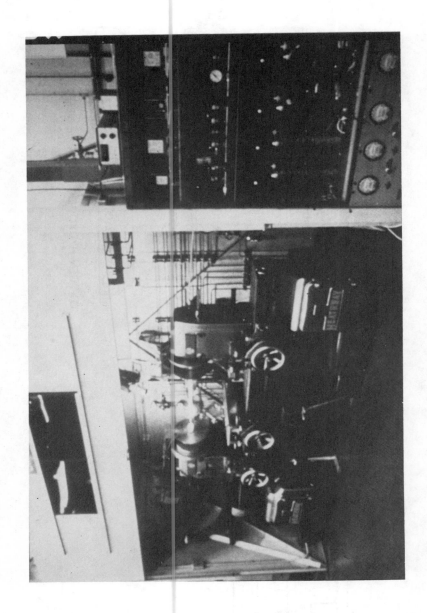

Figure 7-12 Photographs of glass-working lathe during preform fabrication process.

heterogeneous (different phases, gaseous precursors, and solid-tube wall) reactions take place. From the heterogeneous reaction a thin glassy film is deposited on the tube wall in the hot zone (see Fig. 7-13). The homogeneous oxidation reaction produces a finely divided particulate glass material called "soot." As the hot soot flows downstream some of it is attracted to the cold walls of the tube (which the torch has not yet heated) where it is deposited as a thin porous layer. The rest of the soot flows out the exhaust end of the tube. The torch is moved toward the downstream portion of the tube and as it passes over the soot deposit it "zone-sinters" it to a clear glass layer. When the torch reaches the exhaust end of the tube it is returned to the inlet end and the process is repeated.

For deposition of a graded-index core the flow of the dopant $GeCl_4$ is systematically increased with each pass of the torch while keeping the flows of $SiCl_4$, and $POCl_3$, relatively constant. This produces an increasing GeO_2 concentration and therefore an increasing index of refraction within each successive layer of core material. Therefore multiple passes (typically 50 to 100) as described above produce a piecewise continuous graded-index profile as shown in Fig. 7-14.[8] The last step in the MCVD process is to collapse the tube into a preform rod. This is done by decreasing the torch carriage velocity while permitting the tube temperature to increase (for a fused silica tube, 1900°C). As heat softens the tube, surface tension shrinks it. Normally three or four passes of the torch, each at a lower speed, are necessary to collapse the tube into a preform rod.

There are some very attractive features and some negative aspects of the MCVD process which we will now discuss. First, raw materials for all of the above processes are available in high-purity form. The reactants for the MCVD process are vaporized before they are transported into the silica tube. Further purification of the reactants occurs because, as shown in Fig. 7-15, the vapor pressure of many of the transition-metal chloride impurities is much lower than that of $SiCl_4$ or the other dopant chlorides.[2] Second, since the MCVD process is performed inside of a tube, in a controlled environment, very low water-content glass deposition can occur. In addition, since both the deposition and sintering of the glass is carried out in the same traverse of the torch, the chances of bubble entrapment is greatly reduced. The drawbacks of the MCVD process are related to deposition rates and starting tube needs; these are in turn related to manufacturing economics. Current research related to the MCVD process is concerned with developing techniques for improving the efficiency of the soot deposition rate. A thermophoresis model[12] has been developed that explains why soot collects on the tube wall. The deposition efficiency as shown in Eq. (7-7) is improved by decreasing the tube wall temperature downstream of the torch.

$$E \propto \left(1 - \frac{T_{min}}{T_{reaction}}\right) \qquad (7\text{-}7)$$

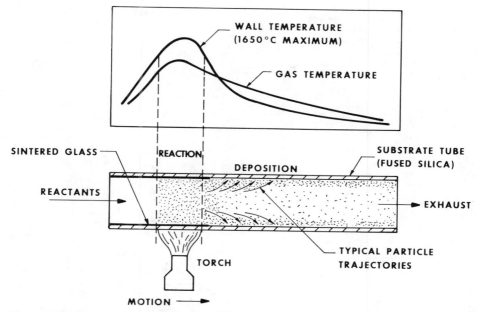

Figure 7-13 Illustration showing deposition pattern of reaction products.

where E is the deposition efficiency

$T_{\min}$ is the minimum tube temperature

$T_{\text{reaction}} = 1500$ K

Figure 7-16 shows the flow pattern of the soot deposition when the hot zone is broadened and downstream cooling is used. Deposition rates of 0.3 to 0.45 g/min have been reported using this technique.

Another experimental technique using an RF plasma generated within the tube to increase the soot deposition rate and an external torch to sinter the glass is shown in Fig. 7-17. An alternate plasma approach also incorporating both internal and external heating of the tube is the Philips process shown in Fig. 7-18.[1,13,14] To fabricate a graded-index preform, a nonrotating 12-mm-ID SiO_2 tube is placed in a furnace at 1100°C and approximately 2000 glass layers are deposited on its inner wall by the heterogeneous reaction of metal halides (no soot is formed). Very rapid traverse of the plasma (8 cm/s) can be used to create very thin glass layers resulting in a very well controlled index profile. Both the conventional MCVD process and the plasma augmented process have produced very low loss fibers (< 1 dB/km at 1300 nm) with high bandwidths (~ 3 GHz-km).

7-5-2 Outside Process

The outside preform fabrication process is subdivided according to whether the soot deposition occurs laterally or axially on a bait rod.

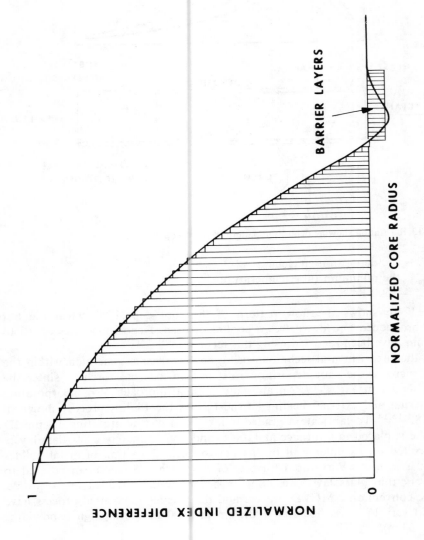

Figure 7-14 Drawing of piecewise continuous normalized refractive-index profile.

166

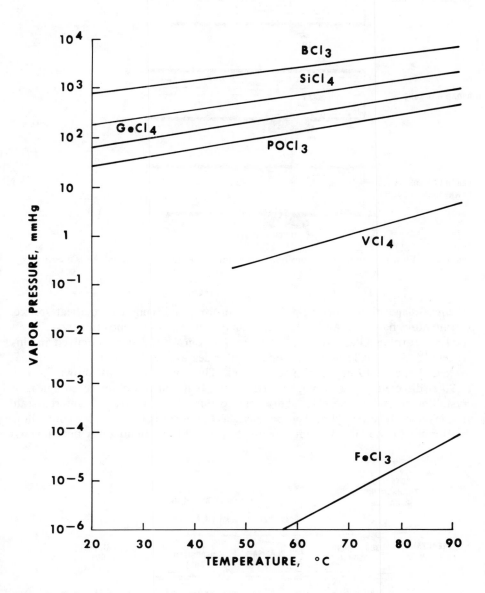

Figure 7-15 Graph showing vapor pressure of chlorides as a function of temperature.

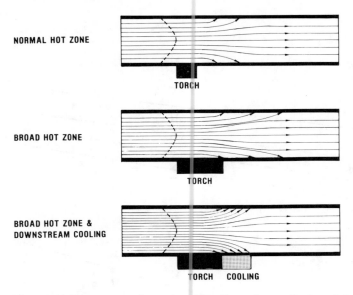

Figure 7-16 Flow pattern of soot deposition illustrating application of thermophoresis model.

a **Lateral deposition (Corning process)** A process involving a flame heat source, a removable bait rod, and a lateral orientation for soot deposition was developed at Corning Glass Works.[15] Figure 7-19 shows the steps involved in this process.[10] First $SiCl_4$ and the dopant chlorides are hydrolyzed in a methane-oxygen flame to form a hot soot stream. The soot stream as shown in Fig. 7-19*a* is directed at a rotating and traversing bait rod (graphite, fused silica, or crystalline ceramic). The glass soot sticks to this rod in a partially sintered state and, layer by layer, a cylindrical porous glass preform is built up. By controlling the dopant halides in the soot stream it is possible to build up a multilayered

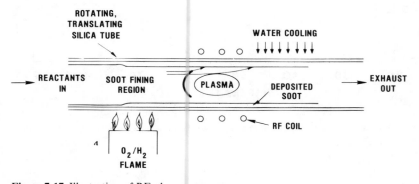

Figure 7-17 Illustration of RF plasma process.

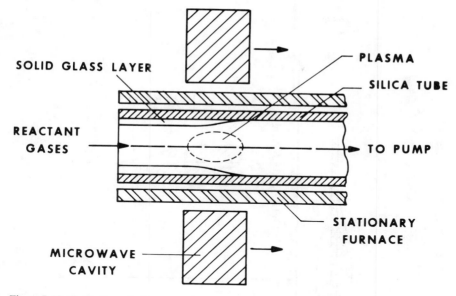

SOLID GLASS LAYER

PLASMA

SILICA TUBE

REACTANT GASES

TO PUMP

STATIONARY FURNACE

MICROWAVE CAVITY

Figure 7-18 Illustration of microwave plasma process (Philips process).

($\sim$ 200 layers) graded-index profile (Fig. 7-19b) in the core region of the preform. When the soot deposition is completed, the porous preform is slipped off the bait rod. As shown in Fig. 7-19c this porous glass preform is then zone-sintered at approximately 1500°C by passing it through a furnace hot zone in a controlled atmosphere such as helium. The resultant bubble-free clear glass preform with a small central hole in it (where the bait rod was removed) is subsequently drawn into a fiber. The central hole disappears (Fig. 7-19d) during the fiber-drawing process which occurs at much higher temperatures ($\approx$ 1800 to 1900°C).

The average soot collection efficiency for the lateral deposition outside process is approximately 50 percent. The effective deposition rate for soot collected on the preform is about 2 g/min.[2] In this process both the preform core and cladding material are deposited. This is in contrast to the MCVD process in which the starting fused silica tube becomes the cladding material. Since the cladding comprises approximately 75 percent of the total preform material, one must multiply the MCVD deposition rate by four to effectively compare it with the Corning outside process. A very attractive feature of the outside process is that large preforms can be made which readily yield more than 10 km of fiber. A disadvantage of the lateral process as described above is the high hydroxyl-impurity content in the fiber core glass introduced by the flame combustion products during soot deposition. This causes undesirable fiber absorption losses at long wavelengths. This problem has been solved in the laboratory by employing gaseous chlorine-drying during the zone-sintering process. Figure 7-20

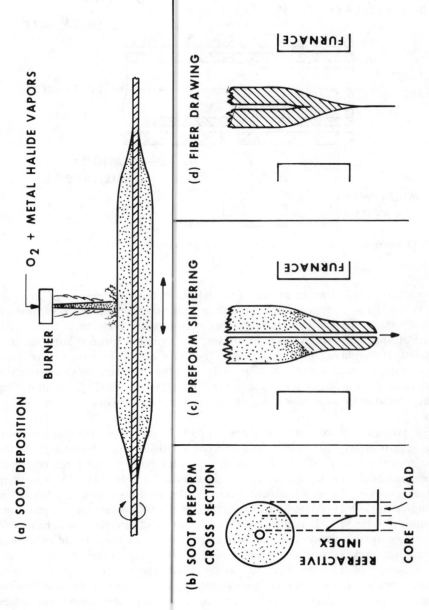

(a) SOOT DEPOSITION

O_2 + METAL HALIDE VAPORS

BURNER

(b) SOOT PREFORM CROSS SECTION

REFRACTIVE INDEX

CORE CLAD

(c) PREFORM SINTERING

FURNACE

(d) FIBER DRAWING

FURNACE

Figure 7-19 Illustration of outside lateral deposition process (Corning process).

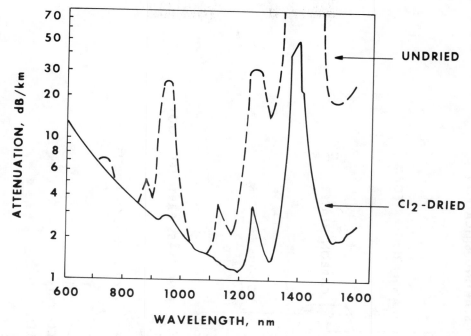

Figure 7-20 Spectral attenuation of an outside laterally deposited fiber.

shows a comparison of the spectral attenuation of an undried and chlorine-dried high NA ($\approx$ 0.3) fiber made by the outside lateral deposition process.[10] Fiber produced by the outside process using lateral deposition have been reported having low losses ($<$ 1 dB/km at 1300 nm) and bandwidths as high as 3 GHz-km.[2]

b **Axial deposition (VAD process)** The axial deposition or, as it is more commonly called, the VAD (vapor phase axial deposition) process was developed in Japan by workers at Nippon Telephone and Telegraph Corporation (NTT).[16] The process as shown in Fig. 7-21[17] involves simultaneous flame deposition of both core and cladding glass soots onto the end (axially) of a rotating fused-silica bait rod. As the porous soot preform grows it is slowly drawn through a graphite resistance furnace (carbon heater) where it is consolidated into a transparent glass preform by zone-sintering. Very large preforms have been made with this technique which have yielded approximately 20 km[18] of fiber at soot, a deposition rate of 0.5 g/min. Because of axial deposition the VAD process has the potential for being a continuous preform-making process. Due to the simultaneous sintering of the hole-free preform without handling, excellent control of the attenuation of the resultant fibers has been achieved. Hydroxyl impurity has been removed using the chlorine gas-drying process previously described.

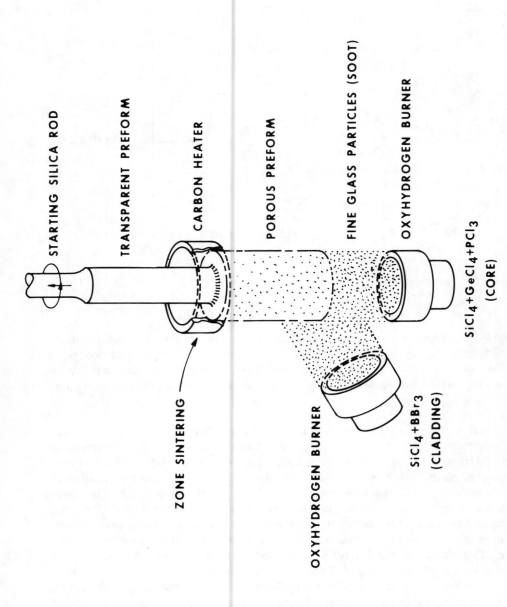

STARTING SILICA ROD

TRANSPARENT PREFORM

CARBON HEATER

POROUS PREFORM

FINE GLASS PARTICLES (SOOT)

OXYHYDROGEN BURNER

ZONE SINTERING

OXYHYDROGEN BURNER

$SiCl_4 + BBr_3$
(CLADDING)

$SiCl_4 + GeCl_4 + PCl_3$
(CORE)

Figure 7-21 Illustration of vapor axial deposition process (VAD process).

Although early fibers made with the VAD process had relatively low bandwidths (<400 MHz-km), recent advances in preform process control has produced fibers with comparable loss and bandwidth to fibers made by the MCVD or lateral-deposition processes.

7-6 FIBER-DRAWING (HIGH-SILICA FIBERS)

Once a preform has been made, the next step is to draw the preform into a fiber on a fiber-drawing machine. The drawing process must yield a fiber whose diameter is precisely controlled (typical diameter variation $< \pm 2\%$). In addition the fiber's strength must be preserved by applying a protective coating which shields the newly drawn fiber from mechanical abrasion and adverse effects of the atmosphere. The elements of a fiber-drawing machine are shown schematically in Fig. 7-22. The preform is fed by a preform drive mechanism into a heated region where it necks down to form a fiber which is pulled from the heat zone. The diameter of the fiber is measured at a point shortly after it is formed, and this measured value is input to a control system. Within the controller, the measured fiber diameter is compared to a desired value, and an output signal is generated to adjust the drawing drive-speed such that the fiber diameter approaches the desired value. After the diameter is measured, a protective coating is applied to the fiber. The coating material is then cured on the fiber before it reaches the drawing mechanism. After the coated fiber passes through the drawing mechanism (typically a capstan) it is stored on a spool for future testing and subsequent packaging operations. Figure 7-23 is a photograph of a Western Electric fiber-drawing machine.[19]

We will now consider the individual components of a fiber-drawing machine. First the various heat sources used for fiber-drawing will be discussed and then the design requirements associated with the components used to obtain precise diameter control and proper coating of the fiber will be described.

7-6-1 Heat Sources

The heat source used for drawing fused-silica fibers must be capable of raising the temperature of a preform to 2000°C. The atmosphere in the heat zone surrounding the molten material must be free from contaminants and must have a minimal amount of thermal turbulence. This is to ensure that the fiber's strength is not degraded and that its diameter variations are kept to a minimum. There are four types of heat sources that have been used to draw high-silica fibers as shown in Fig. 7-24.

a **Oxyhydrogen torch** The oxyhydrogen torch (Fig. 7-24a) is the simplest heat source and the one used for drawing fibers in the early stages of fiber technology.[20] It does not introduce contaminants in the vicinity of the molten preform,

SCHEMATIC OF FIBER–DRAWING MACHINE

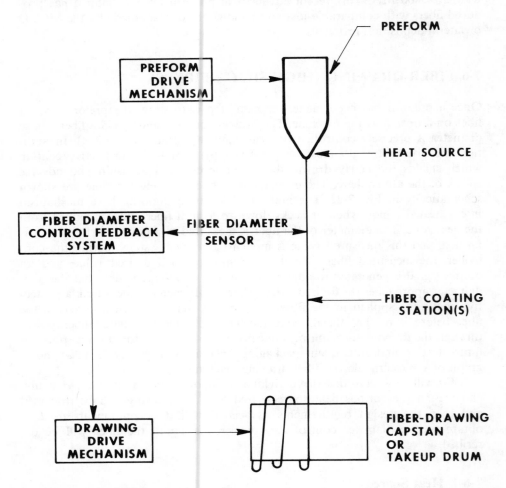

Figure 7-22 Schematic of fiber-drawing machine.

but it induces large variations in the fiber diameter (typically $> 5\%$) due to turbulence of the torch flame and the open environment surrounding the neck-down region. The mode of heating of the oxyhydrogen torch is by conduction from the flame to the glass.

b **CO_2 laser** (Fig. 7-24b) The energy from a CO_2 laser at 10.6 μm wavelength is absorbed by the surface of a preform and its interior is heated by reradiation and conduction. The laser heat source has been successfully used in laboratory experiments.[21] It is a very clean energy source that produces fibers whose

Figure 7-23 Photograph of Western Electric fiber-drawing machine.

diameters are well controlled. While the laser has proved to be a useful laboratory tool other energy sources such as the furnaces described below have much lower cost-to-energy ratios. Because of this, CO_2 lasers have found only limited use as a heat source for producing fibers in a production environment.

c **Graphite or tungsten resistance furnaces** (Fig. 7-24*c*) A resistance furnace uses either a tungsten or graphite element which is heated resistively to heat the preform by blackbody radiation. Because the preform must be heated to approximately 2000°C to soften the glass and draw a fiber, the furnace heating

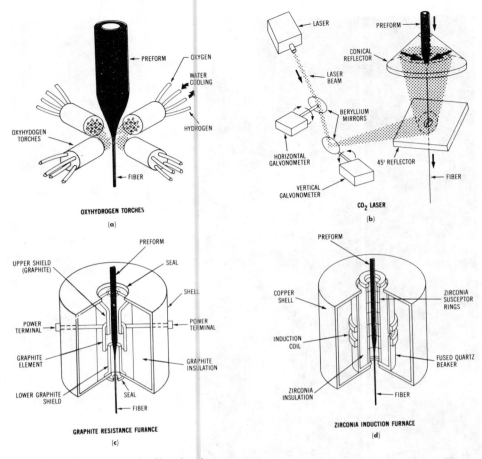

Figure 7-24 Heat sources for fiber-drawing.

element must be surrounded by a protective gas such as argon to prevent its oxidation. The flow of gas must be carefully controlled to prevent disturbances of the molten glass neck-down region. Such disturbances would be translated into variations in the diameter of the resultant fiber. In addition, contamination of the preform surface may occur due to the heating element's high operating temperature. This contamination can cause the drawn fiber to have reduced strength.

d **Zirconia induction furnace** A preform can also be heated by blackbody radiation if RF energy is inductively coupled to zirconia (ZrO_2) susceptor rings as shown in the furnace pictured in Fig. 7-24*d*. This furnace configuration has the advantage that zirconia does not require a protective inert atmosphere, and consequently the preform is drawn in a turbulence-free uncontaminated environment. High-strength fibers with good diameter control ($< \pm 2\%$ variation) can be drawn with the zirconia furnace.[22]

7-6-2 Fiber Coating

The primary function of a fiber coating is to preserve the intrinsically high strength of the newly drawn fiber. To avoid contamination or damage to the fiber's surface a protective coating must be applied to the fiber immediately after it is formed. There are three different types of coating material systems that are in use to coat fibers today. The first class of materials, which includes a group of polymer epoxy acrylates, is cured by ultraviolet radiation. A second class of materials are thermosetting; an example of a material in this class is silicone. The third class includes solvent-based materials such as lacquers and various polymers. The epoxy acrylate coatings are cured by passing the coated fiber through an ultraviolet curing lamp system. The thermosetting and solvent-based coating materials are thermally cured by passing the coated fiber through a small oven. The coating that is applied should not induce microbending losses

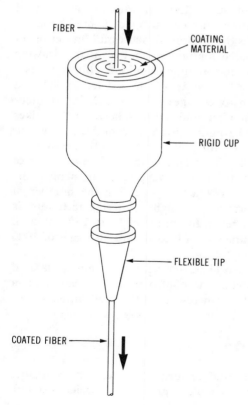

FIBER

COATING
MATERIAL

RIGID CUP

FLEXIBLE TIP

COATED FIBER

Figure 7-25 Drawing of coating cup showing application of coating materials.

due to a hard, rough-coating fiber interface. A soft coating with a relatively low Young's modulus or a multilayer coating with a very soft silicone inner buffer layer and an extruded polymer (typically nylon) outer layer[9,23] are commonly used coating systems. Figure 7-25 is an example of a coating cup used to apply a UV-cured epoxy acrylate coating. The coating process can be a limiting factor in the drawing process. At typical draw speeds in the range of 0.5 m/s to 1.5 m/s[19] the most important factors related to coating are the proper curing of the material and the centering of the fiber in the coating. If a fiber is badly off-centered in the coating its surface may be damaged during the coating process. Off-centered or improperly cured coatings can effect a fiber's strength and cause microbending loss.

7-6-3 Diameter Measurement and Process Control

A number of noncontact diameter measurement techniques[1,19] have been developed and are commercially available to measure fiber diameter. These include shadowgraph methods, laser-scanning techniques, lateral interferometry, and light-scattering techniques. To properly control the fiber diameter to $\pm 2\%$ of the nominal OD the diameter measurement system should have the ability to measure fiber diameters in the range of 90 to 150 μm with an accuracy of $\pm 0.3\%$ at a rate in excess of 100 measurements per meter of fiber. The laser-scanning and light-scattering techniques have proved successful in terms of meeting the measuring requirements needed for precise control of the drawing process. As shown in Fig. 7-26a the laser-scanning technique utilizes a laser beam that is repeatedly scanned across a limited area onto a detector. When a fiber is placed in the moving beam, intensity changes are detected. Sharp intensity spikes correspond to the edges of the fiber, and the time between the spikes is proportional to the fiber diameter. The light-scattering technique, shown in Fig. 7-26b, involves illuminating the fiber with a laser beam and detecting the intensity of light scattered by the fiber as a function of angle.[24] The diameter of the fiber is proportional to the phase of the rapidly varying component of the scattering pattern. The diameter can be obtained by counting the number of intensity peaks within a fixed angular range. The light-scattering technique is capable of making measurements on a fiber in the range of 50 to 225 μm, with a resolution of 0.2 μm, an absolute accuracy of $\pm 0.26\%$, and at a rate of 1000 measurements per second.[19,25]

To obtain precise control of the drawn fiber, the measured diameter is used as an input to a diameter control system. The control system is based on a conservation of mass model of the neck-down region of the preform as shown in Fig. 7-27a. The relationships between the physical variables is given by[19] ,

$$D_f^2 V_f = D_p^2 V_p + \int_{-\infty}^{t} d\omega \qquad (7\text{-}8)$$

where D_f, V_f, D_p, and V_p are the fiber and preform diameters and velocities respectively. The term ω is a random variable representing mechanical and

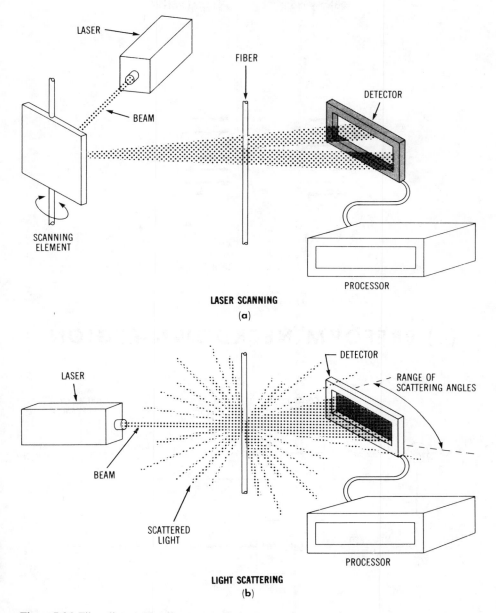

Figure 7-26 Fiber diameter measurement systems.

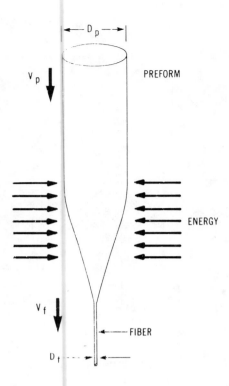

(a) PREFORM NECKDOWN REGION

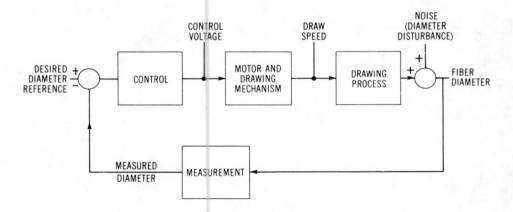

(b) BLOCK DIAGRAM OF DIAMETER-
CONTROL SYSTEM

Figure 7-27 Geometry of mathematical model and block diagram of diameter control systems.

thermally induced disturbances as well as variations in diameter which occur while the process is establishing its equilibrium condition.

The components that make up the diameter control system are shown in Fig. 7-27b. Each block represents the dynamic relationship between physical variables. For example, a voltage input to the motor power amplifier of the draw mechanism affects the velocity of the draw mechanism and hence the fiber velocity. In turn, a change in fiber velocity will produce a change in the fiber diameter. The fiber diameter is measured, this value is compared to a desired value, and a control signal generated which will drive the fiber diameter toward the desired value.[26] This system used in a production environment produces fibers whose diameters vary by less than $\pm 2\%$.

Example 7-1 Estimating fiber length drawn from a preform Let us calculate the length of a 125-μm-diameter fiber that can be drawn from a 1-m-long 12-mm-diameter preform. Using the principle of conservation of mass

$$\rho_{\text{preform}} V_{\text{preform}} = \rho_{\text{fiber}} V_{\text{fiber}}$$

where ρ and V are respectively the density and volume of the preform and fiber. Since the densities at the preform and fiber glass are equal

$$V_{\text{preform}} = V_{\text{fiber}}$$

$$\pi r^2_{\text{preform}} L_{\text{preform}} = \pi r^2_{\text{fiber}} L_{\text{fiber}}$$

$$L_{\text{fiber}} = \frac{r^2_{\text{preform}}}{r^2_{\text{fiber}}} L_{\text{preform}}$$

$$L_{\text{fiber}} = \frac{(6 \times 10^{-3})^2}{(62.5 \times 10^{-6})^2} \quad (1)$$

$$L_{\text{fiber}} = 9.2 \text{ km}$$

7-7 FABRICATION OF MULTICOMPONENT GLASS FIBERS (DOUBLE CRUCIBLE METHOD)

Multicomponent glass fibers are fabricated by first producing separate glass feed rods from purified glass melts of the core and cladding compositions. These rods are then used as feedstock in a double crucible drawing apparatus (see Fig. 7-28) where the composite fiber is drawn from the bottom orifices.

The feed rods are produced by starting with purified powders which are premixed, heated in a crucible until they fuse, and then agitated to produce a homogeneous glass melt. The feed rod is formed by dipping a seed rod into the melt and pulling it slowly upward through a cooling ring. The glass pulls up after the seed rod and solidifies to form a glass rod typically 5 to 10 mm in diameter and a few meters long.[4]

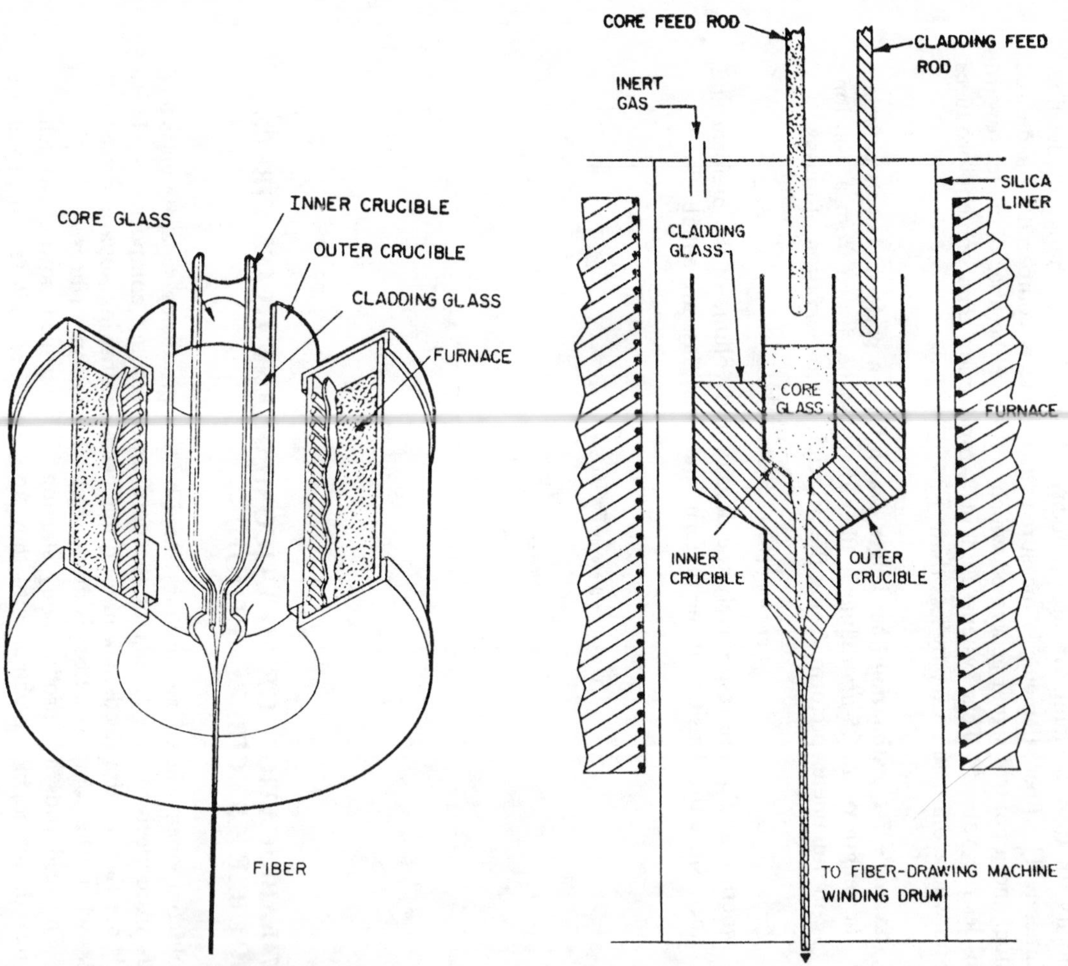

CLADDING FEED ROD

SILICA LINER

FURNACE

CORE FEED ROD

OUTER CRUCIBLE

CORE GLASS

INERT GAS

CLADDING GLASS

INNER CRUCIBLE

TO FIBER-DRAWING MACHINE WINDING DRUM

(b) GRADED-INDEX FIBER

INNER CRUCIBLE

OUTER CRUCIBLE

CLADDING GLASS

FURNACE

CORE GLASS

FIBER

(a) STEP-INDEX FIBER

Figure 7-28 Double crucible configurations.

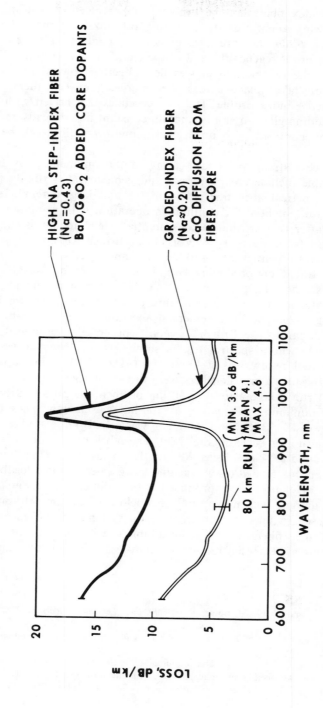

Figure 7-29 Spectral loss curves of multicomponent glass fibers.

Graded-index fibers can be drawn from the feed rods using the double crucible drawing apparatus. By extending the nozzle of the outer crucible as shown in Fig. 7-28b, the core glass comes into contact with the cladding glass some time before it reaches the end of the cladding nozzle from which the fiber is drawn. As the two molten glasses flow together toward the drawing neck, ionic diffusion takes place across the interface between them, producing a graded refractive-index profile. The two crucibles can be fed with feed rods of core and cladding glass so as to maintain constant liquid heads and to facilitate fiber diameter control.[1] Also under these conditions, fiber can be drawn continuously.

The process strengths of fabricating multicomponent glass fibers with a double crucible include compositional and geometrical flexibility (for example, very high numerical apertures of 0.4 to 0.5 and large-core fibers are readily made), and the potential for continuous operation with a minimum of process steps. The latter two attributes can potentially lead to consistency of product and low manufacturing costs.[10] Workers at British Telecom have shown that this process has potential for reproducibility and large-scale production.[27] They have concentrated on producing two fiber types. Using Na_2O—B_2O_3—SiO_2 base glasses, they have obtained 0.43 NA step-index fibers (75-μm core diameter) with an attenuation minimum of 10 dB/km as shown by the upper curve in Fig. 7-29. The high numerical aperture was achieved by adding BaO and GeO_2 dopants. The British Telecom workers also produced graded-index fibers (0.2 NA) whose spectral loss is shown as the lower curve in Fig. 7-29. These fibers had bandwidths of 400 to 900 MHz-km. By using rapid diffusion of CaO from the fiber core the fibers were drawn at speeds greater than 0.5 m/s. In one pilot run, where a total of 80 km of fiber was produced over a five-day period, the minimum attenuation at 800-nm wavelength was 3.6 dB/km, the maximum was 4.6 dB/km, and the mean was 4.1 dB/km as indicated by the bar marks on the lower curve in Fig. 7-29. The fabrication process has been operated on a round-the-clock basis. Melting feed rods during the day and drawing fibers with an unattended draw machine using an automated feedback system at night, 250 km of fiber were produced with a dimensional control of the fiber OD of ± 1 μm and with minimum losses below 5.5 dB/km. Although high-silica fibers are used in most telecommunication systems in existence today, multicomponent glass fibers made by the double crucible method appear to have a place in future systems that require medium-loss relatively low bandwidth fibers.

REFERENCES

1. S. E. Miller and A. G. Chynoweth: *Optical Fiber Telecommunications*, Academic Press, Inc. New York, 1979.
2. B. Bendow and S. Mitra: *Fiber Optics, Advances in Research and Development*, Plenum Press, New York, 1979.
3. R. L. Gallawa, J. E. Midwinter, and S. Shimada: "A Survey of Word-Wide Optical Waveguide Systems," Topical Meeting on Optical Fiber Communication, *OSA*, Paper TuA1, March, 1979.
4. J. E. Midwinter: *Optical Fibers for Transmission*, John Wiley & Sons, New York, 1979.

5. J. A. Jefferies and R. J. Klaiber: "Lightguide Theory and its Implications in Manufacturing," *West. Electr. Eng.*, Winter, 1980.
6. K. A. Stacey: *Light Scattering in Physical Chemistry*, Academic Press, New York, 1956.
7. R. D. Maurer: "Glass Fibers for Optical Communication." *Proc. IEEE*, **61**: 452–463, April, 1973.
8. F. P. Partus and M. A. Saifi: "Lightguide Preform Manufacture," *West. Electr. Eng.*, Winter, 1980.
9. W. B. Gardner: "Microbending Loss in Coated and Uncoated Optical Fibers," Topical Meeting on Optical Fiber Transmission, *OSA*, Paper WA3-1, 1975.
10 P. C. Schultz: "Progress in Optical Waveguide Process and Materials," *Appl. Opt.*, **18** (21): 3684–3693, Nov. 1, 1979.
11. J. B. MacChesney, et al.: "A New Technique for Preparation of Low-Loss and Graded-Index Optical Fibers," *Proc. IEEE*, **62**: 1280 (1974).
12. K. L. Walker, G. M. Homsy, S. R. Nagel, and F. T. Geyling: Electrochem. Soc. Mtg., Abstract 137, Fiber Optics Symposium, Pittsburg, Pa., October, 1978.
13. P. Geittner, D. Kuppers, and H. Lydtin: *Appl. Phys. Lett.*, **28** (11): 645–646, June 1976.
14. D. Kuppers, J. Koenings, and H. Wilson: *J. Electrochem. Soc.*, **123** (7): 1079–1083, July 1976.
15. D. B. Keck and P. C. Schultz: "Method of Producing Optical Waveguide Fibers," U.S. Patent 3 711 262, 1973.
16. T. Izawa, T. Miyashita, and F. Hanawa: U.S. Patent 4 062 665, "Continuous Optical Fiber Preform Fabrication," December 1977.
17. T. Izawa, S. Kobyashi, S. Sudo, F. Taka, N. Shibata, and M. Nakahara: Japanese Nat. Conv. Inst. Electron. Commun. Eng. Paper 909, March, 1978.
18. S. Sudo, M. Kawachi, T. Edahiro, and T. Izawa: *Electron. Lett.*, **14** (17): 534, Aug. 17, 1978.
19. D. H. Smithgall and D. L. Myers: "Drawing Lightguide Fiber," *West. Eng.*, Winter, 1980.
20. W. G. French, J. B. MacChesney, and A. D. Pearson: "Glass Fibers for Optical Communications," *Ann. Rev. Mater. Sci.*, **5**: 373–393 (1975).
21. R. F. Jaeger: "Laser Drawing of Glass Fiber Optical Waveguides," *Ceram. Bull.* **53** (3): 270–273 (1976).
22. F. V. DiMarcello and A. C. Hart: "Furnace Drawn Silica Fibers with Tensile Strengths > 3.5 GN/m^2 (500 kpsi) in One km Lengths," *Electron. Lett.*, **14** (18): 578–579, August 1978.
23. D. Gloge: "Optical Fiber Packaging and its Influence on Fiber Straightness and Loss," *BSTJ*, **54** (2): 245 (1975).
24. L. S. Watkins: "Scattering from Side-Illuminated Clad Glass Fibers for Determination of Fiber Parameters," *JOSA*, **64**: 767 (1974).
25. D. H. Smithgall, L. S. Watkins, and R. E. Frazee: "High Speed Non-Contact Fiber Diameter Measurement Using Forward Light Scattering," *Appl. Opt.*, **16** (9): 2395–2402, September 1977.
26. D. H. Smithgall: "Application of Optimization Theory to the Control of the Optical Fiber Drawing Process," *BSTJ*, **58** (6): 1425–1435, July/August 1979.
27. K. J. Beales et al.: "Preparation of Low Loss Graded Index and High N.A. Step-Index Compound Glass Fiber by the Double-Crucible Technique," Abstract 38-G-79, p. 378, Ceramic Society Annual Meeting, Cincinnati, Ohio, May, 1979.

PROBLEMS

7-1 Describe four requirements that material systems must satisfy for them to be used in the fabrication of communication fibers. List two types of glass systems which fulfill these requirements and the types of fiber produced by each system.

7-2 List and briefly describe five transmission-loss mechanisms in an optical fiber.

7-3 Refer to Fig. 7-3. What is the dominant loss mechanism in a system whose operating wavelength is (*a*) 0.80 μm? (*b*) 1.37 μm? (*c*) 1.55 μm?

7-4 Consider the wavelength range between $\lambda = 0.60$ μm and $\lambda = 1.00$ μm. If a system designer wants to minimize the effects of impurity absorption loss, at what wavelength in this range would he choose to operate the system if the dominant impurity is Fe^{2+}? OH^-?

7-5 Consider a glass in which P_2O_5 is used as a dopant to change the refractive-index profile of a high-silica preform. How does the working temperature of the P_2O_5 doped glass compare with that of a SiO_2 silica glass?

7-6 A glass system is to be made into a preform and drawn into a fiber. What thermal property must the system possess if the thermally induced stresses are to be beneficial to the fiber? What mechanical property will the system possess to ensure minimal problems with preform manufacture and fiber drawing?

7-7 Describe three methods of preform fabrication. Include starting materials, heat sources or fabrication temperatures used, and the technique used to make the preform for each method.

7-8 Draw a block diagram of the process used to draw the preform into a fiber.

7-9 What are three properties of any heat source used in a fiber-drawing machine? What fiber parameters are affected by these properties? Discuss the four heat sources listed in the text in terms of these properties and also give the mode of heating used in each one.

7-10 Approximately how much fiber will be obtained from a 15-mm-diameter 1-m-long preform if the fiber diameter is 100 μm? 175 μm?

7-11 Assume an ideal fiber-drawing process. What is the diameter of a fiber drawn from a 10-mm-diameter preform with a velocity of 0.1 mm/s if the fiber takeup velocity is 0.75 m/s?

7-12 A fiber coating must provide a fiber with two features. What are they? List three types of coating material systems.

EIGHT

FIBER MEASUREMENTS

8-1 INTRODUCTION

In this chapter we will describe the techniques for measuring the transmission characteristics of optical fibers. We will concentrate on the evaluation of a fiber's loss, pulse-delay distortion (bandwidth), and refractive index profile. Optical characterization of fibers typically serves two different purposes. On the one hand the acquired data is used by a fiber designer to improve the properties of the preforms used for fiber fabrication. On the other hand a systems engineer requires data which ensures that realistic fiber parameters are used in the design calculations of an optical transmission system. Often data obtained from different measurement techniques is needed to satisfy the requirements of both the fiber designer and the systems engineer. In this chapter we will illustrate both categories of measurements by describing a few of the more commonly used measurement techniques for evaluating the characteristics of low-loss, multimode optical fibers.

8-2 TRANSMISSION-LOSS MEASUREMENTS

We have observed in Chap. 7 that various absorption and scattering-loss mechanisms contribute to the total transmission loss of an optical fiber. A fiber designer is concerned with measuring both the absorption and scattering components as well as the total loss of an optical fiber. Data obtained from these measurements would be used by the fiber designer to diagnose problems in the fabrication process and to improve the fiber's characteristics. On the other hand, an engineer whose job it is to design a fiber optic system is interested in obtaining data related to the total transmission loss of a fiber.

In this section we will describe a two-point cutback method[1,2] used for measuring the total transmission loss of a fiber. In subsequent sections we will discuss both scattering- and absorption-loss measurements. In addition, we will describe two nondestructive methods for measuring the transmission loss of a fiber.

Multimode fibers contain several hundred propagating modes, each with different loss and delay characteristics. Because of differential mode attenuation and mode coupling, the total loss measured in multimode optical fibers depends on how the source-launching conditions distribute the power among the propagating modes of the fiber. Figure 8-1 is a plot of the log of the power in a fiber as a function of fiber length for different source-launching conditions.[3] After a length L_c, called the mode-coupling length of a fiber, an equilibrium or "steady-state" mode distribution is established whose loss (in decibels per

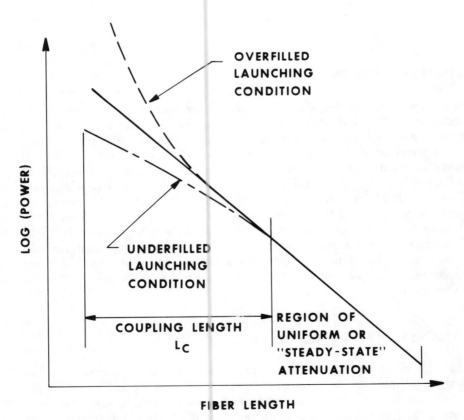

Figure 8-1 Power vs. fiber length in a multimode fiber for different input-launching conditions.

kilometer) is independent of the fiber length measured.[4] Typical coupling lengths can[5] range from tens of meters to more than 10 kilometers.

The transmission loss of an optical fiber is determined by measuring the total power at two points in the fiber separated by a length L as shown in Fig. 8-2. The attenuation of a fiber of length L is given by

$$A = 10 \log \left(\frac{P_{NE}}{P_{FE}}\right) \qquad \text{dB} \qquad (8\text{-}1)$$

with P_{FE} representing the power at the output or far end of the fiber (point B) and P_{NE} the power at the near-end cutback point A. In an effort to obtain a length-independent attenuation measurement of a fiber, launch conditions that approximate the fiber's equilibrium mode distribution (EMD) are required.[6] When a fiber is excited with its EMD, an attenuation constant α can be defined as

$$\alpha = \frac{A}{L} = \frac{10}{L} \log \left(\frac{P_{NE}}{P_{FE}}\right) \qquad \frac{\text{dB}}{\text{m}} \qquad (8\text{-}2)$$

α represents a length-independent steady-state loss which can be[4] extrapolated to arbitrary fiber lengths.

The presence of cladding modes, leaky modes, and lossy higher-order modes in a fiber can cause the measured loss to significantly exceed the equilibrium mode distribution loss. To establish the proper launching conditions in a loss measurement, beam optics[7] or a mode filter[8] as shown in Fig. 8-3 is used.

The validity of choosing a particular launching method is established by determining how well the loss measurements scale with fiber length. Fiber
tion experiments[9] with low mode coupling fibers indicate that
ing accuracy of 0.1 dB/km can be achieved using a mode filter that
es, at point A, the long length power ($\approx$ EMD) distribution of the
rfilled at its input end.

diagram of an automated spectral loss test set that precisely meas-
s of multimode optical fibers at wavelengths from 0.63 to 1.51 μm is
ig. 8-4.[10] A spectrally rich tungsten-halogen light source is chopped
ency synchronous with the detection system), filtered, and then fo-
the end of the fiber being measured. The light intensity is detected at
end of the test fiber by a dual detector which is a silicon–lead-sulfide
Because of the range of wavelengths over which loss measurements are
o different detectors are used, each of which is sensitive to a different
the optical spectrum. The silicon detector is sensitive to wavelengths in
e 0.6 to 0.9 μm, and the lead-sulfide detector from 0.9 to 1.5 μm. The
rom the detector is fed into a lock-in amplifier. The detector–lock-in
r combination responds only to light modulated at the mechanical
r frequency, thus providing a phase-sensitive detection scheme insensitive
bient light. The output of the amplifier is coupled to interface and control
tronics for processing and range selection. When a two-point measurement
made the light transmitted through the fiber (point B) is measured at selected

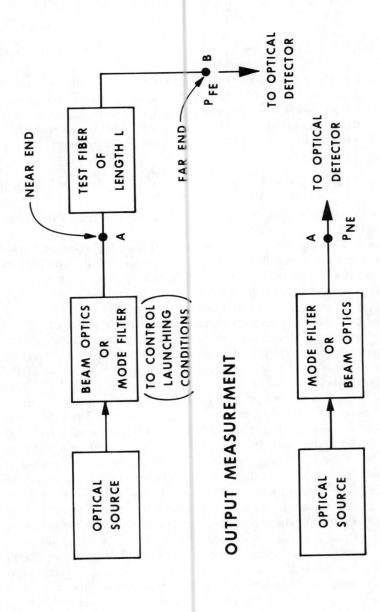

Figure 8-2 Schematic of two-point attenuation measurement.

190

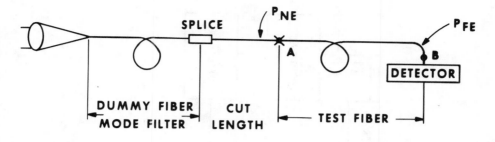

(a) DUMMY FIBER MODE FILTER

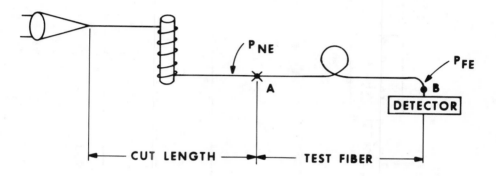

(b) MANDREL WRAP MODE FILTER

Figure 8-3 Attenuation measurement illustrating the use of mode filters.

wavelengths. These output readings are then stored in the calculator. The fiber is then broken at point A and the light transmitted through the short input length is measured at these wavelengths. Next the calculator computes the loss of the fiber at each selected wavelength using Eq. (8-1). Assuming linear length scaling, this spectral-loss data is plotted as a function of wavelength (loss in decibels per kilometer versus λ) as shown in Fig. 8-5.

Round robin studies[8] in which fibers were measured on a number of different test sets in different laboratories indicate that when standardized launching conditions are used, the interlocation precision of a two-point loss measurement is about 0.2 to 0.3 dB/km. The intralocation precision (ability to repeat a measurement on a given test set) is about 0.1 to 0.15 dB/km.

As mentioned in Chap 7, a convenient way to model the spectral response of a fiber is as follows:[5,10]

$$\alpha = A\lambda^{-4} + B + C(\lambda) \qquad (8\text{-}3)$$

where A is the Rayleigh scattering coefficient. It is a measure of the Rayleigh

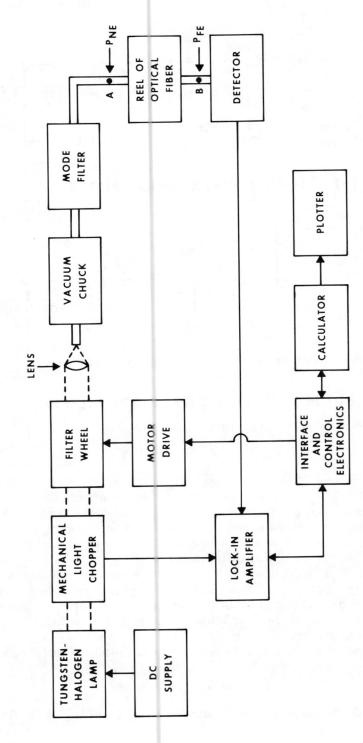

Figure 8-4 Block diagram of automated spectral loss test set.

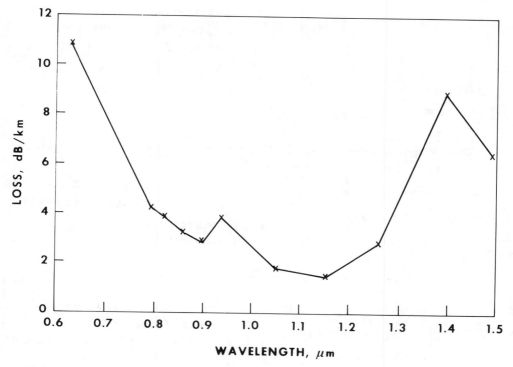

Figure 8-5 Spectral-loss curve.

scattering loss of the fiber. B is a wavelength-independent loss contribution which is affected by launch conditions, waveguide imperfections, and micro-bends. $C(\lambda)$ represents wavelength-dependent loss contributions caused by impurities (OH and transition metal ions, for example), drawing-induced effects, and the ultraviolet and infrared absorption tails. Modeling the spectral-loss curve of a fiber with Eq. (8-3) facilitates the identification and separation of the different loss mechanisms in a fiber.

8-3 SCATTERING AND ABSORPTION LOSS MEASUREMENTS

When a spectral transmission loss measurement of a fiber does not provide sufficient information to a fiber designer, independent measurements of the scattering and absorption loss of the fiber are also made. To measure the scattering loss of a fiber, the scattered light from a short length of fiber is collected and compared with the light traveling in the fiber core, as shown in Fig. 8-6. The fiber is surrounded with an index-matching fluid so that all of the scattered light (except the forward- and back-scattered light in the core) is detected.

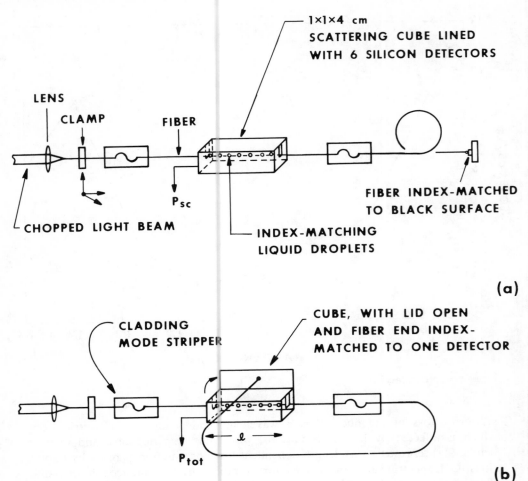

Figure 8-6 Scattering-loss measuring setup.

Practical scattering cells use either an enclosure lined with solar cells,[11] or an integrating sphere and photodetector.[12] Figure 8-6 shows a scattering cube lined with solar cells (Tynes' cell) that is used for measuring the scattering loss of a fiber. After measuring the scattered power P_{sc}, the fiber end is placed into the cell and the power transmitted in the core P_{tot} is determined. The scattering loss can be calculated from the following formula:[5]

$$\alpha_{sc} = \frac{4.34 \times 10^5}{l} \frac{P_{sc}}{P_{tot}} \quad \frac{\text{dB}}{\text{km}} \tag{8-4}$$

where l is the length of the fiber in the scattering cube in centimeters.

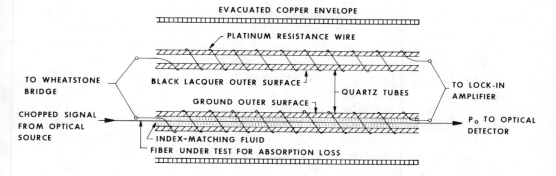

EVACUATED COPPER ENVELOPE

PLATINUM RESISTANCE WIRE

TO WHEATSTONE BRIDGE

BLACK LACQUER OUTER SURFACE

QUARTZ TUBES

TO LOCK-IN AMPLIFIER

CHOPPED SIGNAL FROM OPTICAL SOURCE

GROUND OUTER SURFACE

P_o TO OPTICAL DETECTOR

INDEX-MATCHING FLUID

FIBER UNDER TEST FOR ABSORPTION LOSS

(a) DIAGRAM OF CALORIMETER
(Structure is 20cm long and terminates in a thermal insulator. Tube is 1.5mm)

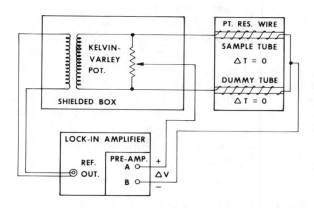

PT. RES. WIRE

KELVIN-VARLEY POT.

SAMPLE TUBE
$\Delta T = 0$

DUMMY TUBE
$\Delta T = 0$

SHIELDED BOX

LOCK-IN AMPLIFIER

REF. OUT.

PRE-AMP.
A
B

ΔV
+
−

(b) DIAGRAM OF TEMPERATURE MEASUREMENT SYSTEM FOR CALORIMETER MEASUREMENTS.

Figure 8-7 Calorimeter for measuring the absorption loss of fibers.

A precision of ± 0.2 dB/km can be achieved in scattering-loss measurements using laser sources.[5] The accuracy of a scattering-loss measurement depends on careful calibration of the scattering cube and the mode spectrum propagating in the fiber.

The absorption loss of a fiber can be determined as the difference between its total and scattering loss, or it can be measured directly using a calorimeter.[13,14] One calorimetric technique[13] that has been used to separate the scattering and absorption components of loss in optical fibers is illustrated in Fig. 8-7. Two quartz tubes of small diameter (typically 20 cm long and 1 mm in diameter) are used: the surface of one is blackened to sense the combined heating effect of both the scattered and absorbed power; the surface of the other tube is ground to pass the scattered radiation and sense the heating effect due to the fiber absorption only. The fiber to be measured is threaded through either the blackened tube (to measure total loss) or the ground tube (to measure absorption loss). Chopped optical power is launched into the fiber and the temperature changes due to the total or absorption loss in the fiber produce resistance changes in the platinum wire wrapped around the particular tube used. The phase-sensitive detector shown in Fig. 8-7 measures the small voltage imbalance that the resistance change induces in the Wheatstone bridge circuit.

Assuming that the tubes are surrounded by vacuum and hence that heat transfer occurs only via radiation, the relation between the bridge imbalance voltage ΔV and the fiber loss α can be derived

$$\alpha = C \frac{\varepsilon R}{PV} \Delta V \tag{8-5}$$

where ε is the surface emissivity, R is the radius of the tube used, V is the bridge voltage, and P is the optical power through the fiber. C is a constant of the calorimeter which can be derived as a combination of physical and material constants and bridge parameters or obtained from a calibration procedure by measuring ΔV caused by the heating due to a wire with a known α.

Using this calorimetric method, one can measure either the total loss or absorption loss (depending on which tube the fiber sample is placed in) at any place along a fiber with 20-cm spatial resolution. Subtracting the absorption loss from the total loss yields a value for scattering loss that is in reasonable agreement[13] (within seven percent) with direct scattering loss measurements made with a scattering cube.[11]

8-4 NONDESTRUCTIVE LOSS MEASUREMENTS

The two-point attenuation measurement described in Sec. 8-20 is a precise and, with properly chosen launching conditions, accurate method for measuring the transmission loss of a fiber. It is, however, a cutback method that has the disadvantage of being a destructive technique. That is, a short length of fiber at the input end is removed (typically a 1 m cutback length) from the test fiber to obtain the input power measurement. Under certain circumstances, for example when a fiber is packaged with a connector on its end or when it is in a cable installed in a duct, a nondestructive loss measurement technique is preferable to the two-point method. Two promising nondestructive loss-measurement methods (insertion-loss and optical time domain reflectometry (OTDR)) will be described in this section.

Figure 8-8 is a block diagram illustrating the measurement of the insertion-loss of a fiber. In an insertion-loss measurement, one first determines the magnitude of an input power level by inserting a short length of reference fiber between the source and the detector. Next the output power level is measured

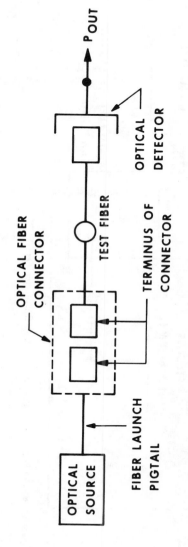

(a) OUTPUT MEASUREMENT

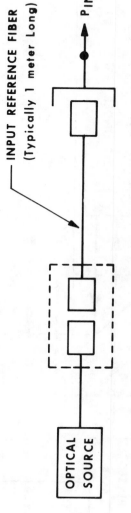

(b) INPUT REFERENCE MEASUREMENT

Figure 8-8 Block diagram illustrating the measurement of insertion loss of a fiber.

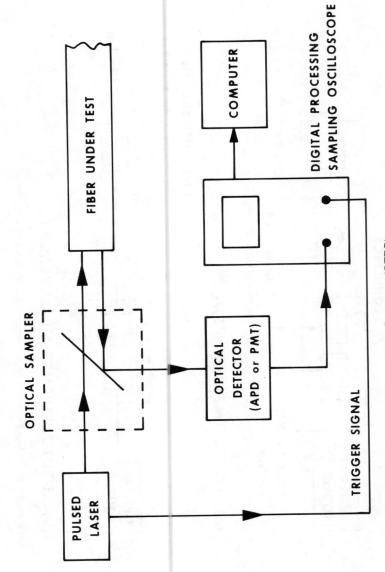

Figure 8-9 Block diagram of optical time-domain reflectometer (OTDR).

by removing the reference fiber and connecting the test fiber between the source pigtail and the optical detector. The insertion loss (IL) is then

$$IL = 10 \log \frac{P_{in}}{P_{out}} \quad \text{dB} \tag{8-6}$$

In the simplest version of an insertion loss measurement, after determining the magnitude of the near-end reference power level, and assuming reasonable source stability, fiber losses can be deduced from the far-end test fiber output reading alone. A comparison of the insertion-loss technique with the two-point method indicates that differences of the order of 0.5 dB/km or greater can occur if the coupling and resulting excitation conditions of the reference fiber differ from that of the test fiber.

The second nondestructive technique, optical time domain reflectometry (OTDR), has proved to be a very useful field-oriented loss-measurement method for determining the existence and location of fiber breaks and for measuring both splice and transmission loss in an installed fiber system.[5,15,16] OTDR is essentially an optical pulse echo system as shown in Fig. 8-9. An optical probe pulse (typically 5 to 10 ns half-power width) from the laser is injected into the fiber to be measured. The probe pulse undergoes scattering continuously along the length of the fiber, producing a low-level reflected signal. The degree of scattering is dependent on the amount of transmission loss in the fiber and is primarily caused by Rayleigh scattering from inhomogeneities in the glass. The reflected signals propagate back to the input end of the fiber where they are detected by a photodetector (usually an avalanche photodiode (APD)) and displayed on a sampling oscilloscope.

Figure 8-10 is an oscilloscope trace showing the decay of the back-scattered light observed in a 1.5-km long low-loss fiber as a function of time.[17] The back-scattered signal as a function of time is a direct measure of the fiber's attenuation versus length. Plotted on a semilog scale the slope of the curve yields the average attenuation of the fiber. One can also analyze the oscilloscope trace to locate loss irregularities along the length of a fiber. Figure 8-11 shows a semilog plot of the back-scattered signal of a fiber illustrating how an

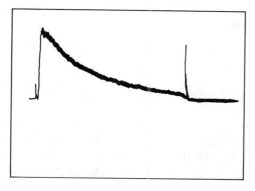

Figure 8-10 Oscilloscope trace of back-scattered signal (OTDR).

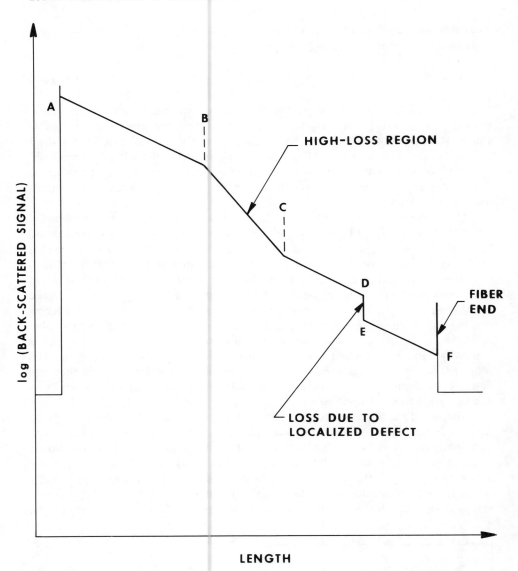

Figure 8-11 Semilog plot of back-scattered signal illustrating region of high loss and loss due to localized defect.

OTDR can be used to locate a high-loss region (*BC*) in a fiber or a localized defect (*DE*).

In addition the location of breaks in a fiber can be precisely measured with an OTDR. To determine the location of a fault in a fiber, the round trip time *t* of the probe pulse from the fiber input face to the fault and back to the fiber input is measured on the oscilloscope. The location of the fault, *L*, measured from the input end of the fiber is then determined from

$$L = \tfrac{1}{2}(c/n_1)t \tag{8-7}$$

where n_1 is the core-refractive index and c is the speed of light in free space. To locate a fault to within one meter of its true position requires an optical pulse width $\Delta t < 10$ ns. The power reaching the detector, P_d, is given by[5]

$$P_d = TRP_o 10^{-2\alpha L/10} \tag{8-8}$$

where P_o is the output power of the laser source, T is the transmittance of the optical system including fiber-coupling efficiency and optical sampler losses, α is the total transmission loss of the fiber in decibels per kilometer, and R is the reflection coefficient at the fault. If the fiber break had a flat perpendicular end, its reflection coefficient, calculated from Fresnel's equations, would be four percent (-14 dB). If the fiber break produced a nonperpendicular jagged end or one cleaved at an angle, the reflection coefficient would be considerably smaller than four percent.[18] Commercially available fault location OTDR's are capable of probing an equivalent length of fiber equal to 25 to 30 dB with a GaAlAs laser diode operating at 0.825 μm and an avalanche photodiode detector.

A typical reflection coefficient for a break has been found to be 0.005[19] and the transmittance of a system is approximately -16 dB (-6 dB due to the loss of the optical sampler and -10 dB fiber-coupling loss).

8-5 DELAY DISTORTION; BANDWIDTH MEASUREMENTS

Most applications of fibers in communication systems utilize some form of digital envelope modulation of an optical signal. Accordingly delay distortion, and how it affects the fiber performance, is usually characterized in terms of the degradation of an optical pulse propagating through the fiber (time-domain characterization). An alternate description in terms of the fibers baseband frequency characteristic can also be given. This frequency-domain characterization can be obtained by applying Fourier transform analysis to the time-domain signals or by direct measurement of the transfer function of the fiber in the frequency domain.

A fiber's characteristics are typically displayed as shown in Fig. 8-12, in terms of its power transfer function $H(\omega)$, or equivalently in terms of its impulse response $h(t)$, where $H(\omega)$ and $h(t)$ are Fourier transform pairs given by

$$H(\omega) = \int_{-\infty}^{\infty} h(t)e^{-j\omega t}\, dt \tag{8-9}$$

and

$$h(t) = \frac{1}{2\pi} \int_{-\infty}^{\infty} H(\omega)e^{j\omega t}\, d\omega \tag{8-10}$$

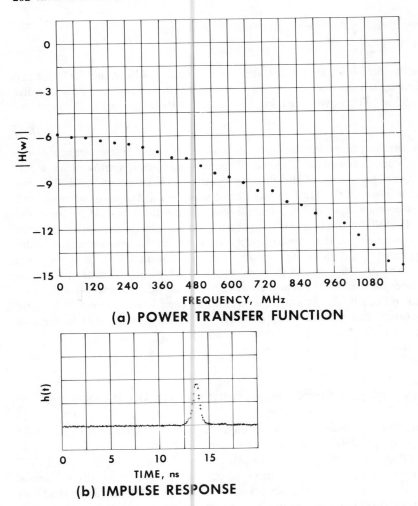

Figure 8-12 Fiber characteristics: $H(\omega)$, power transfer function; $h(t)$, impulse response.

and where ω is the radian base-band frequency of the envelope of the modulated optical carrier.

In the time domain, the shape of the impulse response is characterized by computing its rms pulse width (2σ) defined by[5]

$$\sigma^2 = \frac{1}{p} \int_{-\infty}^{\infty} h(t)t^2 \, dt - \tau^2 \qquad (8\text{-}11)$$

where

$$\tau = \frac{1}{p} \int_{-\infty}^{\infty} h(t)t \, dt \qquad (8\text{-}12)$$

is the pulse delay and

$$p = \int_{-\infty}^{\infty} h(t) \, dt \qquad (8\text{-}13)$$

is the energy in $h(t)$.

In the frequency domain the 3-dB bandwidth (half-power width) of the magnitude of the power-transfer function ($|H(\omega)|$) is usually given as a figure of merit of a fiber's performance.

The measurement of the delay-distortion characteristics of a fiber is critically affected by several factors. The measured bandwidth is strongly influenced by the presence of mode coupling and the modal distribution of the power launched into the fiber. In addition, the source line width enters into the results because of the fiber's chromatic (material) dispersion. For multimode fibers the component of delay distortion due to chromatic dispersion is often small compared to that caused by the differential group velocities and loss rates of the propagating modes.

In the next two sections of this chapter we will illustrate both the time-domain and frequency-domain measurement techniques for measuring the delay distortion characteristics of a fiber and will attempt to indicate the advantages and disadvantages of each approach.

8-6 TIME-DOMAIN MEASUREMENTS

The measurement of the delay distortion characteristics of a fiber using the time-domain technique is shown in Fig. 8-13. A narrow pulse (ideally a unit impulse function) of optical power, $f(t)$, is used to excite a fiber and detector in tandem, and produces an output voltage $g(t)$. The output voltage $g(t)$ is a distorted version of the input signal $f(t)$ due to the combined frequency responses of the fiber being measured and the optical detector. The frequency response of the fiber is extracted using a two-point measurement technique as shown in Fig. 8-14.[10]

Both $g_1(t)$ and $g_0(t)$, respectively the detected output pulses through the full length of fiber and through a short reference length, are measured. The corresponding Fourier transforms $G_1(\omega)$ and $G_0(\omega)$ are calculated using the formula

$$G(\omega) = \sum_{n=0}^{N-1} g(nT)e^{-j\omega nT} \qquad (8\text{-}14)$$

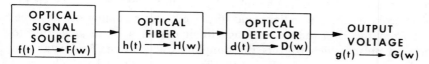

Figure 8-13 Block diagram of time-domain technique for measuring fiber delay distortion.

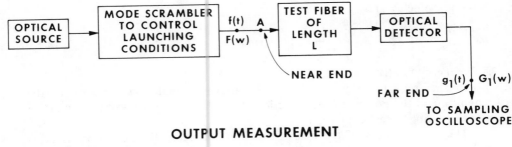

OUTPUT MEASUREMENT

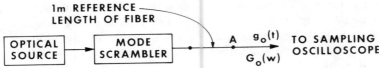

INPUT REFERENCE MEASUREMENT

Figure 8-14 Block diagram of two-point delay distortion measurement.

where $g(nT)$ are the digitized samples of $g(t)$ for each time interval T. The frequency response of the fiber, $H(\omega)$, is then calculated as

$$H(\omega) = \frac{G_1(\omega)}{G_0(\omega)} = \frac{H_1(\omega)}{H_0(\omega)} \tag{8-15}$$

It is assumed in Eq. (8-15) that there is a linear relationship between the detector output voltage and input power. This assumption is generally valid for most PIN detectors. Also, since the reference fiber is short compared to the test fiber length, for the frequency range of interest

$$H_0(\omega) \approx 1 \tag{8-16}$$

The transform of $H(\omega)$ back into the time domain therefore becomes $h_1(t)$, the fiber's power response to a unit impulse.

Figure 8-15 is a block diagram of a delay-distortion measurement set. This type of measurement set typically uses a pulsed semiconductor laser such as a GaAlAs double heterostructure laser operating at 0.825 μm wavelength. The laser is pulsed at a 10 to 25 kHz repetition rate to produce optical pulses of 100 to 200 ps duration. A mode scrambler[20] is often used at the output of the laser to produce an approximately uniform excitation condition among the propagating modes of the test fiber. After the optical pulse has propagated through the fiber it is detected by the photodiode and displayed on a sampling oscilloscope. An output from the laser-pulser clocking circuit causes a pulse generator to send a delayed pulse, which triggers the sampling oscilloscope. This delay can be adjusted to be equal to the delay of the fiber under test and its value read from a setting on the pulse generator. The output of the oscilloscope is con-

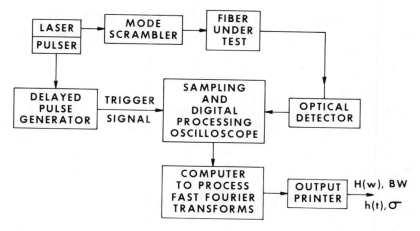

Figure 8-15 Delay distortion measurement test set.

verted internally into digital form and read into a computer which can process, store, and display the information. State of the art measurement sets of the configuration shown in Fig. 8-15 have an upper limit to their frequency range of 3 to 4 GHz.[10]

Example 8-1 Relation between bandwidth and time-domain rms pulse width
When the time domain technique is used to measure the bandwidth of a fiber, the output pulse will often closely approximate a gaussian shape. If we assume a pure gaussian output pulse in the time domain, we can derive a relation between pulse width in the time domain and bandwidth in the frequency domain.

If the time domain pulse $f(t)$ is pure gaussian, the following transform relationship holds:

$$f(t) = \frac{1}{\sigma \sqrt{2\pi}} e^{t^2/2\sigma^2} \leftrightarrow F(\omega) = e^{-\sigma^2 \omega^2/2}$$

A relationship between the full-width half-maximum bandwidth (BW) and the rms pulse width 2σ (see Fig. 8-16) can be obtained from the Fourier transform of the pulse. Since BW is essentially the frequency at which $|F(\omega)| = \frac{1}{2}$

$$|F(\omega)| = \frac{1}{2} = e^{\frac{\sigma^2(2\pi BW)^2}{2}}$$

$$\ln\left(\tfrac{1}{2}\right) = -\tfrac{1}{2}(2\pi BW\sigma)^2$$

Solving for the rms pulse width in terms of the 3-dB bandwidth

$$2\sigma = \frac{\sqrt{2\ln 2}}{\pi BW} \tag{8-17}$$

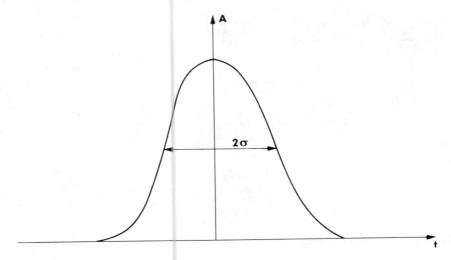

Figure 8-16 Gaussian shaped pulse.

The bandwidth BW and the rms pulse-width 2σ are related by Eq. (8-17). The actual output pulse will not have a pure gaussian shape, so the relationship is approximate for a real fiber.

8-7 FREQUENCY-DOMAIN MEASUREMENTS

Bandwidth measurements can be made directly in the frequency domain using the two-point method, by externally modulating a continuous-wave light carrier (see Fig. 8-17) or directly modulating an LED with a frequency-tunable sinusoidal signal.[5] These frequency-domain techniques assume that the fiber's modes may be considered as independent baseband channels so that the Fourier transform of the impulse response yields

$$H(\omega) = |H(\omega)| e^{-j\omega\tau_0} e^{j\theta(\omega)} = \sum_{v=1}^{N} |C_v|^2 e^{-j\omega\tau_v} \Delta t \qquad (8\text{-}18)$$

where ω is the baseband radian frequency of the envelope of the modulated optical carrier. $H(\omega)$ is the complex power transfer function, $|C_v|^2$ is the output power in the vth mode, and τ_0 is the average delay common to all modes. Figure 8-17 illustrates an experimental arrangement for directly measuring the magnitude of a fiber's baseband frequency response. Light from a xenon arc lamp is passed through one of a set of narrow band interference filters and is focused into an LiTaO$_3$ electrooptic crystal which modulates the incoherent continuous-wave light carrier on a frequency tunable sinusoidal envelope.[3] Using the two-point method the test fiber and short reference fiber output powers are detected with a sensitive photomultiplier tube, and the baseband

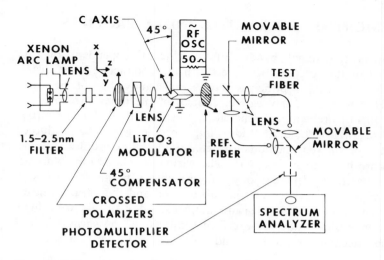

Figure 8-17 Experimental arrangement for measuring the magnitude of a fiber's transfer function directly in the frequency domain.

frequency modulation components are displayed by a spectrum analyzer. The component at the modulating frequency ω from the reference fiber is taken as $P_{ref}(\omega)$ and the same component from the test fiber as $P_{out}(\omega)$. The fiber output power is divided among N modes and only the terms at the modulating frequency ω are measured with the spectrum analyzer.

The reduction of the sine-wave envelope intensity, $P_{out}(\omega)/P_{ref}(\omega)$ gives

$$\frac{P_{out}(\omega)}{P_{ref}(\omega)} = |H(\omega)| = \mathrm{Re}\left(\sum_{v=1}^{N} |C_v|^2 e^{-j\omega\tau_v}\right) \tag{8-19}$$

where $|H(\omega)|$ is the magnitude of the power transfer function of the fiber. It is also known as the magnitude of the fiber's baseband frequency response. Current measurement techniques in the frequency domain yield only $|H(\omega)|$ but it is possible, using phase-sensitive detection, to obtain $\theta(\omega)$.[21] A knowledge of both the magnitude and phase of $H(\omega)$ enables one to calculate the fiber's impulse response $h(t)$ from Eq. (8-10). Wavelength-dependent measurements of a fiber can be made using the test set shown in Fig. 8-17. Using different interference filters whose center wavelengths range from $\lambda = 0.65$ μm to 1.6 μm the test fiber's baseband-frequency response can be measured as a function of wavelength. Wavelength-dependent bandwidth measurements can also be made using time-domain techniques. A Raman[22] or color-centered laser[23] can produce narrow pulses in the time domain over a broad range of wavelengths. The ability to make wavelength-dependent bandwidth measurements is important for the proper design of dual window fibers. A dual window fiber has a high bandwidth in the 0.8 to 0.9 μm and 1.3 to 1.55 μm regions of the spectrum. Such a fiber can be used in systems in a very flexible manner with a variety of semiconductor sources.

8-8 MEASUREMENT OF REFRACTIVE INDEX PROFILES

In multimode fibers the signal bandwidth is critically dependent on the refractive-index distribution of the fiber core. With ideal refractive-index distributions multimode fibers can, in principle, have signal bandwidths of the order of 10 GHz-km. However, extremely careful control of the index profile is required to achieve this theoretical goal. Therefore, precise methods for measuring index profiles are required if the desired ideal index profiles are to be produced. There are a number of different methods for determining index profiles.[24] Some of these methods are itemized in Fig. 8-18. The various methods for obtaining index profiles are based on different physical principles. In this text we will describe two techniques, the interferometric slab method and the refracted near-field method, which allow one to measure a fiber's index profile with high precision. For the interested reader an excellent summary of the various index-profile measurement techniques can be found in the paper by D. Marcuse and H. Presby.[24]

8-8-1 The Interferometric Slab Method

Interferometry is potentially a very accurate method for measuring refractive-index distributions. The slab method, which uses interferometry, is considered by many as the "standard" method used for comparison when judging the accuracy of other profiling techniques. Figure 8-19a shows a schematic view of a thin slab that is cut out of a fiber. The end faces of the slab must be parallel, that is, the thickness of the slab must be constant over the entire slab area to within a fraction of the wavelength of light. Light rays passing through the slab, parallel to its axis, have a phase retardation associated with them that depends upon the optical path length L that they travel

$$L = n(r)d \tag{8-20}$$

and

$$\phi = kL \tag{8-21}$$

where ϕ is the phase retardation of the light wave, d is the slab thickness, and $k = 2\pi/\lambda$.

- **TRANSMITTED NEAR-FIELD METHOD**

- **REFLECTION METHOD**

- **REFRACTED NEAR-FIELD METHOD**

- **INTERFEROMETRIC SLAB METHOD**

- **TRANSVERSE INTERFEROMETRIC METHOD**

- **FOCUSING METHOD**

Figure 8-18 Commonly used refractive-index profile-measurement techniques.

To measure the profile of a fiber, a slab is prepared and placed in one arm of an interference microscope and a homogeneous reference slab, with a refractive index n_2, is placed in the reference arm of the microscope as shown in Fig. 8-19b. The two branches of the microscope form an interferometer. If the fiber slab and reference slab were identical, the light paths through the two branches of the interferometer would have identical optical path lengths and, after recombining, would interfere uniformly over the width of the light beam, either reinforcing or partially cancelling each other. It would be difficult to make measurements with such a perfectly adjusted microscope. For this reason, the mirrors are tilted slightly so that the phase fronts in the two arms are tilted relative to each other, forming parallel bands of interference fringes. This fringe pattern is shown in Fig. 8-19c(i). The dark bands are where the two tilted phase fronts interfere destructively. When one of the homogeneous slabs is replaced with the fiber slab sample, distortions of the fringe pattern appear as shown in Fig. 8-19c(ii). The shift S of a fringe depends on its position in the fiber core, that is, $S(r)$ is a function of r. From the fringe shift $S(r)$ and the fringe spacing D we can calculate the refractive index. This calculation is based on the fact that the distance D between adjacent straight fringes corresponds to a relative phase shift 2π between the two light beams of the interferometer. The fringe shift $S(r)$ corresponds to the relative phase difference ψ between the phase retardations in the fiber slab and the reference slab, where

$$\psi = k[n(r) - n_2]d \tag{8-22}$$

Therefore we can write

$$\frac{2\pi}{D} = \frac{\psi}{S(r)} \tag{8-23}$$

The refractive index of the core can then be obtained as

$$n(r) = n_2 + \frac{\lambda S(r)}{Dd} \tag{8-24}$$

The fringe shift information can be measured with a reticle in the eyepiece of the microscope and the index computed using Eq. (8-24). The process can be automated for quality control purposes using the apparatus shown in Fig. 8-19d.[25]

In practice the accuracy of the interferometric slab method is usually limited by the accuracy with which the slab thickness can be measured. Accuracies better than one part of the refractive index in 10^4 are realizable.[24] The drawbacks of this technique are that it is destructive to the fiber under test and that it requires precise and time-consuming fiber sample preparation.

8-8-2 Refracted Near-Field Method

In Chap. 5 we discussed the fact that the output light intensity in a short length of fiber would be proportional to the difference of the refractive index of the

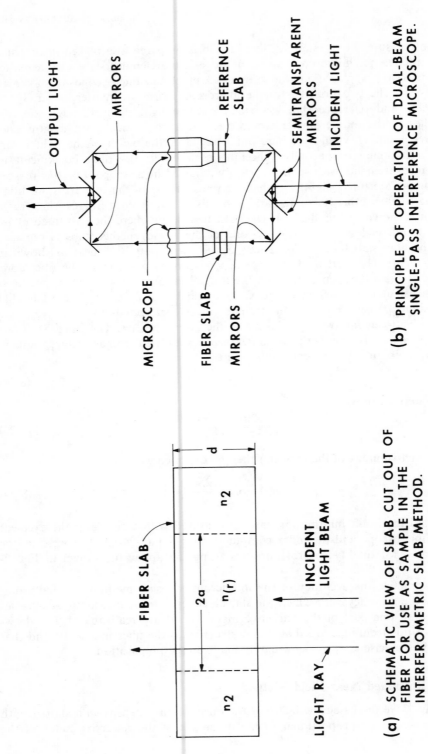

(b) PRINCIPLE OF OPERATION OF DUAL-BEAM SINGLE-PASS INTERFERENCE MICROSCOPE.

(a) SCHEMATIC VIEW OF SLAB CUT OUT OF FIBER FOR USE AS SAMPLE IN THE INTERFEROMETRIC SLAB METHOD.

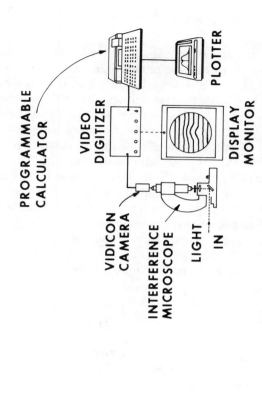

PROGRAMMABLE
CALCULATOR

VIDEO
DIGITIZER

PLOTTER

DISPLAY
MONITOR

VIDICON
CAMERA

INTERFERENCE
MICROSCOPE

LIGHT
IN

(d) AUTOMATIC VIDEO ANALYSIS SYSTEM FOR REFRACTIVE-INDEX PROFILING OF FIBER SAMPLES.

(i)

(ii)

S

D

(c) FIELD OF VIEW OF INTERFERENCE MICROSCOPE (i) WITHOUT AND (ii) WITH GRADED-INDEX SLAB SAMPLE.

Figure 8-19 Interferometric slab method.

core and cladding if the fiber's propagating modes carried equal amounts of power. A technique for measuring the refractive index profile of a fiber has been implemented; it is based on the above principle[26] and is known as the transmitted near-field method. In practice the transmitted near-field method requires a correction due to leaky modes, and only approximates equal power excitation of the propagating modes. A method that is complementary to the transmitted near-field method, but does not require a leaky-mode correction or equal-mode excitation, is known as the refracted near-field technique. The refracted near-field method, developed by Stewart,[27] utilizes the light that is not guided but escapes from the fiber core into the cladding to determine the refractive-index profile of the fiber. A way of implementing the refracted near-field technique is shown in Fig. 8-20. The profile shape is established by moving a tiny light spot (illuminating the fiber input) across its face and measuring the light intensity escaping sideways through the core boundary as a function of the radial position of the sharply focused input light. Consider a light beam focused on a spot

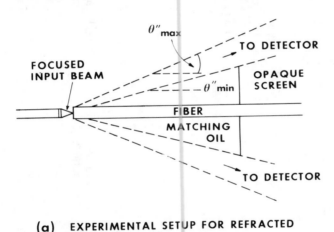

(a) EXPERIMENTAL SETUP FOR REFRACTED NEAR-FIELD METHOD.

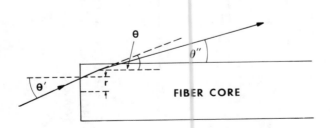

(b) RAY TRAJECTORIES IN ANALYSIS OF REFRACTED NEAR-FIELD METHOD.

Figure 8-20 Refracted near-field method.

at a distance r from the fiber axis with a convergence angle that is much larger than the angle that can be trapped by the fiber core. After entering the fiber some of the light remains in the core. The light escaping from the core is partly a result of power leakage from leaky modes. This part of the radiated power is undesirable since it is not known how much of this leaky power reaches the detector and how much remains in the fiber core. For this reason an opaque circular screen is used to prevent light, leaving below a minimum angle θ''_{min}, from reaching the detector. This minimum angle translates into a corresponding angle θ'_{min}. However, care must be taken that all the light with $\theta' > \theta'_{min}$ reaches the detector. To ensure this condition it is advisable to use input apertures to limit the convergence angle of the input beam to a suitable $\theta' = \theta'_{max}$. The fiber must be immersed in matching oil to prevent reflection at the outer cladding boundary. The refractive index of the fiber core can be determined after the following quantities have been measured: the refractive index of the cladding, the minimum angle θ''_{min} defined by the circular screen placed in front of the detector, and the maximum angle θ'_{max} of the incident cone of light. The detected light power $P(r)$ must be measured as a function of the position of the input beam and $P(a)$ obtained from the $P(r)$ curve as the power detected when the input beam is focused into the cladding. The refractive index profile of the core, $n(r)$, can then be obtained from the following formula:[25]

$$n(r) = n_2 + n_2 \cos \theta''_{min}(\cos \theta''_{min} - \cos \theta'_{max}) \frac{P(a) - P(r)}{P(a)} \qquad (8\text{-}25)$$

Equation (8-25) can be written as

$$n(r) = k_1 - k_2 P(r) \qquad (8\text{-}26)$$

observing the fact that $n(r)$ is proportional to $P(r)$ allows one to directly calibrate the experimental system and obtain the constants k_1 and k_2. A calibration scheme developed by White,[28] in which he monitors the power that passes the opaque screen as it is translated along the optical axis, has proved successful. A practical implementation of the refracted near-field technique has demonstrated that changes in the refractive index of the four parts in 10^{-5} can be measured.[29]

REFERENCES

1. D. B. Keck and A. R. Tynes: "Spectral Response of Low-Loss Optical Waveguides," *Appl. Opt.*, **11**: 1502 (1972).
2. A. H. Cherin, L. G. Cohen, C. A. Burrus, W. S. Holden, and P. Kaiser: "Transmission Characteristics of Three Corning Multimode Optical Fibers," *Appl. Opt.*, **13**: 2359 (1974).
3. J. E. Midwinter: *Optical Fibers for Transmission*, John Wiley and Sons, New York, 1979.
4. P. Kaiser: "NA-Dependent Spectral Loss Measurements of Optical Fibers," *Trans. IECE Japan*, **61**: 225, March 1978.
5. S. E. Miller and A. G. Chynoweth: *Optical Fiber Telecommunications*, Academic Press Inc., New York, 1979.
6. P. Kaiser and D. L. Bisbee: "Transmission Losses of Concatenated, Connectorized Fiber Cables," Fiber Communication Conference, Paper TuE2, *OSA*, Washington, D.C., March 1979.

7. G. T. Holmes: "Propagation Parameter Measurement of Optical Waveguides," *SPIE Conf. Proc.*, Washington, D.C., April 1980.
8. A. H. Cherin and W. B. Gardner: "Measurement Standards for Multimode Telecommunication Fibers," *Proc. SPIE Tech. Symp.*, Washington, D.C., April 1980.
9. A. H. Cherin, E. D. Head, C. R. Lovelace, and W. B. Gardner: "Selection of Mandrel Wrap Mode Filters for Optical Fiber Loss Measurements," *Fiber Integrated Opt.*, January 1982.
10. L. M. Boggs and M. J. Buckler: "Testing Lightguide Fiber," *West. Eng.*, Winter 1980.
11. A. R. Tynes: "Integrating Cube Scattering Detector," *Appl. Opt.*, **9**: 2706 (1970).
12. F. Ostermayer and W. W. Ward Benson: "Integrating Sphere for Measuring Scattering Loss in Optical Fiber Waveguides," *Appl. Opt.*, **13**: 1900 (1974).
13. F. T. Stone, W. B. Gardner, and C. R. Lovelace: "Calorimetric Measurement of Absorption and Scattering Losses in Optical Fibers," *Opt. Lett.*, **2**: 48, February 1978.
14. K. I. White: "A Calorimetric Method for the Measurement of Low Optical Absorption Losses in Optical Communication Fibers," *Opt. Quant. Electron.*, **8**: 73 (1976).
15. J. Guttmann and O. Krumpholz: "Location of Imperfections in Optical Glass-Fiber Waveguides," *Electron. Lett.*, **11**: 216–217 (1975).
16. M. K. Barnoski and R. M. Morrison: "Fiber Waveguides, a Novel Technique for Investigating Attenuation Characteristics," *Appl. Opt.*, **15** (9): 2112–2115 (1976).
17. S. D. Personick: "Photon-Probe, An Optical Fiber Time Domain Reflectometer," *BSTJ*, **56** (3), March 1977.
18. D. Marcuse: "Reflection Losses from Imperfectly Broken Fiber Ends," *Appl. Opt.*, **14**: 3016–3020, December 1975.
19. Y. Ueno and M. Shimizu: "Optical Fiber Fault Location Method," *Appl. Opt.*, **15** (6), June 1976.
20. W. F. Love: "Novel Mode Scrambler for Use in Optical-Fiber Bandwidth Measurements," Paper ThG2 in Tech. Digest, Optical Fiber Communication Conference, *OSA*, Washington, March 6–8, 1979.
21. C. Boisrobert, A. Cozannet, and C. Vassallo: "Sweep Frequency Transfer Function Measurement Applied to Optical Fibre," *IEEE Trans. Instrum. Meas.*, **IM-25** (1976).
22. R. H. Stolen: "Fiber Raman Lasers" in *Fiber and Integrated Optics*, Ed. D. B. Ostrowsky, Plenum Publishing Co., New York, 1979.
23. C. L. Tang: *Methods of Experimental Physics Volume 15—Part B*, Academic Press Inc., New York, 1979.
24. D. Marcuse and H. Presby: "Index Profile Measurements of Fibers and Their Evaluation," *Proc. IEEE*, **68** (6), June 1980.
25. H. M. Presby, D. Marcuse, and H. Asthe: "Automatic Refractive Index Profiling of Optical Fibers," *Appl. Opt.*, **14**: 2209–2214, July 15, 1978.
26. F. Sladen, D. Payne, and M. Adams: "Determination of Optical Fiber Refractive Index Profiles by a Near-Field Scanning Technique," *Appl. Phys. Lett.*, **28**: 255–258, March 1, 1976.
27. W. J. Stewart: A New Technique for Measuring the Refractive Index Profiles of Graded Optical Fibers," Tech. Digest of the 1977 Int. Conf. on Integrated Optics and Optical Fiber Communication, July 18–20, 1977, Tokyo, Japan.
28. K. I. White: "Practical Application of the Refracted Near-Field Technique for the Measurement of Optical Fiber Refractive Index Profiles," *Opt. Quant. Electron.*, **11**: 185 (1979).
29. M. J. Saunders: "Optical Fiber Profiles Using the Refracted Near-Field Technique: A Comparison with Other Methods," to be published.

PROBLEMS

8-1 The loss of a fiber is measured with two test sets. One uses a laser source and one uses an LED source. Would you expect the measured loss to be the same on both test sets? Why?

8-2 The loss of two pieces of the same fiber, each of which is longer than the coupling length L_c, is measured. How would the attenuation per unit length of the two pieces compare? Would there be a difference in the measurements if one piece was shorter than L_c?

8-3 Describe the procedure for making a two-point loss measurement. What launch conditions must be established to ensure a length-independent attenuation measurement? How are these launch conditions established?

8-4 How does the spectral loss set in Fig. 8-4 ensure that the measured loss is due only to the input light from the test set?

8-5 A fiber designer wishes to compare the effects of scattering and absorption in a fiber.

    (a) If a spectral loss measurement of the fiber is available how can it be used to determine scattering effects vs. absorption effects?

    (b) Assume no spectral loss measurement is available. How can scattering loss and absorption loss be measured directly?

8-6 List two techniques that are used to measure the loss of a fiber in an installed cable. Why is the two-point loss measurement undesirable in this case?

8-7 Why do the loss values obtained with the insertion-loss method differ from those obtained with the two-point loss method?

8-8 A break occurs during installation of a fiber whose loss is 3 dB/km. The optical time-domain reflectometry technique is used to locate the break. The output of the laser source in the OTDR is 250 mW and the detected power from the break is 3 μW. Use the typical system values given in the text to estimate how far away the break is.

    Hint: Check the units in your calculation. Some quantities may need conversion.

8-9 The time-domain technique is used to measure the bandwidth of a fiber. If the output pulse is that given in Fig. 8-21, estimate the fiber's 3-dB bandwidth.

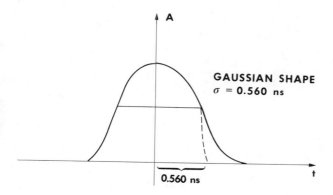

Figure 8-21 Gaussian-shaped pulse, Prob. 8-9.

8-10 Why is the use of a mode scrambler especially important in a bandwidth measurement?

8-11 What is the purpose of the spectrum analyzer in the frequency-domain bandwidth set in Fig. 8-16? What frequency range would be necessary for a spectrum analyzer in a set used to measure multimode fibers?

8-12 The interferometric-slab method is used to measure the refractive index of a fiber. The fiber is found to have an index profile given by $n(r) = n_1(1 - r/a)$. Sketch the output from the interference microscope for this case.

8-13 In the refracted near-field method of profile measurement, what light from the fiber should be detected? What precautions must be included in the measurement to ensure that the correct power is detected?

8-14 In a time-domain delay distortion measurement, σ_{out} and σ_{in} are respectively the rms pulse widths of the output and input pulses.

Show that

$$\sigma_h^2 = \sigma_{out}^2 - \sigma_{in}^2$$

where σ_h is the rms width of the impulse response function $h(t)$.

Hint:

$$P_{out}(t) = \int_{-\infty}^{+\infty} P_{in}(t - \tau)h(\tau)\, d\tau$$

and σ can be written as

$$\sigma^2 = \int_{-\infty}^{+\infty} t^2 P(t)\, dt - \left[\int_{-\infty}^{+\infty} tP(t)\, dt\right]^2$$

NINE

PACKAGING OF OPTICAL FIBERS

9-1 INTRODUCTION

The use of optical fibers as a low-loss, high-bandwidth transmission medium is predicated on the ability of engineers to package and connect them in an economical way and in a manner that will protect them from a hostile field environment. The mechanical properties of fibers along with those factors that alter a fiber's transmission characteristics (micro and macrobending) strongly influence how optical fibers are packaged. In this chapter we will briefly describe the factors that influence the packaging of fibers. In addition we will illustrate fiber packaging by giving examples of a number of current fiber optic cable designs.

9-2 MECHANICAL CONSIDERATIONS

The survival of long lengths of optical fibers exposed to stresses arising from the manufacture and installation of optical cables is crucial to the economically successful application of long-distance optical communication systems. Long lengths of glass fibers must be strong enough to survive these short-term stresses and must also be able to withstand the long-term stresses and environmental conditions encountered during a long service life. The short-term strength of glass is limited by the material's brittle nature. Its long-term strength is limited by the process of static fatigue. Brittle behavior leads to a dependence of a fiber's strength upon the existence of flaws (cracks) on the surface of the

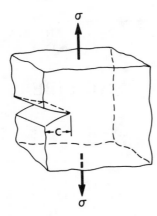

Figure 9-1 Geometry of crack tip on glass surface.

glass.[1] Since the surface flaw size and location is random throughout a fiber, the strength of the fiber becomes a statistical property. Fiber failure due to static fatigue results from stress-induced growth of surface flaws in the presence of moisture. Static fatigue will cause a decrease of the fiber's strength with time.

The brittle failure of a glass material takes place with very little plastic deformation, and occurs at applied stresses far below the theoretical strength of the material. In a brittle material the existence of fine cracks can cause a concentration of stress at the crack tip that far exceeds the applied stress. Griffith[2] demonstrated that the fracture stress of a piece of glass containing a thin edge crack of depth C, as shown in Fig. 9-1, is given by

$$\sigma = \left(\frac{2E\gamma}{\pi C}\right)^{1/2} \tag{9-1}$$

where E is the Young's modulus of the glass and γ is its surface energy. Fracture stress is inversely proportional to the square root of the crack depth C. Strength decreases with increasing flaw size. The dependence of fracture strength on crack size is illustrated in Fig. 9-2. Extreme care must be taken while manufacturing a fiber because merely touching the fiber will damage its surface and reduce its strength to approximately 50 kips/in². For this reason protective plastic coatings are applied to freshly drawn fibers to guard against the spontaneous surface microcracking that results from mechanical contact.

System requirements dictate that the minimum guaranteed strength in long fibers (> 1 km) is important rather than the fiber's strength in short lengths. The statistical behavior and the length dependence of fiber strength has been described from short-length data by a Weibull[3] distribution. Data on the strength of long fibers indicate that the flaws responsible for failure are often caused by isolated irregularities, that is, statistical anomalies which occur during the preform-making or fiber-drawing operations. Because large flaws are not usually a part of strength distributions obtained from short-length data (usually gauge lengths of 0.10 to 0.60 m) estimates of the strength of long-fiber behavior

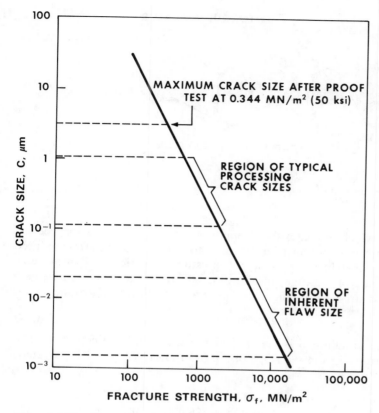

Figure 9-2 The effect of flaw size on fiber strength.

from short-length tests are generally not sufficiently accurate for system needs.[4] To overcome some of the shortcomings of predicting long-length-fiber behavior from short-length strength tests, a fiber proof-testing process is usually used to ensure that long lengths of fiber exceed a defined minimum strength. During proof-testing, fibers are subjected to a tension stress greater than that expected during cable manufacturing and installation.[5] The proof stress is also chosen high enough to ensure a long service life in humid atmospheres. Figure 9-3 shows proof-test apparatus consisting of double capstan arrangements between the supply and takeup positions. Stress is generated by a hysteresis clutch between the two double capstans, and is applied to the fiber continuously as it moves between the two capstans. Thus every section of a reel of fiber is proof-tested. Fibers that break during proof-testing are discarded ensuring that the remaining fibers, that will later be packaged within a cable, all have strengths exceeding the proof stress.[1,6] Proof-testing is usually performed as the last step of the fiber-drawing operation.

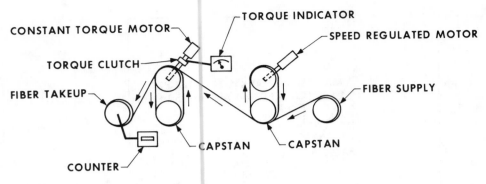

Figure 9-3 Proof-testing apparatus.

Static fatigue which degrades the strength of glass fibers over a long period of time can ultimately cause an installed fiber to fail due to the stress-induced growth of surface flaws in the presence of moisture. Equation (9-2) provides a conservative estimate of the time to failure of a fiber due to static fatigue as a function of applied stress (stress on a fiber in an installed cable, for example)

$$\log t = a\sigma + b \tag{9-2}$$

where t is the time to failure, σ is the applied stress, and a, b are constants. The value of a is determined from the slope of a plot of $\log t$ versus σ. The constant

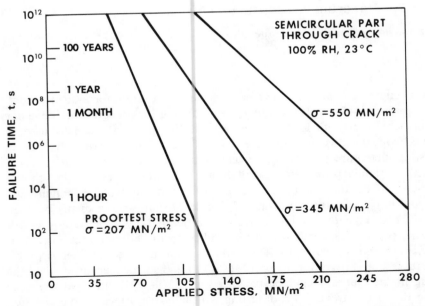

Figure 9-4 Diagram for estimating long-term static fiber performance from proof-test stress.

b depends on the crack tip environment, the glass composition, and the proof-test stress. One can determine a and b experimentally and develop design diagrams as shown in Fig. 9-4. For a given applied stress on the fiber, this figure allows one to determine the times to failure for different levels of proof stress.[1] Using curves of the type shown in Fig. 9-4 a fiber optic cable designer can set a proof-test level to ensure that the static fatigue life of the fibers will exceed a certain minimum life value.

9-3 FIBER TRANSMISSION CONSIDERATIONS

In the process of packaging optical fibers, their transmission characteristics can be affected by the bending of the fiber axis. Bending of a fiber's axis can cause coupling of energy between guided modes in a multimode fiber and can cause radiation losses in both multimode and single-mode fibers.[7] Random bending of the fiber axis (on a microscopic scale), as shown in Fig. 9-5, is called microbending.[6,8] These microscopic random deviations (typically a few microns) of the fiber axis $f(z)$ can be analyzed in terms of their Fourier spectrum. One can then identify spectral components with specific spatial frequencies which are detrimental to the guidance properties of the fiber and cause microbending loss. For a multimode fiber with a near-parabolic graded-index profile only one spectral component having a spatial frequency Ω given by Eq. (9-3) causes microbending loss[6]

$$\Omega = \frac{(2\Delta)^{1/2}}{a} \tag{9-3}$$

For $\Delta = 1.5$ percent and $a = 25$ μm, the spatial frequency that will cause microbending loss is $\Omega = 6.93$ mm^{-1}.

The packaging of an optical fiber can impose random bends on the fiber axis and cause loss (the term "packaging loss" is often used) due to microbending. A fiber-coating system should be chosen that can offer protection from microbending loss. Ideally a coating system which has a hard outer shell that

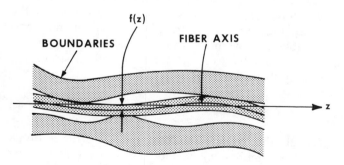

Figure 9-5 Fiber geometry due to microbending.

makes the fiber resistant to conforming to environmental surfaces and a soft inner compliant buffer which makes the roughness of adjacent surfaces should be used.[6] The coating itself should be as uniform and smooth as possible to avoid creating microbends due to coating irregularities. It has been shown both analytically[6] and experimentally[8] that the microbending loss of a suitably coated fiber is proportional to $1/\Delta^x$ where x can be at least two and possibly as high as six. For a given coating, increasing Δ will decrease a fiber's susceptibility to microbending loss. In addition, long-period bending, typically in the range of a few centimeters or less, results in added macrobending loss.[6] Periodic bends of this type can readily occur due to stranding or other periodicities in the cable structure. To maintain the transmission characteristics of optical fibers, an optical cable should be designed and manufactured with properly packaged fibers in such a manner as to control macrobending and microbending losses.

9-4 FIBER CABLE DESIGN

A primary concern in designing an optical fiber cable, as shown in Fig. 9-6, is to protect the fibers from damage during manufacture, installation, and use. As pointed out in Sec. 9-2 the strength of optical fibers is inherently random and depends on the maximum surface flaw depth in the glass. In addition static fatigue can degrade the strength of glass fibers and cause stress-induced growth of surface flaws in the presence of moisture. The cable designer uses the strategy of specifying a proof-test level for the fibers that guarantees a minimum tensile strain capability of the fibers in the cable. The chosen proof-test level allows the fibers in the cable to survive manufacture, installation, and in-place use, with appropriate allowance for static fatigue. (See Figs. 9-7 and 9-8, which are similar to Figs. 9-2 and 9-4 but plotted in terms of applied strain.)[9] A cable is designed to withstand a maximum rated cable load during installation without exceeding the minimum tensile strain capabilities of the fibers in the cable. A typical fiber strain proof-test level (an indication of the minimum tensile strain) is about 0.5 percent. Because of their fragility and small elongation capability it is desirable to avoid significant tensile loading of glass fibers in a cable. In most of the optical fiber cable designs used thus far, load-bearing tensile reinforcing members are incorporated in the cable to carry most of the tensile load.

The tensile load that an optical cable can withstand for a given strain S is given as a first approximation by the expression

$$T = S \sum_{i=1}^{N} E_i A_i \tag{9-4}$$

where E_i and A_i are respectively the Young's modulus and the cross-sectional area of a cable component (fiber, reinforcing member, sheath, or filler). The summation in Eq. (9-4) is extended over all of the cable components. This

I PROTECT FIBERS FROM DAMAGE DURING MANUFACTURE,
INSTALLATION AND USE:

    A. TENSILE REINFORCEMENT MEMBERS REQUIRED TO
AVOID EXCEEDING TENSILE STRAIN CAPABILITY OF
FIBERS.

    B. CABLE TENSILE DESIGN MUST ACCOUNT FOR STATIC
FATIGUE DURING:
       1. SHORT-TERM LOADING — INSTALLATION
       2. LONG-TERM LOADING — MANUFACTURING &
                             INSTALLATION–INDUCED
                             RESIDUAL LOADING

    C. BEND, IMPACT, AND CRUSH REQUIREMENTS MUST BE
SATISFIED BY CABLE CROSS-SECTIONAL DESIGN

II MAINTAIN FIBER TRANSMISSION PROPERTIES:

    A. DURING CABLE MANUFACTURE

    B. OVER A WIDE RANGE OF INSTALLATION AND
ENVIRONMENTAL CONDITIONS

III. FIBER COUNT:

    A. FIBER PACKING STRATEGY, UNIT DESIGN

    B. HANDLING AND SPLICING METHODS

Figure 9-6 Optical cable design considerations.

equation illustrates that if the reinforcing members have a high Young's modulus and a sufficient cross-sectional area they will bear the main part of the tensile load.

Common materials for the reinforcing members are steel, Kevlar®,† and fiberglass in the order of decreasing tensile modulus. The material and the amount of reinforcement are designed to provide enough tensile stiffness within the small elongation limit of the fibers.[9,6] The higher the modulus, the less reinforcing material required for a given tensile strength.

† ®Kevlar is a registered trademark of Dupont.

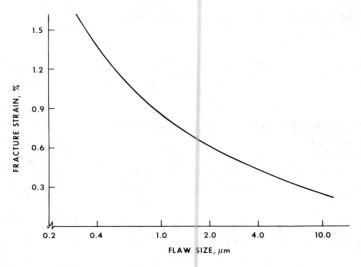

Figure 9-7 Fracture strain vs. flaw size in high-silica fibers.

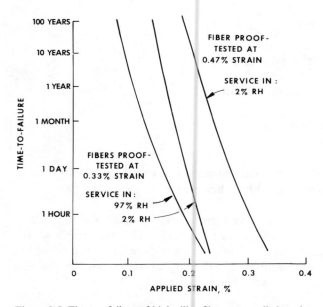

Figure 9-8 Time to failure of high-silica fibers vs. applied strain.

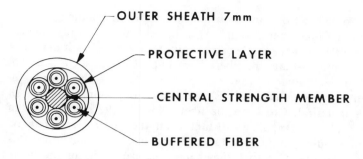

(a)   LAYERED DESIGN (SCALE 4:1)

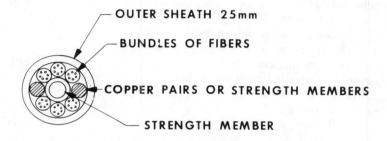

(b)   BUNDLED DESIGN (SCALE 1:1)

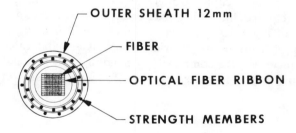

(c)   RIBBON DESIGN (SCALE 2:1)

Figure 9-9 Cable designs showing placement of strength members.

Tensile reinforcement can be located at the center of the cable, as shown in Figs. 9-9*a* and *b*, to form a central strength member design, or in the outer sheath layers (Fig. 9-9*c*) to form an external-strength-member design. Central strength members are used for stranded cable designs where the optical fibers are stranded around the strength member during manufacturing. External strength members permit compact placement of fibers in the cable core region.

They offer greater protection from abrasion and are stiffer in bending than an equivalent central-strength-member design.[6] Also, because fibers do not deform plastically they have little capacity to absorb energy. Hence the sheath design of any optical fiber cable must isolate the fibers from impact loads, such as a tool accidently dropped by a craftsman that strikes the cable, or the fibers will fracture. In addition to these considerations, the small elongation capability of optical fibers makes it desirable to keep the fibers close to the neutral axis of the cable. When a cable is bent, fibers distant from the neutral axis can be subject to significant bending strains. A standard approach for alleviating this problem is to strand the fibers so that they follow helical paths in the cable with a lay length comparable to the minimum cable-bending radius.

The choice of the materials used in an optical fiber cable are not only predicated on mechanical design considerations, but must be carefully chosen to minimize the added microbending loss due to cable manufacture and environmental conditions. In storage and in service, optical cables will be exposed to a large temperature range. It has been shown that thermally induced dimensional changes, specifically axial compressive strains, are responsible for microbending loss.[9,10] Axial compressive strains result from linear thermal expansion of the cable as the temperature is lowered and from shrink-back of the polymeric components at high temperatures.[9] Since the coefficient of linear thermal expansion of glass is small, thermal contraction of the cable at low temperatures is due almost entirely to the effective coefficient of expansion of the remaining cable components. Using reinforcing materials with low thermal expansion coefficients can reduce the effective coefficient of thermal expansion of an optical cable and, in turn, the added microbending loss at low temperatures.[10]

Finally the number of fibers in a cable strongly affect the cable design. When only a few fibers are required individual packaging of the fibers in a design such as the one shown in Fig. 9-9a is attractive. When the fiber count is low the handling and splicing of fibers on an individual basis is a manageable task. As the number of fibers increases, the complexity of handling, splicing, and organizing individual fibers in the field increases rapidly. Packaging groups of

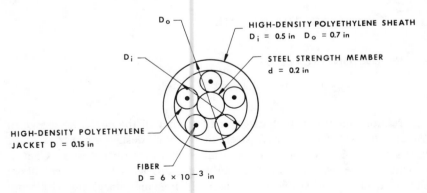

Figure 9-10 Optical cable, Example 9-1.

fibers using a ribbon design (see Fig. 9-9c) and mass splicing techniques looks attractive for cables with fiber counts above approximately twenty.[6]

Example 9-1 Calculation of tensile load on a fiber optic cable This example illustrates how to calculate the tensile load on a fiber optic cable for a given applied strain. For an applied strain of 0.15 percent and a cable of the type shown in Fig. 9-10, we will use Eq. (9-4) to calculate the tensile load T.

$$T = S \sum_{i=1}^{N} E_i A_i$$

Obtaining the Young's modulus from tables gives

Cable component	Young's modulus, lb/in^2
Steel	30×10^6
Glass fiber	10×10^6
High-density polyethylene	0.15×10^6

Using the dimensions given in Fig. 9-10, the contribution $E_i A_i$ for each component of the cable is

Cable component	EA (lb)
Steel	9.42×10^5
Fiber	2.82×10^2
Jacket	2.65×10^3
Sheath	2.82×10^4

There are five jacketed fibers so the tensile load is approximated as

$$T = 0.0015[9.42 \times 10^5 + 5(2.82 \times 10^2 + 2.65 \times 10^3) + 2.82 \times 10^4] \text{ lb}$$

$$= 0.0015(9.8486 \times 10^5)$$

$$= 1477 \text{ lb}$$

9-5 EXAMPLES OF CABLE DESIGNS

Three different types of optical cable designs are illustrated in Fig. 9-9.[9] The first, a layered design, shown in Fig. 9-9a, is efficient for small fiber counts below about twenty. Typical cables have a central strength member, and one

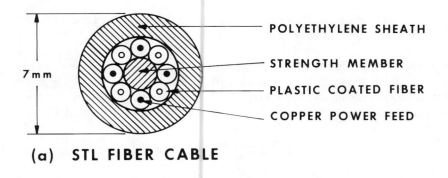

POLYETHYLENE SHEATH

STRENGTH MEMBER

PLASTIC COATED FIBER

COPPER POWER FEED

7 mm

(a) STL FIBER CABLE

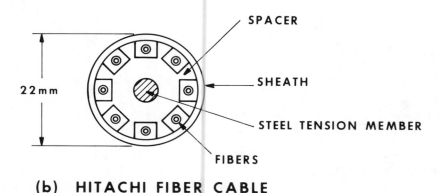

SPACER

SHEATH

STEEL TENSION MEMBER

FIBERS

22 mm

(b) HITACHI FIBER CABLE

Figure 9-11 Layered-cable designs.

layer of four to eight fibers. Copper conductors can be interspersed with optical fibers and the concept can be extended to two layers to increase the fiber count. Examples of layered-cable designs manufactured respectively by STL (Standard Telecommunication Laboratories) and Hitachi are shown in Figs. 9-11a and b.[11,12] These designs are compatible with single-fiber splicing techniques. The second cable design, shown in Fig. 9-9b, is known as a bundle design. In the bundle design, which is an extension of the layered design, groups of two to eight fibers are packaged into a unit. These units are usually stranded around a central strength member and can be mixed with other units containing copper conductors or strength members. Examples of bundled-cable designs are shown in Fig. 9-12. Figure 9-12a shows an Hitachi cable with five units each containing six fibers.[12] Figure 9-12b is a cable used by NTT (Nippon Telegraph and Telephone) in their fiber optic field trial in Tokyo.[13] The cable contained 48 fibers and had eight units. Bundled designs are suitable for a wide range of fiber counts and are usually spliced on a single-fiber basis. The third optical cable packaging scheme utilizes a ribbon design as shown in Fig. 9-9c. In this design coated fibers are packaged into a linear array (ribbon) of from 6 to 12 fibers

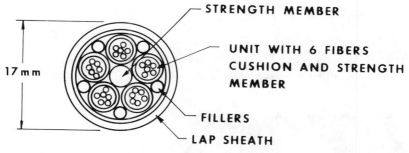

(a) HITACHI CABLE

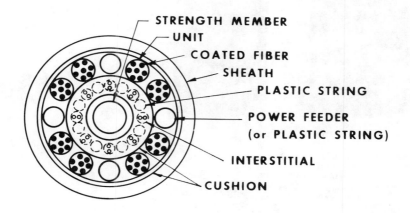

ITEM	CABLE WITH PF
COATED FIBER DIAMETER	0.9 $\pm$ 0.1mm
UNIT DIAMETER	5.5mm
POWER FEEDER DIAMETER	1.2mm
STRENGTH MEMBER DIAMETER	5.5mm
SHEATH	LAP
SHEATH DIAMETER	30mm

WEIGHT: 620-740kg/km (WITHOUT PF)
700-800kg/km (WITH PF)

(b) NTT CABLE

Figure 9-12 Bundled-cable designs.

GLASS CORE AND CLADDING   MYLAR TAPE

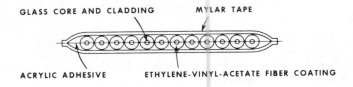

ACRYLIC ADHESIVE   ETHYLENE-VINYL-ACETATE FIBER COATING

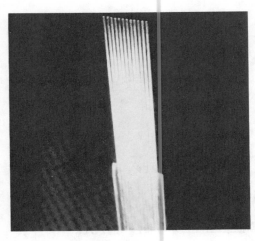

Figure 9-13 Optical fiber ribbon.

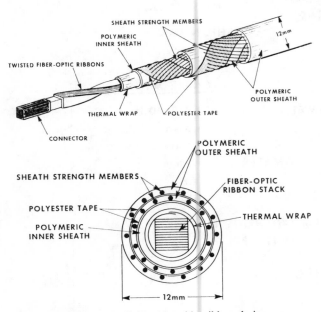

Figure 9-14 Bell system lightguide cable, ribbon design.

with protective tape on its top and bottom as shown in Fig. 9-13.[14] Groups of ribbons can be placed in the core of the cable. A sheath with external strength members completes the cable structure. Figure 9-14 shows the Bell System ribbon-based fiber optic cable.[15] A cable of this type containing 144 fibers has a diameter of 12 mm. The ribbon structure is space-efficient and is suitable for a wide range of fiber counts. The advantages of a ribbon design becomes evident when large numbers of fibers in excess of twenty are needed in an application. This design is well suited for mass-splicing techniques and can be factory-connectorized for ease of handling and installation in the field.[14]

REFERENCES

1. B. K. Tariyal and J. T. Krause: "Ensuring the Mechanical Reliability of Lightguide Fiber," *West. Eng.*, Winter, 1980.
2. A. A. Griffith: "The Phenomena of Rupture and Flow in Solids," *Philos. Trans. R. Soc. London, Ser. A*, **221**: 163 (1920).
3. W. Weibull: "A Statistical Theory of the Strength of Materials," *Proc. R. Swedish Inst. Eng. Res.*, no. 151 (1939).
4. D. Kalish, B. K. Tariyal, and R. O. Pickwick: "Strength Distributions and Gage Length Extrapolations in Optical Fibers," *Amer. Ceram. Soc. Bull.*, **56**: 491 (1977).
5. B. K. Tariyal, D. Kalish, and M. R. Santana: "Proof Testing of Long Length Optical Fibers for a Communications Cable," *Amer. Ceram. Soc. Bull.*, **56**: 204 (1977).
6. S. E. Miller and A. G. Chynoweth: *Optical Fiber Telecommunications*, Academic Press Inc., New York, 1979.
7. D. Marcuse: *Theory of Dielectric Optical Waveguides*, Academic Press Inc., New York, 1974.
8. W. B. Gardner: "Microbending Loss in Optical Fibers, *Bell Syst. Tech. J.*, **54**: 457–465, February 1975.
9. M. I. Schwartz, P. F. Gagen, and M. R. Santana: "Fiber Cable Design and Characterization," *Proc. IEEE*, **68**(10), October 1980.
10. Y. Sugawara, T. Kobayashi, M. Tanaka, A. Mogi, K. Inada, and K. Ishchara: "Attenuation Increase Mechanism of Jacketed and Cabled Fibers at Low Temperatures," *Proc. Opt. Comm. Conf.*, pp. 12.4-1–12.4-4, Amsterdam, September 1979.
11. S. G. Foord and M. A. Lees: "Principles of Fibre-Optical Cable Design," *Proc. IEEE*, **123**(6), June 1976.
12. Hitachi Monography, 1977 International Conference on Integrated Optics and Optical Fiber Communication, Osaka, Japan, July 22, 1977.
13. The Japan Industrial and Technological Bulletin, Special Issue No. 6, 1980, Tokyo, Japan.
14. M. J. Buckler, M. R. Santana, and M. J. Saunders: "Lightguide Cable Manufacture and Performance," *BSTJ*, **57**(6), July/August 1978.
15. P. F. Gagen and M. R. Santana: "Design and Performance of a Crossply Lightguide Cable Sheath," International Wire and Cable Symposium, Cherry Hill, New Jersey.

PROBLEMS

9-1 What mechanisms cause the possibility of mechanical failures in optical fibers over the short term and over the long term?

9-2 A freshly drawn fiber is wound directly on a reel. The fiber is proof-tested and its fracture strength is found to be very low. What could be added to the process to increase the fracture strength of the fiber?

9-3 Draw a block diagram of a fiber proof-test apparatus. What information does the proof-test level provide an installation engineer?

9-4 If a fiber develops a 7-μm crack during the drawing process, what would you expect to happen to that fiber if it is proof tested at 50 kips/in^2? If another fiber has a 1000-MN/m^2 fracture strength, what crack size would be observed in that fiber?

9-5 Consider a fiber under an applied stress of 175 MN/m^2. What is the minimum time that fiber will remain intact if the fiber has passed a proof-test stress level of 345 MN/m^2? How long will it last if the proof-test stress level was 550 MN/m^2?

9-6 For a multimode graded-index fiber with a near parabolic profile, an index difference of 1.3 percent, and core radius 31 μm, what spatial frequency will cause microbending loss? How can the effects of the random bends be minimized?

9-7 Assume that microbending loss decreases as Δ^3. What happens to the relative microbending loss if Δ is increased from 1.3 to 1.6 percent?

9-8 List three primary considerations in an optical cable design.

9-9 A cable designer is responsible for two cables. One is for a data link which will need five fibers. The other cable is for communication purposes and will contain one hundred fibers. Describe how the two cable designs will differ in terms of fiber packaging, strength members, and splicing techniques.

9-10 Suppose the tensile load requirements on the cable in Example 9-1 are reduced so that the maximum tensile load will be only 750 lb. What component could be reduced to allow for this and what would be its reduced size?

SOURCE COUPLING, SPLICES, AND CONNECTORS

10-1 INTRODUCTION

The proper design of an optical communication system using optical fibers as the transmission medium requires a knowledge of the transmission character-istics of the optical sources, fibers, and interconnection devices (connectors and splices) used to join lengths of fibers together. In this chapter we will investigate the coupling of energy from an optical source into fibers, and the effects of intrinsic and extrinsic splice-loss parameters on the transmission characteristics of an optical fiber link. In addition, we will give examples of different types of optical fiber connectors and splices and describe how the transmission loss of an interconnection device is measured.

10-2 SOURCE COUPLING INTO AN OPTICAL FIBER

In this section we will investigate the factors that influence the coupling of power from an optical source into a fiber. Let us define the coupling efficiency of a source into a fiber as

$$\eta_c = \frac{P_F}{P_S} \qquad (10\text{-}1)$$

where P_F is the power injected into the fiber and P_S is the output power of the source. The factors affecting η_c can be broadly divided into two categories, as shown in Fig. 10-1. The first category, loss due to unintercepted illumination,

FACTORS INFLUENCING SOURCE COUPLING EFFICIENCY INTO A FIBER

1. UNINTERCEPTED ILLUMINATION LOSS
   - (a) AREA MISMATCH BETWEEN SOURCE SPOT SIZE AND FIBER CORE AREA
   - (b) MISALIGNMENT OF SOURCE AND FIBER AXIS

2. NUMERICAL APERTURE LOSS
   - (a) CAUSED BY THAT PART OF THE SOURCE EMISSION PROFILE THAT RADIATES OUTSIDE OF THE FIBER'S ACCEPTANCE CONE

Figure 10-1 Factors influencing η_c (coupling efficiency of a source into a fiber).

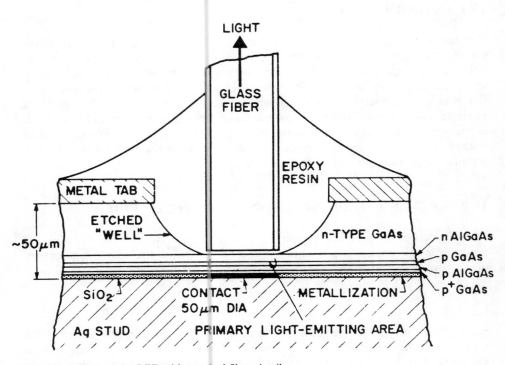

Figure 10-2 Burrus type LED with attached fiber pigtail.

can be caused by the source's emitting area being larger than the fiber's core area. Unfortunately, the brightness of an image on the fiber core cannot exceed that of the source[1] and so an intermediate lens cannot focus all the light into the core. Even if the source is smaller than the core, you can still have problems with unintercepted illumination if separation and misalignment of the source and fiber axes allow emitted light to miss the core and become lost. Coupling loss due to unintercepted illumination can be eliminated, however, if the source-emitting area and the fiber-core area are properly matched and aligned. Figure 10-2 shows a fiber "pigtail" permanently mounted and properly aligned on a Burrus[2] type light-emitting diode. This configuration essentially eliminates loss due to unintercepted illumination. The second category of coupling loss that affects the efficiency of source-coupling into a fiber is due to mismatches between the source beam and fiber numerical apertures. This type of mismatch is shown schematically in Fig. 10-3. For fiber optic communication systems two types of light sources, light-emitting diodes (LED's) and injection laser diodes (ILD's) are typically used. To calculate the coupling loss due to numerical aperture mismatch, we must first describe the radiation characteristics of LED's and ILD's. Radiation patterns of light sources are usually plotted on a polar diagram as shown in Fig. 10-4. A lambertian source whose radiant intensity varies with the cosine of the angle between a line perpendicular to it and another line drawn to an observation point is often used to model the radiation pattern of a surface-emitting LED. The radiation pattern of a lambertian source can be expressed as

$$I = I_0 \cos \phi \qquad (10\text{-}2)$$

where I_0 is the radiant intensity along the line $\phi = 0$. Some sources such as

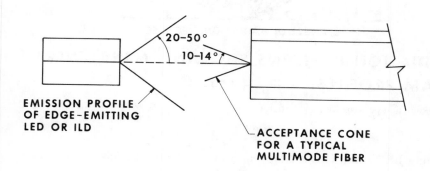

NUMERICAL APERTURE MISMATCH OF
SOURCE AND MULTIMODE FIBER

Figure 10-3 Schematic showing numerical aperture mismatch of source and fiber.

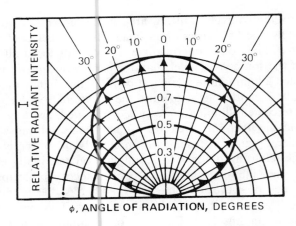

(a) RADIATION PATTERN OF A LAMBERTIAN SOURCE
$$I = I_o \cos \phi$$

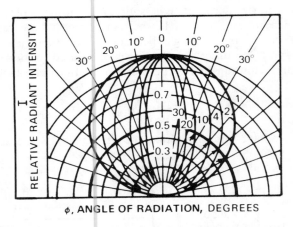

(b) RADIATION PATTERNS SHOWING NARROWER BEAM PROFILES, $I = I_o (\cos \phi)^m$

Figure 10-4 Radiation patterns with lambertian type profiles.

edge-emitting LED's and ILD's exhibit narrower radiation patterns that can be approximated by the equation (see Fig. 10-4b),

$$I = I_0(\cos \phi)^m \tag{10-3}$$

The radiation pattern obtained from an edge-emitting LED is elliptical in cross section with half-power beam divergence angles of approximately $\pm 60°$ and $\pm 30°$. The radiation pattern obtained from a double heterojunction laser diode

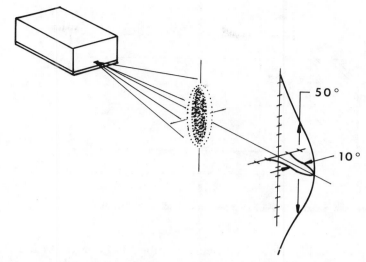

(a)

SCHEMATIC REPRESENTATION OF FAR-FIELD RADIATION PATTERN OF INJECTION LASER DIODE (ILD)

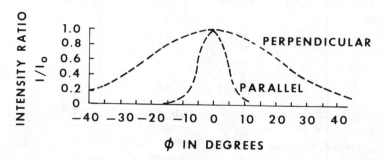

(b)

FAR-FIELD INTENSITY PATTERN OF ILD MEASURED IN PLANES PARALLEL AND PERPENDICULAR TO THE JUNCTION

Figure 10-5 Radiation pattern of an injection laser diode (ILD).

is also elliptical in cross section but narrower in beam width than an LED. For example, the typical half-power beam divergence angles of an ILD are $\pm 25°$ and $\pm 5°$ perpendicular and parallel to the junction plane, respectively (see Fig. 10-5).

Let us now consider the problem of coupling energy from an LED into a multimode graded-index fiber. We will assume that the LED is a lambertian source in direct contact with the fiber core and covering its entire cross section

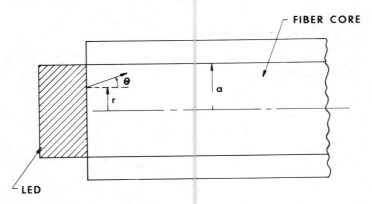

Figure 10-6 Schematic of LED shown in contact with fiber end.

as shown in Fig. 10-6. Each element of the LED of area dA radiates the amount of power ΔP in the θ direction[3]

$$\Delta P = B \cos \theta \, dA \, d\Omega \qquad (10\text{-}4)$$

$B \cos \theta$ is the brightness of a lambertian radiator and $d\Omega$ is an element of solid angle equal to

$$d\Omega = \sin \theta \, d\theta \, d\phi \qquad (10\text{-}5)$$

dA is an element of surface area equal to

$$dA = r \, dr \, d\phi \qquad (10\text{-}6)$$

Because of numerical aperture mismatch between the LED and the fiber, not all of the light from the LED is captured by the fiber core. Source rays whose angles are too steep to be trapped by the fiber propagate through the core boundary into the cladding. The trapping angle for the energy from the source into the fiber at each position r in the fiber core is obtained if we consider the ray angle associated with a given mode at cutoff. From our knowledge of the components of the propagation vector associated with a given mode, we can obtain the ray angle associated with this mode as (see Fig. 6-9)

$$\cos \theta(r) = \beta/n(r)k_0 \qquad (10\text{-}7)$$

The cutoff value of the propagation constant β for each mode is

$$\beta_c = n_2 k_0 \qquad (10\text{-}8)$$

Using Eqs. (10-7) and (10-8), the critical angle for trapping source rays at each radius r of the core is

$$\theta_c(r) = \arccos \left[n_2/n(r) \right] = \arcsin \left\{ 1 - \left[\frac{n_2}{n(r)} \right]^2 \right\}^{1/2} \qquad (10\text{-}9)$$

To obtain the total power the LED injects into the fiber core we must integrate Eq. (10-4)

$$P_f = B \int_0^a r\, dr \int_0^{2\pi} d\phi \int_0^{2\pi} d\phi' \int_0^{\theta_c(r)} d\theta \sin\theta \cos\phi \qquad (10\text{-}10)$$

For the graded-index fiber we will use the power-law profile description of $n(r)$ given by Eq. (6-34). This enables us to obtain an explicit expression for $\theta_c(r)$ which can be used in Eq. (10-10). Integrating Eq. (10-10) will yield an expression for the total power injected into the fiber

$$P_f = (2\pi^2)\left(\frac{\alpha}{\alpha+2}\right) Ba^2 \Delta \qquad (10\text{-}11)$$

To obtain the coupling efficiency η_c we require P_s, the total output power of the LED. For an LED of area πa^2 radiating into a half-space solid angle 2π, P_s becomes

$$P_s = \pi^2 a^2 B \qquad (10\text{-}12)$$

Using Eqs. (10-1), (10-11), and (10-12), the coupling effciency of an LED source into a fiber is

$$\eta_c = \frac{P_f}{P_s} = \frac{2\alpha\Delta}{\alpha+2} \qquad (10\text{-}13)$$

For a parabolic index profile with $\alpha = 2$

$$\eta_{c\,\text{parabolic}} = \Delta \qquad (10\text{-}14)$$

For a step-index profile with $\alpha = \infty$

$$\eta_{c\,\text{step}} = 2\Delta \qquad (10\text{-}15)$$

The coupling efficiency of a step-index fiber is twice that of a parabolic-index fiber. In either case the coupling efficiency is low for a fiber with a small Δ. For a typical value of $\Delta = 0.01$ the coupling efficiency is one to two percent, that is, only one to two percent of the LED's light is trapped in the core of a fiber. Often the coupling efficiency of a fiber is written in terms of a fiber's numerical aperture. Using the expression for the numerical aperture (Eqs. (6-48) and (6-51))

$$NA = n_1 \sqrt{2\Delta} \qquad (10\text{-}16)$$

We can rewrite Eq. (10-13) in terms of the numerical aperture. If we assume $n_1 \approx 1.5$, then the coupling efficiency is approximately equal to

$$\eta_c = \left(\frac{\alpha}{\alpha+2}\right)(NA)^2 \qquad (10\text{-}17)$$

For a step-index fiber the coupling efficiency of a nonlambertian source whose radiation pattern is characterized by Eq. (10-3) with $m > 1$ can be obtained[4] as

$$\eta_c = \left(\frac{m+1}{2}\right)(NA)^2 \qquad (10\text{-}18)$$

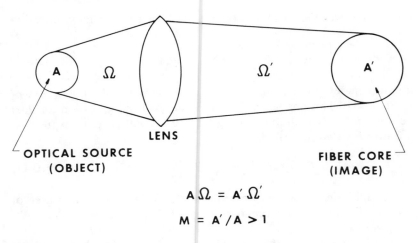

$$A\,\Omega = A'\,\Omega'$$

$$M = A'/A > 1$$

Figure 10-7 Schematic of imaging system to improve source-coupling efficiency ($M = A'/A > 1$).

Using a source with a more directional radiation pattern will increase the value of m in Eq. (10-18) and in turn increase the source-coupling efficiency. Sources such as edge-emitting LED's and ILD's which are more directional emitters, will have a higher coupling efficiency than a lambertian source. ILD's with a properly aligned fiber pigtail will have a source-coupling efficiency of 10 to 20 percent. For the case where the emitting area of the source is smaller than that of the fiber core, imaging optics can improve the source-coupling efficiency. Figure 10-7 shows a source and fiber with an intervening lens.[5,6] If the ratio of the fiber core area to the area of the emitting surface of the source is greater than unity ($M = A'/A > 1$) the effective solid angle of collection from the source can be changed from Ω to $M\Omega$. This represents a gain in the source-coupling efficiency. Figure 10-8 illustrates a number of different lens arrangements that have been used, and their associated source-coupling efficiencies. For the interested reader, an excellent summary of different lens systems and their associated source-coupling efficiencies can be found in Ref. 6.

Example 10-1 Coupling efficiency This example illustrates how to calculate the coupling efficiency η_c of an LED or laser source coupled into a step-index fiber. Consider a step-index fiber of parameters $a = 20$ μm, $n_1 = 1.458$, $\Delta = 1.4$ percent being excited by a lambertian LED of brightness 2.8×10^2 W/cm^2/sr. P_s, P_f an η_c are calculated as follows:

The total power P_s is

$$P_s = \pi^2 a^2 B$$

$$= 15 \text{ mW/sr}$$

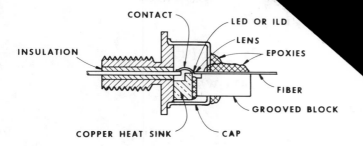

(a) LED OR ILD WITH A LENS INCORPORATED IN THE SOURCE PACKAGE

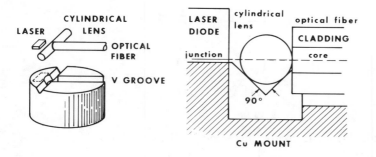

(b) ILD WITH CYLINDRICAL LENS-COUPLING SOURCE ENERGY INTO GRADED-INDEX FIBER

$$\eta_c \approx 40 \text{ TO } 50\%$$

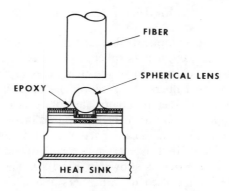

(C) LED WITH SPHERICAL LENS-COUPLING SOURCE ENERGY INTO FIBER

$$\eta_c \approx 8 \text{ TO } 10\%$$

Figure 10-8 Lens systems to increase source-coupling efficiency.

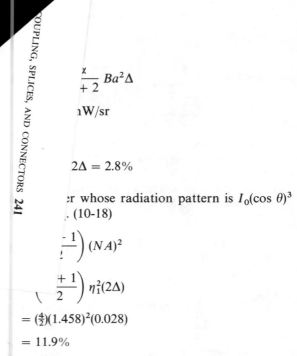

$$\frac{\alpha}{+2} Ba^2 \Delta$$

$$\mu W/sr$$

$$2\Delta = 2.8\%$$

r whose radiation pattern is $I_0(\cos \theta)^3$
. (10-18)

$$\left(\frac{-1}{}\right)(NA)^2$$

$$\left(\frac{+1}{2}\right)\eta_1^2(2\Delta)$$

$$= (\tfrac{4}{2})(1.458)^2(0.028)$$

$$= 11.9\%$$

The coupling efficiency is greatly increased by the use of a laser instead of a lambertian LED.

10-3 INTRINSIC AND EXTRINSIC SPLICE-LOSS PARAMETERS

The practical implementation of optical fiber communication systems requires the use of interconnection devices such as splices or connectors. A connector, by definition, is a demountable device used where it is necessary or convenient to easily disconnect and reconnect fibers. A splice, on the other hand, is employed to permanently join lengths of fiber together. The losses introduced by splices and connectors are an important factor to be considered in the design of a fiber optic system since they can be a significant part of the loss budget of a multi-kilometer communication link. In this section we will divide losses of splices and connectors into two categories as shown in Fig 10-9. The first category of losses is related to the technique used to join fibers and is caused by extrinsic (to the fiber) parameters such as transverse offset between the fiber cores, end separation, axial tilt, and fiber end quality. The second category of losses is related to the properties of the fibers joined and is referred to as intrinsic (to the fibers) splice loss. Intrinsic parameters include variations in fiber diameter (both core and cladding), index profile (α and Δ mismatch), and ellipticity and concentricity of the fiber cores.

EXTRINSIC SPLICE LOSS FACTORS

- TRANSVERSE OFFSET
- LONGITUDINAL OFFSET
- AXIAL TILT
- FIBER END QUALITY

INTRINSIC SPLICE LOSS FACTORS

- FIBER DIAMETER VARIATION
- α MISMATCH
- $\triangle$ MISMATCH
- ELLIPTICITY AND CONCENTRICITY OF FIBER CORE

Figure 10-9 Intrinsic and extrinsic splice-loss factors.

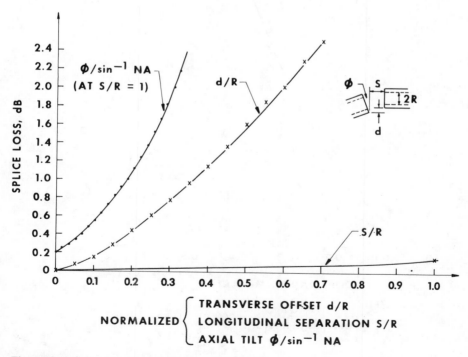

Figure 10-10 Splice loss due to extrinsic parameters.

A number of analytical models have been developed[7,8] and controlled experiments performed[8,9] to determine the effect the various intrinsic and extrinsic parameters have on splice loss. Figure 10-10 compares the relative influence on splice loss of the major extrinsic parameters of transverse offset, end separation, and axial tilt, for multimode graded-index fibers. Splice loss is significantly more sensitive to transverse offset and axial tilt than it is to longitudinal offset. For example, a transverse offset of 0.14 core radii or an axial tilt of 1 degree (for a fiber with an $NA = 0.20$) will produce a splice loss of 0.25 dB. A longitudinal offset of one core radius will produce a loss of only 0.14 dB. Fiber end quality has a minimal effect on splice loss if proper fracturing or grinding and polishing

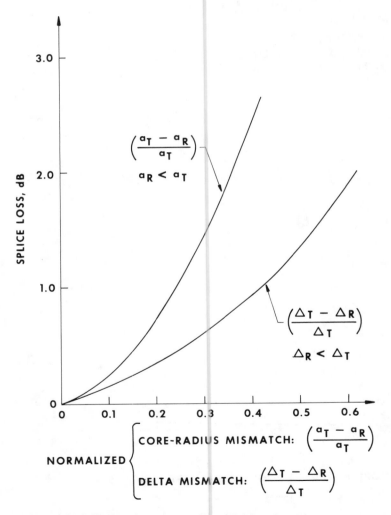

Figure 10-11 Splice loss due to core radius and delta mismatch.

end-preparation techniques[3] are used in conjunction with an index-matching material. A matching material with a refractive index approximately the same as that of the core is used to reduce the Fresnel reflection loss caused by the glass-air interfaces between the coupled fibers of a joint.

The mismatch of intrinsic multimode graded-index fiber parameters can also significantly affect the loss of a splice. Figure 10-11 illustrates how splice loss is affected by core radius or Δ mismatch and Fig. 10-2 shows how it is affected by α mismatch. These curves were obtained using a model in which a gaussian distribution of the power within the solid angle defined by the local numerical aperture at any point on the fiber core was assumed.[8] Splice loss is most sensitive to a mismatch of Δ or core radius (transmission from a high-Δ to low-Δ or large-core to small-core fiber). A normalized Δ or core-radius mismatch of 0.1 will produce a splice loss of approximately 0.2 dB. Correspondingly, a 25 percent mismatch in α will produce a splice loss of less than 0.2 dB. Sensitivity of splice loss to α mismatch is therefore substantially less than that for Δ or core-radius mismatch. Although generally less significant, other intrinsic mismatch parameters, such as core ellipticity[8] and concentricity, do contribute to the total loss of a splice.

In summary, parameters both intrinsic and extrinsic to the fibers being joined can affect splice loss. The most important extrinsic parameters that cause loss are transverse offset and axial tilt. One must carefully design both connectors and splices to very tight tolerances to minimize these extrinsic parameters. The most sensitive intrinsic factors that cause splice loss are the Δ and core-radius mismatch of the fibers being joined. To minimize the effect intrinsic

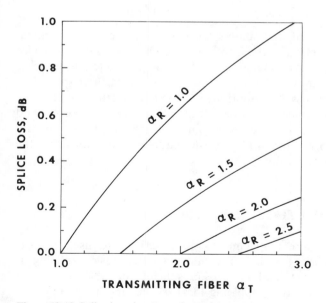

Figure 10-12 Splice loss due to α mismatch.

parameters have on splice loss, tight manufacturing tolerances on the fibers used in a low-loss communication system must be maintained. For example, a core diameter tolerance which yields fibers that vary by less than five percent of their nominal diameter is common in the fiber optics industry today.

Example 10-2 Intrinsic and extrinsic splice loss Consider a splice with a measured short length splice loss of 0.4 dB.

If the fiber parameters, a, α, and Δ are known for the transmitting and receiving fibers, the contribution of the total splice loss due to individual intrinsic effects can be calculated using the ideas presented in Sec. 10-3. For example, if the transmitting fiber parameters are $a = 25$ μm, $\Delta = 1.58$ percent, and $\alpha = 2.1$, and the receiving fiber parameters are $a = 24$ μm, $\Delta = 1.45$ percent, and $\alpha = 2.0$, we can calculate the splice loss due to individual intrinsic parameter mismatches as follows.

From Figs. 10-11 and 10-12 we can compute the losses due to parameter mismatches

$$\frac{a_T - a_R}{a_T} = 0.04$$

$$\frac{\Delta_T - \Delta_R}{\Delta_T} = 0.03$$

Loss due to core mismatch $= 0.09$ dB

Loss due to delta mismatch $= 0.06$ dB

Loss due to α mismatch $= 0.02$ dB

At this point one is tempted to assume a linear relationship between intrinsic and extrinsic parameters, that is, to calculate the total intrinsic splice loss as the sum of the losses due to the individual parameter mismatches (0.17 dB) and then to subtract this loss from the total measured splice loss to obtain the extrinsic loss contribution (0.23 dB). Unfortunately the assumption of a linear relationship between these parameters is incorrect and will yield only an approximate solution to our problem. To properly obtain the combined effects to intrinsic and extrinsic parameters one must use the computer model described in Ref. 8.

10-4 SINGLE- AND MULTIFIBER SPLICES

There are basically two different splicing techniques that are used to permanently join individual fibers together. The first technique, fusion splicing, is currently the most widely used method. Fusion splicing, or welding as it is sometimes called, is accomplished by applying localized heating at the interface between two butted, prealigned fiber ends, causing them to soften and fuse

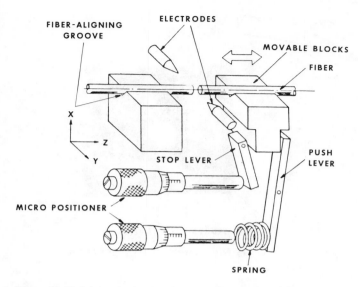

Figure 10-13 Schematic showing fusion splicing using an electric arc.

together. Figure 10-13 is a schematic diagram showing how fibers are welded together using an electric arc.[13] Obstacles associated with fusion splicing are related to the imperfect preparation of fiber ends, the difficulties associated with prealigning the fibers to be spliced, and the tensile strength of the fused fiber. Implementing the fusion process with fibers that have imperfect ends (surface roughness, angle, or lips) can result in a distortion of the core and formation of small air bubbles.[10] To avoid these problems, automated fusion test sets have been developed[11] with the following features:

1. an optical viewing arrangement to simplify fiber prealignment[12]
2. a prefusion process using a low-energy arc discharge to round the fiber ends and avoid bubble formation[10]
3. a controlled inward movement of the fibers during fusion to prevent necking at the fused joint[13]

The tensile strength of a fused fiber has been reported to be approximately 60 percent of the strength of the uncoated fiber before fusion.[6] The decrease in strength is attributed to the combined effects of surface damage due to handling, surface defect growth during heating, and residual stresses induced as a result of changes in chemical composition.[14] Completed fused splices should be incorporated in a protective package and stored with little or no tensile loading to avoid mechanical problems in the vicinity of the splice. Despite some of the difficulties associated with fusion splicing it is one of the most promising techniques currently available for permanently joining individual fibers. Average

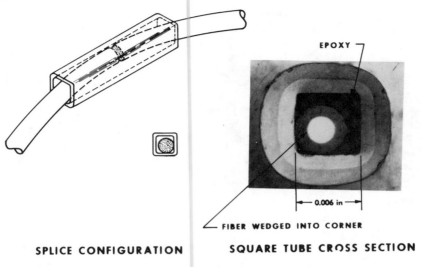

EPOXY

0.006 in

FIBER WEDGED INTO CORNER

SPLICE CONFIGURATION   **SQUARE TUBE CROSS SECTION**

Figure 10-14 Loose tube splice.

splice losses, for identical fibers, of 0.1 dB or less have been obtained with the fusion technique.[6]

The second class of permanent splices utilizes an alignment member (a V groove for example) and adhesive bonding to join individual fibers together. Two examples of this type of splice are shown in Figs. 10-14 and 10-15. A simple technique of fabricating low-loss laboratory type splices uses a loose fitting tube with a square cross section.[15] To assemble a loose tube splice, two fibers with good ends are inserted halfway into each end of a square cross section tube. The fibers are placed on a flat surface and bent in a curved pattern. This causes forces to be generated that rotate the tube so that a diagonal of the square cross section is in the same plane as the bent fibers. The fibers are therefore self-aligned in the same corner of the tube. The bent fibers are then pushed into the tube until they touch each other and index-matching epoxy is wicked into the tube to complete the splice. In the laboratory, graded-index fibers have been spliced together using loose tube splices with an average splice loss of 0.07 dB.

The second example of a permanent splice that utilizes an alignment member is called a Springroove® splice and is shown in Fig. 10-15.[6] This splice uses a bracket containing two cylindrical pins as the alignment element (groove) for the fiber ends being spliced. The diameter of the cylindrical pins is selected to ensure that the upper rim of the fibers is protruding above the cylinders, as shown in Fig. 10-15b. An elastic element (a spring) is used to keep each fiber end pressed in the groove and a drop of commercial optical epoxy is added to complete the splice. A histogram of loss data resulting from laboratory tests performed utilizing Springroove® splices is shown in Fig. 10-15c. The average

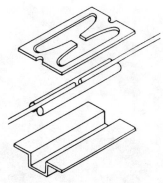

(a) EXPANDED VIEW OF SPRINGROOVE® SPLICE

(b) SCHEMATIC OF CROSS SECTION OF SPLICE

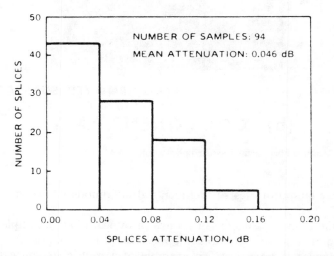

(c) HISTOGRAM OF LABORATORY SPLICE LOSS DATA

Figure 10-15 Springroove® splice.

(a) ASSEMBLED SPLICE

COVER PLATE

TOOLING PIN

VACUUM SLOT

GROOVED SUBSTATE

(b) COMPONENT PARTS

Figure 10-16 Multiple fiber vacuum-assisted plastic splice (VAPS).

loss for these laboratory tests using identical multimode graded-index fibers was 0.046 dB.[16]

The simultaneous splicing of groups of optical fibers (multiple fiber splice) is often required when a multifiber optical cable is damaged and rapid restoration of service is necessary. An example of a multifiber splice used to join optical fiber ribbons (12-fiber linear arrays) is shown in Fig. 10-16.[17] This vacuum-assisted continuous groove plastic splice (VAPS) consists of an injection-molded plastic cover plate and a grooved substrate (Fig. 10-16b). The grooves in the substrate are used to align individual fibers in one ribbon with their respective mates in a second ribbon. Both the substrate and cover plate have vacuum slots, transverse to the direction of the grooves, to facilitate assembly of a ribbon splice. A cross section of the splice is shown in Fig. 10-17a. A properly designed mold and careful attention to molding pressures during cooling are necessary to fabricate plastic parts with the dimensions and tolerances required to produce low-loss optical splices. To fabricate an optical ribbon splice, first the tape and coating are removed from the fibers in a short section at the end of the ribbons. The fiber ends are then prepared using a controlled fracturing technique.[18] After a substrate is placed in the assembly tool, the prepared ribbons are each in turn placed on the substrate and oriented until an easily recognizable alignment pattern is observed between the fibers and the edge of the grooves in the substrate. Vacuum-assist is then used to hold the fibers in their grooves and to enable the formation of a butt joint. The next step in the assembly process is to close the splice. This is currently accomplished by placing fast-setting epoxy in the trough of the substrate and then adhering the coverplate to the substrate with the aid of the assembly tool. After the splice is removed from the assembly tool index-matching gel is injected through a slot in the cover plate to complete the splice-assembly procedure. The entire process of splicing 12 fibers including ribbon preparation and splice fabrication is accomplished in 20 minutes. Figure 10-17b is a histogram of splice-loss data for the vacuum-assisted plastic splice. The average loss for these laboratory measurements using identical multimode graded-index fibers was 0.18 dB.

10-5 SINGLE- AND MULTIFIBER CONNECTORS

There are a wide variety of fiber connectors being used to interconnect both individual fibers and optical fiber cables. In this section we will describe five connectors, each of which uses a different principle of operation.

The molded biconical plug connector[19,20] shown in Fig. 10-18 is widely used as part of a jumper cable for a variety of central office applications in the Bell system. The heart of this connector is a biconical sleeve which accepts two plugs and aligns the axes of the fiber ends that are centrally located in these plugs. An inherent advantage of the conical alignment configuration is that virtually no abrasive wear occurs with repeated engagement of the plug and alignment sleeve. No contact occurs between the mating parts until the plug is fully seated within the biconical alignment sleeve. Both the plugs and the alignment sleeves are transfer-molded using a filled thermosetting epoxy to enhance dimensional accuracy and stability. Each plug is molded directly onto a fiber. Careful prepositioning in the transfer mold ensures that the fiber core is concentric within a few micrometers to the tapered end surface of the plug. After molding, the end of the fiber is ground and polished. To complete a connection the two plugs are inserted into the biconical alignment sleeve as shown in Fig. 10-18b. The lowest average measured insertion loss obtained with identical

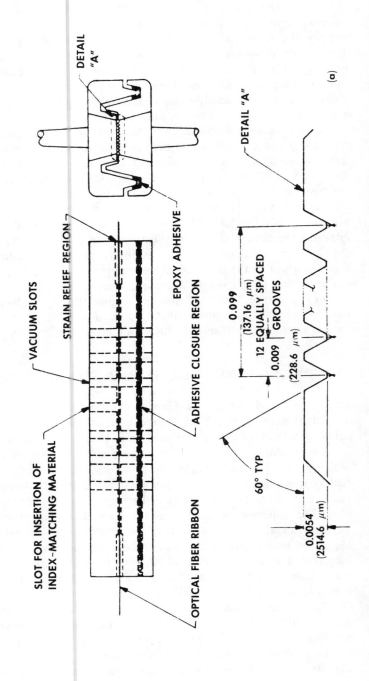

SLOT FOR INSERTION OF
INDEX-MATCHING MATERIAL

VACUUM SLOTS

STRAIN RELIEF REGION

EPOXY ADHESIVE

ADHESIVE CLOSURE REGION

OPTICAL FIBER RIBBON

DETAIL "A"

DETAIL "A"

0.099
(137.16 μm)

12 EQUALLY SPACED
GROOVES

0.009
(228.6 μm)

60° TYP

0.0054
(2514.6 μm)

(a)

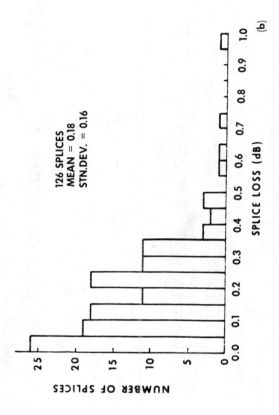

Figure 10-17 (*a*) Cross section of vacuum-assisted plastic splice. (*b*) Histogram of splice loss data (VAPS).

253

(a) SINGLE-FIBER BICONICAL CONNECTOR

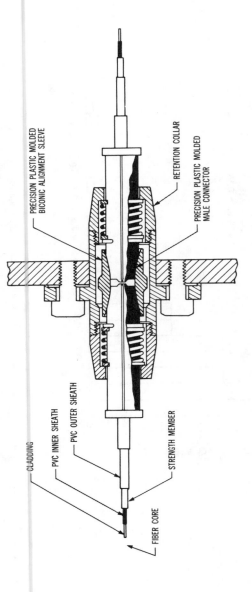

PRECISION PLASTIC MOLDED
BICONIC ALIGNMENT SLEEVE

RETENTION COLLAR

PRECISION PLASTIC MOLDED
MALE CONNECTOR

CLADDING

PVC INNER SHEATH

PVC OUTER SHEATH

STRENGTH MEMBER

FIBER CORE

(b) CROSS SECTION OF BICONICAL CONNECTOR

Figure 10-18 Single-fiber biconical connector.

254

50 μm/125 μm graded-index fibers ($NA = 0.23$) for this connector was 0.11 dB.[21] Fresnel reflection loss can be virtually eliminated in this connector by allowing physical contact of the carefully polished fiber end faces. The next connector design that we will discuss uses a three-ball alignment configuration to center a fiber in a ferrule arrangement shown in Fig. 10-19a.[22] The fiber is located in a groove formed by two balls and held in place by a third ball. To ensure correct location of the two fiber ends they are located with a microscope and recessed with respect to the end plane of the three balls. The fibers are then permanently attached with an adhesive. The geometrical characteristics relating the fiber end recess and ball radius are shown in Fig. 10-19b. By pressing together the two sets of three balls, at a relative rotation of 60°, automatic alignment of the two fibers is brought about. It should be noted that the only high-precision components in this connector are the tungsten carbide balls that are inexpensive and easily manufactured with tolerances of ± 1 μm. Average insertion losses of 0.5 to 1.0 dB have been reported using a 50-μm-core graded-index fiber. A modification of the three-ball connector using fiber bead termin-ations is shown in Fig. 10-19c. The beads, whose spherical flame-polished sur-faces reduce coupling losses due to imperfect fiber cleaving, are produced using an electric arc discharge.[23] An inexpensive molded plastic connector using a three-ball insert and fiber-bead terminations had an average loss of 0.8 dB.

The third connector design shown in Fig. 10-20 is an adjustable eccentric cylindrical sleeve connector.[24] The fibers are mounted eccentrically on two displaced cylinders, which in turn are held in position in a groove by a spring coil. By rotating the cylinders two optimum coupling positions are possible. The most interesting and unique part of this connector is the light monitoring and alignment system that is used to obtain the optimum coupling position.

The fiber is housed in a capillary tube whose terminations facing the con-nector are cut at 45° angles as shown in Fig. 10-20b. The end of the capillary tube acts as a beam splitter reflecting scattered light due to fiber misalignment toward a monitoring detector. Optimum connector coupling is achieved by rotating the two connector parts relative to each other until a minimum signal, picked up by the monitoring detector, is obtained. Average insertion losses of 0.098 dB have been reported for this connector using identical 63 m-core diam-eter graded-index fibers ($NA = 0.18$).[24] An adjustable factory-installed connector of a similar type would be useful for joining single-mode fibers since alignment accuracies of the order of 1.0 μm are necessary to achieve low-loss connections.

The last two connectors that will be described are multiple-fiber connectors. The first of this type is the silicon chip array connector shown in Fig. 10-21.[19] This connector is used in conjunction with the ribbon type structures shown in Figs. 9-12 and 9-13. The connector consists of two array halves, two negative chips with metal backing, and two spring clips (see Fig. 10-22). An array half is formed by permanently affixing two positive preferentially etched silicon chips[25] to the end of a ribbon. The fiber ends are then simultaneously prepared by grinding and polishing the end of the array. The connector halves are assembled on a cable prior to shipment from a factory. A craftsperson assembles a connec-

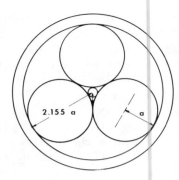

(a) FIBER LOCATED IN GROOVE FORMED BY
THREE CONTACTING BALLS

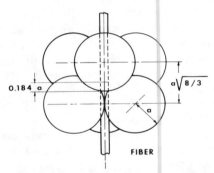

(b) TWO INTERLOCKING, SELF-ALIGNING
SETS OF THREE BALLS

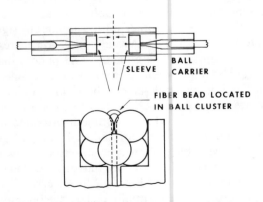

(c) THREE-BALL FIBER-BEAD CONNECTOR

Figure 10-19 Single-fiber three-ball connector.

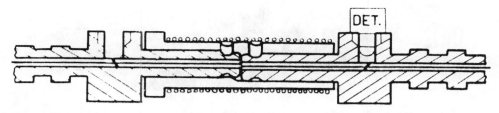

(a) ADJUSTABLE ECCENTRIC CYLINDRICAL CONNECTOR WITH SCATTERED-LIGHT MONITOR

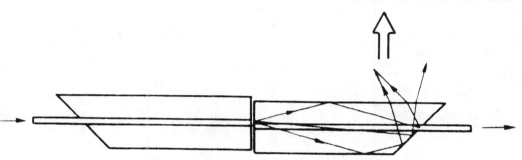

(b) PRINCIPLE OF SCATTERED-LIGHT MONITOR

Figure 10-20 Single-fiber adjustable eccentric cylindrical connector.

tor in the field by simply aligning two array halves with two negative chips as shown in Fig. 10-22. The connector is then held together with spring clips and a matching material is inserted to complete the connection. The array connector can be disconnected and reconnected in the field although it was not designed for use where many connect–disconnect operations are required. It is essentially a splice that can be reentered when testing, or when rearrangement of fibers is necessary. This connector has had wide field use in the Bell system. Its average insertion loss is 0.1 dB using identical 50-μm/125-μm diameter graded-index multimode fibers (laboratory tests). Field data indicate that the loss (which includes both intrinsic and extrinsic splice-loss parameters) for the silicon chip array connector is 0.3 dB.

The second multifiber connector consists of a cylinder with grooves machined along its surface parallel to its axis, as shown in Fig. 10-23.[26] To obtain the two matched halves of the connector the cylinder is cut in two. The fibers to be coupled are glued into the grooves so that the fiber end faces are flush with the front of the cylinders. The cylinders are supported by steel needles and their azimuthal alignment is achieved by placing a third steel needle in an aligning V

(a) 12-FIBER SILICON CHIP ARRAY CONNECTOR

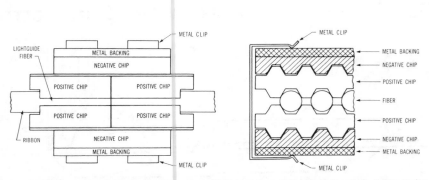

(b) SIDE VIEW AND PARTIAL CROSS SECTION OF ARRAY CONNECTOR

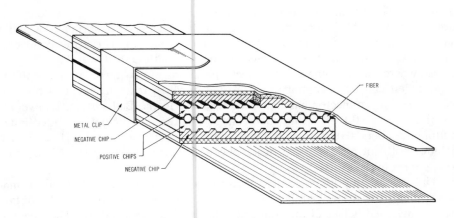

(c) CROSS SECTION OF ARRAY CONNECTOR

Figure 10-21 Multiple-fiber silicon-chip array connector.

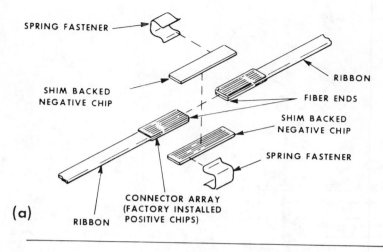

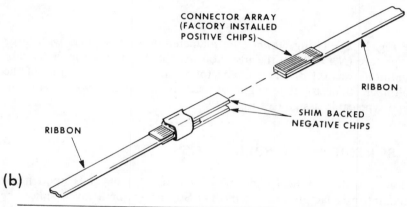

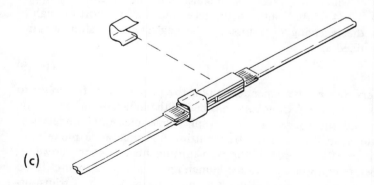

Figure 10-22 Silicon-chip array connector assembly sequence.

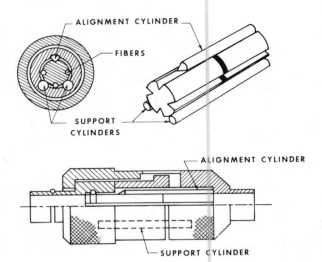

Figure 10-23 Multifiber V groove connector with cylindrical cross section.

groove (see Fig. 10-23). Using 60-μm core diameter step-index fibers with large numerical aperture ($NA = 0.56$), the insertion loss of this connector under laboratory conditions was 0.1 dB. This connector is an interesting example of the type of multifiber connector that might be used in conjunction with a conventional layered type cable design (see Fig. 9-9).

10-6 MEASUREMENT OF SPLICE LOSS

The insertion loss of an optical fiber splice or connector depends upon many extrinsic and intrinsic factors as described in Sec. 10-3. For a given splice the measured loss can be significantly affected by the kind of source used, the launching conditions, and the characteristics of the fibers on either side of the splice.[27-29] Let us consider the transmission-splice loss measurement arrangement shown in Fig. 10-24. If the length of the receiving fiber is short enough (a few meters so that the receiving fiber loss can be neglected), a "short-length" splice loss can be defined as

$$L_s = 10 \log (P_2/P_1) \qquad (10\text{-}19)$$

For multimode fibers, L_s may be dependent upon the proximity of the splice to the source. If there is a long transmitting fiber with sufficient mode-mixing between the splice and the source, L_s is the splice loss measured under near steady-state conditions; in this case the transmitting fiber acts as a mode filter isolating the splice from the source. If the transmitting fiber is short, however, L_s is strongly dependent upon the source-launching conditions. Figure 10-25 shows the loss of a splice measured with and without a long length of transmitting fiber as a function of the source-input beam numerical aperture. A large

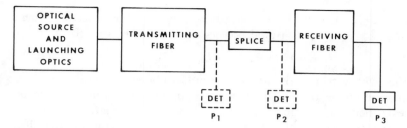

Figure 10-24 Transmission splice-loss measurement.

variation in the measured value of L_s (greater than a factor of three in this case) can occur if the source-launching conditions are not isolated from the splice by a long transmitting fiber.[27]

An additional splice effect exists when a long length of fiber follows a splice. The modal power distribution along a fiber is generally disturbed by a splice. This will cause the receiving fiber to have a loss that is different from its loss measured under steady-state conditions. Since this difference in fiber loss is a direct result of the splice, it can be considered as part of the total splice loss. We may define a "long-length" splice loss, L_l, as

$$L_l = L_s + \delta L_R \tag{10-20}$$

where δL_R is a change from its steady-state value of the receiving fiber's loss

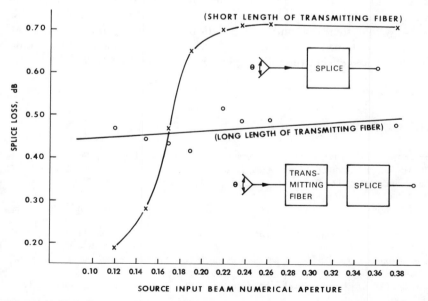

Figure 10-25 Splice loss with and without a long length of transmitting fiber vs. input-beam numerical aperture.

caused by the splice. L_l can be expressed in terms of the receiving fiber's steady-state loss, L_R^{ss}, and the measured powers P_1 and P_3 (see Fig. 10-24) as

$$L_l = 10 \log P_3/P_1 - L_R^{ss} \quad \text{dB} \qquad (10\text{-}21)$$

For a splice with extrinsic loss between identical fibers, L_l is greater than L_s by as much as a factor of two. For a splice in which intrinsic parameter mismatches exist between the fibers, L_l can be less than or greater than L_s. In fact, L_l can even be less than zero. This can occur when transmitting fiber underfills the numerical aperture of the receiving fiber, as, for example, when a small-Δ small-core fiber is spliced to a large-Δ, large-core fiber.[29] In general, L_s is a well-defined localized quantity for a given splice, whereas L_l is a function of the length, the degree of mode mixing, and the differential mode attenuation of the receiving fiber.

For evaluating the quality of splices and connectors, L_s is measured under steady-state conditions (using a long transmitting fiber and identical short receiving fiber). This is the number that is usually quoted as the loss of a splice or a connector. As we have discussed, L_s does not fully account for the effect of a splice on a system. Workers in this field are currently attempting to develop models[7,8] to account for the total effect of a splice on the system loss. The ultimate objective of loss measurements is to enable the system designer to predict losses that will occur in a fiber optic system. To accomplish this end requires that allowance be made for many variables, for example, fiber parameter variations, the type of source and fiber lengths used, and the number and relative location of the splices and connectors in the system. It is impractical to incorporate all of these variables into a standard measurement. The current strategy in system-loss budget calculations is to use L_s and an empirical correction factor (obtained from statistical data on installed systems) to account for the distributed loss effect caused by a splice or connector on a system.

REFERENCES

1. M. Born and E. Wolf: *Principles of Optics*, Pergamon Press, Oxford, England, 1965.
2. C. A. Burrus and B. I. Miller: "Small-Area, Double-Heterostructure Aluminum-Gallium Arsenide Electroluminescent Diode Sources for Optical Fiber Transmission Lines," *Opt. Comm.*, **4**: 307 (1971).
3. S. E. Miller and A. G. Chynoweth: *Optical Fiber Telecommunications*, Academic Press Inc., New York, 1979.
4. M. K. Barnoski: *Fundamentals of Optical Fiber Communications*, Academic Press Inc., New York, 1976.
5. H. Kressel: *Semiconductor Devices for Optical Communication*, Springer-Verlag Press, New York, 1980.
6. Technical Staff of CSELT: "Optical Fibre Communication," Centro Studi e Laboratori Telecommunicazioni, Torino, 1980.
7. C. M. Miller and S. C. Mettler: "A Loss Model for Parabolic-Profile Fiber Splices," *BSTJ*, **47**(9): 3167, November 1978.

8. S. C. Mettler: "A General Characterization of Splice Loss for Multimode Optical Fibers," *BSTJ*, **58**(10): 2163, December 1979.

9. T. C. Chu and A. R. McCormick: "Measurements of Loss Due to Offset, End Separation and Angular Misalignment in Graded Index Fibers Excited by an Incoherent Source," *BSTJ*, **57**(3): 595, March 1978.

10. M. Hirai and N. Uchida: "Melt Splice of Multimode Optical Fibre with an Electric Arc," *Electron. Lett.*, **13**(5): 123, March 1977.

11. K. Sakamoto et al.: "The Automatic Splicing Machine Employing Electric Arc Fusion," Proc. 4th Eur. Conf. Opt. Comm., p. 296, September 1978.

12. A. J. J. Franken et al.: "Experimental Semi-Automatic Machine for Hot Splicing of Glass Fibers for Optical Communication," Philips Tech. Rev., **38**(6): 158 (1978/79).

13. I. Hatakayana and H. Tsuchiya: "Fusion Splices for Optical Fibers by Discharge Heating," *Appl. Opt.*, **17**(12): 1959, June 15, 1978.

14. J. F. Dalgleish: "Splice Connectors, and Power Couplers for Field and Office Use," *Proc. IEEE*, **68**(10), October 1980.

15. C. M. Miller: "Loose Tube Splices for Optical Fibers," *Bell Syst. Tech. J.*, **54**, Pizis, September 1975.

16. G. Cocito et al.: "COSZ Experiment in Twin: Field Test on an Optical Cable in Ducts," *IEEE Trans. Commun.*, **COM-26**(7), July 1978.

17. A. H. Cherin, P. J. Rich, C. J. Aloisio, and R. R. Cammons: "A Vacuum-Assisted Plastic Repair Splice for Joining Optical Fiber Ribbons," *BSTJ*, **58**(8), October 1979.

18. A. H. Cherin and P. J. Rich: "An Injection-Molded Plastic Connector for Splicing Optical Cables," *BSTJ*, **55**(8), October 1976.

19. T. L. Williford, K. W. Jackson, and C. Scholly: "Interconnection for Lightguide Fibers," *West. Electr. Eng.*, Winter 1980.

20. P. K. Runge and S. S. Cheng: "Demountable Single-Fiber Optic Connectors and Their Measurement on Location," *BSTJ*, **57**(6): 1771–1790, July/August 1978.

21. P. Kaiser, W. C. Young, N. K. Cheuvg, and L. Curtis: "Loss Characterization of Biconic Single-Fiber Connectors," NBS Symp. Opt. Fiber Meas., Boulder, Colorado, October 1980.

22. P. Hensel: "Triple Ball Connector for Optical Fibers," *Electron. Lett.*, **13**(24): 734–735 (1977).

23. D. B. Payne and C. A. Millar: "Triple Ball Connector Using Fibre-Bead Location," *Electron. Lett.*, **16**(1): 11–12, Jan. 3, 1980.

24. V. Vucins: "Adjustable Single-Fiber Connector with Monitor Output," Third Eur. Conf. Opt. Commun. pp. 100–102, Munich, Sept. 14–16, 1977.

25. C. M. Schroeder: "Accurate Silicon Spacer Chips for an Optical-Fiber Cable Connector," *BSTJ*, **57**(1), January 1978.

26. J. Guttman et al.: "Multi-Pole Optical Fibre Connector," First Eur. Conf. Opt. Fibre Commun. pp. 96–98, London, Sept. 16–18, 1975.

27. A. H. Cherin and P. J. Rich: "Measurement of Loss and Output Numerical Aperture of Optical Fiber Splices," *Appl. Opt.*, **17**(4), Feb. 15, 1978.

28. R. B. Kummer: "Lightguide Slice Loss—Effects of Lanuch Beam Numerical Aperture," *BSTJ*, **59**(3), March 1980.

29. R. B. Kummer: "Precise Characterization of Long Non-Identical-Fiber Splice Loss Effects," Sixth Eur. Conf. Opt. Commun., York, England, September 1980.

PROBLEMS

10-1 Describe two factors that affect source-coupling loss.

10-2 Sketch the radiation patterns of a lambertian surface-emitting LED and an injection laser diode whose radiation pattern is given by Eq. (10-3) with $m = 10$. Which source would you expect to have higher coupling efficiency?

10-3 A fiber is excited by a surface-emitting LED. Calculate the input power, coupled power, and coupling efficiency if the fiber and LED can be described as follows:

$$a = 30 \ \mu m$$
$$\Delta = 1.5\%$$
$$\alpha = 1.95$$
$$B = 2.0 \times 10^2 \ W/cm^2/sr$$

10-4 A step-index fiber is excited by a nonlambertian source whose radiation pattern is characterized by Eq. (10-3) with $m = 7$. By what factor does the coupling efficiency increase relative to excitation by a lambertian source?

10-5 What is meant by extrinsic and intrinsic splice loss? Give examples of each one.

10-6 Calculate the individual intrinsic and extrinsic splice-loss effects (in decibels) for a splice whose transverse offset is 10 percent, axial tilt is 10 percent, and Δ mismatch is 10 percent? For the transmitting fiber $\alpha = 1.6$ and for the receiving fiber $\alpha = 1.5$. Assume longitudinal offset is 0 and fiber cores of equal diameter. Which mechanism would the splice designer want most to improve?

10-7 Describe two methods of splicing individual fibers together. What are some advantages and disadvantages of each method?

10-8 A farmer cuts through an optical communication fiber with his plow and 144 fibers are broken. What method could be used to join these fibers? What would you expect the average added loss in each fiber path to be?

10-9 List three single-fiber connectors and an advantage of each one. When is a connector used instead of a splice?

10-10 Describe the terms "short-length" and "long-length" splice loss. What factors affect each one?

10-11 The loss of a splice is measured with two sources—one whose numerical aperture is 0.14 and one whose numerical aperture is 0.28. If the loss is measured without a mode filter, what will be the difference in the two measurements? What will be the loss difference if a mode filter is used? (Refer to Fig. 10-25.)

FIBER SYSTEM EXAMPLES

11-1 INTRODUCTION

In this chapter general design considerations for optical fiber systems are dis
cussed. We will review the characteristics of fibers, sources, detectors, and
commonly used system modulation formats with the intent of illustrating how
appropriate components are selected for different system applications. Examples
of intracity, and undersea digital pulse code modulated (PCM) telecommunication systems are given. In addition a fiber optic system which transmits video
signals using analog modulation of an optical carrier is illustrated.

11-2 SYSTEM DESIGN CONSIDERATIONS

We have briefly discussed, in Chap. 1, the various components that make up a
fiber optic communication system (see Fig. 1-6). Although we are primarily
interested in examining the properties of optical fibers in this text, they com-
prise only one component of a communication system. A complete system, even
in its simplest form, consists of an optical source which can be modulated, an
optical detector, and light-conducting fibers. In addition, the system will require
light-coupling methods, fiber protection, splices, connectors, and physical hardware of all sorts. The optical sources may be LED's or lasers, the detectors may
be PIN diodes or APD detectors, and the fibers may be multimode (step index
or graded index) or single mode. Out of this array of components, some of
which are incompatible, one can assemble a wide variety of systems. Although
not covered in detail in this text, processing electronics (both terminals and line

regenerators or amplifiers) and an assortment of specialized test equipment may be needed to complete the system.

Fiber systems can be classified in a number of ways. One general classification refers to the mode of transmission: digital or analog, for example. Besides the digital–analog distinction, we can classify systems according to their range. Communication systems can be divided quite arbitrarily into short- and long-range systems. Short-range systems are less than one kilometer in length and are intended for use, for example, within a building forming a link between two pieces of equipment. Long-range systems are generally one kilometer in length or much longer. They are intended for interbuilding, intracity, intercity, and undersea application. The length of a system (repeater spacing) and mode of transmission (bit rate of a PCM digital system, for example) will determine the quality of fiber (in terms of the attenuation and bandwidth) and the type of source and photodetector used.

In the next four sections of this chapter we will review the characteristics of fibers, sources, detectors, and commonly used system modulation formats with the intent of illustrating how different combinations of components can be matched for different system configurations.

11-3 FIBER CHARACTERISTICS

In Chap. 7 we discussed the various loss mechanisms (see Fig. 7-3) that contribute to the spectral loss of a typical optical fiber. Rayleigh scattering and loss due to the UV and IR absorption tails are the intrinsic loss mechanisms in a fiber that can never be eliminated. As a consequence of this these are the mechanisms that place a lower limit on the loss of a fiber. Table 11-1[1] shows, for Ge-P-SiO$_2$-core fibers, the lowest theoretical loss due to intrinsic loss mechanisms, and the best measured loss reported to date.

The loss numbers in Table 11-1 provide an optimistic lower bound for the attenuation of optical fibers. In addition to intrinsic fiber losses, extrinsic loss mechanisms such as absorption due to impurity ions, and microbending loss due to jacketing and cabling, can add loss to a fiber.

Table 11-1 Best attenuation results—dB/km in Ge-P-SiO$_2$-core fibers

| Wavelength | $\Delta \approx 0.2\%$ (single-mode fibers) | | $\Delta \approx 1.0\%$ (graded-index multimode fibers) | |
	Theoretical limit	Best measured results	Theoretical limit	Best measured results
850 nm	1.90	2.1	2.20	2.20
1300 nm	0.32	0.38	0.44	0.44
1500 nm	0.18	0.20	0.22	0.23

There are three mechanisms that can cause delay distortion and in turn limit the bandwidth of a fiber. They are:

1. modal delay distortion (see Secs. 4-9, 5-13, and 6-9)
2. chromatic (material) dispersion (see Secs. 5-8, 5-13, and 6-9)
3. waveguide dispersion (see Sec. 5-8)

For a multimode fiber, the group velocities of the propagating modes are most nearly equalized when the fiber profile shape parameter α has an optimum value α_0. α_0 depends on both the glass composition and the wavelength. For a fiber with $\alpha = \alpha_0$, the minimum rms pulse spreading σ_m that could occur per unit length of fiber is given by[2]

$$\sigma_m \approx 0.14\Delta^2 \qquad \mu s/km \tag{11-1}$$

for a fiber with $\Delta = 1\%$, $\sigma_m \approx 14$ ps/km. In practice, small perturbations from the ideal profile are generally present in a fiber. These perturbations lead to a much larger σ_m than that predicted by Eq. (11-1).[3] An empirical relationship between the bandwidth (BW) of a fiber and its rms impulse response width σ is given by[5]

$$BW \approx \frac{180}{\sigma} \tag{11-2}$$

Where the bandwidth is expressed in gigahertz-kilometers and σ in picoseconds per kilometer. Figure 11-1 shows a sharp peak in the bandwidth at the optimum value $\alpha = \alpha_0$. Optimizing α reduces modal distortion, but to eliminate it completely, a single-mode fiber is necessary.

Delay distortion due to chromatic dispersion is caused by the variation of the refractive index of the glass with wavelength and the relative bandwidth of the source as described in Eq. (5-74). The rms chromatic pulse spreading σ_c occurs within each mode of a fiber and can be combined with the pulse spreading due to model delay distortion σ_m to give a total rms pulse spreading σ_t.[4]

$$\sigma_t \approx (\sigma_m^2 + \sigma_c^2)^{1/2} \tag{11-3}$$

In the region where chromatic dispersion approaches zero (see Fig. 5-6) σ_c will be minimized but will not be zero due to the finite line width of the source. For example, Fig. 11-2 shows the bandwidth of a fiber excited with an LED source (an LED spectral width $= \lambda^2/40$ μm is used) in the zero chromatic dispersion region of the fiber.[6]

Waveguide dispersion, which is associated with the guidance effects of the fiber structure, is generally only important in single-mode fibers. Increasing Δ or decreasing the core radius for a given single-mode-fiber design, has the effect of increasing the zero material dispersion wavelength. For a given system wavelength, variations in fiber parameters can result in reducing the system bandwidth from its optimum value.

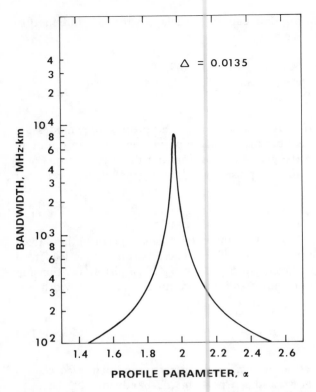

Figure 11-1 Theoretical dependence of bandwidth on profile parameter α.

Table 11-2 Best bandwidth results in Ge-P-SiO2-core fibers

				Single-mode fibers		Graded-index multimode fibers, $\Delta \approx 1\%$		
	Source			Theo-retical BW	Largest measured BW	Theo-retical BW	Largest measured BW	
Wave-length	Type	rms, $\Delta\lambda$, nm	σ_c, ps/km	GHz · km		GHz · km		σ_t, ps/km
850 nm	LED	18	†	†	†	0.1	0.07	1720
850 nm	Laser	0.6	57	3.2	3.3	3.1	3.1	58
1300 nm	LED	42	†	†	†	3.5	7.0‡	52
1300 nm	Laser	1.5	1.5	120	92	13	6.5	14

† Low coupling efficiency rules out the LED as a source with single-mode fibers.

‡ This exceeds the theoretical value for bandwidth because the OH absorption peak at 1.39 μm in the fiber reduces the effective LED linewidth.

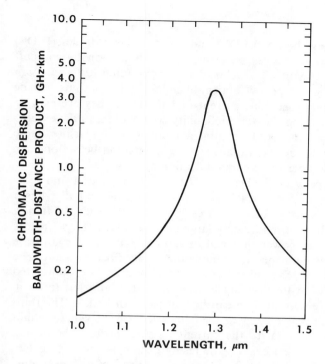

Figure 11-2 Chromatic dispersion bandwidth-distance product plotted as a function of wavelength.

Table 11-2 summarizes the maximum theoretical bandwidth and the largest measured bandwidth to date, for single-mode and graded-index multimode Ge-P-SiO$_2$ fibers.[1]

The theoretical bandwidth figures in Table 11-2 were calculated using Eq. (11-2) with σ_T obtained from Eq. (11-3). For all source-fiber combinations, Table 11-2 gives an optimistic upper bound for the bandwidths.

A system designer can use Tables 11-1 and 11-2 in conjunction with a knowledge of the source power and receiver sensitivity to obtain an indication of the maximum system-repeater spacing. More realistic loss and bandwidth values for fibers along with losses due to source coupling and splices will be given in the system examples later in this chapter.

11-4 SOURCE AND DETECTOR CHARACTERISTICS

In this section we will review the characteristics of optical sources and detectors that are used in fiber optic communication systems.

11-4-1 Optical Sources

Semiconductor light-emitting diodes (LED's) and injection-laser diodes (ILD's) are attractive as optical carrier sources because they are dimensionally compatible with optical fibers; they emit at wavelengths corresponding (0.8 to 0.9 μm and 1.3 to 1.6 μm) with regions of low optical-fiber loss, their outputs can be rapidly controlled by varying their bias current and therefore they are easy to modulate, and finally they offer solid-state reliability with lifetimes now exceeding 10^6 h.[7] Although LED's and ILD's exhibit a number of similarities, there are important differences between them that must be understood before one can select a source for a specific fiber optic communication system.

One major difference between LED's and ILD's is their spatial and temporal coherence. An ILD radiates a relatively narrow beam of light that has a narrow spectral width. In contrast LED sources have a much wider radiation pattern (beam width) and have a moderately large spectral width. These factors govern the amount of optical power that can be coupled into a fiber and the influence of chromatic dispersion on the bandwidth of the fiber medium. The second difference between ILD's and LED's is their speed. The stimulated emission from lasers results in intrinsically faster optical rise and fall times in response to changes in drive current than can be realized with LED's. The third difference between the devices is related to their linearity. LED's generate light that is almost linearly proportional to the current passing through the device. Lasers however are threshold devices, and the lasing output is proportional to the drive current only above threshold. The threshold current of a laser, unfortunately, is not a constant but is a function of the device's temperature and age. Feedback control drive circuitry is therefore required to stabilize a laser's output power. Table 11-3[7] illustrates typical ILD's and LED characteristics found in fiber optic communication systems.

GaAlAs devices (both ILD's and LED's), emitting in the 0.8 to 0.9 μm wavelength region, are commercially available and widely used in optical fiber systems. InGaAsP devices, with their emission wavelengths in the 1.0 to 1.7 μm region, are being developed for application near 1.3 μm and 1.6 μm where fiber

Table 11-3 Optical Source Characteristics

	ILD's	LED's
Output power, mW	1 to 10	1 to 10
Power launched into fiber, mW	0.5 to 5	0.03 to 0.3
Spectral width (rms value), nm	2 to 4	15 to 60
Brightness, W/cm^2/sr	$\sim 10^5$	10 to 10^3
Rise time, 10–90%, ns	≤ 1	2 to 20
Frequency response (-3 dB, MHz)	> 500	< 200
Voltage drop, V	1.5 to 2	1.5 to 2.5
Forward current, mA	10 to 300	50 to 300
Threshold current, mA	5 to 250	NA
Feedback stabilization required	Yes	No

chromatic dispersion and transmission loss are minimal. The high-radiance Burrus type (surface-emitting) LED is well suited for application in systems of low-to-medium bandwidth (< 50 MHz). The power that can be coupled from an LED into a fiber is proportional to the number of modes the fiber can propagate, i.e., to its core area times its numerical aperture squared (see Sec. 10-2). For simple butt-coupling, where the emitting area of the LED is equal to or less than the core area of the fiber, presently available surface-emitting GaAlAs and InGaAsP LED's can launch about 50 μW into a graded-index fiber of $NA = 0.2$ and diameter of 50 μm. The spectral width of an LED is a function of the operating wavelength, the active-layer doping concentration, and the junction current density.[8] The rms spectral width of a typical 0.85 μm GaAlAs Burrus type LED is about 16 nm, while that of a 1.3-μm InGaAsP LED is about 40 nm (spectral width is approximately proportional to λ^2). The modulation bandwidth of an LED depends on the device geometry, its current density, and the doping concentration of its active layer. Higher doping concentration yields higher bandwidth, but only at the expense of lower output power and wider spectral width. Figure 11-3 shows the tradeoff between output power and modulation bandwidth for a group of Burrus type GaAlAs LED's.[9] Typically a 50-μm-diameter LED that can butt-couple 50 μW into a 0.2-NA, 50-μm-core graded-index fiber can be current-modulated at rates up to about 50 MHz.

ILD's are well suited for application in medium- to high-bandwidth fiber optic communication systems. Compared to LED's, injection lasers offer the advantage of narrower spectral width (< 3 nm), larger modulation bandwidth (> 500 MHz), and greater launched power (≈ 1 mW). ILD's are the only source compatible with single-mode fibers. However, ILD's are not as reliable as

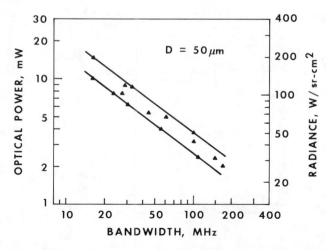

Figure 11-3 Output power vs. 3-dB bandwidth for Burrus type AlGaAs LED's.

LED's, are more expensive, and require feedback circuitry to stabilize their output power against variations due to temperature and aging effects.

11-4-2 Optical Receiver—Photodetectors

The basic purpose of an optical receiver is to detect the received light incident upon it and to convert it to an electrical signal containing the information impressed on the light at the transmitting end.[7,10] The receiver is therefore an optical-to-electrical converter or O/E transducer. An optical receiver consists of a photodetector and an associated amplifier along with necessary filtering and processing as shown in Fig. 11-4. The function of the photodetector is to detect the incident light signal and convert it to an electrical current. The amplifier converts this current into a usable signal while introducing the minimum amount of additional noise to corrupt the signal. In designing an optical receiver one tries to minimize the amount of optical power which must reach the receiver in order to achieve a given bit-error rate (BER) in digital systems, or a given signal-to-noise ratio (S/N) in an analog system. In this section we will describe the characteristics of the photodetectors used in fiber optic systems. Since the performance of an optical receiver depends not only on the photodetector, but also on the components and design chosen for the subsequent amplifier, we will also briefly describe configurations for this amplifier and their associated resulting receiver sensitivities.

In all the installed commercial fiber optic communication systems in existence today the photodetector used is either a semiconductor PIN or avalanche photodiode (APD). These devices differ in that the PIN basically converts one photon to one electron and has a conversion efficiency of less than unity. In an

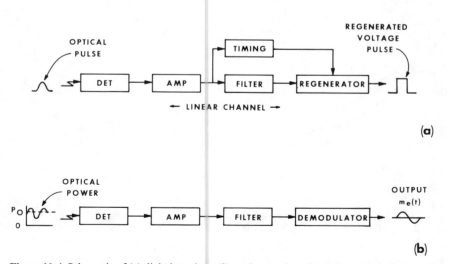

Figure 11-4 Schematic of (a) digital receiver; (b) analog receiver (intensity modulation).

APD carrier multiplication takes place which results in multiple electrons at the output per incident photon.[11]

The reasons for choosing a PIN or APD photodetector are usually based on cost and required receiver sensitivity. The avalanching process in the APD has a sharp threshold which is sensitive to ambient temperature and may require dynamic control of a relatively high bias voltage. The APD control and driver circuits are more expensive than those for the PIN detector, and the APD itself is more expensive than the PIN device. An APD with optimum gain, however, provides about 15 dB more receiver sensitivity than that achieved with a PIN diode.[10]

An excellent spectral match exists between GaAlAs sources operating in the 0.8 to 0.9-μm wavelength range and photodiodes made of silicon (spectral range ≈ 0.5 to 1.1 μm). The silicon PIN diode having no gain but with low dark current ($< 10^{-9}$ A) and large bandwidth (≈ 1 GHz) is best suited for applications where receiver sensitivity is not critical. Silicon APD's are preferable in applications that demand high sensitivity, and those employed in presently installed telecommunication systems have current gains of about 100 and primary dark currents in the 10^{-10} to 10^{-11}-A range.[12] Germanium photodiodes are used in the longer wavelength region (1.3 to 1.6 μm) since the response of silicon decreases rapidly as λ increases beyond 1 μm. Germanium APD's with gain-bandwidth products of approximately 60 GHz have been made but their dark currents are high ($\approx 10^{-8}$ to 10^{-7} A) and their excess noise factors are large.[8,13] InGaAs and InGaAsP diodes have been fabricated and have shown promise in the long-wavelength region. InGaAs PIN diodes have been made with very low capacitance (< 0.3 pf) and acceptably low dark current ($< 5 \times 10^{-9}$ A).[14] However, further work is required in the area of long-wavelength APD's to reduce their high excess noise factor. Table 11-4 summarizes the characteristics of photodetectors used in fiber optic communication systems.

To calculate the system margin for a communication system a knowledge of receiver sensitivity is needed. Receiver sensitivity is determined primarily by the

Table 11-4 Typical photodetector characteristics

	PIN diodes			Avalanche photodiodes	
Characteristic	Silicon	Germanium	In P	Silicon	Germanium
Wavelength range, μm	0.4–1.1	0.5–1.8	1.0–1.6	0.4–1.1	0.5–1.65
Wavelength of peak sensitivity, μm	0.85	1.5	1.26	0.85	1.5
Quantum efficiency, 1%	80	50	70	80	70
Rise time, ns	0.01	0.3	0.1	0.5	0.25
Bias voltage, V	15	6	10	170	40
Responsivity, A/W	0.5	0.7	0.4	0.7	0.6
Avalanche gain	1.0	1.0	1.0	80–150	80–150

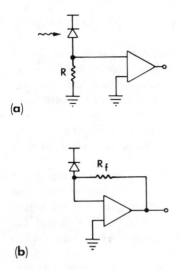

(a)

(b)

Figure 11-5 Schematic of (*a*) high-impedance amplifier design (*b*) transimpedance amplifier design.

characteristics of the photodetector and the low-noise front-end amplifier which is optimized for use with the detector. Figure 11-5 shows two commonly used configurations. To achieve the best receiver sensitivity, the amplifier should have a high input impedance or provide feedback as in a transimpedance amplifier. The first stage can be either a GaAs FET or a silicon bipolar transistor with a suitably adjusted emitter bias.[15]

In the short-wavelength region (0.8 to 0.9 μm) silicon APD's can provide sufficiently high gain and low excess noise to overcome the input amplifier noise. In this wavelength region design of the first amplifier stage is not very critical. A conventional silicon bipolar transistor having an emitter capacitance of 10 pF and a current gain of 150 has been used to build a digital receiver that requires only 10 nW average optical input power (-50 dBm) for a bit error rate (BER) of 10^{-9} at 100 Mb/s.[16]

Since leakage currents (high noise factor) severely limit the use of avalanche gain as a low-noise amplification process in the long-wavelength region (1.3 to 1.6 μm), PIN detectors are usually used.[8] With a PIN diode the microwave GaAs FET is well suited for use in the first amplifier stage because it has a low gate capacitance and high transconductance. It is typically used in a transimpedance configuration and offers wide bandwidth and good dynamic range. The best receivers have been built using InGaAs PIN detectors and GaAs FET's and require an average optical input power of 25 nW (-46 dBm) for 10^{-9} BER at 100 Mb/s.[17]

In Sec. 11.6 curves for receiver sensitivity as a function of bit rate (bandwidth) will be given. These curves, along with curves of power available from LED and ILD sources, will allow us to calculate the net transmission loss tolerable between regenerators (system margin) as a function of bit rate (frequency).

11-5 MODULATION FORMATS

There are a variety of modulation formats that can be used with semiconductor LED's and ILD's in a fiber optic system. In this section we will briefly describe the rudiments of pulse code modulation (PCM) and intensity modulation (IM). These are respectively the most commonly used modulation formats for transmitting digital and analog signals on optical fibers.

11-5-1 Pulse Code Modulation

In a digital telecommunication system the signals are discrete in both time and amplitude. In the simplest case either a pulse or a space (no pulse) is transmitted in each unit of time. The stream of pulses and spaces can be thought of as binary numbers that represent analog signals to which sampling and appropriate coding rules have been applied. To understand this process, consider the example of converting an analog voice signal into a PCM signal. Voice channels in a telephone system are band-limited to a maximum frequency, $f_m = 4$ kHz. To convert the signal it is first sampled at a rate of $2f_m$ (i.e., at the Nyquist rate), in this case 8 kHz. These samples are called PAM (pulse amplitude modulated) pulses. The next step is analog to digital conversion, and this is accomplished using a coder. The coder converts each PAM sample into a binary number called a code word. Typically each sample is converted into a code word containing 8 bits (7-digit binary word plus a signaling bit). As a result of this procedure the voice channel in our example requires a transmission rate of 64 K b/s. The process of time-division multiplexing allows one to combine a number of voice channels on a digital line. Terminals that multiplex many message channels for application to a single digital line are called digital channel banks.[18] Figure 11-6 illustrates the formation of PCM signals and how they are combined in a channel bank. A hierarchy of digital line rates is used in the communications industry and it is summarized below in Table 11-5. Digital multiplexers form the interface between digital transmission facilities of different rates. They combine digital signals from several digital lines in the same level of hierarchy into a single-pulse stream suitable for application to a facility of the next higher level in the hierarchy. This process is illustrated schematically in Fig. 11-7. In a telecommunication network using optical fibers a variety of signals, which can include voice channels, data and video, can be transmitted using a PCM format. Figure 11-8 illustrates the incorporation of various types of signals into the digital hierarchy. Pulse code modulated signals are primarily transmitted over optical fibers at the DS-3 (T3) and DS-4 (T4) line rates. These line rates are respectively 45 and 274 Mb/s. An illustration of a fiber optic system operating at the 45 Mb/s rate is given in Sec. 11-7. A 274-Mb/s system is illustrated in Sec. 11-8.

We will now describe in a qualitative way some of the advantages and disadvantages of using a PCM format with optical fibers.

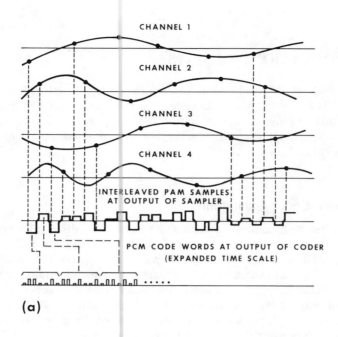

(a)

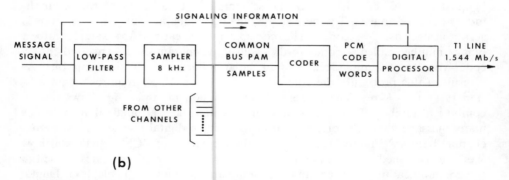

(b)

Figure 11-6 (*a*) Time division multiplexed PCM signal in a channel bank. (*b*) Channel bank block diagram (transmitting portion).

Table 11-5 Hierarchy of digital line rates

Level	Line rate	Number of voice channels
DS-0	64 kb/s	1
DS-1 (T1)	1.544 Mb/s	24
DS-2 (T2)	6.312 Mb/s	96
DS-3 (T3)	44.736 Mb/s	672
DS-4 (T4)	274.176 Mb/s	4032

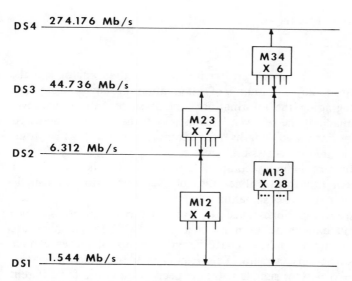

Figure 11-7 Schematic of multiplexers in digital hierachy.

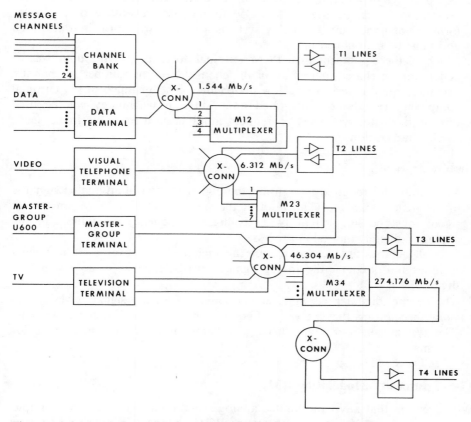

Figure 11-8 Schematic showing the combining of different signals in the digital hierachy.

Advantages of PCM

1. Digital signals can withstand much greater impairments than analog signals. Binary signals tolerate large amounts of attenuation or signal distortion without severely degrading the information content since only a two-level decision has to be made at the receiver. This usually translates into increased repeater spacing (or increased lengths of nonrepeatered links) when comparing digital with analog transmission.
2. Binary digital modulation is highly compatible with a source like an LED or ILD that can switch rapidly. Nonlinearities of the source do not usually affect its suitability for two-level signaling.
3. All signal types are compatible. Once the various types of signals, voice channels, video, and data, have been encoded into PCM format they are represented by a stream of pulses. The different streams of pulses can be combined into a single-pulse stream. This results in a transmission system which can handle a variety of signals without special techniques for different types of signals or loss of capacity.
4. The presence or absence of a pulse on the digital stream is the way in which information is transmitted in a PCM format. Its waveshape or particular form is not important. In analog systems a precise waveform is transmitted and must be maintained.
5. Much of the equipment in a PCM terminal, for example, the quantizer or coder, can be shared among all of the channels. As the number of channels become large this results in a low per-channel cost for much of the terminal equipment. In addition integrated and thin film technology can be used directly in digital systems. The frequent multiple occurrence of circuits lends itself to integration.

Disadvantages of PCM

1. The bandwidth required to transmit the digital version of an analog signal is much greater than the bandwidth of the signal itself. For PCM, an analog signal must be sampled at twice its highest frequency component in the analog-to-digital conversion process.
2. Special facilities are needed to put the digital signals over existing analog facilities and of course the analog signals must be encoded to be placed over digital links.
3. The coding, digital processing, and decoding of analog signals gives rise to noise mechanisms that are very different from those found in analog systems. The system constraints are therefore different from those found in analog systems.

11-5-2 Intensity Modulation (IM)

We have seen that any band-limited analog signal (voice or video, for example) can be transmitted in a digital format via PCM channels. Why should we then concern ourselves with analog modulation techniques and analog systems? The most important factor for choosing an analog modulation format is usually related to economics. If a fiber-guide transmission link, for example, is a subsection of a larger communication system that uses analog transmission, there will be a strong influence favoring the use of analog transmission on the fiber link. The added costs in a digital system of analog-to-digital and digital-to-analog conversion are avoided. Potential applications for analog transmission using optical fibers vary from individual 4-kHz voice channels to a number of frequency-division multiplexed 5-mHz video signals. There are unique requirements associated with analog systems (versus digital) that limit their use. Analog systems usually require a high signal-to-noise ratio (≥ 40 dB) at the receiver and high end-to-end linearity to prevent cross talk between different frequency components of the analog signal.

The simplest form of analog modulation for fiber applications[19,20] is direct intensity modulation (IM). An expression for an IM optical signal at the receiver input is given by[10]

$$p(t) = P_0[1 + \gamma m(t)] \tag{11-4}$$

where $m(t)$ is some analog message, $|m(t)| \leq 1$, and γ is a constant ≤ 1. The optical power is converted to an electrical current by the detector producing the current $i(t)$

$$i(t) = Rp(t) \tag{11-5}$$

where R is the detector responsivity (A/W). This current is amplified and filtered in the receiver. In an intensity-modulated system demodulation is not necessary since the baseband signal $i(t)$ is already simply proportional to the message $m(t)$.

Intensity-modulated signals are very susceptible to harmonic distortion due to nonlinearities in the characteristics of the light source (a properly designed receiver is highly linear). Various means for linearizing the input-output characteristics of optical transmitters such as feedback, feedforward, and predistortion have been proposed with limited practical success.[21] As an alternative to linearization of the transmitter, one can use a modulation scheme such as subcarrier phase modulation which does not require linearity. A subcarrier phase-modulated (PM) signal can be written as[10,19,22]

$$p(t) = P_0\{1 + \cos[\omega t + \gamma m(t)]\} \tag{11-6}$$

where ω is an intermediate frequency. In a subcarrier phase-modulation system a demodulator such as a phase-locked loop or discriminator is needed in the receiver. Analog pulse-modulation schemes such as pulse-position, pulse-width, and pulse-frequency modulation have also been described in the literature.[23] Phase-intensity-modulation and analog-pulse-modulation techniques are very effective in reducing the influence of source nonlinearities on the transmission quality of transmitted signals, on the other hand the penalty you pay is that they require high transmission bandwidth and more costly and complex terminal equipment.

11-6 SYSTEM MARGIN; COMPONENT CONFIGURATIONS

In the last four sections of this text we have reviewed the characteristics of fibers, sources, receivers, and modulation formats used in fiber optic communication systems. In this section we will utilize these component characteristics to illustrate in general terms the calculation of system margin and repeater spacings for digital and analog fiber systems.

Figure 11-9 shows, for digital systems, the average optical power required at the receiver (for BER of 10^{-9}) as well as the power available from optical sources as a function of bit rate.[8] The lower boundary for receiver performance applies for receivers using silicon APD's at wavelengths of less than 1 μm. The upper receiver curve in Fig. 11-9 reflects the performance of PIN FET receivers sensitive in the wavelength range between 1.1 and 1.6 μm. Sources made of GaAlAs and InGaAsP have similar characteristics in terms of modulation speed and power delivered into a fiber. Light-emitting diodes are usually restricted to those applications where the required modulation bandwidths are less than 50 MHz. The separation between the source and receiver bands in Fig. 11-9 is an indication of the gross transmission margin of a system. Practical repeater spans are designed with about 10 dB subtracted from the maximum values given in Fig. 11-9. This will account for variation in the transmitter and receiver components due to temperature variations and aging. As a general rule of thumb the required fiber bandwidth in a digital system is equal to or larger than the specified system bit rate. The noise penalty for using this rule is less than 1 dB.[8] Along with this potential noise source, the 10-dB safety margin also allows for signal degradation from various noise sources in the transmitter and receiver. Once the net transmission loss that is tolerable between regenerators is obtained, the distance between regenerators (link length) can be determined from the loss characteristics of the fibers and interconnection devices used in the

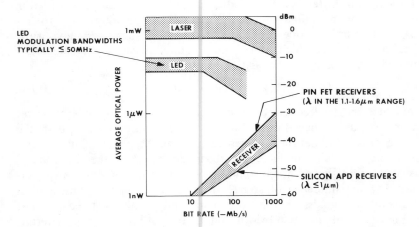

Figure 11-9 Transmission margin vs. bit rate for optical fiber digital transmission systems.

system. We have assumed that the system is loss-limited and that fibers are available with high enough bandwidths to satisfy the system requirements.

As an example, let us assume we wish to design a digital system to operate at 45 Mb/s with a BER $\leq 10^{-9}$ at $\lambda = 0.85$ μm. If we choose a GaAlAs ILD transmitter and a receiver that uses a silicon APD the gross system margin, using Fig. 11-9, would be approximately 53 dB. If we subtract a 10-dB safety factor to account for the various degradation and noise sources, our net system margin would be 43 dB. Typical production fibers would have a loss range at this wavelength after cabling, installation, and splicing of 4 to 6 dB/km. Hence the repeater spacing would range between 7.2 and 10.8 km. A conservative design for a system would have 7-km repeater spacings and use multimode graded-index fibers with a link bandwidth of 60 MHz ($60 \times 7 = 420$ MHz-km fiber bandwidth, assuming linear length scaling) and an installed cable loss of 4 to 6 dB/km. A more detailed treatment of this type of digital system is given in Sec. 11-7.

Optical fibers are currently being used in a wide variety of digital communication system applications ranging from low-speed data links to ocean cable systems operating at hundreds of megabits per second. For each application a designer must choose an appropriate combination of components (sources, detectors, fibers, etc.) to satisfy the system requirements. Table 11-6 illustrates, for a number of fiber optic digital communication systems, typical component choices and their performance range. Some of these systems will be discussed in greater detail in Secs. 11.7 and 11.8. As fiber technology evolves (very high bandwidth graded-index fibers, single-mode fibers, and low-loss inexpensive connectors become readily available) and long-lived sources and detectors become commercially available in the 1.3 to 1.6 μm wavelength region, many of the component choices in Table 11-6 may be modified to improve system performance and lower system costs.

The transmission of wideband analog signals (video signals, for example) on optical fibers using analog-modulation techniques is typically limited to a few kilometers (< 5 km).[20,24] This limited repeater spacing arises primarily from the fact that analog signals and, in particular, video signals must be reconstituted with a large signal-to-noise ratio, typically 40 dB to as high as 57 dB for some applications. To obtain a better understanding of how the signal-to-noise ratio (SNR) constraint limits the system margin, let us consider a plot of carrier-to-noise ratio as a function of detected optical power at a receiver, as shown in Fig. 11-10.[10] In this figure the receiver is thermal noise limited for input power below 10^{-3} mW and limited by quantum noise above input powers of 10^{-2} mW. Using Fig. 11-10 we can obtain the minimum input power at the receiver for a required system SNR. For example, let us assume that we wish to transmit a 4-MHz video signal using an intensity modulated LED and require that we maintain a 57-dB SNR at the input to a PIN FET receiver. Referring to Fig. 11-10, the minimum signal level that must be present at the receiver to ensure a 57-dB SNR is approximately -26 dBm. If the LED couples -13 dBm of power into the fiber the total allowable transmission loss of the fiber link

Table 11-6 Digital communication systems; component choices and performance range

Application	Intracity telephone trunk network	Intracity telephone loop distribution network	Intercity telephone trunk network	Intercity telephone trunk network phase II	Ocean cable system	Low-speed data link	High-speed data link
Bit rate	44.7 Mb/s	44.7 Mb/s	90 Mb/s	274 Mb/s†	274 Mb/s	≤ 1 Mb/s	100 Mb/s
Bit error rate	$< 10^{-9}$	$< 10^{-9}$	$< 10^{-9}$	$< 10^{-9}$	$< 10^{-9}$	10^{-7}	10^{-9}
Source type	Laser	LED	Laser	Laser	Laser	LED	LED
Detector type	APD	PIN	APD	PIN	PIN	PIN	PIN
Fiber type	Multimode graded index	Multimode graded index	Multimode graded index	Single mode	Single mode	Multimode large-core step index	Multimode large-core graded index
Fiber attenuation	< 6 dB/km	< 2.5 dB/km	< 5.5 dB/km	< 0.8 dB/km	< 0.8 dB/km	< 30 dB/km	< 10 dB/km
Fiber bandwidth	> 300 MHz-km	> 300 MHz-km	> 300 MHz-km	> 8 GHz-km	> 8 GHz-km	> 10 MHz-km	> 100 MHz-km
Distance between repeaters	> 5 km	> 8 km	> 6 km	> 20 km	> 30 km	< 2 km	< 0.5 km
Wavelength	0.82 μm	1.3 μm	0.82 μm	1.3 μm	1.3 μm	0.82 μm or 1.3 μm	1.3 μm

† Possible bit rate will typically be in excess of 140 Mb/s.

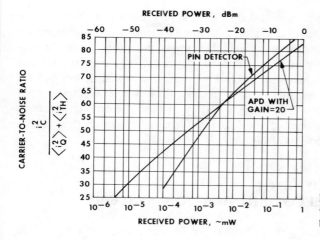

Figure 11-10 Carrier-to-noise ratio vs. received power for a 4-MHz-bandwidth receiver.

Table 11-7 Alternate options for transmitting one television channel, SNR = 57 dB[24]

Modulation format	Optical source	Power launched into fiber, −dBm	Minimum detectable power at receiver, dBm	Allowable transmission loss of fiber link, dB
Intensity modulation (baseband)	LED	−13	−26	13
Intensity modulation (baseband)	Laser	0	−26	26
Intensity modulation (vestigial sideband)	LED	−13	−25	12
Intensity modulation (vestigial sideband)	Laser	0	−25	25
Pulse width modulation	ELED†	−3	−30	27
Pulse frequency modulation	ELED	−3	−30	27
Pulse position modulation	ELED	−3	−30	27
PCM	Laser	0	−46	46

† ELED is an edge-emitting LED

would be 12 dB. If we assume an installed cable loss of 6 dB/km at 0.85 μm the repeater spacing for this system would be 2.2 km. By using more sophisticated modulation techniques and sources with higher input power at longer wavelengths this repeater spacing could of course be increased. However, the system complexity and cost will also increase. Table 11-7 illustrates, for different optical sources, the allowable transmission loss of a fiber link when a single video channel is transmitted (57-dB SNR) using a variety of modulation techniques.[24] A detailed description of an analog modulation system for transmitting video signals and data is given in Sec. 11-9.

11-7 INTRACITY FIBER OPTIC TRUNK DIGITAL TELECOMMUNICATION SYSTEM

Digital fiber optic transmission systems are currently being used for a variety of applications in telephone systems throughout the world. Figure 11-11 is a simplified block diagram showing some of these areas of application. In this section we will describe FT3, the Bell system's first intracity lightwave trunk transmission system. This system is used for interoffice trunking in metropolitan or urban–suburban areas in which the distance between nearest neighbor switching offices is typically between 5 and 10 km.[25] FT3 is a PCM digital transmission system operating at the DS3 line rate (44.7 Mb/s, corresponding to 672 voice channels per fiber). The principle lightwave components of the system are:

1. Graded-index multimode fibers
   50-μm core diameter, 125-μm fiber diameter
   cabled fiber loss < 5 dB/km at 0.825 μm
   bandwidth $\geq$ 300 MHz-km
   numerical aperture $\approx$ 0.23
2. Ribbon-structured 12-mm diameter cables (see Figs. 9-12 and 9-13)
   12 fibers per ribbon
   up to 12 ribbons per cable
3. V groove silicon-chip multifiber ribbon connector (see Figs. 10-21 and 10-22)
   the cables are connectorized in the factory
4. Molded plastic biconic single-fiber connectors (see Fig. 10-18)
5. GaAlAs double heterostructure laser transmitter (0.825 μm wavelength)
   Backface monitor is used to control bias current and maintain fixed average power ($\approx$ −3 dBm delivered to fiber)
6. Silicon avalanche photodiode receiver
   Minimum received power −48.5 dBm

A block diagram of the basic layout of an FT3 system is shown in Fig. 11-12.[25,26] The FT3 system interfaces with existing digital systems via a digital cross connect (DSX). Standard digital transmission signals are fed into the Line Terminating and Multiplexing Assembly (LTMA) from the DSX. In the LTMA,

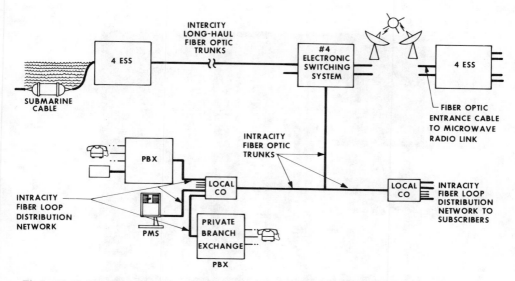

Figure 11-11 Block diagram showing fiber optic telecommunication applications.

output from the modulated light transmitter is coupled into each fiber for outgoing transmission and the incoming light pulses are received by an avalanche photodiode. The Light-guide Cable Interconnection Equipment (LCIE) (see Fig. 11-13a) forms the interface between the outside plant and central office hardware. The outside plant cables and the central office cables are connected here. The LCIE also provides a means for cable rearrangements and, as shown in Fig. 11-13b, single-fiber to multifiber-cable interconnections.[27] Intermediate repeaters are located in central offices or repeater huts and serviced by local powering. The FT3 regenerator (see Fig. 11-14) contains the laser transmitter, the APD receiver, and electrical circuitry for timing recovery, pulse regeneration, and fault location. The same regenerator module serves as a two-way office repeater at terminal locations, and as a one-way line at intermediate repeater sites.

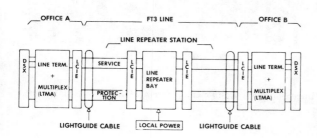

Figure 11-12 Block diagram of FT3 lightwave digital transmission system.

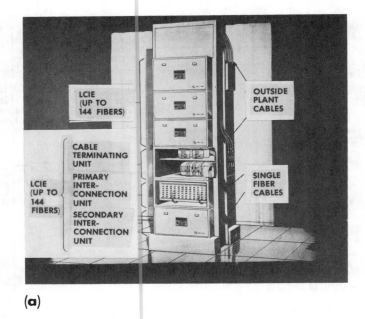

(a)

(b)

Figure 11-13 (*a*) Lightguide Cable Interconnection Equipment (LCIE) (*b*) Ribbon to single-fiber cable fanout located in LCIE.

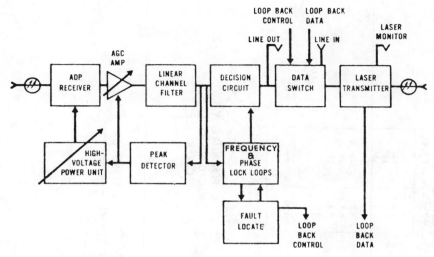

Figure 11-14 Block diagram of FT3 regenerator.

Currently the maximum repeater spacing of the FT3 system is approximately 7 km, although further reductions in fiber loss and other system improvements should increase this distance in the future. An approximate repeater spacing calculation for an FT3 system is as follows:[25]

1. Average transmitter power delivered to fiber	−3 dBm
2. Minimum power at receiver	−48.5 dBm
3. Total system margin	−45.5 dBm
4. End connector loss	3 dB
5. Allowance for splices	7 dB
6. Unallocated system margin	3 dB
7. Allowed cabled fiber loss	45.5 − 13 = 32.5 dB
8. Cabled fiber loss	5 dB/km
9. Repeater spacing	32.5/5 = 6.5 km

The above figures represent extreme values that account for both parameter variations and environmental allowances. End connector losses include the LCIE connector and cabling at both ends of the system as well as the transmitter connector loss. The splice-loss allowance provides for 14 splices (2/km). The cabled-fiber loss includes cabling and temperature effects.

More than 40 FT3 systems are currently operating in the United States. A route map of an installed FT3 system in the Pittsburgh, Pennsylvania area is shown in Fig. 11-15.[28] The route, which is 64 km in length, has 13 regenerator sections. Some of the regenerators are in central offices whereas others are located in huts. Table 11-8 shows some of the characteristics of the route and

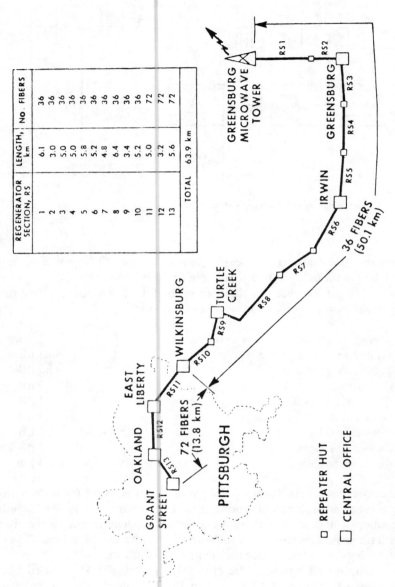

REGENERATOR SECTION, RS	LENGTH, km	NO. FIBERS
1	6.1	36
2	3.0	36
3	5.0	36
4	5.0	36
5	5.8	36
6	5.2	36
7	4.8	36
8	6.4	36
9	3.4	36
10	5.2	36
11	5.0	72
12	3.2	72
13	5.6	72
TOTAL	63.9 km	

□ REPEATER HUT

□ CENTRAL OFFICE

Figure 11-15 Route map of Pittsburgh, Pa. FT3 lightguide installation.

Table 11-8 Characteristics of the Pittsburgh–Greensburg FT3 light-guide route

Regenerator section	Length, km	No. of ribbons	No. of good fibers†	Mean splice loss, dB‡	Mean 825 nm end-to-end loss, dB/km
1	6.05	3	34	0.20	3.85
2	3.00	3	34	0.40	4.20
3	5.00	3	34	0.20	4.00
4	5.00	3	34	0.25	4.30
5	5.75	3	34	0.10	4.10
6	5.20	3	34	0.25	4.05
7	4.75	3	34	0.20	3.90
8	6.40	3	34	0.15	4.00
9	3.40	3	34	0.40	3.65
10	5.20	3	34	0.20	3.70
11	5.00	6	69	0.30	4.80
12	3.20	6	68	0.25	4.10
13	5.60	6	70	0.30	4.25

† No fiber lines were lost as a result of installation and splicing.

‡ Craft measured splice losses with BTL OTDR correction factor (increase included).

summarizes the measured splice and section loss results. The overall average splice loss for this FT3 system was 0.24 dB. This included 387 array splices corresponding to over 4400 individual fiber splices. The average 0.825-μm end-to-end regenerator section loss was 4.15 dB/km.[28] The FT3 intracity fiber optic trunk system has proved to be a practical, economically competitive digital telecommunication system that has operated successfully in telephone companies throughout the United States.

11-8 UNDERSEA DIGITAL FIBER OPTIC TRANSMISSION SYSTEM

A transatlantic digital light-wave cable system (called SL) is currently being designed and tested with a target date for installation in the late 1980s.[29–31] The proposed SL system will be made up of subsystems each of which has 274 Mb/s bit streams transmitted from 1.3 μm lasers over single-mode fibers. The terminal equipment contains a digital multiplexer which accepts data and telegraphy signals directly and telephone signals via digital TASI (Time Assignment Speech Interpolation). In addition, video signals can be accepted through high-speed A-to-D coding and bandwidth reduction equipment. The shore terminal also contains a high-voltage power supply which provides a constant current for repeater powering plus a supervisory terminal. The undersea equipment consists of a cable and a number of regenerators which receive, amplify,

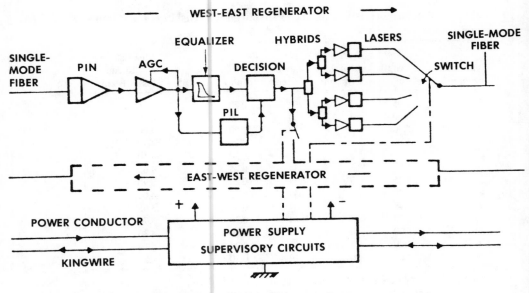

Figure 11-16 Block diagram of undersea lightwave (SL) regenerator.

regenerate, and transmit a digital optical pulse stream into the single-mode optical fibers. Figure 11-16 is a block diagram of an SL regenerator. The system length is 6500 km corresponding to a transatlantic crossing. The optical transmitter for the SL system will be an InGaAsP single-mode laser operating at a wavelength of 1.3 μm. The fiber will be a 10-μm core single-mode fiber. The optical receiver will use an InGaAsP PIN diode and the system will have an expected repeater spacing of about 35 km. The system life is expected to be 24 years with a reliability of 8 years mean time before a failure that requires repair by a cable ship. Obviously this system has unique and extremely stringent engineering requirements that must be satisfied. The undersea light-guide cable, as shown in Fig. 11-17, has been designed to provide the necessary strength and weight for ocean installation and recovery operations. In essence the cable is a power cable with a fiber-containing core at the center. The power conductor is formed from a continuous aluminum tube (the ocean provides the dc return path for power) which also acts as a barrier to water diffusing through the insulation. The steel strand wires are carefully arranged and tightly toleranced to provide a compact structure which isolates the fiber core from the sea pressure. The fiber core is placed at the center of the cable to minimize fiber strain due to cable bending and twisting as well as to provide pressure protection. Although repair operations on an installed system are expected to be infrequent, it is necessary to design the cable to withstand recovery tensions. Under recovery conditions the cable can be strained up to 1.0 percent. In this design the strain of the fibers is essentially the same as that of the cable. Therefore the fibers used in this cable must have more than a one percent strain capability in

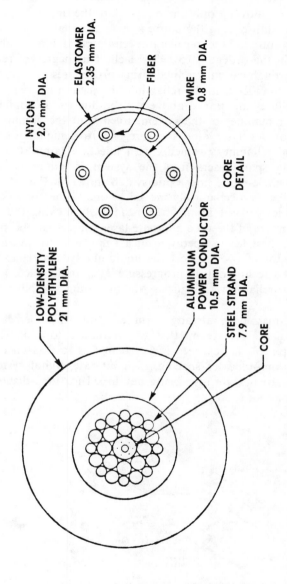

NYLON
2.6 mm DIA.

ELASTOMER
2.35 mm DIA.

FIBER

WIRE
0.8 mm DIA.

CORE
DETAIL

LOW-DENSITY
POLYETHYLENE
21 mm DIA.

ALUMINUM
POWER CONDUCTOR
10.5 mm DIA.

STEEL STRAND
7.9 mm DIA.

CORE

CABLE

Figure 11-17 Undersea fiber optic cable.

continuous lengths of 35 km and meet the attenuation and bandwidth requirements of the system. Meeting these fiber requirements is one of the most challenging aspects of this project and will require expanding the current state of the art of fiber technology. The stringent reliability requirements of the system translates into allowing only three repairs of the undersea portion of the system with a cable ship during the entire system life span. This will require a high level of integration of the regenerator circuitry and a reliability of the integrated circuits in the order of 0.5 FIT's each. This degree of reliability can only be achieved through careful manufacturing procedures and controls. Given the current level of confidence in the reliability of injection lasers it is likely that two of the three failures mentioned above will be due to laser failures, leaving one failure for the remainder of the system. Even with the assumption of two laser failures, up to four laser diodes per regenerator might still be required because of potential reliability problems with injection lasers. One implementation for switching spare lasers into the system if failure occurs (sparing scheme) involves a single-mode fiber optic switch shown in Fig. 11-18.[32] In this switch the output fiber is mechanically moved to one of the corners of a square glass tube in which one of the input fibers resides. By moving the output fiber into the different corners of the tube alternate laser sources can be switched into the system. Today's best lasers operating at 1.3 μm need to improve their life expectancy by a factor of two to meet the minimum system reliability requirements. However, the technology is progressing at a rapid pace, and it is expected that the laser reliability will surpass the minimum reliability requirement within a short time.[29]

As the reader may have already surmised, the SL undersea fiber optic system is a state of the art system that will require a formidable amount of engineering development. It has been included in this text as an example of a second generation long-repeater spacing, high bit rate digital system. Systems with similar characteristics are also being developed for long-distance intercity terrestrial trunking applications.

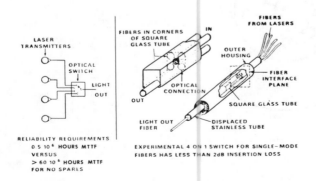

Figure 11-18 Laser-sparing switch.

11-9 ANALOG FIBER OPTIC SYSTEM EXAMPLE

The final fiber optic communication system that will be described in this chapter is interesting both from technological and sociological points of view. It is an analog CATV (cable antenna television) system that utilizes optical fibers in a loop distribution network. The system was sponsored by the Japanese Government and is called Hi-OVIS.[33,34,35] Hi-OVIS stands for Higashi-ikoma Optical Visual Information System. This system was installed in July 1978 and provides cable TV and a wide variety of other video programs to 158 homes in the model town of Higashi-ikoma, a suburb of Osaka, Japan. The network uses a centrally switched star configuration with a program center and a switching subcenter as shown in Fig. 11-19. The program center has a data control computer, a VCR (Video Cassette Recorder), and the transmitter and receiver for rebroadcasting TV signals. In addition eight local studio extension terminals located in various public buildings, such as in the City Hall and in schools and hospitals, can provide input to the center to allow the viewing of local public activities. Signals consisting of TV video, FM audio, and digital data are transmitted to each home subscriber via a subcenter switching network. This subcenter contains a video switching network with 32 inputs and 168 outputs. Two of the 32 inputs are used for the video signal transmission from home terminal video cameras to the center and the remaining 30 inputs are used for the video signal transmission from the center to the home terminal TV monitors. Emanating from the subcenter are 11 distribution cables, each of which can serve 16 subscribers (with 32 fibers per distribution). The final subscriber drop consists of a two-fiber cable (one fiber each for upstream and downstream transmission) brought to an optical junction box where it is connected to the distribution cable. The two fibers running to each subscriber provide one video channel in each direction together with associated sound and signaling channels. The system provides program services which include retransmission of on-air TV programs, independent local TV studio broadcasting with mobile TV camera capability, broadcasting of special video information, interactive video services, and a strong tie-in with various community sectors, i.e., medical services, local shopping information, schools, etc.

Simple analog intensity modulation of an LED source was used for the video, with the sound carried using 25-kHz deviation frequency modulation on a 6-MHz subcarrier. The frequency spectrum diagram for the baseband transmission signals that are intensity modulated on the optical carrier is shown in Fig. 11-20. The output power from the LED into the plastic-clad silica stepindex fibers (theoretical NA = 0.4) was approximately −8 dBm. The detectors used were simple PIN devices and required −26 dBm received power for a video SNR of 52 dB. The typical fiber length in the star-connected network was less than 1 km. The longest transmission distance of the composite video signals was 4 km. The total fiber length was approximately 400 km for the entire repeaterless Hi-OVIS project.

One of the most interesting aspects of the Hi-OVIS project is the innovative

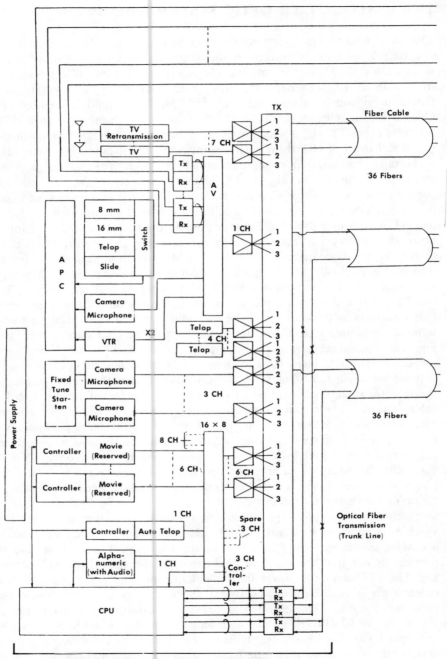

PROGRAM CONTROL CENTER

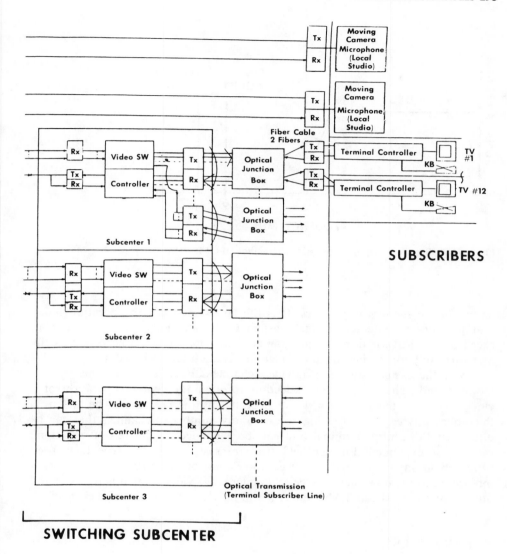

SUBSCRIBERS

SWITCHING SUBCENTER

Figure 11-19 Block diagram of Hi-OVIS.

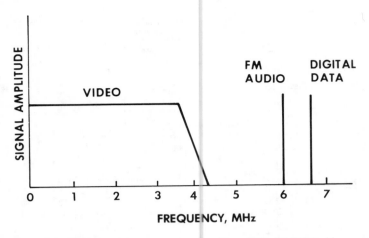

Figure 11-20 Baseband frequency spectrum diagram for Hi-OVIS video system.

nature of the services it provides. It is the largest network in operation today that provides an interactive video system to private homes, and provides an excellent test bed for determining how such systems can be used economically and effectively for a wide range of functions in the future. Viewed as a cable TV network, the system transmits a video channel direct to a customer's video monitor and achieves program selection through the remote operation of a video switch by means of a key pad operated by the customer. The system is thus inherently capable of giving access to any number of channels that can be offered at the central terminal and can be expanded as the central switching capacity is expanded. Further field trials of systems of this type have been proposed in Japan to service between 3000 and 5000 homes. It will be very interesting to see how such a large-scale interactive video system is received and utilized by the public and what effect it will have on the quality of their lives.

REFERENCES

1. W. B. Gardner: "Fundamental Characteristics of Optical Fibers," *ITU Telecommun. J.*, November 1981.
2. I. P. Kaminov, D. Marcuse, and H. M. Presby: "Multimode Fiber Bandwidth: Theory and Practice," *Proc. IEEE*, **68**: 1209–1213, October 1980.
3. D. Marcuse and H. M. Presby: "Effects of Profile Deformations on Fiber Bandwidth," *Appl. Opt.*, **18**: 3758–3763, Nov. 15, 1979.
4. R. Olshansky and D. B. Keck: "Pulse Broadening in Graded-Index Optical Fibers," *Appl. Opt.*, **15**: 483–491, February 1976.
5. M. J. Buckler, Bell Telephone Laboratories, unpublished work.
6. D. Gloge, K. Ogawa, and L. G. Cohen: "Baseband Characteristics of Long-Wavelength LED Systems," *Electron. Lett.*, **16**: 366, 367, May 8, 1980.
7. H. Kressel: *Semiconductor Devices for Optical Communication*, Springer-Verlag Press, New York, 1980.

8. D. Gloge and Tingye Li: "Multimode Fiber Technology for Digital Transmission," *Proc. IEEE*, **68**: 1269–1275, October 1980.
9. T. P. Lee and A. G. Dentai: "Power and Modulation Bandwidths of GaAs-AlGaAs High-Radiance LEDS for Optical Communication Systems," *IEEE J. Quantum Electron.*, **QE-14**: 150–159, March 1979.
10. S. E. Miller and A. G. Chynoweth: *Optical Fiber Telecommunications*, Academic Press Inc., New York, 1979.
11. R. G. Smith: "Photodetectors for Fiber Transmission Systems," *Proc. IEEE*, **68**: 1247-1253, October 1980.
12. M. Saruwatari, K. Asatani, J. Yamada, I. Hatakeyama, K. Sugiyama, and T. Kimura: "Low Loss Fiber Transmission of High Speed Pulse Signals at 1.29 μm Wavelength," *Electron. Lett.*, **14**: 187–189, March 1978.
13. T. Kimura: "Optical Fiber Transmission Research," *Technocrat*, **11**: 32–43, August 1978.
14. T. P. Lee, C. A. Burrus, A. G. Dentai, and K. Ogawa: "Small Area in GaAs/InP PIN Photodetectors: Fabrication, Characteristics and Performance of Devices in 274 Mb/s and 45 Mb/s Light Wave Receivers at 1.3 μm Wavelength," *Electron. Lett.*, **16**: 155, 156, February 1980.
15. S. Machida, J. Yamada, T. Mukai, Y. Horikoshi, T. Miya, and H. Tsuchiya: "1.5 μm Optical Transmission Experiments Using Very Low-Loss Single Mode Fibers," *Electron. Lett.*, **15**: 219–221, April 1979.
16. R. G. Smith, C. A. Brackett, and H. W. Reinbold, "Optical Detector Package," *BSTJ*, **57**: 1809–1822, July/August 1978.
17. D. R. Smith, R. C. Hooper, and I. Garrett, "Receiver for Optical Communication: A Comparison of Avalanche Photodiodes with PIN FET Hybrids," *Opt. Quantum Electron.*, **10**: 293–300, July 1978.
18. Bell Laboratories Technical Staff: "Transmission Systems for Communications," Bell Laboratories Technical Publications, 1971.
19. W. M. Hubbard: "Efficient Utilization of Optical Frequency Carriers for Low to Moderate Bit Rate Channels", *BSTJ*, **52**: 731–765, May/June, 1973.
20. S. D. Personick, N. L. Rhodes, D. C. Hanson, K. H. Chan: "Contrasting Fiber-Optic-Component-Design Requirements in Telecommunications, Analog and Local Data Communications Applications." *Proc. IEEE*, **68**: 1254–1262, October 1980.
21. K. Asatani: "Nonlinearity and its Compensation of Semiconductor Laser Diodes for Analog Intensity Modulation Systems," *IEEE Trans. Commun.*, **COM-28**, February, 1980.
22. A. Albanese and H. Lenzing: "If Lightwave Entrance Links for Satellite Earth Stations," *Proc. ICC '79*, papers 1.7.1–1.7.5, Boston, Mass., June, 1979.
23. M. Sato et al.: "Pulse Interval and Width Modulation for Video Transmission," *IEEE Trans. Cable Telev.*, **3**: 165–173, October 1978.
24. J. E. Midwinter: "Potential Broad-Band Services," *Proc IEEE*, **68**: 1321–1327, October 1980.
25. I. Jacobs: "FT3-A Metropolitan Trunk Lightwave System," *Proc. IEEE*, **68**: 1286–1290, October 1980.
26. N. E. Hardwick and J. L. Baden: "Outside Plant Hardware for Use in FT3 Lightwave Systems," Proc. Int. Wire Cable Symp., 1980, pp. 212–220, Cherry Hill, New Jersey.
27. M. R. Gotthardt: "Lightguide Cable Interconnection Equipment (LCIE)," Third Int. Fiber Opt. Commun. Exp., San Francisco, California, September 1980.
28. M. I. Schwartz: "Design and Performance of the FT3 Lightguide Trunk Transmission Medium," Proc. Int. Conf. Commun., Denver, Colorado, June 1981.
29. C. D. Anderson, R. F. Gleason, P. T. Hutchison, and P. K. Runge: "An Undersea Communication System Using Fiberguide Cables," *Proc. IEEE*, **68**: 1299–1303, October 1980.
30. P. K. Runge: "A High-Capacity Optical Fiber Undersea System," IEE Conf. Publ. 190, Sixth Eur. Conf. Opt. Commun., York, England, September 1980.
31. I. Yaurashita, Y. Negishi, M. Nunokawa, and H. Wakabayashi: "The Application of Optical Fibers in Submarine Cable Systems," *ITU Telecommun. J.*, November 1981.
32. R. B. Kummer, S. C. Mettler, and C. M. Miller: "A Mechanically Operated Four-Way Optical Fiber Switch," Proc. Fifth Eur. Conf. Opt. Commun., pp. 6.4-1 to 6.4-4, Amsterdam, The Netherlands, September 1979.

33. T. Nakahara, H. Kumamaru, and S. Takeuchi: "An Optical Fiber Video System," *IEEE Trans. Commun.*, **COM-26**: 955–961, July 1978.
34. J. E. Midwinter: "Potential Broad-Band Services," *Proc. IEEE*, **68**: 1321–1327, October 1980.
35. K. Y. Chang: "Fiberguide Systems in the Subscriber Loop," *Proc. IEEE*, **68**: 1291–1299, October 1980.

PROBLEMS

11-1 Give an example application of a short-range and a long-range fiber optic system. For each system, choose a fiber, source, detector, operating wavelength, and modulation format.

11-2 What is the approximate bandwidth of a fiber if its index difference $\Delta = 1.5\%$ and its rms chromatic pulse spreading $\sigma_c = 1.5$ ps/km?

11-3 A fiber system requires a bandwidth of 8 GHz-km. The required repeater spacing is 25 km and the system is loss-limited. Choose a fiber, source, and detector which will meet the system design requirements.

11-4 A short-range system is to operate at 700 Mb/s at a wavelength of 1.5 μm. Choose a source and detector for the system and explain your choices.

11-5 Describe the modulation formats PCM and IM. What are some advantages and disadvantages of each format?

11-6 Suppose we wish to design a system to operate at 100 Mb/s with a BER $\geq 10^{-9}$ at $\lambda = 1.3$ μm. If we choose a PIN FET receiver, what is the system margin for an LED source? A laser source? What would the repeater spacing be for each source if we choose a 10-dB safety margin, and the cable loss at 1.3 μm is 2.5 dB/km?

11-7 Describe the services provided by the analog fiber optic system described in Sec. 11-9. What social effects would such a system have on people's lives?

A BRIEF REVIEW OF BESSEL FUNCTIONS

The analysis of the round optical fiber requires, as shown in Sec. 5-2, that solutions be found to a form of Bessel's equation that satisfy the physical requirements imposed upon the fields in the core and cladding. In this appendix a brief review of Bessel's equation and cylinder functions will be given to provide the reader with the background material needed for the analysis of the step-index fiber.

In general, Bessel's equation of order v with parameter λ can be written as[1]

$$x^2 \frac{d^2y}{dx^2} + x \frac{dy}{dx} + (\lambda^2 x^2 - v^2)y = 0 \tag{A1-1}$$

Bessel's equation is an example of the general linear second-order differential equation of the form

$$\frac{d^2y}{dt^2} + P(t) \frac{dy}{dt} + Q(t)y = 0 \tag{A1-2}$$

where

$$t = \lambda x \tag{A1-3}$$

$$P(t) = \frac{1}{t} \tag{A1-4}$$

and

$$Q(t) = \frac{t^2 - v^2}{t^2} \tag{A1-5}$$

If we try a series solution of the form

$$y = t^v(a_0 + a_1 t + a_2 t^2 + \cdots) \tag{A1-6}$$

and substitute it into Eq. (A1-2), we can solve for the coefficients a_0, a_1, ... After a good deal of algebra the resulting power series is

$$y(t) = t^v \left[\frac{1}{2^v \Gamma(v + 1)} - \frac{t^2}{2^{v+2} \Gamma(v + 2)} + \frac{t^4}{2^{v+4} 2! \Gamma(v + 3)} - \cdots \right]$$

$$y(t) = \sum_{m=0}^{\infty} \frac{(-1)^m t^{v + 2m}}{2^{v+2m} m! \Gamma(v + m + 1)} \tag{A1-7}$$

where Γ is the generalized factorial function. For example,

$$\Gamma(n + 1) = n!$$

and

$$\Gamma(x) = \int_0^{\infty} e^{-t} t^{x-1} \, dt$$

The function defined by Eq. (A1-7) is known as the Bessel function of the first kind of order v and is given the symbol $J_v(t)$

$$J_v(t) \equiv \text{Bessel function of the first kind of order } v$$

$$J_v(t) = \sum_{m=0}^{\infty} \frac{(-1)^m t^{v + 2m}}{2^{v+2m} m! \Gamma(v + m + 1)} \tag{A1-8}$$

Bessel functions are tabulated functions that can be found in many handbooks.[3-5] The graphs of $J_0(t)$ and $J_1(t)$ are shown in Fig. A1-1. Their resemblance to the graphs of $\cos t$ and $\sin t$ is interesting. In particular, they illustrate the important fact that for every value of v the equation $J_v(t) = 0$ has infinitely many real roots. Also notice that $J_v(t)$ converges for all values of t for $v \geq 0$. The Bessel function of the first kind is finite at the origin ($t = 0$), that is,

$$J_0(0) = 1$$
$$J_v(0) = 0 \qquad \text{for } v \neq 0 \tag{A1-9}$$

All other Bessel functions are not.

We can define a series that satisfies Eq. (A1-2) by simply replacing v by $-v$ in Eq. (A1-6), that is,

$$J_{-v}(t) = \sum_{m=0}^{\infty} \frac{(-1)^m t^{-v + 2m}}{2^{-v+2m} m! \Gamma(-v + m + 1)} \tag{A1-10}$$

Since $J_{-v}(t)$ contains negative powers of t and $J_v(t)$ does not, it follows that in the neighborhood of the origin $J_{-v}(t)$ is unbounded while $J_v(t)$ remains finite. Therefore $J_{-v}(t)$ and $J_v(t)$ are not proportional to each other and are two independent solutions of Bessel's equation (A1-2).

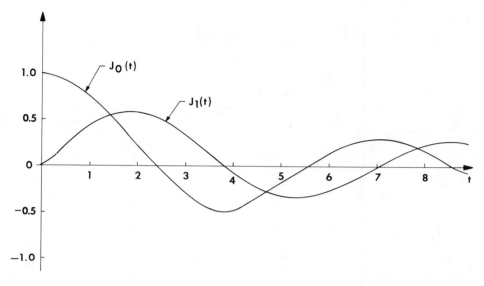

Figure A1-1 Plot of Bessel functions of the first kind, $J_0(t)$ and $J_1(t)$.

A Bessel function of the second kind of order v is defined as follows:

$Y_v(t) \equiv$ Bessel function of the second kind of order v

$$Y_v(t) = \frac{\cos(v\pi)J_v(t) - J_{-v}(t)}{\sin v\pi} \qquad \text{(A1-11)}$$

$Y_v(t)$ is sometimes called a Neumann or Weber function. A plot of the function $Y_v(t)$ is shown in Fig. A1-2. A complete solution of Bessel's equation could be written as

$$Y(t) = C_1 J_v(t) + C_2 Y_v(t) \qquad \text{(A1-12)}$$

For some applications it is convenient to use still another form of the general solution of Bessel's equation. This is based upon the two particular Hankel function solutions

$$H_v^{(1)}(t) = J_v(t) + jY_v(t) \qquad \text{(A1-13)}$$

$$H_v^{(2)}(t) = J_v(t) - jY_v(t) \qquad \text{(A1-14)}$$

where

$H_v^{(1)}(t) =$ Hankel function of the first kind of order v.

$H_v^{(2)}(t) =$ Hankel function of the second kind of order v.

Hankel functions are also known as Bessel functions of the third kind of order v. Hankel functions also have a singularity at the origin. A complete

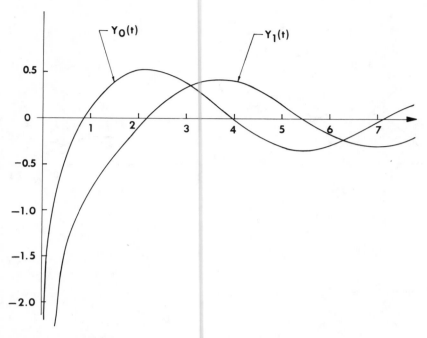

Figure A1-2 Plot of Bessel functions of the second kind, $Y_0(t)$ and $Y_1(t)$.

solution of Bessel's equation can also be written as

$$y(t) = C_1 H_\nu^{(1)}(t) + C_2 H_\nu^{(2)}(t) \tag{A1-15}$$

Collectively, all four functions $J_\nu(t)$, $Y_\nu(t)$, $H_\nu^{(1)}(t)$, or $H_\nu^{(2)}(t)$, or any combination of them, are known as *cylinder* functions. If one does not wish to single out a particular member of the family, one can symbolically write $Z_\nu(t)$ as a solution of Bessel's equation.

There are also other Bessel functions found in the literature known as "modified" Bessel functions. We will be interested in the modified Hankel function for the solution of Bessel's equation in the cladding of the round fiber. For large values of t the modified Hankel function behaves asymptotically like an exponential function.

To obtain a modified cylinder function we let the argument t become jt

$H_\nu^{(1)}(jt) \equiv$ modified Hankel function of the first kind of order ν

$H_\nu^{(2)}(jt) \equiv$ modified Hankel function of the second kind of order ν

It can be shown[2] for large values of t that

$$H_\nu^{(1)}(jt) \sim \left(A \sqrt{\frac{2}{\pi t}} \right) e^{-t} \tag{A1-16}$$

$$H_v^{(2)}(jt) \sim \left(B \sqrt{\frac{2}{\pi t}} \right) e^{+t} \tag{A1-17}$$

where A and B are complex numbers and $\sim$ means "behaves asymptotically as." The modified Hankel function of the first kind $H_v^{(1)}(jt)$ with its exponentially decaying behavior is suitable to describe the evanescent field associated with guided modes in the cladding of the fiber.

There are a number of useful mathematical relationships associated with cylinder functions that will be used in solving the round optical waveguide problem and they are listed below:

$$\frac{d[t^v Z_v(t)]}{dt} = t^v Z_{v-1}(t) \tag{A1-18}$$

$$\frac{d[t^{-v} Z_v(t)]}{dt} = -t^{-v} Z_{v+1}(t) \tag{A1-19}$$

where $J_v(t)$, $J_{-v}(t)$, $Y_v(t)$, $H_v^{(1)}(t)$, or $H_v^{(2)}(t)$ can be substituted for $Z_v(t)$.

A recursion relationship relating different orders of Bessel functions can be written as

$$J_{v+1}(t) = \frac{2v}{t} J_v(t) - J_{v-1}(t) \tag{A1-20}$$

For the interested reader the references[1,3-5] cited at the end of this appendix contain a large number of useful identities associated with Bessel functions.

REFERENCES

1. C. R. Wylie, Jr.: *Advanced Engineering Mathematics*, McGraw-Hill Book Company, New York, 1966.
2. F. B. Hildebrand: *Advanced Calculus for Engineers*, Prentice-Hall Inc., Englewood Cliffs, New Jersey, 1968.
3. H. B. Dwight: *Table of Integrals and Other Mathematical Data*, Macmillan Press.
4. M. Abramowitz and I. A. Stegun: *Handbook of Mathematical Functions*, National Bureau of Standards Applied Mathematics Series 55, U.S. Government Printing Office, Washington, D.C., 1966.
5. E. Jahnke and P. Emde: *Table of Functions with Formulas and Curves*, Dover Press, New York 1945.

TWO

CHARACTERISTIC EQUATION OF STEP-INDEX OPTICAL FIBER

In this appendix the characteristic equation (5-36) for the step-index fiber is derived by expanding the system determinant equation (5-35). Rewriting Eq. (5-35)

$$
\begin{vmatrix}
J_\nu(\kappa a) & 0 & -H_\nu^{(1)}(j\gamma a) & 0 \\
\dfrac{\nu}{a}\dfrac{\beta}{\kappa^2} J_\nu(\kappa a) & \dfrac{j\omega\mu}{\kappa} J_\nu'(\kappa a) & \dfrac{\nu}{a}\dfrac{\beta}{\gamma^2} H_\nu^{(1)}(j\gamma a) & \dfrac{-\omega\mu}{\gamma} H_\nu^{(1)\prime}(j\gamma a) \\
0 & J_\nu(\kappa a) & 0 & -H_\nu^{(1)}(j\gamma a) \\
\dfrac{-j\omega\varepsilon_1}{\kappa} J_\nu'(\kappa a) & \dfrac{\nu}{a}\dfrac{\beta}{\kappa^2} J_\nu(\kappa a) & \dfrac{\omega\varepsilon_2}{\gamma} H_\nu^{(1)\prime}(j\gamma a) & \dfrac{\nu\beta}{a\gamma^2} H_\nu^{(1)}(j\gamma a)
\end{vmatrix} = 0 \quad \text{(A2-1)}
$$

if we let

$$
\begin{aligned}
A &= J_\nu(\kappa a) & D &= H_\nu^{(1)}(j\gamma a) \\
B &= \frac{\nu}{a}\frac{\beta^2}{\kappa^2} & E &= \frac{\nu\beta}{a\gamma^2} \\
C &= \frac{j\omega}{\kappa} J_\nu'(\kappa a) & F &= \frac{\omega}{\gamma} H_\nu^{(1)\prime}(j\gamma a)
\end{aligned}
\qquad \text{(A2-2)}
$$

Using the simplified notation of (A2-2) we can rewrite Eq. (A2-1) as

$$\begin{vmatrix} A & 0 & -D & 0 \\ AB & \mu C & DE & -\mu F \\ 0 & A & 0 & -D \\ -\varepsilon_1 C & AB & \varepsilon_2 F & DE \end{vmatrix} = 0 \tag{A2-3}$$

Expanding the matrix equation (A2-3)

$$A \begin{vmatrix} \mu C & DE & -\mu F \\ A & 0 & -D \\ AB & \varepsilon_2 F & DE \end{vmatrix} -$$

$$D \begin{vmatrix} AB & \mu C & -\mu F \\ 0 & A & -D \\ -\varepsilon_1 C & AB & DE \end{vmatrix} = 0 \tag{A2-4}$$

Further expansion of Eq. (A2-4) yields

$$\mu \varepsilon_2 \, ACDF - A^2 D^2 E^2 - \mu \varepsilon_2 \, A^2 F^2 - 2A^2 BD^2 E$$

$$- A^2 B^2 D^2 - \mu \varepsilon_1 C^2 D^2 + \mu \varepsilon_1 ACDF = 0 \tag{A2-5}$$

Dividing Eq. (A2-5) by $A^2 D^2$ and regrouping yields

$$\left(\frac{C}{A} - \frac{F}{D} \right) \left(\frac{F}{D} \mu \varepsilon_2 - \frac{C}{A} \mu \varepsilon_1 \right) = (E + B)^2 \tag{A2-6}$$

Substituting back into Eq. (A2-6) the original parameters in (A2-2)

$$\left[\frac{j\omega}{\kappa} \frac{J_\nu'(\kappa a)}{J_\nu(\kappa a)} - \frac{\omega}{\gamma} \frac{H_\nu^{(1)\prime}(j\gamma a)}{H_\nu^{(1)}(j\gamma a)} \right] \left[\frac{\omega}{\gamma} \frac{H_\nu^{(1)\prime}(j\gamma a)}{H_\nu^{(1)}(j\gamma a)} \mu \varepsilon_2 - \frac{j\omega}{\kappa} \frac{J_\nu'(\kappa a)}{J_\nu(\kappa a)} \mu \varepsilon_1 \right]$$

$$= \left(\frac{\nu \beta}{a \gamma^2} + \frac{\nu}{a} \frac{\beta}{\kappa^2} \right)^2 \tag{A2-7}$$

with a little bit of algebraic manipulation we can rewrite Eq. (A2-7) as

$$\gamma^2 \kappa^2 \left[\gamma \frac{J_\nu'(\kappa a)}{J_\nu(\kappa a)} + j\kappa \frac{H_\nu^{(1)\prime}(j\gamma a)}{H_\nu^{(1)}(j\gamma a)} \right] \left[\omega^2 \mu \varepsilon_1 \gamma \frac{J_\nu'(\kappa a)}{J_\nu(\kappa a)} + j\omega^2 \mu \varepsilon_2 \kappa \frac{H_\nu^{(1)\prime}(j\gamma a)}{H_\nu^{(1)}(j\gamma a)} \right]$$

$$= \left(\frac{\nu \beta}{a} \right)^2 (\kappa^2 + \gamma^2)^2 \tag{A2-8}$$

Rewriting Eqs. (5-22), (5-23), (5-29), and (5-30)

$$\kappa^2 = k_1^2 - \beta^2 \tag{A2-9}$$

$$k_1^2 = \omega^2 \mu \varepsilon_1 \tag{A2-10}$$

$$\gamma^2 = \beta^2 - k_2^2 \tag{A2-11}$$

$$k_2^2 = \omega^2 \mu \varepsilon_2 \tag{A2-12}$$

Adding (A2-9) and (A2-11)

$$\kappa^2 + \gamma^2 = k_1^2 - k_2^2 = k_2^2 \left(\frac{\varepsilon_1}{\varepsilon_2} - 1 \right) \tag{A2-13}$$

Substituting Eqs. (A2-10), (A2-12), and (A2-13) into (A2-8) yields

$$\gamma^2 \kappa^2 \left[\gamma \frac{J_\nu'(\kappa a)}{J_\nu(\kappa a)} + jk \frac{H_\nu^{(1)\prime}(j\gamma a)}{H_\nu^{(1)}(j\gamma a)} \right] \left[k_1^2 \gamma \frac{J_\nu'(\kappa a)}{J_\nu(\kappa a)} + jk_2^2 \kappa \frac{H_\nu^{(1)\prime}(j\gamma a)}{H_\nu^{(1)}(j\gamma a)} \right]$$

$$= \left(\frac{\nu\beta}{a} \right)^2 k_2^4 \left(\frac{\varepsilon_2}{\varepsilon_1} - 1 \right)^2 \tag{A2-14}$$

Now multiplying (A2-14) by $a^2/k_2^2 \kappa^4$ and noting that $k_1^2/k_2^2 = \varepsilon_1/\varepsilon_2$ we finally obtain

$$\left[\frac{\varepsilon_1}{\varepsilon_2} \frac{a\gamma^2}{\kappa} \frac{J_\nu'(\kappa a)}{J_\nu(\kappa a)} + j\gamma a \frac{H_\nu^{(1)\prime}(j\gamma a)}{H_\nu^{(1)}(j\gamma a)} \right] \left[\frac{\gamma^2 a J_\nu'(\kappa a)}{\kappa J_\nu(\kappa a)} + j\gamma a \frac{H_\nu^{(1)\prime}(j\gamma a)}{H_\nu^{(1)}(j\gamma a)} \right]$$

$$= \left[\nu \left(\frac{\varepsilon_1}{\varepsilon_2} - 1 \right) \frac{\beta k_2}{\kappa^2} \right]^2 \tag{A2-15}$$

Equation (A2-15) is the characteristic equation for the step-index optical fiber and is used in Chap. 5 to determine the types of propagating modes in the guide.

THREE

DERIVATION OF CUTOFF CONDITIONS FOR STEP-INDEX WAVEGUIDE

In this appendix the cutoff condition equations for the various modes of a step-index optical fiber will be derived from its characteristic equation (5-36). Rewriting Eq. (5-36)

$$
\left[\frac{\varepsilon_1}{\varepsilon_2}\frac{a\gamma^2}{\kappa}\frac{J_\nu'(\kappa a)}{J_\nu(\kappa a)} + j\gamma a\frac{H_\nu^{(1)'}(j\gamma a)}{H_\nu^{(1)}(j\gamma a)}\right]\left[\frac{a\gamma^2}{\kappa}\frac{J_\nu'(\kappa a)}{J_\nu(\kappa a)} + j\gamma a\frac{H_\nu^{(1)'}(j\gamma a)}{H_\nu^{(1)}(j\gamma a)}\right]
$$

$$
= \left[\nu\left(\frac{\varepsilon_1}{\varepsilon_2} - 1\right)\frac{\beta k_2}{\kappa^2}\right]^2 \tag{A3-1}
$$

We will follow a procedure developed in Refs. 1 and 2 of rewriting Eq. (A3-1) in a simple form for obtaining its solution right at cutoff. If we introduce the following notation:

$$
J^+ = \frac{1}{\kappa a}\frac{J_{\nu+1}(\kappa a)}{J_\nu(\kappa a)} \tag{A3-2}
$$

$$
J^- = \frac{1}{\kappa a}\frac{J_{\nu-1}(\kappa a)}{J_\nu(\kappa a)} \tag{A3-3}
$$

$$
H^+ = \frac{1}{j\gamma a}\frac{H_{\nu+1}^{(1)}(j\gamma a)}{H_\nu^{(1)}(j\gamma a)} \tag{A3-4}
$$

$$
H^- = \frac{1}{j\gamma a}\frac{H_{\nu-1}^{(1)}(j\gamma a)}{H_\nu^{(1)}(j\gamma a)} \tag{A3-5}
$$

and use the following cylinder function identities:

$$Z'_v = \tfrac{1}{2}(Z_{v-1} - Z_{v+1}) \tag{A3-6}$$

and

$$Z_{v+1}(x) + Z_{v-1}(x) = \frac{2v}{x} Z_v(x) \tag{A3-7}$$

we can show, after a bit of algebra,[1] that the characteristic equation (A3-1) assumes the simple form

$$\left(\frac{\varepsilon_1}{\varepsilon_2} J^- - H^-\right)(J^+ - H^+) + \left(\frac{\varepsilon_1}{\varepsilon_2} J^+ - H^+\right)(J^- - H^-) = 0 \tag{A3-8}$$

We wish to find the solutions of Eq. (A3-8) at mode cutoff. When a mode is cut off its field in the cladding detaches itself from the guide and does not decay, that is, at cutoff $\gamma = 0$. Since for $\gamma = 0$ the argument of the modified Hankel functions vanishes, we need the approximation of these functions for small arguments as γ approaches zero.[3]

$$\lim_{\gamma \to 0} H_0^{(1)}(j\gamma a) = \frac{2j}{\pi} \ln \frac{\Gamma \gamma a}{2} \tag{A3-9}$$

where $\Gamma = 1.781672$ and

$$\lim_{\gamma \to 0} H_v^{(1)}(j\gamma a) = \frac{-j(v-1)!}{\pi} \left(\frac{2}{j\gamma a}\right)^v \qquad \text{for } v = 1, 2, 3, \ldots \tag{A3-10}$$

Substituting (A3-9) and (A3-10) into (A3-4) and (A3-5) results in

$$\lim_{\gamma \to 0} H^+ = \frac{-2v}{(a\gamma)^2} \qquad \text{for } v = 1, 2, 3, \ldots \tag{A3-11}$$

$$\lim_{\gamma \to 0} H^- = -\ln \frac{\Gamma \gamma a}{2} \qquad \text{for } v = 1 \tag{A3-12}$$

and

$$\lim_{\gamma \to 0} H^- = \frac{1}{2(v-1)} \qquad \text{for } v = 2, 3, 4, \ldots \tag{A3-13}$$

We are now in a position to find the solution of the characteristic equation (A3-8) at mode cutoff. For small values of γ and for $v \neq 0$ if we substitute (A3-11) into Eq. (A3-8) we obtain

$$\left[\frac{\varepsilon_1}{\varepsilon_2} J_{v-1}(\kappa a) - \kappa a H^- J_v(\kappa a)\right]\left[a^2\gamma^2 J_{v+1}(\kappa a) + 2v\kappa a J_v(\kappa a)\right]$$

$$+ \left[\frac{\varepsilon_1}{\varepsilon_2} a^2\alpha^2 J_{v+1}(\kappa a) + 2v\kappa a J_v(\kappa a)\right]\left[J_{v-1}(\kappa a) - \kappa a H^- J_v(\kappa a)\right] = 0 \tag{A3-14}$$

We will now use Eq. (A3-14) to develop the cutoff equations for the various modes.

Case 1 $v = 1$ $\mathbf{HE_{1\mu}}$ and $\mathbf{EH_{1\mu}}$ modes

For $v = 1$ and $\gamma \to 0$ Eq. (A3-14) becomes

$$[2(\kappa a)J_1(\kappa a)]^2 \ln \frac{\Gamma \gamma a}{2} = 0 \qquad \text{(A3-15)}$$

The solution of this equation is

$$J_1(\kappa a) = 0 \qquad \text{(A3-16)}$$

The other solution $\kappa a = 0$ is included in Eq. (A3-16) since $J_1(0) = 0$.

Equation (A3-16) is the cutoff equation for the $\mathrm{HE_{1\mu}}$ and $\mathrm{EH_{1\mu}}$ modes. Excluded from this group is the $\mathrm{HE_{11}}$ fundamental mode which is never cutoff.[2]

For $v > 1$ and $\gamma \to 0$ Eq. (A3-14) becomes

$$J_v(\kappa a)\left[\left(\frac{\varepsilon_1}{\varepsilon_2} + 1\right)J_{v-1}(\kappa a) - \frac{\kappa a}{v-1} J_v(\kappa a)\right] = 0 \qquad \text{(A3-17)}$$

Equation (A3-17) has two solutions:

Case 2 $v > 1$ $\mathbf{EH_{v\mu}}$ modes

$$J_v(\kappa a) = 0 \qquad \text{for } \kappa a \neq 0 \text{ and } v = 2, 3, \ldots \qquad \text{(A3-18)}$$

Case 3 $v > 1$ $\mathbf{HE_{v\mu}}$ modes

$$\left(\frac{\varepsilon_1}{\varepsilon_2} + 1\right)J_{v-1}(\kappa a) = \frac{\kappa a}{v-1} J_v(\kappa a) \qquad \text{for } v = 2, 3, 4, \ldots \qquad \text{(A3-19)}$$

In Ref. 2 it is shown that for $v > 1$, $\kappa a = 0$ cannot be a solution of (A3-17) as κ and γ approach zero.

Finally we need to investigate the case for the TE and TM modes for $v = 0$. For small values of γ approaching zero, the characteristic equation (A3-1) becomes

$$\frac{\varepsilon_2}{\varepsilon_1} \frac{\kappa}{\gamma} \frac{J_0(\kappa a)}{J_1(\kappa a)} = -a\gamma \ln \frac{2}{a\gamma\Gamma} \qquad \text{(A3-20)}$$

As $\gamma \to 0$

$$\lim_{\gamma \to 0} \gamma a \ln \frac{2}{\gamma a \Gamma} = 0$$

The solution for Eq. (A3-20) for $\gamma \to 0$ becomes

Case 4 $v = 0$ **TE and TM modes**

$$J_0(\kappa a) = 0 \qquad \text{(A3-21)}$$

The results of this appendix are summarized in Chap. 5 (Eqs. (5-56) through (5-60)).

REFERENCES

1. S. P. Schlesinger, P. Diament and A. Vigants: "On Higher Order Hybrid Modes of Dielectric Cylinders," *IEEE Trans. Microwave Theory Techn.* **MTT-8**, March 1960.
2. D. Marcuse: *Light Transmission Optics*, Van Nostrand Reinhold Co., New York, 1972.
3. E. Jahnke and P. Emde: *Tables of Functions with Formulas and Curves*, Dover Press, New York, 1945.

FOUR

DERIVATION OF THE CHARACTERISTIC EQUATION FOR THE LP MODES IN A WEAKLY GUIDING STEP-INDEX FIBER

Starting with expressions for the transverse field components in a weakly guiding step-index fiber, the characteristic equation for the LP modes will be derived. Rewriting Eqs. (5-77) to (5-79), the transverse field components can be expressed as in the core, $r < a$

$$E_y = \frac{\eta_0}{n_1} H_x = \frac{A J_l(\kappa r)}{J_l(U)} \cos l\phi \qquad \text{(A4-1)}$$

and in the cladding, $r > a$

$$E_y = \frac{\eta_0}{n_2} H_x = \frac{A H_l^{(1)}(j\gamma r)}{H_l^{(1)}(jW)} \cos l\phi \qquad \text{(A4-2)}$$

where A is the electric field strength at the core-cladding interface and

$$U = \kappa a \qquad \text{(A4-3)}$$

$$W = \gamma a \qquad \text{(A4-4)}$$

We can derive the longitudinal components of the fields E_z and H_z from H_x and E_y using Eqs. (3-6c) and (3-7c)

$$E_z = \frac{j\eta_0}{k_0 n_{1,2}^2} \frac{\partial H_x}{\partial y} \qquad \text{(A4-5)}$$

where n_1 applies for the field in the core and n_2 the field in the cladding of the fiber

$$H_z = \frac{j}{k_0 \eta_0} \left(\frac{\partial E_y}{\partial x} \right) \tag{A4-6}$$

Substituting Eq. (A4-1) into (A4-5) we will derive E_z in the core of the fiber to show the detailed procedure for obtaining the longitudinal components of the fields. In the fiber core $r < a$

$$E_z = \frac{jA}{k_0 n_1} \frac{\partial}{\partial y} \left[\frac{J_l(\kappa r)}{J_l(U)} \cos l\phi \right] \tag{A4-7}$$

Using

$$\frac{\partial}{\partial y} = \sin \phi \frac{\partial}{\partial r} + \frac{\cos \phi}{r} \frac{\partial}{\partial \phi} \tag{A4-8}$$

in Eq. (A4-7) we obtain

$$E_z = \frac{jA}{k_0 n_1} \left[\frac{1}{J_l(U)} \right] \left[\kappa J_l'(\kappa r) \cos l\phi \sin \phi - \frac{l}{r} J_l(\kappa r) \sin l\phi \cos \phi \right] \tag{A4-9}$$

$$\frac{\partial}{\partial (\kappa r)} [J_l(\kappa r)] = \tfrac{1}{2}[J_{l-1}(\kappa r) - J_{l+1}(\kappa r)] \tag{A4-10}$$

$$\left(\frac{2l}{\kappa r} \right) J_l(\kappa r) = J_{l-1}(\kappa r) + J_{l+1}(\kappa r) \tag{A4-11}$$

$$\cos l\phi \sin \phi = \frac{\sin (l + 1)\phi - \sin (l - 1)\phi}{2} \tag{A4-12}$$

$$\sin l\phi \cos \phi = \frac{\sin (l + 1)\phi + \sin (l - 1)\phi}{2} \tag{A4-13}$$

yields

$$E_z = \frac{-jA}{2k_0 a} \left[\frac{U}{n_1} \frac{J_{l+1}(\kappa r)}{J_l(U)} \sin (l + 1)\phi + \frac{U}{n_1} \frac{J_{l-1}(\kappa r)}{J_l(U)} \sin (l - 1)\phi \right] \tag{A4-14}$$

Following the same procedures the other longitudinal components of the fields in the core and cladding can be obtained and are written below.

In the core $r < a$

$$H_z = \frac{-jA}{2k_0 \eta_0 a} \left[U \frac{J_{l+1}(\kappa r)}{J_l(U)} \cos (l + 1)\phi - U \frac{J_{l-1}(\kappa r)}{J_l(U)} \cos (l - 1)\phi \right] \tag{A4-15}$$

In the fiber cladding $r > a$

$$E_z = \frac{A}{2k_0 a} \left[\frac{W}{n_2} \frac{H_{l+1}^{(1)}(j\gamma r)}{H_l^{(1)}(jW)} \sin (l + 1)\phi - \frac{W}{n_2} \frac{H_{l-1}^{(1)}(j\gamma r)}{H_l^{(1)}(jW)} \sin (l - 1)\phi \right] \tag{A4-16}$$

and

$$H_z = \frac{A}{2k_0 \eta_0 a} \left[W \frac{H^{(1)}_{l+1}(\gamma r)}{H^{(1)}_l(jW)} \cos (l+1)\phi + W \frac{H^{(1)}_{l-1}(\gamma r)}{H^{(1)}_l(jW)} \cos (l-1)\phi \right] \quad \text{(A4-17)}$$

To obtain the characteristic equation for the LP modes the boundary conditions associated with the tangential components of the fields must be applied at the core-cladding interface, that is, the electric and magnetic field z and ϕ components must be matched at the interface. We must now obtain the ϕ component of the fields to proceed with the application of the boundary conditions. We have postulated transverse components of the field E_y and H_x given by Eqs. (A4-1) and (A4-2). If we obtain the transverse fields using Eqs. (3-9) to (3-12) from E_z and H_z (Eqs. (A4-14) and (A4-15)) the results are not identical with the postulated transverse fields but differ by a small order Δ compared to them.[1] We will neglect this small difference as we proceed in our derivation of the characteristic equation. It is this approximation that determines the accuracy of our assumption of linearly polarized modes. To obtain the ϕ component of the fields we use

$$E_\phi = -E_x \sin \phi + E_y \cos \phi \quad \text{(A4-18)}$$

$$H_\phi = -H_x \sin \phi + H_y \cos \phi$$

Noting that $E_x \approx 0$ we substitute (A4-1) and (A4-2) into (A4-18) to obtain, in the core, $r < a$

$$E_\phi = \frac{AJ_l(\kappa r)}{J_l(U)} \cos l\phi \cos \phi$$

$$E_\phi = \frac{A}{2} \left[\frac{J_l(\kappa r)}{J_l(U)} \right] [\cos (l+1)\phi + \cos (l-1)\phi] \quad \text{(A4-20)}$$

and in the cladding, $r > a$,

$$E_\phi = \frac{A}{2} \left[\frac{H^{(1)}_l(j\gamma r)}{H^{(1)}_l(jW)} \right] [\cos (l+1)\phi + \cos (l-1)\phi] \quad \text{(A4-21)}$$

for the magnetic field $H_y \simeq 0$. From Eq. (A4-19) H_ϕ is, in the fiber core,

$$H_\phi = \frac{-An_1}{\eta_0} \frac{J_l(\kappa r)}{J_l(U)} \cos l\phi \sin \phi$$

$$H_\phi = \frac{-An_1}{2\eta_0} \left[\frac{J_l(\kappa r)}{J_l(U)} \right] [\sin (l+1)\phi - \sin (l-1)\phi] \quad \text{(A4-22)}$$

and in the fiber cladding,

$$H_\phi = \frac{An_2}{2\eta_0} \left[\frac{H^{(1)}_l(j\gamma r)}{H^{(1)}_l(jW)} \right] [\sin (l+1)\phi - \sin (l-1)\phi] \quad \text{(A4-23)}$$

Matching the tangential fields at $r = a$, we equate the $(l + 1)$ and $(l - 1)$ terms separately. In the limit as $\Delta \ll 1$, $n_1 \approx n_2$. Using $n_1 = n_2$ we obtain for the $l + 1$ terms using Eqs. (A4-14)–(A4-17),

$$U \frac{J_{l+1}(U)}{J_l(U)} = jW \frac{H_{l+1}^{(1)}(jW)}{H_l^{(1)}(jW)} \tag{A4-24}$$

and for the $l - 1$ terms,

$$U \frac{J_{l-1}(U)}{J_l(U)} = jW \frac{H_{l-1}^{(1)}(jW)}{H_l^{(1)}(jW)} \tag{A4-25}$$

Equations (A4-24) and (A4-25) are two equivalent forms of the characteristic equation of the LP mode of a weakly guiding step-index fiber. To see the equivalence of the two equations we can use the recursion relationship for cylinder functions

$$Z_{l+1}(t) = \left(\frac{2l}{t}\right) Z_l(t) - Z_{l-1}(t) \tag{A4-26}$$

where the Bessel or Hankel functions can be substituted for Z. When this recursion relationship is used in Eq. (A4-24) to replace the functions of order $l + 1$ with functions of order $l - 1$, Eq. (A4-25) is obtained. The characteristic equation (A4-25) is used in Sec. 5-10.

REFERENCE

1. D. Gloge: "Weakly Guiding Fibers," *Appl. Opt.*, **10**(10), October 1971.

FIVE

DERIVATION OF
MODAL WAVEGUIDE DELAYS
IN A WEAKLY GUIDING STEP-INDEX FIBER

Starting with Eq. (5-148) we will derive a general equation for the waveguide delay of each of the modes in a weakly guiding step-index fiber. This general equation will then be used to calculate the arrival time difference, $\Delta\tau_m$, between energy propagating in the mode with the largest waveguide group delay and the least delay. We begin our derivation by rewriting the expression for waveguide delay τ_m, given by Eq. (5-148)

$$\tau_m = \frac{L}{C} \frac{V}{k_0} \frac{d}{dV} (n_2 k_0 \Delta b) \tag{A5-1}$$

Writing the derivative of (A5-1) in terms of V, from Eq. (5-139)

$$V = \sqrt{2} n_2 k_0 a \sqrt{\Delta} \tag{A5-2}$$

and

$$\frac{d}{dV} (n_2 k_0 \Delta b) = \sqrt{\Delta} \frac{d}{dV} (n_2 k_0 \sqrt{\Delta} b) \tag{A5-3}$$

Writing Eq. (A5-3) in terms of V we obtain

$$\frac{d}{dV} (n_2 k_0 \Delta b) = \frac{\sqrt{\Delta}}{\sqrt{2} a} \frac{d(Vb)}{dV} \tag{A5-4}$$

315

and

$$\tau_m = \frac{L}{C} n_2 \Delta \frac{d(Vb)}{dV} \tag{A5-5}$$

Our task now is to obtain an expression for $d(Vb)/dV$. The task of obtaining this expression is a bit circuitous. We will first write b in terms of U, W, and V. From Eq. (5-137)

$$b = \frac{W^2}{V^2} \tag{A5-6}$$

and

$$\frac{d(Vb)}{dV} = \frac{d(W^2/V)}{dV} = \frac{2W}{V}\frac{dW}{dV} - \frac{W^2}{V^2} \tag{A5-7}$$

We now must find an expression for dW/dV by using the characteristic equation for the guide. If we take the derivative of the characteristic equation (5-89) with respect to V and use

$$Z_{l+1}(x) = \left(\frac{2l}{x}\right)Z_l(x) - Z_{l-1}(x) \tag{A5-8}$$

and

$$J_l'(U) = \frac{-l}{U} J_l(U) + J_{l-1}(U) = \frac{l}{U} J_l(U) - J_{l+1}(U) \tag{A5-9}$$

we obtain

$$U(A-1)\frac{dU}{dV} + W(B-1)\frac{dW}{dV} = 0 \tag{A5-10}$$

where

$$A = \frac{J_{l-1}(U)J_{l+1}(U)}{[J_l(U)]^2} \tag{A5-11}$$

and

$$B = \frac{H_{l-1}^{(1)}(jW)H_{l+1}^{(1)}(jW)}{[H_l(jW)]^2} \tag{A5-12}$$

We now wish to write B in terms of A. Multiplying Eqs. (5-79) and (5-80) we obtain

$$B = \frac{-U^2}{W^2} A \tag{A5-13}$$

Substituting Eq. (A5-13) into (A5-10) yields

$$UA\frac{dU}{dV} - \frac{U^2}{W} A\frac{dW}{dV} = U\frac{dU}{dV} + W\frac{dW}{dV} \tag{A5-14}$$

but

$$V^2 = U^2 + W^2 \qquad \text{(A5-15)}$$

and

$$U\frac{dU}{dV} + W\frac{dW}{dV} = V \qquad \text{(A5-16)}$$

Also

$$\frac{dU}{dV} = \frac{V}{U} - \frac{W}{U}\frac{dW}{dV} \qquad \text{(A5-17)}$$

Substituting Eq. (A5-16) and (A5-17) into (A5-14) and solving for dW/dV we obtain

$$\frac{dW}{dV} = \frac{W}{V}\left(1 - \frac{1}{A}\right) \qquad \text{(A5-18)}$$

Now, finally substituting (A5-18) into (A5-7) we obtain

$$\frac{d(Vb)}{dV} = \frac{W^2}{V^2}\left(1 - \frac{2}{A}\right) = b\left(1 - \frac{2}{A}\right) \qquad \text{(A5-19)}$$

or, in terms of the definition of A from equation (A5-11), we have

$$\frac{d(Vb)}{dV} = b\left\{1 - \frac{2[J_l(U)]^2}{J_{l-1}(U)J_{l+1}(U)}\right\} \qquad \text{(A5-20)}$$

and

$$\tau_m = \frac{L}{C}\,n_2\,\Delta b\left\{1 - \frac{2[J_l(U)]^2}{J_{l-1}(U)J_{l+1}(U)}\right\} \qquad \text{(A5-21)}$$

Equation (A5-21) is the general expression for waveguide delay for a weakly guiding step-index fiber. τ_m is different for every guided mode.

Far from cutoff $b \to 1$, while $J_l(U) \to 0$ according to Eq. (5-94). For $V \to \infty$ Eq. (A5-20) approaches unity for all modes.

In Fig. A5-1, $d(Vb)/dV$ (equation (A5-20)) is plotted for the first 20 modes of the fiber.[1] It is apparent from the figure that the modes with $l = 0$ and $l = 1$ have zero waveguide delay at cutoff. Marcuse has shown[2] that the cutoff value of $d(Vb)/dV$ for modes $l \geq 2$ can be written as

$$\frac{d(Vb)}{dV} = \frac{2(l-1)}{l} \qquad \text{(A5-22)}$$

Using Eq. (A5-22) the arrival time difference between the mode with the largest waveguide group delay and the least delay ($l = 2$, $d(Vb)/dV = 1$) is

$$\Delta\tau_m = \frac{L}{C}\,(n_1 - n_2)\left(1 - \frac{2}{l_{\max}}\right) \qquad \text{(A5-23)}$$

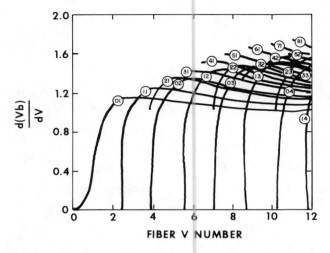

Figure A5-1 Plot of normalized waveguide group delay, $d(Vb)/dV$, as a function of fiber V number.

From Fig. 5-11, l_{max}, the largest value of l that can occur for the V at which the fiber operates, can be written as

$$l_{max} = \frac{2V}{\pi} \tag{A5-24}$$

Finally substituting Eq. (A5-24) into (A5-23) yields

$$\Delta\tau_m = \frac{L}{C}(n_1 - n_2)\left(1 - \frac{\pi}{V}\right) \tag{A5-25}$$

Equation (A5-25) appears in the text as equation (5-149) and is used to calculate the difference in the arrival times of the leading and trailing edges of the resultant output pulse propagating through a weakly guiding multimode step-index fiber.

REFERENCES

1. D. Gloge: "Dispersion in Weakly Guiding Fibers," *Appl. Opt.*, **10**(11), November 1971.
2. D. Marcuse: *Theory of Dielectric Optical Waveguides*, Academic Press Inc., New York, 1974. (For the interested reader, the procedure followed in this appendix was developed in this text.)

CALCULATION OF THE NUMBER OF MODES IN A MULTIMODE GRADED-INDEX FIBER WITH A POWER LAW PROFILE

In this appendix we will start with Eq. (6-32) and derive an expression for the number of modes in a multimode fiber with a power-law refractive-index profile. Rewriting Eq. (6-33)

$$m(\beta) = \int_0^{r_2} [k^2(r) - \beta^2] r \, dr \tag{A6-1}$$

where $m'(\beta)$ is the number of bound modes having a propagation constant greater than β. The radius r_2 at which $k(r) = \beta$ defines the upper limit of the integration in Eq. (A6-1). Using the power-law profile given by Eq. (6-34) the refractive index in the core of the fiber is

$$n(r) = n_1 \left[1 - 2\Delta \left(\frac{r}{a} \right)^\alpha \right]^{1/2} \tag{A6-2}$$

To solve Eq. (A6-1) we need an expression for r_2 in terms of a, Δ, β, and k_1. We obtain r_2 when $k(r) = \beta$ as follows:

$$\beta = k(r) = \frac{2\pi n(r)}{\lambda_0} \tag{A6-3}$$

or, solving for $n(r)$,

$$n(r) = \frac{\beta \lambda_0}{2\pi} \tag{A6-4}$$

Substituting (A6-4) into (A6-2) and solving for r_2 we obtain

$$r_2 = a \left[\frac{(1 - \beta^2/k_1^2)}{2\Delta} \right]^{1/\alpha} \qquad \text{(A6-5)}$$

Now writing $k^2(r)$ in terms of $n(r)$, for substitution into (A6-1) we obtain

$$k^2(r) = k_1^2 \left[1 - 2\Delta \left(\frac{r}{a} \right)^\alpha \right] \qquad \text{(A6-6)}$$

and Eq. (A6-1) becomes

$$m(\beta) = \int_0^{r_2} \left[k_1^2 \left(r - \frac{2\Delta}{a^\alpha} r^{\alpha+1} \right) - r\beta^2 \right] dr \qquad \text{(A6-7)}$$

where r_2 is given by Eq. (A6-5). Upon integration Eq. (A6-7) becomes

$$m(\beta) = \frac{k_1^2 r_2^2}{2} - \frac{k_1^2 2\Delta r_2^{\alpha+2}}{a^\alpha(\alpha+2)} - \frac{r_2^2 \beta^2}{2} \qquad \text{(A6-8)}$$

Substituting (A6-5) into (A6-8) for r_2 produces

$$m(\beta) = \frac{k_1^2 \left\{ a \left[\frac{1}{2\Delta} \left(1 - \frac{\beta^2}{k_1^2} \right) \right]^{1/\alpha} \right\}^2}{2} - \frac{k_1^2 2\Delta \left\{ a \left[\frac{1}{2\Delta} \left(1 - \frac{\beta^2}{k_1^2} \right) \right]^{1/\alpha} \right\}^{\alpha+2}}{a^\alpha(\alpha+2)}$$

$$- \frac{\left\{ a \left[\frac{1}{2\Delta} \left(1 - \frac{\beta^2}{k_1^2} \right) \right]^{1/\alpha} \right\}^2 \beta^2}{2} \qquad \text{(A6-9)}$$

Equation (A6-9) can be simplified after performing some straightforward algebra to be

$$m(\beta) = a^2 \Delta k_1^2 \left(\frac{\alpha}{\alpha+2} \right) \left(\frac{k_1^2 - \beta^2}{2\Delta k_1^2} \right)^{(\alpha+2)/\alpha} \qquad \text{(A6-10)}$$

Since $m(\beta)$ is the number of bound modes having a propagation constant greater than β, if we let $\beta = \beta_c = n_2 k_0$ we can calculate the total number of propagating modes in a fiber. Notice, in Eq. (A6-10), that

$$\frac{k_1^2 - \beta_c^2}{2\Delta k_1^2} = \frac{k_0^2(n_1^2 - n_2^2)}{2\Delta k_0^2 n_1^2} = 1 \qquad \text{(A6-11)}$$

since

$$\Delta = \frac{n_1^2 - n_2^2}{2n_1^2} \qquad \text{(A6-12)}$$

Therefore, substituting (A6-11) into (A6-10), the total number of propagating modes in the fiber becomes

$$N = a^2 \Delta k_1^2 \left(\frac{\alpha}{\alpha + 2} \right) \tag{A6-13}$$

Equation (A6-13) is identical to (6-37) used in Chap. 6. We can also rewrite Eq. (A6-10) in terms of N

$$m(\beta) = N \left(\frac{k_1^2 - \beta^2}{2 \Delta k_1^2} \right)^{(\alpha + 2)/\alpha} \tag{A6-14}$$

Equation (A6-14) appears as Eq. (6-38) in the text.

INDEX